THE CIVIL WAR AND NEW YORK CITY

The Civil War
and New York City,

Ernest A. McKay

Syracuse University Press

First Edition 1990
90 91 92 93 94 95 96 97 98 99   6 5 4 3 2 1

This book is published with the assistance of a grant from the John Ben Snow Foundation.

The paper used in this publication meets the minimum requirements of American National Standard for Information Sciences—Permanence of Paper for Printed Library Materials, ANSI Z39.48-1984. ∞™

Library of Congress Cataloging-in-Publication Data

McKay, Ernest A.
    The Civil war and New York city / Ernest A. McKay. — 1st ed.
      p.   cm. — (New State book)
    Includes bibliographical references.
    ISBN 0-8156-0246-4
      1. New York (N.Y.)—History—Civil War, 1861–1865.   I. Title.
F128.44.M46   1990   90-32799
974.7'103—dc20   CIP

Manufactured in the United States of America

In memory of my brother

DONALD STUART MCKAY

ERNEST A. MCKAY taught at the State University of New York, Maritime College, and now teaches at the University of South Carolina at Aiken. He is the author of a number of books and articles, including *A World to Conquer* (1981), *Henry Wilson, Practical Radical* (1971), and *Essays on the American Revolution* (1976).

Contents

Illustrations

Preface

The Civil War and New York City are two popular and enduring subjects for both scholars and general readers. Countless books have been written about each of them, and their fascination appears to be endless. Oddly, despite such massive attention over the years, this is the first comprehensive book about the city during the war. A few aspects have been well treated by others such as the draft riot and the attempt to burn New York, but none has covered the effect of the war on the life of the city from start to finish. Such a synthesis, I believe, provides a fresh perspective along with new material based on previously unused manuscript collections.

The purpose of this book is to tell about the thoughts and actions of important and unimportant people who lived through the tragedy of these terrible years. It is presented as a panoramic view in a chronological manner to give a sense of events, and reactions to them, as they unfolded. The facts produce many surprises and frequently lay bare the inconsistencies of human behavior. And underlying the facts were the persistent illusions held by both supporters and critics of the war. Sudden shifts of opinion, often founded on misinformation, confusion, and ignorance of the future, caused innumerable ironies among New Yorkers who saw a war with different eyes than those of us who look backward in safety with clearly defined principles and loyalties.

Since the days of the Dutch, Manhattan was a heterogeneous place where clashes of ideas commonly produced vitality in a city mainly devoted to commerce. Prejudices and differences existed, but they were usually set aside to conduct the work of the day and created a semblance of tolerance. As the Civil War approached, tensions between the North and South sharpened sentiments within the city about war and peace. In a city traditionally friendly to the South, the new strains and crosscurrents of thought were amplified and sometimes seemed intolerable. These imbalances of ideas were an additional burden to the more normal complexities of urban life amid a rapidly growing population. Health, housing, poverty, and the most recent wave of immigrants were among the multitude of municipal problems that still had to be borne, war or no war.

New York City has always defied logical classification, but particularly so in the years between 1860 and 1865. A close look at the city in that troubled time exposes the errors of false images. Stereotypes of hardheaded businessmen and hard-boiled politicians frequently failed to follow expected patterns. Unquestioned devotion to the Union and seeds of sedition or near sedition were habitually voiced by striking personalities. Sometimes realists, wrongheaded or not, desperately sought peace while more ethereal individuals called for blood. The city had no shortage of articulate saints and sinners who contributed color along with confusion and conviction. Fernando Wood and his brother Benjamin were only two among many dramatic figures who were adept at stirring furious emotions. The city dwellers, in the main, gave their support to the Union, and they gain our admiration, but it was not an easy decision for them. Even after minds were made up, many remained disturbed and disconsolate.

Heroics took a holiday from the city now and then, but searching for solutions to the imponderable questions of war and peace was eternally energetic. Freedom of expression existed regardless of arbitrary arrests, and attempted restrictions on speech and press were futile. The discordant voices were an embarrassment to the Union more than once. At the same time, they were a living demonstration of freedom. It was America's strength, not its weakness.

Consistently, among the many inconsistencies, irony continually flaunted logical expectations. One instance was the behavior of one of the most vocal groups who opposed the war—the recently arrived Irish-Americans. Their bitter criticism of the war and the national administration was more than offset by their casualties in the ranks of the Union army. In battle after battle they numbered among the maimed or killed. Consistency of thought and action was truly a paste jewel.

Indifference to the immorality of slavery seemed prevalent throughout the city. Yet within four years there was almost an unconscious evolution of thought among many citizens. Imperceptibly they reached new viewpoints that were more sensitive to the evils of slavery and the condition of blacks. The transformation, as one diarist revealed, usually took place quietly in people's inner lives without public fanfare.

New York City was filled with compromisers before and during the war. Their efforts were in vain, and they often seem ignoble to us, but their prescience about the horror of war may teach us some lessons for the future. We automatically condemn war while we continue to glorify it wittingly and unwittingly. Despite our protestations, we still take more pride in combat and less pride in efforts to prevent bloodshed. We lose patience with compromisers when war seems to be the only alternative. The historical interpretation that politicians failed to prevent the Civil War is not new, but perhaps the compromisers stopped trying too soon. As J. H. Plumb once wrote, "First we must get rid of the insane notion that all negotiation is preliminary to appeasement."

Acknowledgments

Historians are always indebted to innumerable anonymous librarians, and I am no exception. Librarians have been consistently courteous and invaluable in my pursuit of this work. I also appreciate the help of Phyllis Barr, director of archives and museum curator at the Parish of Trinity Church in the City of New York. My former colleague Professor Karen Markoe of the State University of New York Maritime College read an early draft and made many useful comments. Trudie Calvert deserves my thanks for her care as copy editor. My wife, Ellen, in this venture from the start, has been a source of encouragement, a diplomatic critic, and a helpful partner every step of the way.

THE CIVIL WAR AND NEW YORK CITY

1

The Long Wait

The mayor of the City of New York was the picture of an aristocrat dining at Delmonico's. The deep blue eyes, sleek hair, slender build, and polished manner of His Honor Fernando Wood blended with the fashionable surroundings and favorably impressed people of refinement. Yet this same man was equally at ease drinking beer with his less elegant but ardent admirers at the Volks Garten or claiming the affection of the Dead Rabbits, the most notorious gang in the city. Some people said that the mayor was the handsomest man they had ever seen. Others said that he was the most corrupt. John Bigelow, a prominent editor, was sure he was both. It was certain, however, that Wood was a far more perplexing person than anyone had reason to believe from the appearance that emanated from his ever affable, always unruffled ways.

So many scandalous tales circulated about this mayor who led the city into the new decade of the 1860s the wonder was that he had been elected. The stories that floated around about his wicked doings made it easy to suspect that there must be some truth to the murky rumors. Before turning to politics, Wood had been engaged in a series of business ventures that hardly increased his reputation for honesty. His charm and duplicity had carried him a long way from the wine and cigar store on Pearl Street and the grocery and grog shop at Washington and Rector streets that he operated as a young man. Contemporaries said that he arranged to have stevedores paid off in his shop and then sold them bad malt liquor. Later, he entered the shipping business, and one of his ships was among the first to reach San Francisco after the discovery of gold in California. But his success was always accompanied by shadowy stories of swindles and false pretenses.[1]

In a rough city known for its rough politics, Wood served two terms as mayor from 1855 to 1857. When vicious infighting with jealous mem-

Fernando Wood, mayor of New York City at the start of the Civil War. (Courtesy of the New-York Historical Society)

bers of Tammany Hall led to his defeat for reelection in 1857, he walked out of their midst and formed his own greedy tribe, Mozart Hall. His audacity paid off, and Wood won a third term at City Hall in 1859. He was well placed to shape public opinion. His Quaker background might have been taken as a sign of his absolute integrity and birthright interest in peace in a troubled time, but skeptics saw him in a different light. Politics had not interfered with Wood's interest in business. To the contrary, they went hand in hand as his political friends helped him prosper in real estate. William Marcy Tweed, a young, energetic politician with his own ambitions, begrudgingly envied Wood's enterprise. "I never yet went to get a corner lot," he said, "that I didn't find Wood had got in ahead of me."[2] And in Wood's second term, the state legislature took the police out of his control because the department was so debased and inefficient.

Fellow Democrat Samuel Tilden, cool and analytical, tried to explain Wood's most recent victory at the polls to his friend the elder statesman Martin Van Buren. Horrified by Wood's behavior, he readily admitted that he could not compete with Wood's finely honed organization. He told the former president that Wood had the support of "the lower stratum of Irish" combined with special interests and some job-seeking Republicans.[3] It was an unbeatable alliance.

The appearance or reality of corruption did little to harm Wood's blossoming career. Even the White House did not seem to be outside the range of possibility as the mayor cast his eyes on the national arena. During the year, Wood, ever on the make, had bought the *Daily News* to help boost his chances for the Democratic nomination for vice-president of the United States. And in December 1860, the forty-eight-year-old Wood, once divorced and once widowered, strengthened his ties with the best people of the city by taking for his third wife the cultivated sixteen-year-old Alice Fenner Mills, daughter of a rich New York merchant. His new father-in-law was well established with the thriving Broad Street grocery firm of Atwater, Mumford and Company, and he had great expectations for the new member of his family.

The contradictions in the character of Fernando Wood reflected the contradictions in the city itself. Any elegance, integrity, or leadership that emerged from the largest city in the Union was frequently marred by ugliness, rascality, or subservience. Virtue and vice, energy and lethargy, luxury and poverty were in continual combat. The rest of the nation reacted to the city with a mixture of respect and disdain. To some, it was a symbol of success, to others a symbol of greed. There was never unanimity of thought whenever New York City was the subject. Still, for all its sore spots and provincial pride and prejudice, New York was a place of power and home for some of the most influential citizens in the country. Their thoughts and actions affected the entire nation. Wall Street's premiership in finance was well established, but by 1860 prominence in other fields was equally important. The words of clergymen, intellectuals, and editors echoed throughout the land while the labors of manufacturers, shipbuilders, and merchants found markets in every corner of the country. And there was politics. The city seemed to breed politicians. Although some never raised their sights above seeking favors for clubhouse cronies, others more shrewd and durable sharpened their talents on the broader scene. As sectional tensions increased between North and South, New York politicians had much to say to a national audience even though they rarely spoke in unison.

These voices came from a disparate city of eight hundred thousand people that Wood ruled, or at least reigned over. It was a partially settled Manhattan that had always vibrated with well-defined contrasts and never projected a homogeneous image such as Quaker Philadelphia or Calvinist Boston. Instead, differences had historically clashed within its borders, ethnic, economic, political, and religious. Strong resentments and violent opinions were a part of daily life. Yet somehow the residents endured each other side by side.

Above Fifty-ninth Street there were few buildings except flimsy squatter shacks. Joseph Choate, a young New Englander starting a law practice in the city, walked to 100th Street one day and for the first time saw the wretched living conditions of Irish workingmen who typified the recent wave of immigrants. It was a rude shock for a young man who spent his evenings with the elite Schuylers, Morrisses, and Jays. The Irish lived with their pigs in "miserable cabins," and Choate seriously believed that his old pigsty would have made a better home.4 Not surprisingly, New York was considered one of the unhealthiest cities in the world.

Central Park, a project the mayor supported, was taking shape under the eye of the architect Frederick Law Olmsted, but it had a long way to go before completion. Nevertheless, it was a major attraction. A dreary area, twice the size of Hyde Park in London, was becoming transformed into a beauty spot that rivaled the loveliness of the Thiergarten. The winding walks of the Ramble, the graceful bridges, and the carefully tended flowers and shrubs fascinated visitors. One of the projects under construction in the park was a reservoir. In the not too distant future, sluices would open to let 107 acres of Croton water rush into the tremendous pool that was called the greatest piece of masonry in the country.[5]

Since the arrival of the Dutch in the seventeenth century, the movement uptown from the Battery was unrelenting. The untidy and raucous city was always under construction. The demolition of old structures disturbed some sensitive New Yorkers who realized that historic relics of another time were lost forever. Nonetheless, they were unable to stop the destruction. Pleas for preservation were abruptly dismissed. Buildings were torn down, others were put up. Blasting the rockbound earth for new foundations never ceased. Steadily the town crept northward. Even Columbia College moved to Forty-ninth Street.

Most of the prosperous families had given up their pleasant residences at the foot of the island and left it to financiers during the day and saloon keepers at night. Commerce, of course, was the main reason for the city's existence. It gave the city vitality and excitement, and there was no doubt that New York was the financial and commercial center of the country. It was more than a mere municipality limited by geographical demarcations. The beautiful view of the harbor from downtown clearly announced that the city meant business. And the city's business was really the nation's business. The bay and East and Hudson rivers were alive with clipper ships, steamships, and assorted riverboats and barges loading and unloading cargo. Shipments from all parts of the country were sent abroad. Wheat arrived from the West through the inland waterways, and cotton came from the South by coastal ships. Exports of produce and merchandise from the port were 30 percent higher in 1860 than any previous year on record at the customhouse. At the same time, increasing quantities of products arrived from the rest of the world for transfer throughout the republic. A. A. Low and Brothers was the nation's largest importer of tea, an old staple. But more and more machinery arrived from Europe to meet the demands of the new industrial world. Estimates claimed that 75 percent of the nation's imports passed through New York harbor.[6]

In the past five years, activity in sugar refining, machine and engine building, garment making, and publishing had also taken giant leaps. Local investment in manufacturing during that period jumped 550 percent, and New York had become the leading American city in the value of its manufactured goods. According to some inhabitants, the city achieved this success despite the heaviest taxes on the continent for a "municipal government worse than any."⁷ Near the docks in the early hours of the morning, herculean truck horses strained every muscle backing heavy wagons up to loading platforms in the narrow, congested, dimly lighted streets. Along the waterfront the rows of tall masts impressed anyone who took a moment to appreciate the spectacle. Too often, however, there was little time for reflection as people scurried around the busy streets. They had business to conduct in nearby shops and offices.

Along the East River, for about a mile and a half from Pike Street to Thirteenth Street, some of the finest shipbuilders in the country operated their yards. Among them were Smith and Dimon, Brown and Bell, Jacob Westervelt, and William Webb. The demand for clipper ships had made the past ten years an exhilarating era for them. Each year they had launched fifty to a hundred vessels, and often twenty or thirty of these handsome ships were under construction at once. The yards were a hive of activity, and the quantity of lumber consumed was staggering. New York white oak and white pine, Long Island locust, New England oak and chestnut, and live oak and pitch pine from the South were stacked everywhere. New York City owners in the packet, tea, or California trade bought most of the ships, but the brilliant William Webb probably constructed more tonnage for foreign accounts.

Webb's independent, impatient, and imaginative mind did not seem to mesh with naval authorities in Washington at a time when his services might have been especially valuable. Recently, they had turned down his plans for a speedy seventy-four-gun steam frigate. Undaunted, Webb, a small, pugnacious-looking man with a flat nose and bald head, sailed to Russia, where he received a friendlier reception and a million-dollar order to build the frigate that would be hailed as the highly successful *General Admiral*.⁸

Men in the same business followed the maxim that true birds of a feather flocked together as they formed their own little worlds downtown. Jewelers gathered on Maiden Lane, leather dealers congregated near Beekman and Cliff streets, and wholesale grocers were usually found on Water and Front streets. Cotton brokers were active on Pearl Street.

Traders saw good times and bad. The Panic of 1857 was still fresh in their memories, but optimism was the prevailing note for the future. The country was growing, and money men sought new investments. There was much to do, railroads and ships to build, transatlantic lines to form, and goods to exchange, and this city of businessmen had every intention of playing a major part in the national growth. New York was even important for agriculture. A mainstay of the export trade was the enormous amount of cotton shipped abroad. It was one of the reasons the city had such close ties with the South.

Behind this industrial and commercial restlessness was the presence of Wall Street to extend credit for the country's expanding economy. In the previous decade, New York had surpassed Boston as the financial leader in the United States and had achieved a new status as second in the world only to London. City bankers who offered credit on convenient terms attracted entrepreneurs from far and wide, in effect making New York the capital for capitalists. Financing the cotton trade had become one of their significant services.[9]

Wall Street speculators gambled on widely varying scales. Some, with extraordinary vision, took grand risks that affected the national economy for good or ill. Sometimes they seemed to scoff at money as well as public opinion, making daring judgments that made or lost fortunes. Railroad stocks and bonds were of particular interest to them. Others, with faded dreams and lower horizons, simply hoped to eke out a living for the day. The differences of these operators were often mirrored in their dress. At the august Stock and Exchange Board, gloves and boutonnieres were in style, while nearby, shabbier characters executed their transactions in shady gambling dens and dark cellars. On William Street, twenty-one, roulette, and keno were popular ways to make or, more likely, lose money.

Commercial men visiting the city often stayed at one of the large hotels downtown. The luxurious Astor House across from City Hall on Broadway catered to well-heeled travelers. Inside the Greek Revival building there was a garden, fountain, and stunning dining room, where a guest might choose from twelve varieties of poultry or forty brands of Madeira. The hotel, on the same side of the street as the venerable St. Paul's Church, had a more unusual neighbor on the other side of Broadway. P. T. Barnum continually introduced shocking attractions to lure crowds to his American Museum. Barnum said his monomania was to make the museum the town wonder and the town talk. And he succeeded. He had educated dogs, "industrious fleas," jugglers, ventriloquists, tableaux, gypsies, rope dancers, dioramas, and panoramas.[10]

One of Barnum's features was "Miss Jane Campbell, the Celebrated Giant Girl, the largest Mountain of Human Flesh ever seen in the form of a woman." Perhaps it was vulgar, but it intrigued the naive and even the not so naive. In October 1860, the worldly Prince of Wales, later King Edward VII, took time out from his busy social schedule to visit the museum. He saw the female giant, Siamese twins, the living skeleton, the fat boy who kissed his hand, and "The Infant Drummer Boy." The royal visitor was delighted.

The City Hall, where the mayor, aldermen, and councilmen transacted their reputable and disreputable affairs, was a graceful Federal style building, mainly marble, with broad, sweeping stairs to a well-proportioned portico, which was the centerpiece of a pleasant park. The clock in the Georgian tower, built by Messrs. Sperry and Company, was regarded as one of the most accurate timekeepers in the world.[11] The Common Council, the legislative body for the city, consisted of a Board of Aldermen, sometimes called the "Forty Thieves," and a Board of Councilmen. The members, mostly ward heelers, were not known for either industry or integrity. Nevertheless, they had an eye for the odd dollar, and an eager politician who exerted himself granting favors could be well rewarded. Some critics said these representatives of the people were drawn from barrooms, brothels, and political societies. Although the characterization may have been slightly harsh, no one could truthfully say that their ethical standards were of the highest order.

Broadway, paved with slippery Belgian blocks, was a continual hazard for the hundreds of horses that drew carriages, wagons, and stages. The small stages that operated below Fourteenth Street carried only a few people, and dozens of them cluttered the street. The driver had a seat on the roof. When passengers wanted to stop, they pulled a leather strap tied to his leg. Passengers who jammed into dirty, smelly horse cars that fought their way up and down the avenue took for granted signs that read "No Colored People Allowed on This Car." Segregation in the city was a common practice, especially in churches and theaters.

Broadway bustled with a variety of retail stores that offered the latest in fashions. The city was a logical place for such outlets because most of the dry goods imported into the United States arrived in New York and the manufacture of ready-made clothes was increasing. Women preferred to walk on the west side of the street, where the better shops were located. As a result, the east side of Broadway became known as the "wrong side."

A. T. Stewart had made a name for himself as a merchant and was probably as rich as the real estate tycoon William B. Astor. Stewart started with a small store opposite City Hall Park, and soon ladies flocked to his place for fine laces. He was a tough boss who paid extremely low wages and fined his employees when they violated his rules. He preferred to hire good-looking male clerks because he believed women enjoyed gossiping with them. In time they became known as "Stewart's nice young men." Although a martinet, Stewart was fair and capable of making huge charitable donations. Later, he built a "marble palace" on Broadway near Chambers Street and finally a six-story building at Tenth Street and Broadway, which was called the largest dry goods store in the world.[12]

On the way uptown, other fine hotels lined Broadway. The St. Nicholas Hotel at Spring Street had been built a few years before at a cost of more than a million dollars. It was six stories high and could accommodate about a thousand guests. The magnificent chandeliers, candelabra, and mirrors created an aura of luxury. The mirrors cost about $40,000 and the silver service and Sheffield plate another $50,000. The telegraph office was strategically located in the barroom to enable men of affairs to send messages to almost any part of the country while enjoying their comfort. The Metropolitan at Broadway and Prince Street was proud of its thirteen thousand yards of deep carpeting and twelve miles of gas and water pipes. It also had "sky parlors," an unexcelled feature, where ladies could look down at the activities in the street below. The Fifth Avenue Hotel, opposite the greenery of Madison Square, had a "perpendicular railway" that could carry guests from one floor to another. The city could aways be counted on to produce surprising innovations.[13]

In the evening Broadway turned from merchandising to entertainment. Carriages drew up to theaters and music halls that dotted the avenue and let off their well-dressed patrons. The amiable Joseph Jefferson might be playing opposite the beautiful auburn-haired Laura Keene in *Our American Cousin* at her own theater, later known as the Olympic. Lester Wallack, a dashing actor and entrepreneur, usually attracted an elite audience at his theater near Broome Street. He had made his presence known some years before as Sir Charles Coldstream in Dion Boucicault's *Used Up*. Wallack was under pressure to keep up with the times, and he would soon move his theater to Broadway and Thirteenth Street. Way uptown at the corner of Thirtieth Street was the popular Wood's Museum and Metropolitan Theater.[14]

A less grand area for shopping and amusement was in the Bowery, north of City Hall, which ran parallel to Broadway from Chatham Square to Eighth Street. It was a busy place for pawnbrokers and lottery dealers. Shows sometimes believed to be too indecent for more respectable theaters were popular here, but most were perfectly harmless. The Bowery Theater was the oldest in the city and struggled to stay alive. Some of the actors and actresses had seen better days and others were as yet undiscovered, but no one could say that the Bowery was dull. Strangers could find fun, lively and now and then tawdry, at Tony Pastor's Opera House or at one of the many congenial beer gardens. On Sunday, the beer gardens hummed with activity. Families took tables for the day and played cards, dominoes, or dice. Usually there was a good band with brass instruments, a harp, violin, drums, and a piano, and there was lots of singing. The beer, served by teenaged girls, flowed steadily, and the consumption was immense. But fun was not so innocent in other parts of the Bowery, where it merged with cruelty at cock pits and rat dens, where unfeeling gamblers laid down heavy bets.

Not far away, another neighborhood was internationally renowned. More infamous than the Bowery, the Five Points at the intersection of Worth, Park, and Baxter streets, which ran into Mulberry, Mott, and Center streets, was a hub for the debased, criminal, and poor. Danger lurked everywhere in these dark streets, where the sale of rum, next to thievery and vice, was big business. This was where Fernando Wood's friends the Dead Rabbits hung out in dismal, overcrowded wooden firetraps. Filthy bunks were available for the night in damp, putrid cellars for five or ten cents. Only Church Street on the lower west side could come close to matching the reputation of Five Points as a center of evil. That area swarmed with prostitutes and had a well-established history.

During the American Revolution it was known as the "Holy Ground" because Trinity Church owned much of the land. The city was not a peaceful place. No one was safe from crime. In 1860, seventy-one thousand
crimes were recorded, and the number increased in the next five years.[15]

The rich people in town lived in brownstone mansions on Murray
Hill and along Fifth Avenue as far as Fifty-ninth Street. Brownstone had
become a symbol of respectability and helped define class distinctions.
The upper reaches of society were small and closely knit. Everyone knew
everyone else or about everyone else, and their business and social relations were frequently interwoven. They were well aware of their privileges and had every intention of preserving them. There were dangers,
however, in regarding the elite as a solid block of select people with uniform opinions. Within their circle jealousies, prejudices, and rivalries
contributed to the formation of different perspectives. Politically, many
had been Whigs, others were Democrats, and still others had become,
reluctantly or otherwise, Republicans. Nonetheless, an invisible wall
made up of a wide assortment of nuances protected the social elite from
the crudities of the lower orders. Their class could be penetrated, but
only by sufficient means. In the end, money always gained respect, and
as long as someone had an overabundance of money, criticism of social
shortcomings could be sublimated if not completely forgotten.

The monotony of brown fronts would be broken only when A. T.
Stewart built a mansion of palatial white marble on the corner of Fifth
Avenue and Thirty-fourth Street. Above Forty-eighth Street, the pave-
ment on the avenue was unfinished. Still, it was the wealthiest street in
the country. Park Avenue failed as a high-style competitor of Fifth Avenue. It was a railroad street for the Harlem line, and alongside the tracks
were stables, tenements, and a variety of barnyard animals.

Forty-second Street had not yet become a famous thoroughfare. If
it received any attention, it was for the unpleasant garbage dumps and,
even worse, the nauseous slaughterhouses that boiled bones and separated fat on the far east side. Cattle were often driven across town from
the west side. Nearby at Fortieth Street and First Avenue there was a
squatter colony known as "Dutch Hill." The inhabitants, who kept goats,
pigs, cows, and children, worked in quarries and manure heaps in the
neighborhood.[16]

New York did not appear to be any more hospitable to the middle
class then than now. It seemed to be a city of contrasts, the rich and poor.
Yet the middle class was present and increasing in size. The city was a

magnet for white-collar workers in banks, shops, and a multitude of other firms that needed ever larger clerical staffs. On Lexington Avenue there were many small brick houses where middle-class owners took in middle-class boarders. Yorkville, among other middle-class neighborhoods was a village occupied mainly by hardworking Germans and their descendants. It revolved around Third Avenue for about a mile or so between Forty-fifth and Sixty-fifth streets and bordered countryside to the north which stretched up to another village, Harlem, at 115th Street.

Middle-class shoppers often took the Sixth Avenue horsecars to between Carmine and Twenty-third streets. Among their favorites were Altman's, Stern's, and Macy's. Rowland H. Macy had opened a store on the street floor of a four-story brick building at 204–206 Sixth Avenue near Fourteenth Street in the fall of 1858. Although his store was not situated among the major retail shops, he wisely selected a site that had the advantage of good transportation. An omnibus line also crossed Fourteenth Street. The frequently muddy streets were a deterrent for any shopper, and Macy, a strong believer in advertising, placed an ad that read, "Ladies, if walking is too bad, just take the cars."

Macy, a former whaler from Nantucket, had failed in business in Boston and met with indifferent results in a store in Haverhill, Massachusetts. His new establishment was no match for Lord & Taylor or A. T. Stewart, but he was beginning to attract attention with his lively ads that stressed the connection between low prices and paying cash. "All Articles Marked, Way Down at Macy's," he advertised. Macy's timing was good. Profits were climbing again as factories, railways, and other companies started to hire more people. Macy, like other retailers, was a specialist. He concentrated on fancy dry goods such as ribbons, laces, embroideries, handkerchiefs, and hosiery. Soon he would add new items and become the owner of one of the first true department stores in the country.[17]

This city that bustled with optimism for the future and led the nation in so many ways also experienced a sense of uneasiness. Wall Streeters, always acutely aware of the latest current event, were among those who now increased their tendency to be wary. The prospect of an upcoming presidential campaign did not please many of them because it would drag up old issues and rehash delicate subjects that they believed were better left alone. Political talk, they feared, increased tensions and gave extremists an excuse to become more hostile. Businessmen, as a rule, wanted peace and quiet. Their associations with the South had been profitably established, and they did not want disturbing influences to upset the relationship. An economic study made in 1860 declared that "all the profitable branches of freighting, brokering, selling, banking, insurance, etc, that grow out of the Southern products, are enjoyed in New York."[18] It would be better for business to live and let live. Any clash between the industrial North and the agricultural South was not evident in New York City.

For thirty years or more, since at least Andrew Jackson's time, the same issues appeared and reappeared in political campaigns to stir emotions. States' rights, slavery, abolition, secession, the Union, and admission of territories had been political themes time and again. Men who prided themselves on practicality asked why it was necessary to antagonize the South. Now, another presidential campaign would embroil citizens and divide them once more.

Fernando Wood knew that most New Yorkers recognized the importance of the South to the city. For years the port of New York had thrived on the cotton-carrying trade. It was estimated that five cotton states brought at least $200 million worth of business to the city each year. But they also knew that there was a loose credit system tied to this pot of gold. Somewhere between $150 and $200 million worth of credit to southerners was outstanding.[19] Talk of war or secession, no matter how foolish or exaggerated, was to be avoided. They could ruin the city.

As an astute politician, Wood also knew that not all the southern sympathizers in the city were capitalists. Among his followers were new Americans who had arrived from Europe in recent years, especially the thousands of Irish. By 1860, almost half of the city's population was foreign-born, and two hundred thousand of them were Irish. Never one to let principle stand in the way, Wood had been known to send newly arrived immigrants to court with a note, "Please naturalize the bearer."[20] It was a quick and effective way to build a political following. The Irish were devoted to Wood for his favors, unaware that he had once been a member of the antiforeign Know-Nothing society. As a large part of the laboring class that did the menial jobs, the Irish had their own problems making a living. They had no interest in abolition, which would fill the labor market with a new class of job seekers to replace them or undercut their miserable wages. Life was already too severe.

Wood had personal ties to the South, too. He had once worked in Virginia and easily accepted the southern views of life and politics. He saw nothing wrong with slavery. Neither the cruelty nor the immorality of the system troubled him. At the state Democratic convention in February 1860, Wood made his sentiments clear when he vigorously stressed that much of the wealth accumulated in New York came from slave labor. "The profits, luxuries, the necessities, nay even the physical existence," he said, "depend upon the products only to be obtained by the continuance of slave labor and the prosperity of the slave master."[21]

Wood spoke for many of New York's most respected citizens. Sometimes they cloaked their concern for their pocketbooks in talk about the Constitution or states' rights. Other times they blatantly expressed their true feelings and showed complete disinterest in the moral question or high-flown language of political philosophy. Charles O'Conor, considered one of the ablest lawyers in the city, argued that slavery was just and ordained by nature. He thought it was "benign in its influence on the white man and on the black man" and worth perpetuating. The *New York Evening Day-Book,* a defender of the white laboring class, felt no qualms in declaring that slavery was one of the happiest occurrences in human affairs. The Negro, the newspaper said, was in "his natural position of social subordination." The *Herald* pictured slaves as contented and comfortable and looked upon antislavery fanaticism as "nigger worship."[22]

New Yorkers also closed their eyes to the slavers who fitted out ships in their port and transported slaves from Africa to Cuba. The enormous profits that were possible in this merciless trade attracted certain callous merchants and the city became a major center for illegal slavers. Some of them were backed by southern syndicates. These smugglers, called "blackbirders," often met at Sweet's Restaurant on Fulton Street to talk over their sinister affairs. They always had much to discuss. There were clearance papers needed from the customhouse, bribes to pay, supplies to buy, and false identifications to arrange. One slave ship sailed under the colors of the New York Yacht Club. For men who knew that they conducted their business under the threat of a death penalty, they were surprisingly open, almost flagrant, in their ways. Their confidence came from the knowledge that no one had ever been hanged under the law for carrying on the nefarious trade.

Inspectors of slave ships never seemed to find evidence that could block their sailing. They looked the other way. Excess lumber for slave decks or the unusual number of water casks were all quietly ignored. And the blackbirders had extra assurance of safety from United States District Attorney James I. Roosevelt, who said that President James

Buchanan would "probably pardon" anyone convicted of illegal slave trading. Roosevelt came to the conclusion that the public no longer considered slavers as pirates and the death penalty could not be supported. In October 1860, a case against the slave ship *Erie* that came before the federal court in New York demonstrated the apathetic attitude of judge and jury. Under examination, the mate was uncertain of his nationality, could not explain what had happened to the ship's missing papers, or what the ship's mission was when he signed on. It did not matter. He and his captain were set free.

Religious groups in the city suffered from the strain of the slavery issue, too. Some of their institutions had no qualms about supporting slavery. The highly regarded American Tract Society broke in two, and the New York branch became proslavery. The Boston branch became antislavery. This break in the devout society laid bare the misconception so frequently voiced that the God of the North frowned on slavery.

Sympathy for slavery in the city was not exclusive to any one religious denomination. The pious Samuel F. B. Morse, a talented artist and inventor of the telegraph, believed that slavery was a divine institution, and as a matter of conscience he considered abolition a sin. The son of a famous orthodox Congregational minister and geographer, he had formed this belief after careful study of the Scriptures. Morse was an unusual man with a complex personality. The rigidity of his religion did not restrain his vivid imagination in a multiplicity of artistic and scientific ways, though he remained remarkably narrow on many social and political issues. In 1836, a victim of his prejudices, he had run unsuccessfully for mayor as a candidate of the nativist Know-Nothings. Shortsightedness often matched his farsightedness. He feared "dreamers of abolitionism, of women's rights . . . spiritualism-socialism . . . and similar visionary schemes." His former pastor, H. G. Ludlow, wrote to him, "My abhorrence of your proslavery notions cannot be less intense than your abhorrence of my antislavery ones."[23] Morse's convictions about slavery were equaled by others such as James W. White, an Irish immigrant with a totally different background. White later became a justice of the New York City Superior Court and founded *the Freeman's Journal,* a Roman Catholic newspaper. The title of his paper was an odd choice because he stridently defended slavery.

The forthcoming presidential campaign in 1860 was bound to confuse issues and bewilder voters. It was a rare year when four major candidates ran for the highest office in the land. The Democrats had split and nominated two standard-bearers, one from the North and the other from the South. The northern candidate was the "Little Giant" from Illinois, Senator Stephen Douglas. He thought that popular sovereignty, which would allow people in the territories to make their own decisions about slavery, was the answer to a thorny problem. Instead, it had caused him to break with President Buchanan over the admission of Kansas into the Union and roused southern animosity. Many New York City Democrats were ready to drop their support of Douglas and back a candidate from the South for the sake of a strong, united ticket.[24] But it was not to be. The riled southern Democrats bolted the convention and nominated their own man, the Kentuckian John C. Breckinridge, who was Buchanan's vice-president.

Democrats represented the vast majority of voters in the city, and when united they could determine the election in the state. This made the city vitally important in national elections when the state's electoral vote could be critical. Locally, however, Democrats were prone to bicker among themselves and split. Petty feuds and personal jealousies were always likely to break out at any moment. Now the disorganization of their national party made them wonder even more where their loyalty and self-interest belonged.

A third presidential candidate also attracted Democrats in the city. He was John Bell of Tennessee, the nominee of the Constitutional Union party, which rose from the remains of the old Whigs and nativist Know-Nothings. Horace Greeley, the antislavery editor of the *New York Tribune*, called it "The Old Gentlemen's Ticket." Bell was a conservative supporter of slavery, who gave his first allegiance to the Union. His party platform favored "no political principles other than the Constitution of the country, the union of the states, and the enforcement of the laws." Although Bell's strongest followers were in the border states, there was a mildness in his candidacy that appealed to many New Yorkers. He might restrain hotheads and provide the moderation they so desperately wanted.

The Republicans dismayed city dwellers. It had been assumed that their nominee would be the intelligent Senator William H. Seward from upstate New York. The failure of this assumption proved that the behavior of convention delegates cannot be predicted. Suddenly, Abraham Lincoln, the man of the people, emerged as the candidate who could appeal to northern and western states. Lincoln's success at the convention could be partially attributed to a bitter Horace Greeley, who turned against his former friend Seward. Lincoln was a dark horse, but he was not completely unknown in New York City. He knew the importance of recognition in the East and earlier in the year had accepted an invitation to address the Young Men's Republican Union. Despite the overwhelming number of Democrats in the city, the shades of political opinion were countless. To offset proslavery, prosouthern sentiment there was a vocal minority opposed to slavery. Some were against its spread in the territories, and some were extreme abolitionists. Many of them wanted to see and hear Lincoln, who had attracted national attention in his unsuccessful senatorial campaign against Douglas in Illinois.

On that famous visit no one met Lincoln when he stepped off the ferry at Cortlandt Street. Instead, he unobtrusively found his own way to the Astor House. The next day was Sunday, and Lincoln took a two-cent ferry ride to Brooklyn to hear the renowned antislavery preacher Henry Ward Beecher at the Plymouth Church. In the afternoon, someone showed him the sights, and he was exposed to the squalid Five Points as a place of interest.

Rain and snow made moving around the city difficult on Monday, but Lincoln visited Knox Great Hat and Cap Establishment at Broadway and Fulton Street, where he received a free silk top hat. Then he went to Matthew Brady's famed photo studio at 643 Broadway and posed for his picture. By evening the weather grew worse. It was snowing heavily. Nevertheless, fifteen hundred people came to hear Lincoln speak at the Great Hall of the brownstone building on Fourth Avenue and Eighth Street erected by the eccentric industrialist Peter Cooper for the betterment of the working class. Each person in attendance that evening paid twenty-five cents for the privilege, and the audience was generally sympathetic.

William Cullen Bryant, editor of the *Evening Post*, introduced Lincoln, who wore a tight black frock coat and new boots. The audience seemed to have a sense of curious anticipation as they waited to hear the tall, awkward midwesterner. Would he prove to be, as some people said, simply an uncouth politician from the backwoods? Before long, most of them were enthralled by the stranger. Partly it was his sincere presence, partly his carefully selected words, and partly his well-modulated voice. His listeners were pleased that he was conciliatory toward the South and sought peace. But there was also a firmness in his speech that appealed to those who opposed slavery, and he electrified the gathering. "If slavery is right," he said that night, "all words, acts, laws, constitutions against it are themselves wrong." Bryant thought he made the best political speech he had ever heard in his life. Four newspapers thought the event was important enough to print Lincoln's speech the next day. Some of his remarks would remain among his most memorable and quotable such as "Let us have faith that right makes might." Unquestionably, he had made a vivid impression upon many Republicans, and historians have frequently referred to this visit as increasing Lincoln's political stature. But the neglected side of the story is that he did not convert the majority of New Yorkers to his way of thinking about slavery, territories, or the Republican party. As the *Evening Post* had written that same month, "The City of New York belongs almost as much to the South as to the North."[25]

Republicans in the city who had supported Seward for president were crushed when Lincoln received the nomination. Disappointment intensified their ambivalent feelings about the party candidate. They were baffled by the midwesterner's personality and lack of experience. Despite Lincoln's appearance in New York, he was still unknown to most easterners, who did not believe he was a proper nominee. The petty snobbery expressed by some influential men was appalling. John Bigelow, a part-owner of the *Evening Post,* wrote to his English friend William Hargreaves that Lincoln was not a man who would be "a la mode at your splendid European courts." His style and appearance were not even beyond the "reach of criticism in our Atlantic drawing rooms."[26]

August Belmont believed the election of Lincoln would be a catastrophe. Belmont was firmly established in the city's financial and social circles and exuded ultimate self-confidence. In addition to his own considerable ability, he had two things in his favor. He was the American representative of the Rothschild banking family and husband of the beautiful and gracious Caroline Perry, daughter of the naval hero Commodore Matthew Perry, who had led the expedition that opened relations with Japan. Belmont took on the job of national campaign manager for Douglas and worked closely with Tammany Hall. Surprisingly, even he had trouble raising money for his candidate. Some of his friends on Wall Street regarded Douglas as a threat to their business relations with the South and shunned association with him.

Belmont invited a group of influential citizens to his art-filled home on Fifth Avenue and Eighteenth Street "to save the Union from the calamities of the election of Lincoln," which he believed would bring bloodshed. His guests at this private meeting were a mixed group that included such down-to-earth politicians as "Honest John" Kelly, the very rich William B. and John Jacob Astor, and the staid Samuel Tilden. Belmont's aim was to form a coalition of Bell, Breckinridge, and Douglas supporters to control New York's electoral vote against Lincoln. The gathering appeared to be in general accord, and they organized the Volunteer Democratic Association of New York for this purpose.[27]

The chairman of the National Democratic Campaign Committee, Congressman Clement L. Vallandigham, came to town to speak for Douglas at Cooper Institute. The Ohioan's language and views, more extreme than his candidate's, featured abuse of Negroes and frightened his listeners by claiming that the Republicans favored emancipation. The merchants, conservatives, and loyal Democrats in attendence shuddered over these shared fears. When Vallandigham remarked that he would never vote a dollar that might shed a drop of blood in a civil war, he received the expected loud and long applause.[28]

In October, William Yancey, the fire-eater from Alabama, a Breckinridge booster, found sentiment in the city strong for his candidate. The *Herald, Journal of Commerce, Daily News,* and *Evening Day-Book* eagerly endorsed the southerner. Yancey appeared in the busy forum at Cooper Institute, where he was enthusiastically cheered not only when he proclaimed his loyalty to the Union but also when he threatened to resist "to blood" any administration that trampled on the rights of the South. When he said that the South asked nothing "but that you will not allow anyone to steal away her niggers," he was greeted with laughter and applause. He asked if he had said anything unreasonable, and the audience cried out, "No, No!" His mellifluous words presented a pretty picture of slavery in the South as he spoke of happy sons of toil who loved their masters, contributed to the wealth of the world, and were the best population under the sun if the "philosophers" would only leave them alone. He told his listeners that the arch of the Union was crumbling and that the burden of responsibility rested with them. The decision of union or disunion, he charged, was in the hands of New York.[29] Yancey went home with a glow of satisfaction after his warm welcome. He could only

conclude that no one in the city was ready to throw down the gauntlet to
the South.

Later in the month, prices dropped sharply on the stock market.
Some brokers believed that politicians had created the break to demon-
strate the dire consequences of a Republican victory. True or not, John
Jacob Astor, a son of William B. Astor, backed away from the Democrats.
He had attended Belmont's meeting and had appeared to back a coali-
tion ticket. Now, he and Shepherd Knapp, president of the National
Bank, announced that they would vote for Lincoln. It was a reluctant de-
cision, but they felt that the election might otherwise end in the House of
Representatives and cause months of delay and suspense.

As election day approached, employers were not subtle about telling their employees how to vote if they wished to keep their jobs. Some
companies printed circulars warning their employees not to vote for Lincoln because it would hurt them and their families. Southern customers
would cut off their business, and there would be little work. Fear of black
competition in the labor market was widespread, and Democratic politicians forecast the dreadful economic consequences of a Republican victory. James Gerard, a well-known lawyer and candidate for Congress,
warned his "friends from Ireland" that Republicans were abolitionists,
and if they were not defeated the result would be "negro labor dragging
you from your free labor." The irony of the complaint did not occur to
those who pictured the dire results of blacks replacing white working
people. Twenty years before, most longshoremen, hod carriers, coach-
men, bootblacks, barbers, and waiters had been black men. And black
women had been maids, cooks, laundresses, and seamstresses. In the intervening years, blacks were eased out of these jobs and replaced by
Irish.[30]

Selfish interests were overriding. James Gordon Bennett's *Herald*
had called Lincoln a "vulgar, village politician," and now the newspaper
intimidated workingmen by writing, "If Lincoln is elected you will have
to compete with the labor of four million emancipated negroes."[31] To
Bennett, Black Republicanism, fostering the equality of races, was as evil
as free love. He saw no possibility for black and white people to live and
work together harmoniously. Only bloodshed would result.

The Republicans tried to make up for their weakness in the city
with noise and hullabaloo. The Wide Awakes, a Republican organization
of young men, created excitement in their black and silver suits as they

marched in a torchlight parade on Fifth Avenue. The Republican press had anticipated fifty thousand marchers in the show of strength. A. H. Satterlee, however, watched the procession near Bleecker Street and estimated that there were not more than nine or ten thousand, and he guessed that nearly half of them were from out of town. Whatever their number, the Wide Awakes put on a good show even if they did not promote many votes. Later in October, anti-Lincoln supporters of Bell, Breckinridge, and Douglas put on a grander parade up Broadway to Fifth Avenue and then down Fourth Avenue and the Bowery. Dressed in red shirts, carrying lanterns, and shooting off roman candles, they marched until the early hours of the morning. Satterlee watched this spectacle too and calculated that there were more than thirty thousand participants.[32]

Voting on election day was a slow process and was complicated by a separate ballot in New York State on the issue of equal voting rights for blacks. About 80 percent of the blacks could not vote because they did not own property worth $250. For years, efforts had been made to remove this qualification from the state constitution, and now the people were to vote on an amendment to correct the injustice. The New York City and County Suffrage Committee of Colored Citizens campaigned diligently for support against this rank discrimination.[33]

Lines formed early and moved at a snail's pace. Even early voters often had to wait two hours to cast their ballots. In the morning George Strong found a queue that extended a block away from the polls. He gave up for the time being. When he returned in the afternoon, he was pleased to wait only an hour. Numbers of latecomers, less fortunate, were unable to vote before the polls closed.[34]

Dishonest practices may have reached new heights on this election day, but there was scarcely any question that the Democrats would carry the city. Despite the almost certain outcome, widespread reports of fictitious names on the voting lists were common. In the Twelfth Ward, for example, five hundred of the thirty-five hundred names on the register were said to be fraudulent, and in the Seventeenth Ward, the names of two boys, six and seven years old, were among the many that were falsely registered.

Not surprisingly, neither the ballyhoo of the Wide Awakes nor the solemn presence of Lincoln brought Republicans success in New York City when the votes were counted. The heavy drizzle early on election day cleared and crowds gathered in Printing House Square to wait for the returns. As the hours passed, they learned that although Lincoln carried the state by a small margin, he lost the city by about 30,000 votes. Lincoln had been clearly rejected by New York City. Democrats also took consolation in the defeat of equal suffrage for blacks, which was voted down 337,934 to 197,505. Later, Archbishop John Hughes of New York told Bishop Patrick Lynch of Charleston that Lincoln had not been elected by Black Republicans but by three Democrats.

The election of Lincoln immediately increased speculation in the city about whether southern states would secede. The South Carolina legislature wasted no time in calling for a convention in December to declare the state's intentions, and on the streets of New York everyone asked, "Do you think the South will secede?" Alfred Satterlee wrote in his diary, "If S. C. would only go *alone* out of the Union it would be a good riddance." But William Cullen Bryant, happy over the election, was convinced that only silly people expected disunion.[35]

Although rumors of secession were incessant, few people knew that an obscure army officer, Major Robert Anderson, had received orders from the army headquarters in New York City on November 13 to take command of the troops and forts in Charleston Harbor. Some New Yorkers did not even realize that the headquarters for the United States Army was in their city rather than Washington, D. C. Winfield Scott, the commanding general of the army, had made that move when his relations with Secretary of War Jefferson Davis had soured during the Pierce administration.

Before leaving for the South, Anderson, who had been born in Kentucky and was married to a Georgian, conferred with Scott. They reviewed the strength of the forts and the possibility of evacuating Fort Moultrie on the mainland and concentrating their position at Fort Sumter in the harbor. Anderson recommended increasing the forces in the forts, but the aging and ailing general had already given that advice to President Buchanan and had been turned down. At the same time, Scott wisely rejected the amateurish offer from Moses Grinnell, James Hamilton, and John Williams, rich New Yorkers, to form a volunteer garrison of four hundred artillerymen at their expense to hold Fort Moultrie.[36] Scott left for Washington the next month to step up his demands for more vigorous military preparation. Neither Secretary of War John B. Floyd nor the president was anxious to listen.

Meanwhile, panic struck Wall Street. The fear was that the southern states would repudiate their northern debts. Reports and rumors, denials and confirmations cluttered the conversations of all businessmen. No one knew what to believe, but there was no question that the confusion had an effect on the market. Southern editorials about suspending northern debts gave the calmest businessman the jitters. Then the governor of Georgia recommended the confiscation of property owned by northerners. More ominous were the laws introduced in some southern states to postpone payment of debts. John A. Stevens, president of the Bank of Commerce, which controlled more than $10 million in capital, tried to reassure the public that this was a mere flurry and that everything would soon return to normal. Still, uneasiness remained.[37]

Frightened merchants tried to settle outstanding accounts and prepared to take losses. So as to make an immediate collection, some businessmen accepted unusually small percentages of the amount owed them. The price of flour dropped a dollar a barrel and prices of rice, cotton, and corn dropped too. Wheat went down to twenty cents a bushel. The dry goods business was at a standstill and some manufacturers held up their operations in bewilderment. Unemployment in the winter months increased, and even the Brooklyn Navy Yard ordered layoffs.

Over the years New York merchants had made good friends with customers and suppliers in the South, whom they now tried to reassure that all would be well and that they had the highest regard for the South. In their anxiety, the thought of peaceable secession did not disturb many of them as much as the possibility of their own imminent bankruptcy. Concessions to the South, at the very least, were necessary. If compromise did not work, it would be better to carry on sound trade relations with a new confederacy than to bear financial disaster. William Aspinwall, one of the richest and most respected men in the city, was willing to see the South leave the Union in peace. William B. Astor agreed with him.

Businessmen were not the only New Yorkers ready to see the South leave the Union. The impetuous Horace Greeley, a Republican, who later complained that President Buchanan trembled at the rustling of a leaf, wrote in the *Tribune* that he deplored the southern madness, but if seven or eight states wanted to depart, "Let them go!" He philosophized that he could not take any other side without clashing with the revered "Rights of Man." When Greeley expressed his opinions, logical or illogical, consistent or inconsistent, he addressed a large part of the nation. His weekly and semiweekly editions of the *Tribune* were condensations of the daily and were mailed to readers from Maine to California. The *Tribune* had a total circulation of about three hundred thousand, the largest of any newspaper in the world, and it was estimated that it was read by a million people. Yet Greeley probably did not think that southerners would take him up on his dare to secede. Disunion was beyond his comprehension, and he had convinced himself that aside from a few hotheads, Union sentiment was strong in the South. Such disbelief in the South's declared intentions was common in the city. After all, the South had cried "wolf" for years.[38]

Greeley's confidence in the South's loyalty to the Union prompted him to make some seemingly practical suggestions concerning secession. Two days after Lincoln's election, he admitted that the South had a right to secede, but he pleaded for time and insisted that any such step should be taken with calm deliberation. He wanted the South to discuss the issue carefully, reflect upon the consequences, and then vote. "Let the act of secession be the echo of a popular fiat," he wrote. In this way, either separation could be achieved without bloodshed or support for the Union could be clearly expressed. Greeley's reasonableness, shared by many in the city, undoubtedly stemmed from his certainty of a favorable outcome for the Union. And he may have been right. But it did not matter. No one, North or South, listened sufficiently to cast aside heated passions and act on the plan.

The New York *Times*, edited by keen-minded Henry Raymond, an active Republican politician, also flirted with the concept of peaceable secession. Moderation had always been the key word for Raymond and the *Times*. His paper had announced in its first issue that it did not intend to write as if in a passion. But moderation and passion were matters of judgment that did not prevent the *Times* from presenting uncommon views on occasion.

It seemed less surprising when other papers, such as the *World, Express, Journal of Commerce,* and *Daily News,* favored peaceable secession. They had frequently shown sympathy for the South in the past. The editor of the *World,* an independent newspaper at the time, weary of never-ending southern threats, suggested an amendment to the Constitution that would allow states to depart amicably. He sensibly argued that if

Texas had not been annexed, or if South Carolina had not ratified the Consitution, or Florida had not been bought from Spain, the nation would have still prospered.

Gerard Hallock's *Journal of Commerce* disapproved of journalists and clergymen whose code of morality considered meddling in other people's business a Christian duty. History and science proved, the paper claimed, that an inferior race had to be placed in a condition of slavery. Immediate freedom for the blacks would create a series of events too horrible to contemplate. Only the owners of slaves could free them, and interference from northerners would do more harm than good. The *Journal of Commerce* was proud of its practicality and expressed the opinion that the southern states should be allowed to secede with the benediction of the North.

The editor of the *Daily News* was the mayor's younger brother Benjamin, and he had consistently shown sympathy for the South. He was willing to let the South secede because peaceable secession was far preferable to him than civil war. Ben Wood had a flair for his work, and his words often appealed to recent immigrants and workingmen. The Wood brothers had a touch of the theatrical which made them sprightly personalities even when presenting disturbing ideas. Theater and politics have much in common, and the Woods were skilled performers. Henry Wood, a third brother, exhibited this family trait more strongly than the other two. He was a theatrical promoter and partner in Christy's Minstrels.

The popularity of the *Daily News* was understandable because its pages were relatively concise at a time when turgid columns were the general practice. It also gave far more attention to the increasing interest in sports than other newspapers. Baseball, cricket, the turf, sculling, and sailing received prominent space. Despite irritation with the recent trend of events, the editor also retained a sense of humor, a continual wonder about irony, and bafflement over intolerant Puritans who considered themselves good Christians.

James Gordon Bennett, publisher of the always lively and provocative *Herald,* went along with the idea of peaceable secession for awhile too. If separated, the South could move into Mexico and the North could annex Canada. New York City would become the capital of the northern empire and the center of commerce for three continents. Bennett found the idea appealing. But he had another fanciful scheme too. He proposed a reorganization of the Union with a southern constitution that would exclude New England.[39]

Twenty or more newspapers published in the city offered citizens a broad range of opinions. Free expression was rampant. When the *Evening Post* reported that abolitionists were more concerned with morals than politics and wanted immediate emancipation, the *Caucasian* reminded its readers that the presence of ten thousand prostitutes in the city created a more serious moral problem closer to home.

No one could say that New York newspapers and newspapermen were not opinionated, but they had the advantage of offering plenty of alternatives. News reports were usually heavy on opinions and short on facts. Objectivity was not a major concern. This was an age known for some of the greatest editors in American journalism, but reporters, the workingmen of the press, were looked upon as a shiftless crowd. They were often seen at their favorite haunt, Pfaff's Cave, drinking Charles Pfaff's fine lager, eating heavy German food, and idling away their time.

As the strain between North and South accentuated, most New Yorkers wanted some sort of reasonable compromise. August Belmont was sure that except for a few "ultra radicals" the people favored concessions. He wrote to Governor William Sprague of Rhode Island that he had spent an evening with some leading Republicans, including one of the Astors, Moses Grinnell, and Hamilton Fish. "They were unanimous," he said, "in their voice for reconciliation, and the first steps have to be taken by the north."[40] Belmont may have underestimated the strong sentiments of local Republicans who opposed the extension of slavery in the territories and placed limits on concessions. There was no doubt, however, that compromise was much discussed throughout the city and received widespread approval.

John Cochrane, a New York City congressman, proposed legislation similar to the suggestions of Senator John J. Crittenden of Kentucky. Cochrane wanted to divide the territories along the Missouri Compromise line of 36° 30° and prohibit slavery to the north and permit slavery to the south. He was also receptive to interstate slave trade, unrestricted travel of owners with their slaves in free states, and the abolition of personal liberty laws designed to nullify the return of fugitive slaves.

Belmont, thinking himself a realist, favored the Cochrane and Crittenden ideas. He believed compromise was the only answer to the problem and rallied support for such proposals to prevent chaos. He was convinced that the breakup of the nation into two confederacies was "too preposterous to be entertained." Belmont was reassured when he learned that the masterful upstate Republican politician Thurlow Weed, who often spoke for the propertied interests in the city, also favored compromise. Belmont wrote, "In our own city and State some of the most prominent men are ready to follow the lead of Weed. Restoration of the Missouri line finds favour with most of the conservative Republicans, and their number is increasing daily." He was undoubtedly heartened when William Seward presented a memorial in the Senate from thirty-eight thousand residents of the city pleading for compromise.[41]

Belmont's appraisal of the situation may have been accurate, but there were those who disagreed. William Cullen Bryant worried that Seward was conspiring with Wall Streeters in the interest of compromise. He tried to offset Seward's advice by assuring Lincoln that Republicans without Wall Street connections were vehemently opposed to making concessions concerning slavery and that the restoration of the Missouri Compromise would destroy the Republican party.[42]

Anxious citizens who wanted to foster a compromise with the South sent out a call to leaders in the city and state for a meeting on December 15. They were looking for a way to escape what appeared to be an approaching disaster. Replies were so numerous that two buildings had to be engaged on Pine Street for the large crowd presided over by Charles O'Conor, who asked, "Can we obtain a little time?" The appeal was desperate. O'Conor believed that a voice from New York City would be recognized as the voice of a friend because a "mighty majority" in their midst favored justice for the South. Daniel Dickinson spoke of the need to repeal obnoxious laws that offended the South and to transform public opinion that had been dominated by demagogues and "ministers of depravity." Hiram Ketcham, a highly regarded businessman, assured the distinguished group that if a conflict arose, the city's residents would stand by their brethren, the white race.

The need to reassure the South seemed to be paramount. The preface to the resolutions, which unanimously endorsed the return of fugitive slaves and the extension of southern rights in territories, left no doubt about the intent of those who attended the meeting to appease the South. They proclaimed an abhorrence equal to any southerner's for the "aggression and insult visited upon you by abolitionists and their abettors during the last thirty-five years." As friends, however, they called for a delay of action so that cooler heads might prevail. A committee was appointed to carry these sentiments to the South. John Dix urged Horatio Seymour to go south with leading citizens such as James Beekman and Stewart Brown to induce friends in that section to suspend their moves toward secession. These were serious pleas for peace by powerful men outside of the regular political channels. They sought a practical solution to a knotty problem as they were accustomed to do in their businesses or professions. They hoped the matter could be negotiated. But neither the North nor the South listened.[43]

Tilden, who was present at the Pine Street meeting, did not minimize the danger of disunion. He believed the only hope was to build an effective minority in the South to support the Union. But that would take time. The urgent need was to understand the opposing viewpoint. Tilden wrote to his friend W. B. Ogden, who was on his way to Chicago to meet Lincoln, "Nothing is so difficult in ordinary experience as to see both sides of a question. . . . It is necessary to do more — to imagine ourselves in their position in order to form a policy adapted to their case."[44]

Other New Yorkers futilely fought for time. Alderman Francis Boole pleaded for the South to avoid violence so that differences could be adjusted. Alderman William Peck, completing his term as president of the board, unabashedly told his fellow aldermen that the people of the city might have to assume the responsibility for restoring harmonious relations throughout the Union. This was a tall order, and he may have had an exaggerated opinion of the national influence of the Board of Aldermen, but he expressed the views of many constituents that the city could serve as a calming force in the country. But once again the supplicants went unheeded. In a few days, South Carolina announced its secession, and other states soon followed.[45]

The long lag in time between the election of the president in November and inauguration in March contributed to the anxiety and gloom. Lincoln, aware that he had no authority and that anything he might say could be misinterpreted, remained silent. But even his silence was subject to interpretation. He silently opposed compromise.

The Radical Republicans were less apt to be silent. Zachariah Chandler of Michigan, no friend of compromise, viewed the business world with disgust. He was not bothered by a little bloodshed for the sake of preserving the Union. "From the days of Carthage to those of

James Buchanan," he said, "the great mercantile centres have been peaceable — ever ready to buy immunity but not to fight for it." The weakness of peace-loving commercial men distressed him, and the opinions that flowed from the businessmen's capital of America reaffirmed his disgust.[46]

Rowland H. Macy recognized the tension and despair in the city and used it as a theme to boost sales in one of his ads: "Tremendous Excitement: The Irrepressible Conflict: ... R. H. Macy relies upon ENORMOUS REDUCTION from the usual prices as the GENTLE PERSUADER which will not only relieve him, but carry peace and happiness to EVERY HEARTHSTONE, and LIFT THE CLOUD OF GLOOM which has hung like a pall over the EMPIRE CITY during the last sixty days."[47] This may have been an example of early hucksterism, but the astute Macy showed a sensitivity and understanding of the emotional state of the city.

At this precarious time, Lincoln was not the only silent politician. During the presidential campaign, the mayor had urged New Yorkers to save the city from Abraham Lincoln. Now that the election was over, Wood bided his time as he tried to measure public opinion. Because of all the commotion, he concluded that the better part of valor was to wait before he declared himself. At the moment, nothing was predictable.

2
The New Year

Wall Streeters looked for hopeful signs in the New Year and were pleased when the stock exchange opened with a strong start. A rise of 5 percent on almost all securities appeared to be a good omen for the future. There was a reason for the market's optimistic action. At last the sleepy Buchanan government was taking a firm step against the treasonous behavior of South Carolina. People commonly accepted the illogical belief that military action would bring peace, and rumors were rife that warships had been ordered to Charleston. Public confidence grew with the thought that this show of strength was a first step toward the peace they desperately wanted. It was an open secret that military preparations for this expedition were under way in New York Harbor.

Yet the strengthening of the stock market was at the start of 1861 deceptive. Hope and fear mingled together. For those who studied business conditions there were disturbing signs. The credit rater, Dun, Boyd and Company, saw the need to renew harmony between the mercantile and political interests in the nation. It reported that by the end of the previous summer the country had almost entirely recovered from the effects of the panic of 1857. The nation was unusually free from foreign debt, and prosperity seemed certain. But the last three months of the year were troublesome. Although fewer companies had failed during that time, their liabilities were proportionately greater than during the preceding nine months. Oddly, failures had occurred among companies that had been financially above suspicion. Dun, Boyd did not see any reason to doubt the honesty of southern merchants but warned that there might be delays in the settlement of their accounts. In 1857, the West had suffered severe economic hardship, and New Yorkers eagerly turned to southern trade. Now, the company suggested that northern merchants watch the extension of credit carefully and look once again to the west for new business.[1]

In the next few weeks, New York businessmen wondered about the integrity of southern merchants. Their requests for payment of outstanding bills brought some unusual replies. One read, "I shall pay, of course, every farthing I owe you, in cash, but not till I pay it in the currency of the Southern Confederacy." Another stated, "I cannot return the goods, as you demand, for they are already sold, and the money invested in muskets to shoot you-Yankees."[2] Confidence in southern customers was on the wane.

Mail arrived from insurance holders in South Carolina asking about the effect of secession on their policies. Morris Franklin, president of the New York Life Insurance Company, replied to one of his southern agents that only the insolvency of the company could have any effect on their policies. Nevertheless, he added that the trustees were unanimous in the opinion that their company was not warranted in assuring the risk of death in the event of an "unfortunate hostile collision" between persons living in different states. Still, none of the trustees believed such a collision would take place. Later, when a soldier under Major Anderson at Fort Sumter inquired about the status of his New York Life policy, he was told that he was not covered for risk in the armed services. The reply continued, "We doubt not that there is patriotism enough in our trustees to waive the legal question which might arise under the policy and pay the amount insured." It would be considered an act of self-defense.[3]

To ease the anxiety of the nation, President Buchanan proclaimed a "Day of Special Humiliation, Fasting, and Prayer" on January 4. It gave the spiritual leaders of the city a chance briefly to take the center stage away from the materialistic-minded. Many businesses closed for half a day, and concerned citizens flocked to churches to pray and listen to the wisdom of the clergy about the condition of the country. The following day, newspapers reported the prayer day's activities in detail and printed sermons delivered by some of the best-known clergymen in the city. The texts revealed that there was no agreement among them and that the Scriptures were used to defend as well as denounce slavery and the South. Dr. Morris Raphall spoke at the Greene Street synagogue during the day of prayer. Although only about 1 percent of the people in the city were Jews, there were about twenty-seven synagogues and many mem-

bers of their congregations had considerable influence. The rabbi severely criticized the well-known antislavery minister Henry Ward
Beecher of the Plymouth Church in Brooklyn. "How dare you," he declared, "in the face of the sanction and protection afforded to slave property in the ten commandments — how dare you denounce slaveholding
as a sin. When you remember that Abraham, Isaac, Jacob, Job—the men
with whom the Almighty conversed, with whose names he emphatically
connects his own most holy name . . . that all these men were slaveholders, does it strike you that you are guilty of something little short of blas-
phemy?" Raphall thought that considering slavery a sin angered the
South and alarmed the North.[4]

The local politicians were busy at the start of the New Year, too.
Some of them could not resist the opportunity to use the Charleston crisis for their own self-promotion. When the Board of Aldermen met at
City Hall, Francis Boole went beyond the realm of municipal affairs and
offered a resolution about the national predicament. He expressed the
affection of New Yorkers for the South and appealed for restraint from
violence while attempts were made to adjust differences. Boole wanted
to send a copy of the resolution to the president, Congress, governor, and
state legislature. It would include a memorial for the state legislature to
call a convention to consider the state of the Union.

Alderman John Brady said he did not understand the object of the
resolution. What good could it possibly do? Boole answered that its purpose was to protect the country, and everyone in the room laughed.
Brady countered that he thought the country could take care of itself,
but Alderman Henry Genet joined the discussion, saying he was not so
sure. He bluntly declared, "We have bigger traitors here than in the
South." Brady asked Boole why he wanted a convention. Did he want to
secede from the state? Everyone laughed again and Genet interrupted,
"That is just what we will do if they don't let us alone." A voice in the
chamber asked Brady what he thought of Major Anderson. He replied
that Anderson was doing his duty and that the people should stand by
the Constitution and the country. "Never allow South Carolina," he said,
"or no slave, or no nigger of any description to interfere with our stars.
. . . I go for my country — irrespective of niggers and South Carolina —
they are only fighting for niggers." Genet, a lawyer, said that the South
Carolinians were fighting for their property. Fighting for a slave was the

same as fighting for a horse. Brady disagreed. He did not believe that Negroes were property and Genet asked, "Why you don't pretend that a nigger is a man do you?" When Brady answered that blacks were men just as everyone else, Alderman James Bagley chimed in, "Brady is a little dark himself." The exchange, insensitive and unbecoming, illustrated the intellectual level of the board members, who treated the episode as a joke and failed to stop the passage of one more worthless resolution.[5]

By now, Mayor Wood concluded that the time was ripe for him to solve the complicated problems that faced the city and nation. His plan, he believed, might startle some people, but he was confident that the commercial interests in the city would see the common sense of his proposal. He was convinced that the dissolution of the Union was a certainty. Once a southern confederacy was formed, he saw the additional probability of California establishing an independent republic with gold as its key to independence. Then the western wheat states would break away. In this event he did not see why New York City should not become independent. Two-thirds of the expenses of the United States government, he claimed, were paid by revenue from the city anyway.

On January 7, Wood lived up to his "Napoleonic love of sensations." He sent a message to the Common Council calling for the secession of the city when the breakup of the nation took place. In the meantime, he expected "a continuance of uninterrupted intercourse with every section" and did not think the city should oppose the South. Other parts of the state had been imbued with the ' 'fanatical spirit" of New England, but New Yorkers, he said, had sympathy for their "aggrieved brethren" in the slave states. "We have not participated in warfare upon their constitutional rights or upon their domestic institutions."[6]

The city that Wood envisioned would be free of the state legislature as well as the national government. In recent years, the legislature had aggressively diluted his power as mayor. The passage of the Metropolitan Police Act, which had taken away his control of the city police, was only one of many infringements on Wood's jurisdiction. The legislature had also established commissions to supervise construction of Central Park and a new City Hall and changed the city charter to give financial responsibility to the comptroller instead of the mayor. Wood regarded these and other adverse actions by the state as unwarranted

usurpations. They infuriated him, and he realized that his secession plan offered the additional benefit of casting off the yoke of the legislature.

Wood justified his proposal on the basis of the colonial charter of
Thomas Dongan, lieutenant governor and vice-admiral of New York,
which was ratified in 1730. He quoted the first article: "New York be,
and from henceforth forever hereafter shall be and remain, a free city
of itself," claiming that statement guaranteed the independence of the
city regardless of whatever government succeeded to the sovereign
power of the English throne. For this purpose, he was willing to forget
the American Revolution. Unshackled, the city, which provided, according to him, the capital, energy, and enterprise of the nation, could
achieve security and prosperity at little cost. Income could be produced
by a tariff on imports, and the free city would have "the united support
of the Southern states." All this was to be obtained without violence.[7]

Wood was neither the first nor the last politician to present this uto-
pian proposal to his constituents. It was an intriguing idea, a bill of di-
vorcement based on commercialism and political opportunity, that was
almost irresistible in the abstract. The scheme captivated those who
believed that their city, superior to all others, had been unnecessarily
subordinated by malevolent men in the lesser cities of Albany and
Washington.

The mayor's bombshell was not received with unanimity, but Wood
had supporters. Among those who favored his plan were the United
States marshal Isaiah Rynders, James E. Kerrigan, recently elected to
Congress, and Gazaway Bugg Lamar, president of the Bank of the Republic. Others had expressed similar views privately. August Belmont
may have quietly influenced the mayor. A short time before, he had written to John Forsyth of Mobile, Alabama, saying that he deplored dissolution of the Union. Nevertheless, he went on, "New York, in such a catastrophe, would cut loose from the puritanical East, and her protective
tariff . . . she would open her magnificent port to the commerce of the
world. What Venice was once on the sluggish lagoons of the Adriatic,
New York would ere long become to the two hemispheres."[8]

Gazaway Bugg Lamar, a major figure in the financial world, was a
native of Augusta, Georgia, who retained a strong sense of loyalty to the
South despite his long residence in the city. He had been the most prominent figure in 1851 in establishing the Bank of the Republic, which

Fernando Wood's southern sympathies roused the ire of one artist, who satirized him as the "Angel of Peace." (Courtesy of the New-York Historical Society)

stood at the corner of Wall Street and Broadway, and he believed that a free city would help avoid a civil war. It was inconceivable to him that New York would give up commercial leadership in the country under any circumstances and he saw Wood's proposal as a way to serve both business and the South.[9]

Congressman Daniel Sickles, always ready to sponsor any idea that might promote his own career, had earlier made a long-winded speech that sounded much the same as Wood's proposal but had not attracted as much notice. If a crisis arose, he did not believe that any man would cross the city line to wage war against a state of the Union. In addition, he opportunistically envisioned a time when the city would eliminate interference from Albany. He despised the state legislators and looked upon them as nothing more than fanatical tax gatherers. The dream of a free city-state appealed to him as it did to the mayor. Sickles pictured a municipality free of all restraints opening its gates to the world's cultures and trade.[10]

Sickles had some ability and political influence, but his exaggerated remarks had not carried as much weight as Wood's. Although Sickles was charming, his character was probably more suspect than the mayor's. He had achieved his greatest fame by shooting his young wife's lover and securing an acquittal for the murder. Since Sickles was a well-known womanizer and frequently absent from home, the jury's verdict appeared more than generous.

Wood's message started a controversy in the press and among politicians. Alderman Isaac Dayton presented a resolution charging that the mayor was "totally at variance with the sentiments of the mass of the people of this city."[11] But his critical proposal lacked support among board members and did not carry when it came to a vote. The *Journal of Commerce* expressed mixed feelings about the mayor's views, and the *Times* considered the idea a matter of "suicide while insane." The *Daily News*, as expected, came to the defense of the plan, and the *Evening Post* ridiculed Wood and asked if the city should take over the New York Central Railroad and the Erie Canal. Greeley's opinion in the *Tribune* was much harsher. "Fernando Wood," he said, "evidently wants to be a traitor, it is lack of courage only that makes him content with being a blackguard." And Tammany Hall used the mayor's proposal as one more reason to attack Mozart Hall. Benjamin Wood saw nothing impractical in his brother's plan. He thought it preferable for New York City to be the marketplace for the South rather than Liverpool or Le Havre, and he believed that trade with the Gulf states would build American instead of European alliances. "The position of Hamburg and the free cities of Germany has not been mean," a *Daily News* editorial commented, "nor has their influence been other than beneficial to German nationality and prosperity. . . . New York will surely be allowed to occupy a similar relation here to the agricultural and manufacturing populations of the interior—the channel of their trade with the rest of the world." The editor presented an attractive picture of future possibilities for the city and insisted that a large majority of rich men agreed with him. He may have been right, but they remained nameless, silent, and unhelpful in gaining public support.[12]

No serious political group took up the mayor's proposition on the day of disunion. The people were still waiting to see what would happen when Lincoln was inaugurated. Yet the plan did not die; it was held in abeyance to be dragged out again if needed. That may have been the most that Wood had expected to accomplish. His desire for the city's secession was genuine, but he was still smarting from his feuds with the legislature and he knew the political pitfalls in carrying out such an extreme idea. At the moment, he was apparently raising a finger to catch the direction of the latest popular breeze.

The vexatious words of Wood and Sickles did not calm a tense city. Wild notions and strange opinions sprang up all over town. Moods and rumors, rather than reason, controlled conversations with little relation to fact. Passing fancies and false impressions, not profound analyses, were the order of the day. The Wall Street lawyer George Templeton Strong noted in his diary, "One hears queer talk in these days of excitement." Minds were unsettled, and anything seemed possible. One of Strong's acquaintances, Edward Bancker, a conservative old Dutchman, thought every man who voted for Lincoln should be hanged. Another, Willy Cutting, "talks mysteriously of an organization to revolutionize the city." He wanted to expand Wood's scheme by including Westchester and Kings counties in the new principality.[13]

During these days of doubt and consternation, Wood apologized to the governor of Georgia because the Metropolitan Police under Superintendent John Kennedy had seized a cargo of almost a thousand muskets on the steamship *Monticello*, which was bound for Savannah. "If I had the power," he wrote, "I should summarily punish the authors of this illegal and unjustifiable seizure of private property." His embarrassment over this episode, real or feigned, was undoubtedly heightened by his delight in placing the police, now under the state's control, in a bad light. It caused him embarrassment of a different sort, however, in the next few years when he was repeatedly reminded by *Harper's Weekly* and other journals of his perfidious behavior on this occasion. But even Wood was probably unaware of the deliberate undercover activities of Gazaway Lamar, who had been secretly commissioned by Secretary of War Floyd to buy these and thousands of other guns for the South. Lamar represented Georgia in this dispute over the *Monticello* shipment, and eventually the guns were released when Governor Joseph E. Brown of Georgia threatened to seize New York ships in the Savannah harbor.[14]

While Wood talked of secession, his Democratic rivals at Tammany Hall found a good excuse to express their devotion to the Union by celebrating the forty-sixth anniversary of Andrew Jackson's victory at the Battle of New Orleans. Guests of all political shades gathered at a hastily organized banquet in the grand ballroom of the St. Nicholas Hotel, where they enjoyed food and drink that was "the best the market affords." William B. Kennedy, the grand sachem, presided beneath a portrait of George Washington and offered a toast for "the day we celebrate," which was followed by stirring band music and a response from Samuel Tilden.

It was the perfect opportunity for Tilden to mention the former president's toast "Our Federal Union, it must and shall be preserved." The comparison with their own perilous times was obvious, and Tilden said he was sure there was not a single man in the room who would not die for the Union. It was an extravagant claim. The staunch loyalty of his listeners was debatable, and before Tilden ended his speech his own dedication seemed to pale. He said he favored any reasonable compromise to prevent disturbing the Union. And he added, "If it should happen that fifteen, or fourteen, or twelve states should be well nigh unanimous that the policy of the North, or a faction of the North was fatal to their interests, I should consider long, I should consider well, before I lighted the torch in this civil war in this glorious union!" It probably did not matter what Tilden said. The guests were well into their cups and did not find Tilden very entertaining. The nation's peril was not of great interest to them that night as they laughed and talked among themselves

during Tilden's speech. Calls for order did not help, and anyone interested in the distinguished lawyer's comments had trouble hearing him
above the din.[15]

While Tammanyites wined and dined, the unarmed *Star of the West,*
a sidewheel merchant steamer, sailed southward to strengthen the Union
position in Charleston Harbor. It was decided that a merchant ship was
preferable to a warship because it would seem less threatening to South
Carolinians. The ship had quietly taken on two hundred troops in the
lower bay and slipped out of New York Harbor. It was cleared for its regular run to Havana via New Orleans, but there was little doubt in the city
that the real destination was Charleston.[16]

Major Anderson, besieged at Fort Sumter, became a symbol of the
federal government's strength. The city could never resist heroes, and
for many he became the hero of the day. An anonymous item in the personal column of the *Times* read, "Major Anderson will be the next President of the United States."[17] That whimsical notion, like so many others
that appeared at this time of crisis, was quickly forgotten.

On January 9, 1861, the hope held for the *Star of the West's* mission
crumbled when South Carolinians fired on the ship and it failed to reinforce Anderson. In a few days, the *Star of the West* was back in New York.
Seventeen shots had been fired at the helpless steamer, but aside from a
few broken planks, the ship had suffered slight damage. Nevertheless,
the craving for a first step toward peace remained unfulfilled. Troops
unceremoniously transferred to a tug and return to Governor's Island.[18]

South Carolina shocked New Yorkers by this act of war, but interest
in compromise continued in the city. A few days later, an antislavery
meeting at Clinton Hall attracted an irritated crowd of hecklers outside
who gave three cheers for South Carolina, three cheers for Governor
Francis Pickens, the secessionist leader, and three groans for Abraham
Lincoln.[19] The protesters may have been only an isolated group of troublemakers, but they were an indication that the attack on the *Star of the
West* had not set off an emotional wave in the city to support the Union
at all costs.

The subject of war was on everyone's lips. It was anticipated and at
the same time disbelieved as too farfetched. Somehow the politicians
would find a common ground for compromise. Still, the Republican
Central Club started to enroll volunteers to meet any government call for

troops. The company was to be known as Company A, Union Volunteers. Reports also circulated that disunion agents were at work in the city and that a Virginian was trying to raise a body of men for a southern regiment.[20]

By the end of January, Georgia, Florida, Alabama, Louisiana, and Mississippi joined South Carolina in secession. Nevertheless, appeals for compromise continued. Peter Cooper had captured the imagination of the masses when he built the Tom Thumb, the first American steam locomotive. Now, he called on the people to use Christian forbearance despite the rashness of the South. In a mellow mood at the age of seventy, he had philosophically concluded that it was a good idea to search for wisdom by reflecting on the past. As he reflected on American history, his faith in compromise grew stronger when he realized that a wise precedent had been established at the first Constitutional Convention. The Constitution could not have been produced or the nation preserved, he discovered, without compromise at Philadelphia in 1787. The North had then acquiesced to slavery in the South, and in return the federal government gained the right to regulate commerce. He was convinced at this critical moment in history compromise might once more avoid death, debt, and desolation.[21] Possible profits that he might make from a war were far from the old ironmonger's thoughts, and he was not unlike most businessmen in the city who were ready to go to great lengths to prevent hostilities. The Chamber of Commerce had unanimously urged Congress to accept the Crittenden Compromise. And another gathering at Cooper Institute pleaded for understanding between the North and South and designated three commissioners to confer with delegates to the conventions of the seceding states.[22] All efforts were to no avail.

Charles Daly, a justice of the Court of Common Pleas of the city of New York, saw the Crittenden Compromise as the only way to avoid civil war. Considering himself humane, he thought a concession by the South to attach slaves to the land so that their families would not be separated might prove helpful. He asked Senator Seward what he would do if Fort Sumter was attacked. Seward replied, "They won't do it, and if they do, it will be time enough to think about it." Seward assured Daly that there would never be a civil war.[23]

William Howard Russell, correspondent for the *London Times*, believed that affluent members of New York City society would do anything rather than fight. He thought they had severe reservations about democracy and did not think much of universal suffrage, free citizenship, or free speech. These aristocrats, he observed, had watched democracy at work in their municipal government, and it looked to them like government by the most ignorant. Equality in large cities had serious drawbacks for them. Russell attended a select dinner in the city that included Horatio Seymour, George Bancroft, Samuel Tilden, and August Belmont, all distinguished Democrats. He gained the impression from their table talk that the Constitution restricted the government from using force to prevent secession.[24]

Assurance of northern sympathy for the South was emphasized and reemphasized. August Belmont and some of his banking and merchant friends told secessionists that the new administration would certainly recognize their property rights in fugitive slaves and that they could count on an equal right to slavery in the territories. Belmont, steadily corresponding with his southern friends, wrote John Forsyth that nobody regretted the election of Lincoln more than he, but he was sure that southern rights would be guaranteed by amendments to the Constitution. He had no authority for making these statements, but in return he asked southerners to avoid extreme behavior that might cause trouble.[25]

Samuel Tilden wrote to a friend in Virginia that the recent presidential election did not really reflect northern opinion but was instead the result of a disorganized Democratic party. He now believed that the Democrats' errors had run their course and that Lincoln's administration would go to pieces. The Democrats would grow stronger and do full justice to the South. If Congress failed to take any constructive action, he thought it would be wise to call a national convention to propose amendments to the Constitution. He calculated that three-quarters of the states would ratify amendments similar to the Crittenden proposal. "Our people," Tilden wrote, "are temporarily misled, but by a vast majority conservative at the bottom. We only need time to bring them to a sound position." Tilden was willing to pacify the South because his vivid imagination clearly foresaw the calamity that a war would bring.[26]

Samuel F. B. Morse, at his new house at 5 West 22 Street, agonized over the possibility of war. In January he wrote to a friend, "There is something so unnatural and abhorrent in this outcry of arms in one great family that I cannot believe it will come to a decision of the sword. Such counsels are in the court of passion, not of reason. Imagine such a conflict, imagine a victory, no matter by which side. Can the victors rejoice in the blood of brethren shed in a family brawl?"[27] Morse was a confounding man. His clear thinking accurately sensed the pain of a civil war, but he remained insensitive to the pain of slavery.

Other Democrats in the city, less intellectual than Belmont, Tilden, or Morse, gave a colorful example of the democracy in action that repelled the elite. Nonetheless, under the raw manners, language, and brogues, many of their beliefs and goals were similar. Representatives of the working class gathered in the drill room at Brookes' Hall on Broome Street to oppose the Republican party, which they claimed was rushing them into the horrors of a civil war. Workingmen, especially Irish workingmen, feared that they would be replaced by blacks. Actually, it was the other way around as Irish and other immigrants continued to squeeze blacks out of their jobs.

Before the meeting at Brookes' Hall began, clusters of men outside the building expressed their intense indignation in abusive language. Listeners could hear such straightforward phrases as "Hang the Republicans," "Niggers ain't as good as I am," and "Oh Lincoln will never be inaugurated. I will be the one to kill him." When the proceedings commenced, the speakers on the platform were almost as belligerent as their audience. The chairman, D. W. Groot, painted a dreary picture of closed factories and claimed that the city was losing $20 million a month in southern orders. Worse was ahead for everyone when Republicans took power. As he spoke pessimistically about what was to become of workingmen and protested against civil war, denounced coercion, and demanded protection for southern rights, someone shouted, "Hang old Lincoln."[28]

Strong language was the stock in trade for one of the speakers, U.S. Marshal Isaiah Rynders from the Fourteenth Ward, an old hand at riling up crowds. The lawyers, preachers, and newspapermen had had their say. Now, he said, it was the workingman's turn. The Black Republicans were traitors. Carried away with his own words, he became more extreme: "If a Democratic Company volunteers to go South to subjugate the South, I say to them, you are traitors to your country." This was too much for one brave soul, who yelled, "You are a political demagogue." Rynders insisted that the man be put out of the hall, and he was forcibly ejected. Liberty had its limits even among Democrats. Rynders went on. The crowd was with him. Soon the meeting passed resolutions supporting a white man's government, extending sympathy for southern resistance, and insisting on a peaceable solution so that the "wheels of business" could move again. Southern slaveholders, they said, were the natural allies of northern laborers. The resolutions went further and showed the Irish influence in the hall. They declared that Great Britain was a domineering influence on America in trying to reduce the white man to the level of Negroes. They pledged to oppose the British, who had "abolitionized" the press and pulpit but were guilty of oppression at home and in Ireland. They charged that while the South had fought in a holy cause for American liberty, the British diverted attention from their own sins by false philanthropy for Negroes in America.[29]

Despite severe criticism of the Republicans, New Yorkers looked forward with curiosity to the visit of Lincoln on his way to Washington. Lincoln was a conundrum. He had said very little during these long months. Perhaps he would make a statement when he reached the city. There was concern for the president's safety. Some citizens feared that his inauguration would end in bloodshed and considered going to the capital to protect him. They were brought up sharply by an article in the *Herald* entitled "Mind Your Own Business," and nothing more was heard of the project.[30]

Young Joseph Choate was now a partner in the Wall Street law firm of Butler, Evarts, and Southmayd making the handsome salary of $3,000 a year against 15 percent of the firm's income. He was anxious to get a look at "Old Abe" when he arrived in the city on February 19 and hoped that the president-elect would make very short speeches and refrain from his undignified practice of kissing girls. Choate succeeded in getting a good look at Lincoln and was not impressed by his stubbed beard, which made him uglier than ever in the lawyer's eyes. He wrote his mother, " 'Handsome is as handsome does,' and if he realizes half the hopes which we entertain for him, we shall forget how bad looking he is." Good looks, however, are a matter of opinion. Alfred Jones, an officer of the Sixth Avenue Railroad Company, saw Lincoln stand up in his carriage and decided that he was "better looking than his portraits."[31]

Lincoln had taken the Hudson River Railroad from Albany and arrived at the new station on Thirteenth Street between Ninth and Tenth Avenues. A procession of public hacks accompanied him downtown to the Astor House. The president-elect, seated in an open barouche drawn by six glistening black horses, may have seen the banner at 351 Broadway that read "Welcome Abraham Lincoln, We beg for compromise."

Walt Whitman, caught in traffic on a Broadway omnibus, was in the crowd of thousands who strained to see the visitor. The young newspaperman and poet, aware of the ranting against Lincoln, was sure that "many an assasin's knife and pistol lurked in hip or breast-pocket there, ready as soon as break and riot came." He thought the crowd sulky and silent as he watched Lincoln step out of his carriage, stretch himself, and quietly look at the mass of solemn people. Whitman was impressed by his "look and gait—his perfect composure and coolness—his unusual and uncouth height, his dress of complete black, stovepipe hat push'd back on the head, his dark-brown complexion, seam'd and wrinkled yet canny-looking face, black, bushy head of hair, disproportionately long neck, and his hands held behind him as he stood observing the people. He looked with curiosity upon that immense sea of faces, and the sea of faces return'd the look with similar curiosity."[32]

Whitman's impression created a striking portrait of the President-elect, but his somber appraisal of the crowd was somewhat overdrawn. The people may have been curious, but they showed more hospitality than hostility. The thousand or more police who turned out in their best uniforms to keep order in the streets found that their day was much easier than anticipated as they exchanged pleasantries with the waiting spectators. Lincoln had many friends in the crowd in front of the Astor House who wanted him to say a few words. He obliged their friendly request by stepping before them for a greeting. He said he had nothing to say at that time and begged to be excused. It was not much of a speech, but he received a loud round of applause.

Later in the day, Lincoln attended a surprise reception at the Astor House and said little more. Yet in a few words he showed an awareness of his position in the national crisis. "I do suppose," he said, "that while the political drama being enacted in this country at this time is rapidly shifting in its scenes, forbidding an anticipation with any degree of certainty today what we shall see tomorrow, that it was peculiarly fitting that I should see it all up to the last minute before I should take ground, that I might be disposed by the shifting of the scenes afterwards again to shift."[33] His remarks were well received even though everyone in the room wanted him to say more.

The next day, Lincoln was up early and, escorted by James Watson Webb, former editor of the *Courier and Enquirer,* and Thurlow Weed, drove to Moses Grinnell's home on the corner of Fifth Avenue and Fourteenth Street, where a large group of well-to-do merchants greeted Lin-

coln. Later in the morning, Lincoln went through the formality of meeting Mayor Wood and members of the Common Council in the handsome
Governor's Room at City Hall. Wood, unabashed by his differences with
Lincoln, stood behind George Washington's writing desk and greeted
the president-elect warmly. In a brief speech, Wood mentioned that the
city's commercial greatness was endangered. "We fear," he said, "that if
the Union dies, the present supremacy of New York may perish with it."
And he expressed hope for the revival of "fraternal relations between
the States."[34]

Lincoln listened to Wood with a thoughtful, dreamy look in his
eyes. In his reply he thanked the mayor for the kind reception in the city
by people "who do not by a large majority agree with me on political sentiment." Politely, he capitalized on Wood's remarks by saying that he
would never willingly consent "to the destruction of this Union, in which
not only the great city of New York, but the whole country has acquired
greatness."[35] At the close of his speech, Lincoln met the members of the
Common Council. Outside an enthusiastic crowd surged about hoping
to catch a glimpse of the next president. The police opened the doors,
and a number of surprised onlookers found themselves greeting Lincoln. As they filed by, they made remarks such as "God bless you," "Stand
firm," "It's a hard day's work you have," and "I hope you will take care of
us. I have prayed for you." Lincoln answered, "But, you must take care
of me." A tall man came toward Lincoln and stretched himself to his full
height. Lincoln turned around and back to back measured his height
with the stranger. That action regaled the crowd, especially when it was
found that Lincoln was two inches taller.[36]

While Lincoln was occupied with his obligations, Mrs. Lincoln en-
joyed a visit to Barnum's Museum. That same evening, Lincoln went to
the Academy of Music to hear *A Masked Ball*, a new Verdi opera. Later,
Mrs. Lincoln received several women in the Ladies Parlor at the Astor
House and listened to a serenade by a German quartet and a National
Guard band.

On February 21, Lincoln and his party left for Baltimore and
Washington. Violence had been avoided during his visit to New York
City, and the stock market showed greater strength. Apparently he had
favorably impressed the business leaders. Yet this was the same city
where he was hanged in effigy from riggings of ships with signs that
read "Abe Lincoln, the Union Breaker" and "Abe Lincoln, dead and
gone to Hell."[37]

Opposition to the forthcoming administration helped unify the discordant Democrats. Their many factions now had common fears of sectional tensions, increased federal interference in their lives, and a threat to their liberty. The "Constitution and the Union" was now their rallying cry.[38]

Republicans in the city were almost as dubious of Lincoln's leadership qualities as the Democrats. His public supporters conversed freely in private about their misgivings, and soon their private feelings became public. Horace Greeley never short of opinions, had visited Lincoln in Springfield and came away with the impression that Lincoln was a simple man. Greeley tended to look down on him. John Bigelow thought Lincoln did not understand the difficulties of his new position and failed to realize his ignorance of the world. He wrote William Hargreaves, "When he reaches Washington he will be likely to get his eyes opened that then he will see that he cannot get along without Seward for the present."[39]

The New York State Republican organization was also plagued with factional fighting between Thurlow Weed, Seward's henchman, and such New York City Republicans as David Dudley Field, George Opdyke, William Cullen Bryant, Hiram Barney, and Horace Greeley. Their differences became sharper when Lincoln selected Seward for secretary of state, thereby creating a vacancy in the Senate. Greeley, always anxious for high public office, saw his opportunity and aggressively sought the nomination. The editor's careless dress, large, pale face, and innocent air disguised his driving energy and ambition for power. Equally deceptive was his humble claim that he was merely a good newspaperman who was not made to be a "scrambler for offices."[40] One of his acquaintances, Count Gurowski, a Polish exile, concluded that the eccentric editor was no more fit to be a senator than to command a regiment.

Weed backed William Evarts, a skillful lawyer, for the Senate in opposition to Greeley. Evarts, originally a Seward supporter, had campaigned for Lincoln and was not afraid to disagree with his business friends who wanted to conciliate the South. But the Weed and Greeley factions merely frustrated each other and forced the compromise selection of Ira Harris from upstate.

As Lincoln's inauguration approached, Henry Bellows, the bright, confident minister to the elite at All Soul's Unitarian Church, was inclined to think that the Gulf states would secede and then return in a couple of years. He probably reflected the views of many of the members of his church. His congregation consisted of some of the richest and most powerful people in New York society, which was why it was often called the "Beef Steak" church. The building was designed in the image of the Basilica of San Giovanni in Monza, Italy, and had alternate layers of terra-cotta and white Caen marble that reminded some people of a zebra. An out-of-town visitor to the church was overwhelmed by the show of wealth in the pews. He felt out of place in the midst of that congregation and decided that New York churches were not interested in preaching to the poor.[41]

George Templeton Strong ran into his old friend Walter Cutting at the opera two days before Lincoln's inauguration. Cutting had decided that the sooner civil war started the better. He was ready to join the fight and give up all his worldly possessions and, if necessary, his life. Why was he willing to go so far? He wanted "to exterminate those damned abolitionists."[42]

March 4 finally arrived, and at last Lincoln was president. His inaugural speech was conciliatory. He sought time just as New Yorkers did to solve the nation's problems. Some were satisfied with the speech. Others believed Lincoln had made a mistake in establishing his theory of "an unbroken Union." And the uncertainty remained.[43]

On this same cold and windy day, secession or war was less frightening to some New Yorkers than a more immediate threat. Infectious diptheria was taking its toll in the city. What appeared to be simple nose colds and sore throats turned into the deadly disease as toxin produced by corynebacterium diptheriae entered the blood and struck at the heart and nervous system. Mrs. Evarts lost a sister, brother-in-law, and two nieces in rapid succession. Another sister came close to death, and her children also suffered attacks.[44] Life in the city was more than politics.

As Lincoln said, the scenes kept shifting. Still, the people waited.

3
Fort Sumter

Salmon P. Chase, the new secretary of the treasury, soon learned that the government was short of money. He advised Assistant Treasurer John J. Cisco, who was in charge of the subtreasury in New York, of the urgent need to sustain the nation's credit. Cisco, a Democrat who had remained in office at the request of Lincoln and Chase, passed the word to Wall Street. Henry Clews, head of a prosperous firm that specialized in buying merchants' acceptances and receivables at a commission, saw the opportunity for a profit in lending the government money. He quickly organized a syndicate to take the balance of a government loan at a price of ninety-four and left for Washington to inform Chase of his support.

Clews met Chase and gave him the welcome news. After the meeting, Clews walked back to the Willard Hotel and began to ponder about the wisdom of his decision. His visit to the capital gave him a different perspective. Frightening rumors pervaded the town, and he saw a trainload of cannon that brought him closer to the reality of war. Suddenly he realized that war was inevitable and that it would be a long and bloody affair. The financial risk overcame him, and he sent a message to his firm to sell all its mercantile paper at once. He also told his office to tell the syndicate to withdraw its offer to Chase. Clew's mind was made up. He was convinced that the price of government bonds would drop a great deal.

The next morning Clews called on Chase again and told him that he believed there would be a long war. In the interest of his clients, he said, he could not carry out the bid that he had made the previous day. The government would have to look elsewhere for money. His clients came first. Clews's attitude was symptomatic. Neither Chase nor Lincoln could look to a coherent group of New York financiers who felt a keen sense of obligation to serve the government in crisis. Clews returned to New York relieved that he had escaped Washington without making any lasting commitment. He was even more pleased with himself when he learned that his office had unloaded almost all of its notes, which amounted to about half a million dollars.[1]

Peter Cooper also had misgivings about the financial condition of the country. He warned Senator John Sherman that negotiating loans to sustain the government would be extremely difficult. He had learned from the "principled money institutions" in the city that the loss of the border states would mean that the government could not obtain loans because securities would depreciate too sharply. Cooper, a long-standing Democrat, urged Republicans to rise above party and agree that southerners had the right to take their slaves into the territories. He believed that they should be reassured concerning "every right and privilege which they can claim legally or in equity."[2]

Despite the gloomy forecasts of Clews and Cooper, Chase received enough offers for a new federal loan to keep him out of trouble for the moment. In the autumn of 1860, a loan committee had been established by an association of banks to help the government, and although often falling short of promise, it was succeeded by other committees when the war began.[3] Nevertheless, Chase continued to receive disturbing news from the financial center of the nation. John Jay, member of an old New York family, wrote to him in alarm that there was danger of insurrection in the city if hostilities broke out. He reminded the secretary of the treasury of Mayor Wood's plan for the city's secession and told him of a report that a secret league of four or five thousand men was in favor of the proposal. Jay urged that the federal government immediately plan to protect the subtreasury and customhouse. He also suggested that the rabble-rouser and southern sympathizer U.S. Marshal Rynders be removed from office at once.[4]

Jay's fears may have been farfetched, but treacherous acts did take place in the city. The respected financier Gazaway Lamar accepted an assignment from Confederate Secretary of the Treasury Christopher Memminger to arrange for printing more than a million dollars in bonds by the National Bank Note Company of New York. Lamar carried out his mission successfully, and the bonds arrived in Montgomery, Alabama, early in April. The banker soon showed his true colors by leaving for the South in May. During the war, he served as paymaster of Georgia troops, adviser to Jefferson Davis, and organizer of a major blockade-running activity.[5]

Commercial and financial activities in the city seemed temporarily suspended. The uncertainty of the situation was destructive to trade. James Gordon Bennett's *Herald*, ready to yield everything to the South to avoid war, stressed the paralyzing effect of idle capital and unemployment. This uncertainty, he said, was more fatal than the worst reality. Merchants could not make forecasts and were afraid to invest. "Suspense is death to all interests." Suddenly everyone seemed more aware of closed stores, empty warehouses, and shabby homes.

Bennett appeared as an alarmist in picturing the horrors that civil war would bring. He saw brother against brother as the depth of degradation. It meant "oceans of blood and millions of treasure." The country would be left exhausted. Prospects were "dark, menacing, and desolate." The grim predictions of the *Herald*, however, were far more prescient than the press that supported Lincoln. The *Evening Post* was confident that if war came it would be short and the government would be reestablished on firmer ground. The *Times* did not believe that any military clash would harm a hair on northern heads. And the independent *World* did not believe it would be too long after the blockade went into effect before the South would beg to be saved. The loss of cotton profits would cripple and humble southerners.[6]

Although the stock market was generally dull during these days, Wall Streeters, as ignorant of the future as everyone else, had a well-developed ability to deceive themselves. Any news dispatch with a glimmer of hope for peace resulted in an upward movement in the market. Late in March money markets eased and stocks improved briefly because there was a growing feeling that the political troubles would be overcome without a conflict of arms. Yet the optimistic sentiment was not sustained, and in another day or two stocks were dull and lower.[7]

The economy of the city was in a strange state, but as always, it remained a city of contrasts. While Arnold Constable sold fine lace for hundreds of dollars a yard there were women in the city who received wages of one to three dollars a week. Unemployment spread and some workingmen, with no alternative, accepted reductions of 85¢ to $1.25 a day in their regular wages. The dry goods and hoop skirt businesses were especially hard hit and roves of tailors lost their jobs. The boot and shoe industry and carriage and harness makers, who had traditionally done a brisk business with the South, were at a standstill.[8]

The *Herald* had no love for the new administration, but Bennett, always mischievous, could not resist jabbing at the critical stand of his two major rivals, the *Times* and *Tribune,* which were supposed to be administration supporters. The *Herald* gleefully observed that both of these Republican papers were blasting Lincoln and shattering "his cabinet to atoms when it is hardly three weeks old." The *Tribune* impatiently complained that the president had not shown his hand for peace or war. But Bennett found the *Times* more bad-tempered: "It denounces the inactivity and imbecility of Mr. Lincoln in vehement language; says the Union is in far worse position than when he came into power; that he has done nothing ever since but administer spoils to greedy politicians, and has let slip the golden opportunity of saving the Union which will never return."[9]

Bennett referred to a *Times* editorial written by Henry Raymond called "Wanted—A Policy!" It marked the low point in relations between the self-assured Republican editor and Lincoln. To Raymond, the Confederates were filled with resolution but the new administration in Washington was marked by irresolution, and his faith in Lincoln's government rapidly waned. Raymond claimed that the Confederacy moved ahead with vigor and intelligence while the federal government did nothing. He warned the president that he must adopt a clear policy or the Union would be destroyed and the country disgraced. This criticism by alleged friends of the administration gave the *Herald* the opportunity to crow, "The Republican journals of New York will probably break the government to pieces before it is six months old." The remarks were intentionally exaggerated, but it was true that Lincoln could not expect steady backing from the New York City press.[10]

Lincoln the politician appreciated the importance of James Gordon Bennett. The publisher, in his mid-sixties, had gained his present eminence only after years of struggle. A native of Scotland, he had once studied for the priesthood in Aberdeen. He abandoned that pursuit when he emigrated to Nova Scotia and then the United States in his early twenties. After a brief stint as a teacher, the tall, quiet young man with a heavy brogue worked as a clerk in a Boston bookstore and, despite his Catholicism, attended some of the town's leading Protestant churches to hear their prominent ministers. Restless and poor, he moved to New York and then to South Carolina, where he worked for the *Charleston Courier.* His experience in the South gave him a friendly feeling for that section which he always retained.

After about two years in Charleston, Bennett returned to New York, where he attempted to buy the *New York Courier* on credit but failed. His first recognition came as a Washington correspondent for the *New York Enquirer.* Once again, however, his ambition led him to publish the *New York Globe,* and once again he failed. This failure was quickly repeated in his unsuccessful ownership of the *Philadelphia Pennsylvanian.* But these were temporary setbacks. At the age of forty, Bennett still dreamed of becoming a publisher. With little money and the odds stacked against him, he started the four-page *Herald,* which he sold for a penny. His office was in a cellar at 20 Wall Street, and his desk was a plank set on two barrels. Unafraid to work long days and nights, he did all the jobs on the paper from reporter to folder.

The *Herald* survived and appealed to a large audience. It gained a spicy reputation for sensationalism after Bennett gave considerable space to a love-nest murder, and circulation climbed. And he did not hesitate to malign his competitors. To Bennett, the editors at the *Times* were "little fidgety tricksters." Those at the *Journal of Commerce* were "pious hypocrites" and at the *Daily News,* "weeping and wailing Jeremiah." He said of Greeley, "The man is certainly mad." Libel of fellow newspapermen was apparently not a worry. Bennett's rivals, of course, heaped like criticism on him. But it was truly a paper battle. The editors and publishers frequently met at public gatherings or at Delmonico's on the friendliest terms. Bennett profoundly believed that the independent press of New York City, ever watchful, could be more influential and effective than the president, cabinet, or Congress.

Bennett was a fresh and controversial breeze in the world of journalism, and by 1861 he was rich and powerful. Although he would have little faith in the forthcoming war, he would soon have more than sixty correspondents reporting from the front. This was the man Lincoln hoped to tame.

Lincoln knew that the widely read *Herald* had the potential to damage the country abroad and give false hope to the South. The president might have considered the publisher who wanted to overthrow the "de-

moralizing, disorganizing, and destructive" Republican party a hostile
critic beyond his reach. Instead, he decided it was time to "bell the cat,"
and he heard that Thurlow Weed was the man to do the job. Lincoln
summoned Weed to the White House and explained the assignment he
had in mind. Weed was not a friend of Bennett, and he had reservations
about his ability to convince the publisher to change his ways. Nevertheless, he accepted the mission and through a mutual friend arranged to
meet Bennett at his country place on Washington Heights.

The two men spent a quiet day discussing the nation's problems.
Weed frankly admitted that Lincoln sought Bennett's help. Bennett, in
defense of his own actions, emphasized that abolitionists were the devils
who had sown the "dragon teeth" and destroyed the "Garden of Eden."
He saw Horace Greeley, William Lloyd Garrison, and Wendell Phillips
as the troublemakers. Weed was far from an abolitionist. Nevertheless,
he differed with Bennett and gave the publisher some inside information based on his own experience. He told of such southern obstruction-
ists as Robert Toombs, Alexander H. Stephens, and Thomas L. Cling-
man, who had tried to persuade President Zachary Taylor to veto a bill
to bring California into the Union as a free state. Weed also stressed the
significance of the census figures, which indicated that numbers alone
worked in favor of freedom over slavery.

Weed was a superb conversationalist. In soft, low tones, he convinced his listeners of his sincerity and benevolence. Yet Bennett remained noncommittal. Although he did not immediately show it, the
publisher could not help but be flattered by the attention he received
from the president. Nonetheless, Bennett still believed that both the
Confederate and Union governments were preparing to plunge the
country into war against the will of three-fourths of the people. Statesmanship seemed to him to be nonexistent, and federal, state, and municipal governments were remarkable only for their "imbecility."[11]

While politicians and publishers debated the idea of compromise
on a theoretical level, a more practical demonstration took place at Pier
13 on the North River. Two deputy marshals, in accordance with the
Compromise of 1850, dragged a fugitive slave toward the SS *Yorktown*
bound for Virginia. The reluctant slave struggled with his captors, and
his cries for help attracted a large crowd. A policeman asked the marshals to produce their official papers, which they had apparently left in

their carriage. While one marshal went for the papers, the slave slipped from the grasp of the other and was last seen running up West Street. The owner, a Mr. Jameson of Lynchburg, Virginia, would have a long wait for the return of his property.

Despite the heartrending scene of the captive slave, compromise still appealed to locally elected politicians as the painless solution to the national problems. A few days later, the Board of Councilmen unanimously adopted a resolution inviting Senator Crittenden of Kentucky, the great exponent of a compromise that recognized the rights of slave-owners, to visit New York as a guest of the city.[12]

Meanwhile, activity increased again in New York Harbor and the surrounding garrisons. Early in April it was evident that preparations for a new military expedition were under way. Crowds watched the *Baltic* take on supplies that piqued their curiosity. Among the items packed on board were bacon, hay, molasses, stove coal, preserved meats, and muskets. More intriguing were the small boats and ammunition for heavy twelve-pound howitzers. The activity was a relief to many people. The uncertainty had caused so much tension that any action was welcome. Joseph Choate noticed that a peace-loving Quaker actually seemed relieved at hearing rumors of war.[13]

The imminence of war was almost the only topic of conversation. In saloons and hotel lobbies, on horsecars and ferryboats, people exchanged rumors and reports about troop movements, their probable destinations, and chances of success. Although the news was still as contradictory as ever, mercurial Wall Streeters now concluded that war was certain. Stock prices varied from hour to hour, but early in April the general trend was down and speculative demand for Treasury bills disappeared.[14]

Although there was still talk about maintaining the Union, the *Journal of Commerce* insisted that occupation of forts in Confederate states would convert the federal government into an oppressor. Benjamin Wood was another who opposed the thought of occupation. He had concluded sometime ago that the southern Confederacy was real, not a paper republic. Now he hoped and prayed for the government to evacuate the forts speedily. He fiercely denounced traitors and considered himself a true Unionist. The traitors he loathed were the fanatics who were leading the country into war. If war came, he said, it would be against slaveholders, not traitors, This was a time for peace. And if the

Confederacy would do business as usual, the North would be foolish not to reciprocate. Wood defended his lack of logic by quoting Alexander Pope, "whatever is, is right." A more apt phrase at the time might have been "whatever is, is wrong."[15]

Navy Captain Gustavus Fox, a Lincoln confidant, was in the city chartering tugs and recruiting men to supply Fort Sumter. The elderly Winfield Scott also worked diligently in his uptown office. Mail and telegraphic dispatches from the War Department were more voluminous every day, and busy clerks and special messengers rushed in and out with an air of urgent business. Finally, on April 9, after much confusion and indecision in Washington, fires were lighted under the *Baltic* boilers and Fox sailed for Charleston accompanied by the *Pawnee* and *Harriet Lane*.[16]

The *Herald*, anticipating war while hoping for peace, warned that great commercial cities would be the first to bear the burden of war. The paper claimed that cities depended on order. Amid disorder, neither life nor property would be safe, "for where the carcass is there will the vultures gathered together."[17]

On the evening of April 12, Walt Whitman went to the Academy of Music to hear Verdi's *Masked Ball*. After the opera, he sauntered down Broadway. It was almost midnight when he heard newsboys cry, "Extra!" He bought a copy and stood under the gaslight near the Metropolitan Hotel reading the startling news. Fort Sumter had been bombarded. Despite previous headlines about approaching war clouds, the report seemed incredible. A group gathered around a lamppost, and someone read the news aloud. The group quietly remained together for a minute or two and then went their separate ways.[18]

George Templeton Strong heard the news about the same time and did not believe that the rebels could be so foolish. He was walking uptown with two acquaintances when he heard the shout, "Extry-a Herald! Got the bombardment of Fort Sumter!!!" They decided it was a newsboy's sales ploy and refused to buy a paper but after walking four blocks more they could not resist the temptation. Newspapers were not known for their accuracy, and that night many skeptics questioned the truth of the report. Prices on Wall Street had been firmer that day and had been regarded as a good omen. Joseph Choate said it looked like a made-up story. Yet it was a peculiar sensation to see and hear the excited newsboys in the streets. Papers were eagerly bought on horsecars, ferries, and in hotel lobbies. Abby Woolsey lived on Brevoort Place and was appalled by the hoarse voices of the boys, which she heard from her room until after midnight.[19]

John Dix, a devout Unionist who had served briefly as Buchanan's secretary of the treasury, attended a meeting of prominent citizens late that night to discuss ways to preserve peace. Some of those present favored a bloodless breakup of the Union. While they talked, a messenger abruptly entered the room and exclaimed, "General Beauregard has opened fire on Fort Sumter." There was absolute silence, and then one man raised his hands and cried out, "My God, we are ruined."[20]

Dumbfounded and disbelieving, the people hungered for more news, but it was slow in arriving. Crowds packed Printing House Square to read the latest bulletin. By the fourteenth, the Metropolitan Police barricaded the streets so that the steam-operated presses could roll out the news without interference. The *Herald* printed more than 135,000 copies that day, the largest print run of any newspaper in America.[21] But it was not until April 15 that the firing on Fort Sumter was confirmed and all doubts disappeared. The tugs that Fox had chartered were delayed by a gale and did not arrive to help the expedition. Helpless, the force merely took off Major Anderson and his men after their surrender and returned to New York.

The worst fears had been realized, and a new scorn for the South prevailed in the city. Some who had been sympathetic to the South were now saying that they were ready to go to any length to uphold the government. Yet the question remained after the initial shock, what would New York City do in the crisis? William Evarts joined five friends in a private office on Pine Street to weigh the situation. They wanted to call a public meeting to support the government but wondered whether they could draw a sufficient crowd. If too few people showed up, the game would appear to be lost. They even worried whether to hire the Academy of Music for fear that they might not fill the house.[22]

The *Times* editorialized that the North was now a unit and wrote, "The crucial test of this is New York City — the spot most tainted by Southern poison." Nevertheless, there was still uncertainty about how New Yorkers would behave. The *Journal of Commerce* called for diplomacy: "Let us learn from the Confederate States what they demand, and if consistent with national honor, grant it, and let them go in peace." The editor, Gerard Hallock, a gentle man, called for courage. He did not want courage to fight but to stop the carnage that threatened to destroy liberty. The *Daily News* and *Day-Book* vehemently expressed similar views. On April 14, Benjamin Wood still declared that New York merchants would refuse to support a war. "The wealthy," he said, "will not supply the means to depreciate the rest of their property by prolonging this unnatural war."[23]

Mayor Wood issued a delicately worded proclamation to the people of the city: "Our country now trembles upon the brink of a precipice and that it requires a patriotic and honest effort to prevent its final destruction ... here at least harmony should prevail." The statement was neither a call to arms nor a strong call for unity. He simply asked for obedience to the laws and public peace. George Templeton Strong thought Wood's proclamation proved that he was a "cunning scoundrel" who "sees which way the cat is jumping" and puts himself right on the record in a vague way while giving the least possible offense to the South.[24]

The proclamation had seemed demagogic because the public peace had not been disturbed. The only appearance of anything like a commotion came when a mob called on the editor of the *Herald* to hang an American flag from its building at Broadway and Ann Street. The emergency was averted when an office boy went scurrying out the back door to buy a flag. When it was raised, Bennett appeared and bowed to the crowd, but his patriotic display had little significance. Despite Weed's meeting with Bennett, the *Herald* was not quick to change its ways. At this late date, the paper still announced its opposition to coercing the South. Bennett was especially sensitive about the border states, which he desperately wanted to keep within the Union, and he hoped his soft words would appease them.

In the immediate aftermath of Fort Sumter, more rumors than ever swirled around the city. The Sixty-ninth Regiment, according to one false report, was ready to leave the city and join the Confederacy. During the recent visit of the Prince of Wales, the Sixty-ninth, made up of Irish immigrants, had refused to participate in his reception and was stripped of its colors. Some believed that the incident soured the regiment and turned its members toward the rebels.[25]

John Kennedy, superintendent of the Metropolitan Police, received numerous warnings that public places were in danger of attack. There were reports that the city water supply would be destroyed and that there would be tampering with the bridges on the Harlem Railroad line. He also heard that the customhouse, subtreasury, and assay office were threatened by southern sympathizers and increased the patrol force in that area. He conferred with Hiram Barney, the newly appointed collector of the Port of New York, but he did not discuss the matter with John Cisco, the able director of the subtreasury, because he thought Cisco was so timid he might be thrown into "spasms" in fear for his safety.[26]

Within a few days the prevailing sentiment in the city was apparent to everyone. All doubts vanished, southern sympathizers disappeared, or at least so it seemed, and in a wild rush of emotion the city rallied around the Union. Fernando Wood's grand design for the city's secession was completely forgotten. Flags and bunting appeared on buildings and in shop windows. Union cockades suddenly became popular and were worn in the streets by men and women. At the Merchants, Corn, and Produce exchanges businessmen declared their determination to stand by the president. The crisis had created an atmosphere that had never been seen in the city.

Pelatiah Perit, president of the compromise-prone Chamber of Commerce, said, "There can be no neutrality now—we are either for the country or for its enemies." Members of the New York Stock and Exchange Board raised an American flag over the rostrum in their trading room and passed a resolution pledging their fidelity to the Union and their "resolute determination to stand by it under all circumstances." Soon they forbid members from dealing in any new securities of a seceding state. Portraits of Major Anderson went on sale for twenty-five cents, and a blue "Union tie" became a new sales item. At the Philharmonic the "Star Spangled Banner" thrilled the audience as never before.[27]

The compelling need for news gave the press in the city a field day. In the first week after Fort Sumter, the *Times*'s circulation jumped from forty-five thousand to seventy-five thousand. Charles Dana, the *Tribune*'s managing editor, announced that the paper would issue an evening edition, and five days later the *Herald* answered the challenge with afternoon editions at 1:30, 3:00, and 4:30. Even then, papers issued extras at the slightest provocation. Sunday newspapers had been frowned upon as sacrilegious, and only the *Herald* had risked condemnation. Now it was followed by the *Times* and *Tribune*. And by May, the Associated Press found it necessary to move to more spacious quarters at 175 Broadway.[28]

One of the first definite signs of the shift in public feeling occurred on April 18 when the Sixth Massachusetts Regiment arrived from Boston on its way to Washington, D.C. Evarts, still suspicious of the depth of Union support in the city, was in the crowd watching the regiment's departure. People jammed the streets along Broadway from Barclay to Fulton Street and the lower end of Park Row. Morgan Dix, rector of Trinity Church, watched the Massachusetts troops go by. They looked like stout men to him, and he noted in his diary that they were "evidently the right stuff."[29] The New Yorkers were silent until the band struck up "Yankee Doodle," and then there was an enormous roar of approval. Cheers greeted the New Englanders as they marched down Broadway with bayonets raised above their heads, and Evarts had little doubt where the people stood. The emotional display also made an indelible impression on John Dix.[30]

The rally to the Union cause came from strange places. Fernando Wood saw the sudden swell of patriotism and came out fervidly for the stars and stripes. He was now ready to rise above partisanship. Congressman John Cochrane, recently so sympathetic to the South, immediately stopped calling for compromise. A rich property owner and former judge, James Whiting, a strong advocate of southern rights, said that the firing on Fort Sumter made his blood boil: "I will give every cent of my property to aid the Government for what do I want of property . . . without a country."[31]

Clergymen of all faiths who had loudly favored the South now spoke up for the government. One of the most prominent was the Roman Catholic Archbishop John Hughes, an opponent of immediate emancipation, who had worked as a slave overseer in Maryland shortly after his arrival from Ireland. He was a stalwart Union man who satirized abolitionists in his official organ, the *Metropolitan Record,* and he wanted each state to eliminate slavery by its own authority rather than by congressional order. The biggest sin in the North, he believed, was the people's concern for iniquity in the South instead of in their own neighborhoods. By the force of his personality, Hughes had gained a unique place in the city politically as well as theologically. He had also started construction on St. Patrick's Cathedral. Although he denied that he was either a wire puller or a politician, he had raised the financially weak and despised Roman Catholic church in the city to a respected and feared position. His confidential secretary said that he was neither a learned man nor a laborious student, but he had a quick insight into character, the power of sarcasm, and a love for the excitement of collision. He was always free with his opinions and ready to use his influence. Now he wanted the war over as quickly as possible and was willing to see a large military force built to accomplish that purpose.[32]

Another influential churchman, Gardner Spring, minister of the fashionable Brick Presbyterian Church on Fifth Avenue and Thirty-seventh Street, dropped his previous southern sentiments. He had always easily accepted the Constitution's recognition of slavery and looked upon abolitionists as anathema. At All Souls, Henry Bellows, an avid Union man, preached a strong antisouthern sermon, and the congregation broke tradition by singing the "Star Spangled Banner" at the end of the service and then loudly applauding. Thanks to the risky work of ship riggers, an American flag flew from the 284-foot spire of Trinity Church on Wall Street, and ten days after the news of Fort Sumter reached the city, virtually all denominations proclaimed the righteousness of the Union cause. War in defense of the country appeared to be sanctified.[33]

Drastic changes of opinion did not seem to embarrass anyone. The city government passed resolutions drafted by the previously secession-minded Dan Sickles that declared "unfaltering loyalty." The *Tribune* stopped writing against coercion of the South, and when Virginia seceded on April 22, the *Herald* wrote that Lincoln's actions were founded on an "inextinguishable love of country." Bennett went further and instructed the journalist Henry Villard to tell Lincoln that he favored the unconditional suppression of the rebellion. Always practical, Bennett backed his feelings with the donation of his 160-ton yacht, *Henrietta*, which served as a Union cutter and for awhile was part of the blockading squadron off Port Royal, South Carolina. Public opinion, always volatile, had a new ring. William Russell, the London correspondent, was convinced that the South Carolinians would not have bombarded Fort Sumter if New Yorkers had previously acted so strongly in favor of the Union.[34]

The new military spirit that pervaded the city showed itself in dozens of ways. Bookstores prominently displayed soldiers' manuals, books on tactics, and war histories. Print shops sold pictures of famous battles and naval engagements. Theaters concentrated on the drama of war and

martial music. Children carried knapsacks and played drummer boy.
And men and women, unconcerned about their ignorance of such matters, wrangled over grand strategy.

As the war fever reached a crescendo, a few skeptical holdouts refused to believe that the public attitude had changed so drastically. The
Evening Day-Book felt only revulsion over abolitionists suddenly becoming dedicated patriots after they had denounced the Constitution and
Union for years. The editors had not forgotten that William Lloyd Garrison had burned the Constitution in public. These agitators, who had
been scorned as outcasts, were now riding the tide of popular opinion
that swept through the North. The *Day-Book* editors could not understand how these scoundrels could finally have found refuge in patriotism. They also resented talk about preserving the Union by fighting for
it. "Are the people stark mad?" they asked. "Are they crazy? Will they
not pause and listen to reason?" They were certain that Fort Sumter was
merely a "cunningly contrived scheme" that would divide the Union.[35]

The glamour and glory held no appeal for Samuel Morse. He continued to agonize over this war among brethren, and after many sleepless nights he decided to devote his life to achieving peace. He wrote to
his sister who lived in the city that he could not remain a "listless spectator." But his sleepless yearnings were for naught as the momentum
rushed toward war.[36]

John L. O'Sullivan, living in Lisbon and far from the war spirit,
wrote to his old political friend Samuel Tilden that he hoped if any
troops marched south they would all be Republicans. He erroneously assumed that Tilden shared his views. Tilden did not reply, and as the war
progressed O'Sullivan concluded that either Tilden was ignoring him or
the Post Office had intervened in a correspondence between a "traitor"
and a "Copperhead." At the moment, Tilden would not have appreciated the prosouthern label. O'Sullivan also suspected that Tilden suffered from "villainous virtue of prudence" and was too much absorbed
in the party system.[37]

The fervor in the city was so overwhelming that there was little
question that President Lincoln's call for seventy-five thousand volunteers on the fifteenth would be wholeheartedly answered. Perhaps it
would be harder to keep men out of the army than to urge them to join.
George Templeton Strong wrote, "The city seems to have gone suddenly
wild and crazy." Colonel Michael Corcoran, commanding officer of the

Sixty-ninth Regiment, under a cloud in certain parts of the city for his unfriendliness to the Prince of Wales, now showed his fighting ardor. Although charges against him had been dismissed, he had recently suffered the ordeal of a court-martial, and his outfit was in limbo after its colors had been taken away. Corcoran called on the fixer, Thurlow Weed, with a letter of introduction from Archbishop Hughes. He said that if his colors were restored, he and his men could march in twenty-four hours. Weed telegraphed Governor Edwin D. Morgan, and in a short time the Irish received their wish. The regiment left the city with such speed that many of the men had neither uniforms nor arms.[38]

William Evarts and his friends held their mass meeting at Union Square on the twentieth. Estimates of the size of a crowd are always unreliable, and for that day they varied widely from 100,000 to 250,000. But it was a huge affair and a grand success. It was a Saturday, and the proceedings began at 3:00. The Stock Exchange canceled its afternoon session, and most businesses closed down for the occasion. Crowds, mostly men, surged up and down Broadway from Union Square. Along Fourth Avenue masses extended beyond the Everett House at 17th Street.

John Dix presided with the help of eighty-seven vice-presidents. Five stands bedecked in bunting were placed at strategic locations in the square for the twenty orators of the day. Innumerable bands provided martial music, and the presence of Major Anderson and his men created a sensation. They had arrived in New York on the *Baltic,* and Anderson had been serenaded at the Brevoort House, where he stayed, and was the main attraction of the day. To Abby Woolsey, he looked small, slender, old, wrinkled, gray and subdued. On the platform with Anderson was the Sumter flag and splintered staff as grim testimony of the assault on the Union. Jane Woolsey watched the scene from a balcony at the corner of Union Square and Broadway. She could not hear the speakers but knew when they scored a point. Every now and then thousands of hats flew into the air and a roar went up from the crowd. The masses now knew they faced a choice between a government of law or anarchy. Titus Coan, a young medical student, caught up in the contagious excitement and impressed that the best and most influential men in the city were lending themselves and their riches to the war, realized that all his doubts had disappeared. "Is not this a glorious war?" he wrote his mother.[39]

Thousands surged into Union Square and vicinity to show their support at the Great Union Meeting, April 20, 1861. (Courtesy of the New-York Historical Society)

Evarts spoke, saying that he regarded the great demonstration as a business meeting. Aside from the show of strength, the meeting resulted in the formation of the Union Defense Committee with a membership that read like a Who's Who of city leaders. Among them were Hamilton Fish, John Jacob Astor, A. T. Stewart, William Havemeyer, and Edwards Pierrepont. Fernando Wood was on the list as an ex-officio member. The purpose of the committee was to raise funds to help the Union cause.

Edwin M. Stanton nervously wrote to John Dix, with whom he had served in President Buchanan's cabinet, "If there be any remedy—any shadow of hope to preserve this government from utter and absolute extinction — it must come from New York without delay." That help seemed to be on the way.[40]

A few days later, Wood urged the Board of Aldermen to appropriate a million dollars to equip and train volunteers for the army. The board adopted an ordinance to that effect with payments to be made by the comptroller on vouchers approved by the Union Defense Committee. One of the visible supporters of the ordinance, rising to the occasion again, was Dan Sickles.

Thrilled by the outpouring of emotion that had taken place at Union Square, Jane Woolsey expressed the feelings of many when she wrote, "Now we don't feel that the social fabric is falling to pieces at all, but that it is getting gloriously mended."[41] The enthusiasm had created a false sense of unity that masked the disastrous division in the nation.

Bankers, politically conservative and never quick to part with their money, made a concerted effort to show their goodwill. Thirteen banks, led by the Broadway Bank, Bank of Commerce, and Bank of New York, gave a half-million dollars for the defense of the government. Cornelius Vanderbilt, the shipping tycoon, went to his simple office on Fourth Street, sat down at a desk that had space only for cigars and a checkbook, and wrote to Secretary of the Navy Gideon Welles. He offered his ships to the government for a price and asked his lawyer to expand on the proposal. But if the proposal was not acceptable, he was ready to give his ships to the government.[42]

Howard Potter, a new member of the respected firm of Brown Brothers and Company, wrote to his brother-in-law John Brown in Liverpool that he did not see how the war could have been averted. He believed that the people of the North had been incredibly moderate. War was abhorrent, but it had become "holy and necessary." He was certain that to shrink from the war would be infamous and result in "the destruction of everything dear to humanity in these States, in universal anarchy, and a relapse almost into barbarity."[43] His reaction that all efforts for peace had been exhausted seemed reasonable. It was commonly accepted that the political marathon had been run, the political body had been drained, and finally there was no alternative to war. Potter was convinced that further negotiations were impossible.

John Dix held a reception at his home on Twenty-first Street for the heroic Major Anderson. The soldier was a strange kind of hero because he had surrendered his command, and no one was more aware of that fact than the melancholy Anderson. Nevertheless, he was a celebrity, and the rich and famous wanted to meet him. About a hundred of the biggest names in the city swarmed around. Archbishop Hughes was there as well as Episcopal Bishop Horatio Potter, Fernando Wood, Thurlow Weed, Henry Raymond, and John Van Buren. The historian George Bancroft rubbed elbows with Astors, Belmonts, and other magnates. The only talk was of the war. Morgan Dix lingered awhile, thought the party was a great bore, and left.[44] But at the Dix home and all over the city, people of all walks of life looked to each other for strength and assurance.

Women immediately wanted to help in the war effort. William Cullen Bryant considered them the most zealous patriots. They had no interest, he said, in compromise. A letter to the *Times* signed "Nightingale," said, "I am but a woman," but she wanted to know if she could do more than tend babies. She wanted to volunteer, "not to shoulder a musket—but to nurse the sick, bind up the wounded.... Please call attention to us and we will respond."[45] "Nightingale" had written to the right newspaper. The wife of the *Times* editor, Juliette Raymond, a strong-minded, public-spirited mother of seven who was known for her violent temper, was ready to organize the women of the city. On April 22, Henry Raymond, at his wife's urging, placed a call in his paper for women to meet. The intention was to organize to prepare bandages, lint, and other articles for the wounded. The response exceeded all expectations, and the women banded together to work in the Society Library on University Place.

Other women, equally interested in helping the wounded, also organized, and Juliette Raymond suggested that a central committee of women's organizations be formed to reduce confusion and give direction to the movement. Almost at once a circular addressed "To the Women of New York" called a meeting for that purpose. Leading women of "various circles" added their names to Mrs. Raymond's. New York society was relatively small, and the same names appeared time and again as leaders of the movement. The surnames had a familiar ring: Astor, Roosevelt, Cooper, Bellows, Aspinwall, Fish, and Dix, among others. Within a week a large meeting at Cooper Institute founded the Woman's

Central Association of Relief, which would confer with the War Department about ways to give aid and to work with an advisory committee of the Boards of Physicians and Surgeons of the Hospitals of New York and the New York Medical Association for Furnishing Hospital Supplies.[46]

Medical aid, however, was not solely the interest of socially ambitious women. Elizabeth Blackwell, the first woman in the United States to receive a medical degree, had suffered indignities when trying to establish herself in the profession. Prejudice and resentment had led her to found her own private dispensary in 1857, which became the New York Infirmary and College for Women. Now she saw the imminent need for trained nurses, which were almost nonexistent in the city. At Bellevue, the municipal hospital, convalescents or meagerly paid and ignorant attendants cared for patients. Former prisoners, inmates of almshouses, and charwomen accepted the poor pay to help the sick because no other work was available to them. Sometimes prostitutes served as nurses at Bellevue when the police court judge in the Five Points section of the city gave them the option of prison or hospital service for ten days. Other times, female prisoners on Blackwell's Island were brought to Bellevue by barge to help with the nursing.

Dr. Blackwell had conducted a thirteen-month training session for a small number of nurses at her infirmary. Now she prepared a two-month course. In the first month she taught theory at her infirmary; the second month the students gained practical experience at Bellevue or New York Hospital. By the start of the following year, she sent fifty nurses to Dorothea Dix, the superintendent of nurses in Washington. The humane but stern Dix, aware of a strong prejudice against "girls going to war," accepted only women thirty years of age or older. The morals and modesty of young women had to be protected.[47]

The widespread support for the Union in New York City surprised and disappointed the people of the South. They had expected the great financial and commercial center to give them aid and comfort. Confederate newspapers were certain that their betrayal had a mercenary motive. Ten days after the firing on Fort Sumter, the *Richmond Whig* reported that a fellow Virginian in New York City described street scenes that were reminiscent of the Reign of Terror, lacking only a guillotine. The *Richmond Dispatch,* equally bitter, wrote, "New York will be remembered with special hatred by the South for all time."[48]

4
Recruits

Recruiting for the army began at once in New York City. Enlistment offices opened, and patriotic posters went up on walls all over town. The young and poor rushed to the colors. Adventure attracted some while others were glad to find employment even at a private's poor pay of eleven dollars a month. Later there would be bounties for joining and an increase in pay to sixteen dollars a month. Edwin Worthington wrote to his mother, "I could find nothing to do anywhere so ... I went to New York and enlisted." In the rush to recruit, blacks offered their services and were turned down. When they formed a military club for drilling, the police forced them to close. New York City intended to raise a white man's army. [1]

Frederick Law Olmsted encouraged his employees at Central Park to enlist, and he organized a home guard of park police. Joseph Choate joined a drill team so he would know how to handle a musket in case of emergency. He considered himself a patriot, and this was a pleasant precaution, but he had no intention of seeing combat. Others could do the fighting. He had a bright legal career to protect and looked forward to marrying soon. The war interested him as news of the day, but he was typical of those who saw it as an unhappy abstraction. Nearsighted George Templeton Strong joined the New York Rifle Corps with good intentions, but what he and his fellow recruits intended to accomplish other than to assuage a sense of inadequacy remained a mystery. Their egos were probably comforted by drilling for an hour or two and then having dinner with one of the Astors. When there was a possibility of a call to active duty, many of the members dropped out.

The Seventh Regiment, the "darling Seventh," made up of members of high society, wasted no time setting out for Washington, D.C. It departed on April 19 from the brand new armory at Third Avenue between Sixth and Seventh streets. The ornate building cost a quarter of a million dollars and was thought to be the finest armory in the world for volunteers. Well-outfitted in neat gray uniforms with white cross belts and accompanied by their regimental band and three servants in each company, the men of the Seventh eagerly left to defend the nation's capital. The New York Stock and Exchange Board paid part of their expenses by allocating a thousand dollars. The board also passed a resolution praising the "gallantry and patriotism" of two of its members who left with the regiment.[2]

Excitement increased when the news came that the Massachusetts troops had been fired on in Baltimore and it seemed certain that the Seventh would see action within twelve hours. As the regiment marched down Broadway, crowds cheered and friends and strangers filled the soldiers' pockets with tobacco, cigars, wine, and matches. Mothers worried about their sons in the Seventh, but Abby Woolsey was a better judge of the situation. She was sure that the regiment was "greatly pampered" and would only serve as a moral influence in the capital. She saw it as a guard of honor and expected the men to return soon. Nevertheless, her sister Georgeanna busily made roast beef sandwiches and wrapped them in white paper for some of the socialite soldiers to take along as rations.[3]

The Seventh had agreed to serve for thirty days, which was contrary to the president's proclamation calling for three months' service. The exception, it was explained, was necessary because in the urgency of the moment these young men of affairs had not had sufficient time to arrange their personal business. Nevertheless, their brief period of active duty did not seem of concern because almost everyone was confident that the Confederates could be put down in short order. Some misguided young soldiers told John Dix that their biggest problem would be to get the Virginians to fight. "On to Richmond" was the popular cry. The regiment arrived in the capital on the twenty-fifth and paraded down Pennsylvania Avenue, passing in review before the president. Washingtonians, in a gloomy state of mind, appreciated the appearance of the troops, which boosted their downhearted spirits.

In New York City no one knew the whereabouts of the Seventh after its departure or what was going on in the capital. All communication from Washington was broken off for the next two days. Yet the lack of telegraphic dispatches came as a relief to those who believed that no news was better than false, exasperating news. The *Daily News* wrote, "The biggest liar in the land is gagged" and rejoiced that "eyewitnesses" and "persons just from there" with "fictitious news" were also silent. "Would to Heaven," the paper exclaimed, "the whole cavalcade of misrepresenters was like the wires—cut off!" Some people, disgusted with contradictory dispatches, called the telegraph "Electric Liars." In the absence of solid news, third- and fourthhand stories cropped up everywhere and increased the fear that the capital had been taken. Someone heard that an acquaintance of a friend had received letters from two brothers in the rebel army who expected to enter Washington on the twenty-first. The newspapers were no better than the oral rumors. One report denied the next. Morgan Dix made a vow, which he immediately broke, never to read a newspaper again. On the afternoon of the twenty-second, however, dispatches arrived assuring that the capital was safe.[4]

The Seventh Regiment was temporarily quartered at the Willard, National, and Brown hotels. Later, the soldiers bivouacked at the Capitol in the chamber of the House of Representatives, and still later, they made camp at Meridian Hill on the Harpers Ferry Road. The Ladies Havelock Association of New York sent a thousand havelocks, white linen cap covers, to help protect them against the sun, and William Aspinwall donated loose worsted jackets that became known as "Aspinwalls." Rutherford Stuyvesant, unable to join the regiment because of illness, sent two twelve-pounder howitzers in his place, and the Union Defense Committee, prompted by John Jacob Astor, forwarded two rifled twelve-pounders with a supply of ammunition.

Camps sprang up everywhere in New York City. Behind the sea wall at the Battery tents were raised for twenty-five hundred volunteers. Hastily built wooden barracks appeared in City Hall Park. A large tent went up near the striking equestrian statue of George Washington in Union Square. Other barracks were erected in Central Park.[5]

Among the early recruits was sixty-three-year-old John Dix, who had served as a young ensign in the Battle of Lundy Lane in the War of 1812. His faith in the Union had never wavered, and during his brief term as secretary of the treasury he appeared as a strong man in the weak Buchanan administration when he issued the order, "If any man attempts to haul down the American flag, shoot him on the spot." Dix attended the service at Trinity one early spring Sunday and asked the rector, his son Morgan, to join him for a walk after church. He said he had something important to tell him. They walked solemnly up Broadway, and Morgan was surprised to learn that his father had been offered a commission as a major general and had decided to accept. It was a serious step and a sacrifice, but he was determined to help the cause.[6]

Dix developed a military plan to end the war, which called for a strong blockade of the South with no aggressive land action until November. Then he would make a massive simultaneous movement from Washington and Ohio. Yet he knew that the plan might not be accepted by the impatient Americans, who "expected everything done in twenty minutes."[7] He was right. The plan was never used.

Elmer Ellsworth was another soldier who that spring was ready to achieve a victory in twenty minutes or soon thereafter. The previous summer, the handsome young man with curly black hair and dark eyes had fascinated New Yorkers who saw him perform with his men at Madison Square Garden. His outfit was the precision-trained Chicago Zouaves, a volunteer military company patterned after Algerian mountain tribes. The French had been so impressed by these fierce fighters that some parts of their army such as the Chasseurs de Vincennes adopted their methods and colorful uniforms of billowing trousers, loose tunic, and fez. The strictly trained Chicago Zouaves, in turn, imitated the French. They were impressive to watch as they speedily went through their complicated drills. In quick time and double-quick time, they moved rigidly without help from a drumbeat. They presented a great spectacle, and Ellsworth attracted considerable attention during his visit.

In the months following his New York appearance, the ambitious Ellsworth worked in Lincoln's law office in Springfield. When Lincoln moved into the White House, Ellsworth, twenty-four years old, made himself useful and was frequently seen among the president's circle of friends. He received a commission in the army as a second lieutenant but resigned after Fort Sumter so that he would be free to recruit a regiment. He planned to organize a regiment of New York City firemen, knowing they were a pugnacious lot.[8] Ellsworth was as good as his word, and he was like a magnet in drawing men to his side. He set up headquarters in an office building at Broadway and Elm Street and in a few days signed up more than a thousand men. In a meeting at Palace Garden, the recruits unanimously elected Ellsworth as their colonel.

The young colonel had moved so quickly that the state was not in any position to arm the regiment. The newly formed Union Defense Committee came to the rescue. A. T. Stewart was chairman of collections and subscriptions, and he was a difficult man for the well-to-do of the city to resist. Citizens contributed $60,000 to equip the regiment with Sharp's rifles, though unfortunately of ten different models, a sixteen-inch knife the men called an "Arkansas toothpick," and exotic gray, scarlet, and blue Zouave uniforms. Sometimes men were equipped on a more individual basis. A law clerk, for example, received a commission as a first lieutenant in the Fire Zouaves, and his firm presented him with a sword, uniform, and other regalia. Outfitting of the troops was a very haphazard process.

On April 29, with practically no training, the Fire Zouaves, officially known as the Eleventh Regiment, New York State Volunteers, left the city in grand style bound for Annapolis on the steamship *Baltic*. The first departures of regiments were cause for festivities, and before the Fire Zouaves left, there were speeches and presentations by dignitaries. Members of the Union Defense Committee and city officials, including the president of the Fire Department, were on hand. Mrs. John Jacob Astor presented a crimson silk flag to the regiment, and Laura Keene, the celebrated actress, presented another. On the march to the pier, five thousand firemen accompanied the soldiers to see them off.

All went well until a government mustering officer refused to accept the regiment into service because some companies were not regulation size. The high fervor of the day was threatened. Would the dazzling recruits have to return to their homes? That was unthinkable, and General John Wool, commanding officer of the Department of the East, who was present to review the troops, took responsibility for permitting the oversight. The men departed from the pier to the roar of a cannon salute.

During these days of confusion and lack of communication with the capital, General Wool, often regarded as a vain eccentric, frequently exceeded his authority in the interest of expediency. After the mass meeting at Union Square, leading movers and shakers of the city, including John Dix, Simeon Draper, Samuel Blatchford, and Moses Grinnell, called on him for support. All believed that Washington was in danger and something must be done quickly. Working with little information, they presented a plan as members of the Union Defense Committee for chartering ships, furnishing supplies, and sending troops to defend the capital, and Wool cooperated fully with these enterprising and energetic men. Some of their plans may have been unnecessary, some of their actions may have been misdirected, some of their energy may have been wasted. But time was precious, and they accepted responsibility when every moment seemed critical.

Sometimes the excitement of the hour created ridiculous situations. A. T. Stewart found that even church was not sacrosanct. Someone routed him from a Sunday morning service to go to his store to supply five dozen pairs of stockings to a military company that had been ordered to leave the city. Later, the great magnate enjoyed telling his friends how he had been disturbed to make fifteen cents.[9]

Some weeks later, when the first frenetic activity subsided, the secretary of war criticized Wool for taking too much upon himself. Simon Cameron wrote to Wool, "Issuing orders for arms seriously embarrassed the prompt and proper administration of this Department and could not be permitted to continue without a disregard of law, as well as the disarrangement of its activities." The criticism may have had merit, but the secretary apparently forgot the trying conditions under which Wool had worked. The letter seemed strange, too, because the president and some cabinet members had given extraordinary power to the Union Defense Committee at this stage of the war. Secretary of State Seward had given the committee authority to issue or deny passes into war regions such as Washington and Baltimore. Despite Cameron's criticism, Wool had his defenders and remained in command of the Department of the East until July 1863.[10]

When the Zouaves arrived in Washington, they were greeted with mixed emotions even though the rowdy regiment helped put out a fire at the Willard Hotel. Reports of their disorderly conduct spread throughout the capital. Ladies ran for safety and tavern owners worried about unpaid bills and broken property whenever these odd-looking soldiers came into view. A common complaint was that the Zouaves were prone to enjoy a hearty meal and then charge it to the Confederacy. In one overzealous incident, the regiment went through the emotions of electing a Speaker in the new hall of the House of Representatives and declared the Union dissolved. Ellsworth took his men's behavior calmly and treated their pranks lightly. Impetuous himself and ready for a fight, he wanted men with gumption. These outbreaks showed him that his men had spirit. George Strong, more critical, thought a few of the Zouaves would have to be court-martialed and shot before the regiment could be relied upon.[11]

Other regiments quickly formed in New York City, but the state and federal systems were not geared to absorb so many men so fast. Guns, uniforms, and camps were all sadly insufficient. To help meet the crisis, President Lincoln ordered $2 million transferred to the privately organized Union Defense Committee to purchase military supplies even though he had no legal authority to do so. The Bank of New York, among others, subscribed $50,000 to a city loan for equipping volunteers.[12]

The New York State Military Board learned that the federal government would not clothe the troops it recruited. As early as April 23, the board advertised for bids for twelve thousand uniforms. Brooks Brothers, a well-established firm with a reputation for selling superior goods, received a contract to produce them at $19.50 each after giving assurance that it had enough suitable cloth. Two days after signing the contract, however, the firm notified the state that it could not fill the order except by using material that was not army cloth. Under the pressure of time, the state treasurer inspected the substitute and the military board approved the change. Unfortunately, the new cloth was "shoddy," made from scraps that could fall apart with rough wear or adverse weather. The newspapers made the most of what they called a "scandal." Perhaps it was merely an honest mistake. The mild-mannered Brooks brothers, Daniel, Elisha, John, and Edward, negotiated a new contract with Governor Morgan and agreed to replace the shoddy uniforms with the best-quality cloth without charge to the state. The unpleasant episode did not hurt the clothiers' business. Abraham Lincoln and many leading Union generals remained regular customers throughout the war.[13]

The quality of men who offered their services may have been a more serious problem than the quality of uniforms. The confusion and lack of standards allowed men to join the service who were unsatisfactory for duty. George Bliss, later an assistant adjutant general, said that at the start of the war no one knew anything about the business of recruiting and men were "scooped up" rather than enlisted. Physical examinations were cursory at best, a farce at worst. Dr. Franklin H. Hamilton gave lectures at Bellevue Hospital on military surgery and described a number of disqualifications for active service, but his advice did not appear to receive much practical application. Many men passed by the examining doctor in single file without taking off their clothes. No one checked criminal records, and age limits were disregarded. Boys sixteen or less were frequently accepted, and regimental bands took twelve-year-olds. Colonel W. B. Franklin wrote to Secretary of War Cameron that he had reviewed some of the troops recruited by the Union Defense Committee and "at least one-eighth ought to be rejected on account of physical disability, youth, disease, etc."[14]

Although physical examinations were often remiss, Fowler and Wells at 308 Broadway offered enlistees a phrenological examination at half price. The offer was special, for a few days only, for those who defended the flag. The so-called science for reading personality by studying the bumps and hollows of the skull was all the rage.[15]

Thousands of young men enlisted in good conscience, and "young men of respectability" drilled with such outfits as the Lindsey Blues and Belmont Cavalry Troop, but rowdies seemed much more in evidence. They were on a great lark and considered regulations something to be ignored. Billy Wilson, a local personality, who had bolted from Tammany Hall with Fernando Wood and had gained a certain distinction as a former prize fighter and alderman, recruited toughs in a neighborhood that was best known for dog fighting and rat baiting. His Sixth Regiment was called Billy Wilson's Boys. The story went the rounds that Billy told his men not to take their watches with them because there would be plenty of chances to snatch one when they passed through Baltimore. When the regiment set up camp on Staten Island, the residents suddenly suffered a rash of robberies. But Billy, a short young man with broad shoulders and bright black eyes had leadership qualities that impressed his men. For one thing, he made a point of wearing a private's uniform, which appealed to their egalitarian sense.[16]

In mid-June, Billy Wilson's Boys were scheduled to leave the city on the chartered steamer *Vanderbilt*. Before departure the commanding officer unwisely gave three hundred men a twelve-hour furlough with orders to appear at Pier 2 at ten in the morning. When the time arrived, only a handful of soldiers reported and the day was spent rounding up the rest with the aid of police. By evening a hundred men were still missing. In the confusion, Billy Wilson fell, cut his head, and was unconscious for an hour. A physician examined him and gravely announced that constant care must be taken or congestion of the brain would ensue. The durable leader quickly recovered, however, and the *Vanderbilt* sailed the following morning, but about seventy-five men never made the ship.[17]

Billy Wilson's Boys were not an exception. The first and eleventh regiments behaved just as badly, and Colonel G. D'Utassy, commanding officer of the Thirty-ninth Regiment, the Garibaldi Guard, ended up in Sing Sing. He received free pistols from the Union Defense Committee and made a good profit selling them to his officers for $24 each. Later in the war, he allegedly auctioned captured horses and forged a bill against the government for $3,000.[18]

The first barracks and camps in the city were as filthy as they were undisciplined. Sanitation held no interest for these recruits. The Palace Garden at Fourteenth Street and Sixth Avenue was so dirty the officers went home in the evening or spent the night elsewhere. The remaining enlisted men, with little to do, found that nearby saloons were a good place to wile away the hours. Usually their congeniality ended in brawls. Absence without leave was a common occurrence, and large numbers of men refused to board transports before making one last visit home.

A camp at Bellevue Garden for a regiment of sappers and miners was on low, marshy ground and had insufficient shelter. During a cold rainstorm, the men huddled near fences and trees and complained bitterly. Their uniforms consisted of cheap blue overalls and shoes. Colonel James Kerrigan had about five hundred men under his command at the foot of West 44th Street. They were well fed but short of shoes and only the officers had uniforms. At the Turtle Bay encampment, men received ill-fitting uniforms and seethed about having to alter them at their own expense. In contrast to the well-equipped New England troops that marched through the city, many of the New Yorkers appeared to be half-clothed with basted uniforms, wooden-soled shoes, inferior muskets or none at all and no wagons for sick or wounded.[19]

Nevertheless, the ranks swelled and the ethnic appeal helped in recruiting. Louis Blenker, a German émigré, headed one of the German regiments, the Eighth Regiment or Blenker's Rifles. They left the city at the end of May with Blenker making a grand appearance at the head of his troops on a superb horse which he managed skillfully. There were also the Steuben Guard, Sigel Rifles, and DeKalb Regiment. Colonel Wladimir Kryzanowski led the Polish Legion; the Seventy-ninth, dressed in plaid pantaloons, was the Cameron Rifle Highlanders; and Colonel Régis de Trobriand led the Garde de LaFayette, a French regiment, that had a stylish uniform of a red cap, light blue frock coat with red trimming, and red pants. The Garibaldi Guard contained a share of Hungarians, French, Spanish, and Croats as well as Italians. Black bersaglieri hats with a feather and red blouses, however, gave the regiment a distinctly Italian style. The *Herald,* snidely and perhaps with some affection, commented that it included "all the organ grinders of the city."

The Garibaldi Guard, which contained many recruits who were not naturalized, could claim a rare distinction. Most of its officers and men had seen combat, or at least active military service, as followers of Garibaldi a decade or so before in his effort to unify Italy. When they left for Washington on May 28 with haversacks filled with bologna sausage, cheese, and bread, they proudly displayed the original flag that Garibaldi had carried through his battles. The Garibaldi Guard and Italian Legion of about 750 men joined the Netherlands Legion, Polish Legion, Hungarian Legion, and First Foreign Rifles to make up the Thirtyninth Regiment of Infantry.

Archbishop Hughes thought this inordinate pride in outfits named on an ethnic basis was wrong. Instead, he told Seward, numbers alone should be used to identify regiments to avoid "trouble among the troops even before the enemy comes in sight." The archbishop had a point. As an Irishman, he knew that ethnic emotions ran high. The city attracted a variety of people, but each foreign group became a finely etched clan with a romantic loyalty to a real or imagined bond with their homeland. It was their key identification as they lived together, suffered together, and died together, and it generated intense pride that was matched by intense prejudice. Even regimental numbers did not hide images. Everyone knew that the Sixty-ninth was Irish, and the archbishop was clearly partial to it. He told Thurlow Weed, "You are aware that this Regiment is composed almost exclusively of Irish Catholics. I feel a deep interest in the honor & bravery with which they shall conduct themselves during this campaign."[20]

Tammany Hall, a vocal center of patriotism at the start of the war, was among the early organizers of a regiment, and Grand Sachem William Kennedy became the commanding officer. As time went on, Tammany became a bitter critic of the war, but when the need arose its members could always reassure the public of their loyalty to the government by pointing to the record of their regiment, officially the Forty-second New York Infantry. It would fight in thirty-six battles and skirmishes before hostilities ceased, losing almost a hundred men killed and more than six hundred wounded or missing.

Daniel Sickles, in Washington, had ignored his wife's letters to "my own dear Dan." She had heard rumors that he was determined to join the army as a private and wanted to know his plans. "How unsettled, so lonely for us to have you so much away."[21] Soon the congressman came home and joined Company B of the Seventy-first Battalion of National Guard as a private, but not for long. On the day his battalion was to leave New York, friends "persuaded" Sickles that his talents would be put to better use by raising recruits. At the last moment, Sickles sent a letter by coachman to the battalion commander, Colonel A. S. Vosburgh, saying that he had been conscripted for other duties. The same day, as if by magic, he received a commission from Governor Morgan to raise eight companies of volunteers.

Sickles soon became embroiled in a controversy with the governor over the number of men he had raised and, ignoring Morgan, went to Lincoln with a plan to raise a national army. Governors objected to proposals such as this that chipped away at their authority, but the president commissioned Sickles as a colonel of United States Volunteers. His Excelsior Brigade was the only volunteer force in the early part of the war mustered directly into federal service. His successful defiance of Morgan, however, was short-lived. By the end of the year his brigade would become a part of New York State troops. Nevertheless, Sickles was now a colonel and soon a brigadier general.

The less flamboyant John Dix was ready to leave for the "seat of war." He was to command the Alexandria and Arlington Department. His family gathered to see him off, and Mrs. Dix became entirely unnerved and broke down. Even his son Jack, who would soon leave himself, had trouble keeping the tears away. Dix said goodbye repeatedly and then kept coming back for another look at his new baby granddaughter before he finally left.[22]

Many people commented that the city had taken on a Parisian atmosphere. Ellsworth was not the only man to raise a Zouave regiment. There were also the D'Epineuil Zouaves, Hawkins Zouaves, and Anderson Zouaves, and their uniforms cast a romantic glow. Men in colorful and often outlandish outfits swarmed the city streets. Imitations of Arabs and Frenchmen were seen everywhere. The tailors, so recently despondent, found their dark clouds brightening as they went to work making or altering Union uniforms. And some tailors, rumor claimed, were at work making Confederate uniforms.

Other businessmen saw opportunities to help the sagging economy. The jeweler Tiffany, at Broadway and Broome Street, started to produce swords, military insignia, and medals, and a variety of shops offered all sorts of military equipment. Daniel Fish, a profit-seeking gunmaker on Fulton Street, went a little too far. He was arrested for suspicion of treason when the police found correspondence and bills of lading that incriminated him in selling to the Confederacy.[23]

The man with the greatest responsibility for military affairs in the state was Governor Edwin D. Morgan. A self-made success in business in New York City before he turned to politics, Morgan was an able executive who understood the importance of organization and clearly defined authority. Yet he was struggling with disorganization, duplication of effort, and vague or absent lines of authority. He found the chaotic conditions that surrounded the raising of troops maddening, and the patriotic Union Defense Committee was one of his trials. The group's motives were beyond question, but Morgan found its interference with normal procedure intolerable.

The aggressive committee thought that the federal government was too slow in accepting troops and sent a delegation to Washington to tell the president of their dissatisfaction. Intent upon bypassing Morgan, they told Lincoln that they had fourteen regiments in New York City ready to move and that something must be done with them. These tactics infuriated Morgan, but the president was more interested in the wholehearted support of the people than in administrative procedure. He agreed to accept the fourteen regiments and later told Morgan not to check this enthusiasm, "even though it overflows and runs in channels not laid down in any chart."[24]

Aside from duplication of effort, confused instructions, and the departure of the Second Regiment in violation of Morgan's orders, the Union Defense Committee found itself in an embarrassing position. It could not produce fourteen regiments. A War Department representative went to New York to straighten out the mess, and it was finally agreed that the committee would provide eight regiments and the state the remainder. From then on, Morgan gained the upper hand that he claimed as his constitutional right and the committee became less conspicuous. The Union Defense Committee, however, was very valuable during the first year of war in crystallizing public opinion and furnishing supplies.[25]

Less than a month after the Fire Zouaves left New York, Ellsworth moved his restless men to Alexandria, Virginia. His eye was immediately caught by a Confederate flag flying from the Marshall House. He dashed into the hotel, rushed upstairs to the roof, cut down the halyards, and started down the narrow, winding stairway. The hotel owner appeared out of nowhere and shot him with a double-barreled gun. Nearby Zouaves immediately shot and bayoneted the innkeeper, but it was too late to help their leader. The energy, impetuosity, and ambition of the small young colonel vanished in an instant. He was the first commissioned officer to die in the Civil War.

Ellsworth's death cast a pall over New York City. He had created a sensation there, and now he was gone. A service was held in the White House and then the body was taken to New York City. In the funeral procession along Broadway, the Zouave who reportedly avenged Ellsworth's death marched immediately behind the coffin. He had the secession flag that had caused the tragic incident rolled up in a bundle attached to the top of his musket. The body was laid in state in the Governor's Room at City Hall. The same chamber where Lincoln had given hope such a short time before was now filled with sadness. The city's tough firemen were especially touched. Choate unconsciously showed his snobbery by writing to his mother that Ellsworth's death "has stirred up the feeling of the firemen and the other 'roughs' among us to a very excited state and has given a great impetus to enlistments here among the classes which are likely to make the best soldiers."[26]

The army grew larger, but June passed without any significant military action. Horace Greeley, who had written and talked about peaceable secession, now agitated for military movement. His managing editor, Charles Dana, was even more bombastic, and Greeley did nothing to deter him. "Forward to Richmond" became the *Tribune*'s permanent headline on the editorial page. Neither Greeley nor Dana exercised restraint in passing critical judgment on the strategy of the president, War Department, and leading generals. Greeley thought Winfield Scott was an old humbug. The editor was convinced that the war had to be won in a year or the Union was lost, and all he saw was incompetence.[27] The cries for military action by Greeley and Dana drove Benjamin Wood to distraction. He found their militarism particularly grating because he was certain that the world would never hear of a Colonel Greeley or a Captain Dana in any combat zone. They might shed oceans of ink, he said, but they would never shed a drop of blood, and in that analysis he was quite correct.

New Yorkers, like most northerners, saw no reason why the war should not soon be won. August Belmont continued to analyze the situation in economic terms and thought the Confederacy would collapse financially. "In less than a year," he wrote Baron Lionel de Rothschild, "the Confederate states will pay their obligations in treasury warrants, which will have the same ultimate value as the French 'assignats.'" Others, he said, were more insistent; "The business community demands that the war shall be short. . . . Business can stand a temporary reverse. They can easily make arrangements for six months or a year. But they cannot endure a long, uncertain, and tedious contest."[28] Belmont had a sharp mind, and his analysis made sense, but like so many logical thinkers he was wrong. He ignored the ramifications of a war that involved far more than economics.

On May 31, the *Times* published an editorial headlined "A Short War Probable" and insisted that the rebellion must be crushed in the first campaign. On the same day, the Stock and Exchange Board voted a half holiday to welcome and compliment the Seventh Regiment on its return from the capital after supposedly fending off the threat of an enemy attack. A deputation of the Union Defense Committee greeted the regiment at the foot of Cortlandt Street, and John Jacob Astor presented cordial resolutions recognizing its services as though its soldiers were conquering heroes. A. H. Satterlee wrote in his diary, "They look well bronzed and hardened by their experience of campaign life." The Common Council, always good-natured on such occasions, passed and engrossed resolutions referring to the gallantry of the regiment and expressing the "joy and gratitude to our city."[29]

On June 3, the Seventh mustered out, and the men remained at home throughout most of the war performing mainly ceremonial functions. They guarded Baltimore twice, but one of their more notable engagements was to quiet a threatened mutiny by some members of the

Spinola Brigade, who spent too much of their bounty on alcohol. Many officers and men of the Seventh, however, joined other outfits, saw heavy action, and suffered casualties. Before the year was much older, Theodore Winthrop, a cousin of the Woolseys, died in battle at Great Bethel, and Noah Farnham, who succeeded Ellsworth in command of the Fire Zouaves, died at Bull Run, shot in the head.

The disruptive *Daily News* and the provocative *Herald* continued to be more realistic about the future than Republican papers. The clairvoyance of the *Daily News* was not perfect, but its editors foresaw horrendous conditions. They claimed that government expenses of $20 million a month would soon be doubled, the national debt might reach several hundred million dollars, the writ of habeas corpus would be suspended, and tens of thousands of lives would be sacrificed.[30]

Ben Wood was sensitive about the threat to freedom of the press. He had heard that Republicans did not intend to permit any expressions sympathetic to the South, and this distressed him. But any such fears did not curtail his freely offered opinions. A day scarcely went by that he did not assail the administration for warmongering. He refused to give up hope that a compromise might be effected and considered any restriction on his freedom to speak his mind intolerable. Wood believed that when liberty was threatened, free speech and free press served as safety valves. He saw himself and his newspaper as prime defenders of free discussion in the North, and he was probably correct in that perception. Arbitrary arrests, martial law, and suspension of the press were genuine concerns for a free society. Still, it was remarkable that Ben Wood and others were left largely undisturbed when the situation was so critical. It seems unlikely that such freedom would have been tolerated in some later eras of American political life.

Henry Clews had seen the possibility of a long war. By now, Henry Bellows also realized that the conflict would not be settled easily. He told his son, "I suspect our side does not estimate the power of the South & think the affair less serious than it will prove." He had no doubt, however, about eventual success. He thought the cabinet gained confidence "*in* the country and *from* the country. ... Lincoln stock rises. He is not *great,* but very honest and resolute."[31]

Henry Bellows was supremely confident, effervescent, and eloquent—excellent qualities that often produce pomposity. Such mannerisms were common among successful clergymen of the day who preached to the rich and powerful. Underneath the pretentious facade that Bellows projected was an intelligent, hardworking Christian gentleman who was genuinely interested in the brotherhood of man. He enjoyed hobnobbing with the high and mighty, but he used his ambition, clear thinking, and drive for good causes. Although war was anathema to him, he considered "degradation and moral political servitude" greater evils. Bellows knew of the unnecessary loss of life in the Crimean War caused by improper medical care and feared a repetition in the current war. He believed the sanitary conditions in some early camps were so bad that the young recruits would return home sick before meeting the enemy. Shortly after the attack on Fort Sumter, he supported the women's movement led by the determined Louisa Lee Schuyler, a great-granddaughter of Alexander Hamilton, to help the sick and wounded soldiers and participated in the organization of the Woman's Central Association of Relief.[32]

The need for an understanding between private relief groups and the Army Medical Bureau was obvious, but such overtures roused jurisdictional problems and professional jealousies. Dr. R. C. Satterlee, the medical purveyor for the army in New York, turned a cold shoulder to friendly gestures of volunteers. Just as the efforts of the Union Defense Committee upset the governor and the War Department, the Medical Bureau feared outsiders who lacked knowledge of army methods and organization. The intentions of interlopers might be noble, but army doctors set in their bureaucratic ways were genuinely concerned that amateurs might cause confusion or worse and considered themselves competent to handle any situation that arose.

The competency of the Medical Bureau was debatable. Colonel Thomas Lawson, the surgeon general, was a proud veteran of the War of 1812 and was now over eighty years old and ailing. The old doctor pathetically held onto office until his last breath. Over the years Lawson had had a reputation as a martinet, and he kept an eagle eye out for any extravagance. He once went into a rage when he learned that an army post had two sets of surgical instruments. He was anxious to cut the budget to the bone. The medical staff was never large, and at the start of the war, twenty-four surgeons and assistant surgeons left for the South. Only ninety-eight medical officers remained to care for the entire Union army.[33]

Bellows and some of his friends were impatient with the wait-and-see policies of the government concerning medical care. In mid-May,

Bellows, Dr. Elisha Harris, a well-known physician in the city, Dr. W. H. Van Buren, representing the Physicians and Surgeons of the Hospitals of New York, and Dr. Jacob Hanson of the Lint and Bandage Association took a train to Washington to convince high-ranking officials of the need for their services in cooperation with the Medical Bureau. The physical danger of passing through Baltimore was real, and the men expected trouble, but nothing unpleasant occurred.

In the next few days, Bellows and his associates met with a number of top-ranking members of the government to plead their case. Bellows was surprised and pleased to find that they were received with "extraordinary respect" and that their mission was regarded to be of first-rate importance. "Every door has opened to our biddings from the president down all the way through the Cabinet, to the Bureau," he wrote his wife. While others waited, they walked in. He was delighted to mingle with celebrated figures and present arguments for the establishment of a sanitary commission based on the precedent-setting Woman's Central Association of Relief. While Bellows moved from office to office laying the groundwork, Surgeon General Lawson passed away. Bellows looked upon this as a providential departure and intended to influence the appointment of a new man who would be more receptive to their ideas.[34]

In the meantime, Bellows thought the president a "good, sensible honest man, utterly devoid of dignity" and lacking a sense of presence. On their first meeting he found "his smile is sweet, his mind patient, slow, firm—but I doubt his comprehensiveness." Seward appeared to be neither frank nor friendly but able and cunning. The frequently criticized Secretary of War Cameron, who rarely receives a kind word from historians, seemed to Bellows to be the "most business-like and direct of all." Chase, he thought, was "the superior of all in moral elevation," but Bellows had doubts about his insight. The generals were humane and friendly, and Bellows had confidence in Winfield Scott.[35]

The president, contrary to his assurance to Governor Morgan that the Union Defense Committee was important in arousing public support, had reservations about a volunteer group meddling with the medical officers of the army. Nevertheless, when Bellows met with the president a second time, he received a more favorable impression and felt that his respect for Lincoln would probably grow upon acquaintance.[36]

The New Yorkers aimed at establishing a commission that would furnish medical supplies to the army, inspect army camps, and give advice to the Medical Bureau, especially by calling attention to its deficiencies. None of these activities would cost the government any money. Although the inspectors were to be paid professionals, their salaries were to come from the commission, which would support itself with private contributions.

During Surgeon General Lawson's last illness, Surgeon R. C. Wood, more amenable to change than his chief, recognized merit in some of the demands for reform. Better physical examinations, trained nurses, and careful preparation of food were sensible suggestions from outsiders as long as the army remained in administrative control. On May 22, 1861, Surgeon Wood recommended to Secretary of War Cameron the establishment of a government commission "of inquiry and advice ... to act in cooperation with the bureau." The commission was to investigate and advise concerning the sanitary conditions of camps and hospitals and the possible use of female nurses and an ambulance corps. Cameron signed the agreement on June 9 and sent it to the White House. Lincoln approved the proposal with reservations, saying that he thought it might become "a fifth wheel to the coach."[37]

The next day, the commission elected Bellows president and he went to work at once. He wrote up a plan of organization for the "Commission of Inquiry and Advice in Respect of the Sanitary Interests of the United States" and divided the commission into subcommittees. They were to acquaint themselves with accepted principles of sanitation, explore army posts to collect information about "conditions and wants" of the troops, and investigate clothing and health care. As gadflies they would also reiterate neglected orders to the Medical Bureau. Bellows was a good organizer. He could think big, and he had every intention of building an efficient organization that would bring order out of chaos.[38]

The United States Sanitary Commission had an enormous opportunity to do good, but the opportunity to be nothing more than a nuisance was equally enormous. Would the commission simply be a "fifth wheel"? Only time would tell. Frederick Law Olmsted, the architect of Central Park, looking for a more active role to play in the war, accepted an appointment as executive director to manage the day-to-day affairs of the new organization and moved to Washington. The Woman's Central Association of Relief became a branch of the new commission but remained independent in management and money matters and kept its headquarters in New York City. The Ladies Committee met each day at Cooper Institute.

At home, Mrs. Bellows was not so pleased with her husband's new prominence. She knew his weakness for the center stage and bluntly told him not to be so conspicuous. "Some secessionists," she wrote with loving concern, "might be glad to do you violence, so do keep quiet."[39] But Bellows believed that God made the back for the burden and immediately commenced a tour of army camps.

Sometimes Bellows was appalled by conditions he saw; sometimes he was happy to approve of what he saw. He favored the use of female nurses as much as did Elizabeth Blackwell, and in Cincinnati he was distressed to see young soldiers dying on pallets without the comforting presence of a woman. In Cairo, Illinois, he was pleased to see soldiers clearing swamps to improve sanitation, and the condition of the troops surpassed his expectations.[40]

When Dr. Elisha Harris returned to the city, he attended the regular meeting of the New York Sanitary Association and reported on his group's reception in Washington. He was particularly pleased that General Scott was ready to take steps to attach a professional cook to each company. The food had been hard on the recruits because almost everything was fried. Visits to camps by Harris and his friends also led them to the conclusion that the health of the soldiers would be best protected if they wore flannel next to the skin. The doctor said this could not be stressed too much, and the Medical Bureau endorsed the idea. Surprisingly, the committee found that hardships had been endured by soldiers in the capital area but there was relatively little sickness. The most prevalent disease was a mild form of typhoid fever.[41]

The well-to-do Woolsey women, like other women in New York, energetically pitched in to furnish the army with hospital supplies. Jane Newton Woolsey, a native Virginian, who hated slavery, was the mother of seven daughters and one son. Charles, the son, born after his father had died, was soon off to war. Abby Woolsey's first trunk of supplies was sent by steamer to Fort Schuyler in New York Harbor for sick soldiers. It included sheets, drawers, calico gowns, woolen socks, slippers, handkerchiefs, pillow cases, damask napkins, towels, sponges, and four boxes of lint. Her mother made up a tin box of sardines, potted meats, arrowroot, chocolate, guava, cologne, and a jar of prunes.[42]

The Woman's Central Association of Relief selected a hundred "moral" women for training in city hospitals before serving in the army. The candidates agreed to accept supervision willingly and not wear hoop skirts. The Sanitary Commission had gained recognition for them from the War Department, and they were to receive the same pay as privates. The Sisters of Mercy volunteered to help as their sisters had done in the Crimean War, but Archbishop Hughes gently told them that they had better mind their own affairs until their services were needed. When the Sisters of Charity in the diocese expressed a willingness to provide up to a hundred nurses, he objected more strenuously and told them they already had enough to do.[43]

Georgeanna Woolsey wanted to become a nurse, but only "able-bodied and experienced women" were to be taken and she was too young and inexperienced. Nevertheless, she appeared before the examining board and made herself as unattractive as possible by taking the flowers out of her bonnet and the flounce out of her dress. Somehow the board took kindly to her, passed her, and left her application blank where her age should have been given.[44]

Georgeanna went to work at New York Hospital, which occupied a square block on Broadway between Worth and Duane streets. The Earl of Dunmore, a colonial governor of New York, founded the hospital in 1771. The main building of gray stone had two wings and contained separate "apartments" for various ailments and a theater for surgery. For a small annual fee, medical students were allowed to accompany surgeons on their rounds. Private patients received what was generally regarded as the best medical care in the city for about four dollars a week.[45] Georgeanna felt total panic when she visited a male ward for the first time, and she fainted at the sight of a probe, but she did not give up and eventually learned to make beds, cook for the sick, and wash and dress wounds. One of her early assignments was to feed jelly to a young soldier who had apparently enlisted while he was dying.

Female readers of *Mother's Magazine and Family Circle*, published in New York, were called upon to make sacrifices for the good of the Union. The male editors of the magazine, guilty of the worst balderdash, told mothers that it was a Christian war and God would protect their sons. They must "sustain the good Government that God had ordained, blessed and continued to us."[46] Once again, men used religion to support a paradoxical purpose.

The First Lady was busy in the city, too. Congress had appropriated $20,000 for renovating the White House, and she gleefully went on a shopping spree that attracted more attention then and later than the serious efforts of such women as the Woolseys. The New York shops fascinated her, and the buying expedition bolstered her spirits. She stayed at the Metropolitan Hotel, and her forays took her to A. T. Stewart's, Lord and Taylor, Arnold Constable, and George Hearn. She delighted the storekeepers, who extended almost unlimited credit. At Haughwout and Company, Mary Lincoln ordered a Haviland dinner service in "solverino and gold" with the seal of the United States and a duplicate set with her initials. The government paid for both. The president said he would not approve an overrun in the budget, but his wife's exuberant purchases of custom carpets, draperies, furniture, and brocades did just that. Congressmen quietly and politely buried the expense in a later appropriation.[47]

Meanwhile, pressure increased for the Union army to march on Richmond. In a few months the atmosphere in New York City had undergone a revolution. A new militaristic attitude pervaded the streets, and calls for action increased. William Russell, the London *Times* correspondent, noticed the change in behavior after a brief absence. He passed a shop window in front of which a large crowd had gathered and found to his amazement that a blood-stained "Cap of a Secession officer killed in action" was the morbid attraction. And the people's forbearance of long-winded patriotic speeches was remarkable. When Edward Everett spoke for two and a half hours on the issues of the day at the Academy of Music, the audience was enraptured. Alfred Bloor listened intently, and after hearing the entire oration he pronounced Everett "a fine talker."[48]

The appearance of a Confederate ship sailing into New York Harbor in June intensified the warlike attitude. The low, black schooner with raking masts mounted an eighteen-pounder on a swivel amidships and flew the Confederate flag beneath the Stars and Stripes. The raised letters on the front of the cabin read "Savannah." It was a privateer that had been captured off Charleston by the Union warship *Perry* and brought to New York by a prize crew. The men on the *Savannah* had been transferred to the Union ship *Minnesota,* which still remained off Charleston.

The "saucy little schooner" attracted curious crowds to the Battery, and some sightseers hired boats to take a closer look. The arrival of the enemy ship prompted complaints about the government's soft treatment of rebels. Some secessionists had already been captured and "allowed to return to treason" and others still held confidential positions in Washington. The men on the *Savannah,* critics claimed, deserved unsparing treatment as pirates, but it was feared that all precedent pointed to their release and "return to their friends in Charleston."⁴⁹

The United States had always allowed privateering and had not joined other nations in the Declaration of Paris of 1856, which attempted to abolish the practice. Nevertheless, Abraham Lincoln now took a stern stand. He declared that the men of the *Savannah* were "pirates" and therefore subject to the death penalty. Soon thirteen of the *Savannah's* crew members arrived in New York for trial in the Federal Circuit Court. On July 16, a grand jury indicted them for robbery on the high seas, but the trial was postponed until the fall.⁵⁰

Early in July there was a strong belief in the city that the Union army was on the verge of crushing the Confederate forces. The press reported that General Scott planned to occupy Fairfax Courthouse and Manassas Junction in Virginia even if it cost a battle. Yet few believed that the rebels would fight because it was accepted as general knowledge that they did not have sufficient strength. It was more likely that the southerners would fall back to the James River and make their stand in the shadow of Richmond.

The ability of New Yorkers to delude themselves was limitless. It was a common belief that the South had no money to fight a war and that South Carolina had recently withdrawn its troops from Manassas Gap. Slave insurrections were also believed to be imminent and therefore secession states would prohibit their troops from leaving their borders because they were necessary to preserve order at home. The Confederates might risk one severe battle, but it would end in a rout. The thought of a Union defeat was beyond imagination.

As a major battle loomed, Samuel Morse managed to keep himself above the popular clamor. He remained detached and was not ensnared by the war spirit that swept through the city. It was impossible for him to consider the South an enemy. The war made no sense to him, and his logical, scientific mind refused to be caught up in the latest Union sentiments. He wrote to his brother-in-law A. B. Griswold in New Orleans on July 13, "Everybody south of a certain geographic line is an enemy; you live south of that line, ergo you are an enemy; I send you my love, you being the enemy; this gives you *comfort;* ergo I have given comfort to the enemy; ergo I am a traitor, ergo I must be hanged."⁵¹

The advance of General Irvin McDowell into Virginia and reassuring headlines that the rebels were to be overwhelmed at Fairfax and

Manassas were a tonic for less detached minds. Prices on the stock exchange moved higher, and a telegraphic request for a temporary loan of $5 million from the Treasury Department was promptly filled. Later rumors of the evacuation of Fairfax Courthouse by the southerners excited members of the exchange, and the buoyant stocks rose higher. The "remarkable animation" of the stock market was regarded as significant. The *Times* opined, "No other thermometer of public confidence is so sensitive and reliable as the Exchange."[52]

Confidence that the demoralized rebels were easy prey lasted another twenty-four hours and then doubts appeared. Reports of early skirmishes told of a slight repulse of Union troops. No one knew anything for sure. On July 20, the *Times* hedged its assurance and wrote that the popular mind must be "prepared for both fortunes." The indecisive news affected the stock market, too. In the Saturday session stocks receded even before the battle began.[53]

The day before McDowell crossed Bull Run, the battery of artillery of the Eighth New York Militia insisted on being discharged. Their three-month enlistments were up, and they demanded the right to leave. A heavy engagement was clearly at hand, but the volunteers cast aside all pleas to remain. One of the most vocal in his insistence on leaving was Jimmy Lynch, a New York City politician and ally of Fernando Wood. Lynch and his crowd had enjoyed the fun and excitement of answering the call to colors in the city's surge of patriotism. Joining the militia was like answering a fire alarm, but facing the enemy was another matter. The men had their way and received their discharges. The next morning, as the battle began and cannon fire filled the air, they marched to the rear.[54]

McDowell attacked on Sunday, July 21, and his ill-trained forces fought well early in the engagement. New York newspapers reported the rebels routed in the greatest battle ever fought in North America. Headlines claimed a brilliant victory for the Union and a death blow for the secessionists. The *Herald* declared, "Heroism of the Union Forces. ... They Know No Such Word as Fail." When Mrs. Woolsey heard newsboys cry out, "Rebels Defeated! Batteries all taken," she thanked God with relief. A few hours later, she heard of another extra in the street that told a far different story.[55]

When newsboys shouted, "Defeat of the Union Army," no one believed them. The reversal had come so quickly. Suddenly it was "Disaster to the National Army" and "A Panic among the Teamsters and Civilians." Victory abruptly turned into a terrible tragedy. Soaring spirits plummeted to a new low.[56]

New Yorkers, surprised and dismayed, reeled under the bad news and then in a day or two tried to make the best of the situation. But reports about the behavior of New York troops were unpleasant. The Garibaldeans were said to have lost their presence of mind and maltreated innocent people in a rage over their defeat. General McDowell privately wrote to John Bigelow, an old friend, "The first Zouaves are scattered every where and worthless." Frederick Olmsted told William Cullen Bryant, "A large portion of our forces were stricken with a most terrible mental disease, under which all manliness was lost and the utmost cowardice, unreasonableness, and fiendish humanity were developed."[57]

As a counterbalance, heroic stories began to appear about the orderly retreat and lack of panic. The Fire Zouaves allegedly used knives and pistols to destroy the Black Horse Cavalry, a famous southern troop that bragged about picketing the White House. High praise also flowed about the "unflinching" Sixty-ninth, the "dauntless" Seventy-first, and the "manly fighting qualities" of the Seventy-ninth. Although the compensating stories were exaggerated to erase a sense of shame, it was true that not all New Yorkers were shirkers. When the time came to bury those left on the battlefield, many of them were from the sidewalks of New York. One of the Union soldiers buried on a slope of green pasture was Colonel James Cameron, brother of the secretary of war, who commanded the Seventy-ninth Regiment, the Cameron Rifle Highlanders. His men had fought furiously in attack and counterattack. Colonel Michael Corcoran of the Sixty-ninth was missing in action. Soon friends learned that he was slightly injured and a prisoner of war. The fate of Colonel William Kennedy also aroused sympathy. The commanding officer of the Jackson Tammany Guard died the day after the battle in Washington from "congestion of the brain."[58]

The battle that was considered a disaster in the North did not stop the return of the three-month men less than a week later. On the twenty-sixth, the Eighth Regiment arrived by ferry at Cortlandt Street with one of the Black Horse Cavalry horses as a trophy. Later the same day, the Seventy-first Regiment arrived on the steamer *John Potter*. The piers on the Hudson River were jammed, and traffic came to a halt on West Street. The Washington Gray's Home Guard fired a welcome with six howitzers. The uniformed juvenile corps of the Ellsworth and Anderson

Zouaves joined Governor Morgan in the reception that gave the appearance of the return of victorious rather than defeated troops. The wounded of the Seventy-first were carefully placed in carriages, and the regiment marched up Broadway. Flags flew from almost every window, and as the men passed Barnum's Museum, the Barnum Band played "The Bold Soldier Boy."

Members of various Irish societies met at Hibernia Hall to plan a warm welcome for the Sixty-ninth, but the regiment did not show up until the next day. Crowds repeated their greeting as the Irish marched up Broadway to Union Square and down Fourth Avenue and the Bowery to their headquarters. The shabby men wore a variety of hats and shirts and carried heavy knapsacks. The Eighth Regiment, which had marched on parade the day before, had appeared much sturdier and trimmer.[59]

Despite the showy parades, the defeat in battle left New Yorkers in a quandary. The bear market that followed Bull Run turned stronger, and Governor Morgan determinedly called for twenty-five thousand more men. These were signs of positive action and resolution. Nonetheless, false optimism had evaporated and everyone seemed to have second thoughts. John A. Stevens, Jr., son of the president of the Bank of Commerce, felt mortification and placed the blame on "high quarters." He was shocked that after four months the North was "trembling for the safety of the Capital instead of striking terror into the hearts of the rebels." August Belmont wrote that thousands of people regretted having voted for Lincoln. John Bigelow, always ready to find fault, complained that there was nothing "sovereign or commanding" in the president's character. Lincoln did not comprehend the situation and "immensity of interests" at stake. Bigelow wanted a "central mind" to direct the government.[60] As usual, Bigelow's ponderous analysis was off the mark.

The erratic, eccentric Greeley, so recently warlike with his steady cry, "Forward to Richmond," was in an especially poor frame of mind. His newspaper rivals took cruel pleasure in blaming his "crazy and bloodthirsty position" for the disaster at Bull Run because he had placed too much pressure on the government for action. Ever mercurial, Greeley could never be counted on for consistency. He did not respond now by calling for more aggressive military measures. Instead, in a depressed state, he wanted an armistice. The war had already caused too much bloodshed. "The gloom in this city," he wrote, "is funereal — for our dead at Bull Run were many, and they lie unburied yet. On every brow sits sullen, scorching, black despair." During those trying days, Greeley was uncertain about many things, but he was certain that Lincoln was totally incompetent. He soon decided that his having helped elect Lincoln was the greatest mistake in his life.[61]

Archbishop Hughes, a power in the community, was always ready with advice for the administration, but he appreciated the complex problems the president faced and was usually sympathetic. Nevertheless, he wanted the patient Lincoln to show even more patience and consideration for the Confederates in hope of attaining peace. "Conquest is not altogether by the sword," he wrote Seward. The secretary of state astutely let the archbishop know that he forwarded his letters to the president, "who reads all you write with deep interest." Both Seward and Lincoln knew that Hughes could be a valuable ally.[62]

These opinions and criticism of the conduct of the war were relatively mild and came from men who were more or less in the mainstream of affairs. There were others, however, southern sympathizers, peaceable secession people, and deeply disgruntled antiadministration politicians, in the city. With military reversal, their voices, much more extreme, became louder, taking the opportunity to claim that they had been right all along. Benjamin Wood's *Daily News* flatly stated that the North was fighting against the Constitution and its soldiers should lay down their arms. The paper said it was illogical and unjust to brand a man a traitor because he would not admit that there was a need for a civil war. Wood was positive that the predominant sentiment in the city was for peace. Anyone who doubted that, he said, should walk down the street and ask the first twenty people he met or eavesdrop on talk in public places and invite casual conversation. He did, however, admit one reservation: he knew that the tone of public opinion in New York City did not necessarily reflect feelings throughout the North. James McMaster, a devout believer in states' rights, who had bought Archbishop Hughes's interest in the *Freeman's Journal*, denounced the administration in language as sharp as Wood's.

Benjamin Wood's flirtation with treason led a federal grand jury to consider the question of indicting him for disloyalty. Although no indictment was handed down, the jury returned a presentment which expressed its belief that the *Daily News* made statements "calculated to aid and comfort the enemy." Although Wood escaped trial, he as well as the publishers of the *Evening Day-Book, Freeman's Journal,* and less extreme *Journal of Commerce* were penalized in another way. A New York City superior court issued a court order that temporarily banned the papers from the mail for "encouraging the rebels." The *Daily News* suspended publication for twenty months, but in May 1863 the paper would vigorously resume its fundamental opinions and criticism intact. The ban was too much for Gerard Hallock, editor of the *Journal of Commerce.* He sold the paper and never wrote for the press again.[63]

McMaster was a sturdier critic than Hallock, and his continued denunciation of the administration resulted in his arbitrary arrest without a warrant or indictment. In August he was imprisoned in Fort Lafayette at the Narrows, where he remained for about eight months and enjoyed picturing himself as a martyr for freedom of the press. When he was released without trial, he showed no remorse and stubbornly carried on his battle with the government. Francis Lieber, a Columbia College professor and adviser to the government on military law, received his share of vicious barbs in the pages of the *Freeman's Journal* and was under the impression that McMaster was a priest.[64] He was wrong. McMaster, the son of a Presbyterian minister, happily married with four children, had converted to Roman Catholicism.

Everyone and everything seemed to be at odds, and the differences affected the attitude of the entire city. A. H. Livermore wrote to the traveling Henry Bellows in August from his office at 111 Broadway, "We are feeling a little blue these days in N.Y. ... The sputter of treason in the North — a vague misgiving about the loyalty and determination, still more about the ability of the cabinet, the generals, etc."[65] They were all good reasons for feeling a little blue.

5
Money

After Bull Run, Secretary of the Treasury Salmon Chase arrived in New York to rally the money men in the city who had given only luke-warm financial support to the Union. Despite all the fervor since Fort Sumter, New Yorkers, whether they admitted it or not, hoped to continue with business as usual. Their justification was a desire to appease the South. As late as mid-May, Governor Brown of Georgia distressed city bankers by falsely claiming that property of Georgians in New York had been forcibly taken from them. Quite the opposite was true, but in sup-posed retaliation, Brown forbade citizens of Georgia to pay any debts owed in New York and invited them to pay the same amount to the Geor-gia treasury. Brown's actions outraged New York bankers because they were still paying drafts against all funds deposited by Georgians and other southerners. They still did not realize that a life-and-death battle was under way.[1]

These were the bankers to whom Chase looked for financial suste-nance. With the help of Assistant Treasurer Cisco, he hoped to inspire them with a sense of duty. Progress in his conferences was slow, and at one time his mission faltered badly. The bankers were reluctant to invest in a war that had started out so poorly and now, along with other reser-vations, they wanted better military management. Chase wanted a loan of $50 million in "seven-thirty" treasury notes with the privilege of con-verting them into twenty-year bonds. The subscribers would have an op-tion to take $50 million more and then another $50 million for a total of $150 million. The government would pay 7.3 percent interest for the money.

The mood of the bankers who met at the American Exchange banking house was decidedly mixed even though the bonds could be an attractive investment. Savings banks, stocks of New York State, and mortgage bonds for such leading railroads as the New York Central and Erie paid interest rates that ranged from 5 to 6 percent. No investment with reasonable security offered interest as high as 7.3 percent. Stevens of the Bank of Commerce was against accepting Chase's proposal, but Moses Taylor of City Bank supported the secretary. James Gallatin of the National Bank was strongly against the plan, and Shepherd Knapp of Mechanics Bank worried that the property of the banks would become worthless if the government could not fulfill its obligations. The fate of the nation took second place to the fate of the banks. The negotiations were difficult, and the righteous Chase, desperate for agreement, even considered bribery to smooth the way. He wrote Lincoln that it would be necessary to appoint Stevens's son a consulship to Paris. But Lincoln was not tempted and immediately approved John Bigelow's commission to that post as he had originally planned.

After many hours of discussion, Chase finally had his way and his proposal was essentially adopted. The banks in New York, Boston, and Philadelphia formed an association to advance $50 million to the government, and Moses Taylor, a master of complex deals, headed the group. New York, with the largest banking capital, supplied $35 million of this amount.

Chase said to Cisco, "Well, we have fifty million, but how about the next fifty?" Cisco optimistically replied, "The banks will take them, do you not see that they have stepped into the same boat with you?" Cisco was confident that the bankers would lend the entire $150 million. "Then," he said, "will come the suspension of specie payments." Chase answered, "Never, while I am Secretary of the Treasury." But Cisco was right. He was certain that suspension of specie payments and the circulation of paper money were inevitable in the absence of heavy taxation.[2]

Soon after the details of the loan were arranged, the bankers gathered at the Willard Hotel in Washington to congratulate themselves on their efforts. The president of the Bank of Commerce expressed the hope that this loan would be sufficient to end the war. "We are glad," he said, "that we have decided to come thus to the support of the government but we owe a duty to our stockholders and dare not encroach upon their rights ... this is all that can be expected of us." None of his fellow bankers around the banquet table questioned his lack of foresight about the future financial demands of the war.[3]

The bankers did not look upon themselves as shirkers. To the contrary, they thought they were acting as altruistic and patriotic citizens without interest in personal gain. And there was no doubt that they had a legitimate responsibility as stewards of their depositors' money. The bankers never intended to serve as anything more than a medium between the government and the people. In this emergency, however, they actually supplied the money of the few they represented until greater numbers of the population could be enlisted to give financial aid. The business was risky, and the Union defeats that followed Bull Run made it even riskier. They had reason to be concerned.

To those who opposed the war, the loans Chase had negotiated were simply one more step to national bankruptcy. This time, financial bankruptcy had joined moral bankruptcy. The sale of the bonds, they believed, was one more way of deceiving the people and taking advantage of those with little means who purchased them. These critics predicted that the bonds would soon be worthless as the war dragged on.

Others in the city had money worries, too. Some men deserted from the army because of their concern for their families. They were not paid on a regular basis, and many wives and children suffered. The Children's Aid Society was swamped with children of volunteers who drifted about the city streets. Women demonstrated at City Hall and said they would ask their husbands to desert. Unsympathetic citizens, however, complained that the city was too generous in providing for families of volunteers. The city gave needy families three dollars a week plus one dollar for the first child and fifty cents for each additional child, which critics said was more than many of their husbands had earned before enlisting.[4]

The Union Defense Committee set up a center in a large vacant store at 14 Fourth Avenue to administer relief to families of volunteers, and the crowds of applicants were so large that a store next door had to be used, too. By June 10, relief for the head of the family was reduced from three to two dollars a week. On a relative basis, this may have been fair. At this time, many people lived comfortably in a room with board for three and a half to five dollars a week.

Although many of the applicants were in genuine need, the committee discovered a variety of frauds. Women falsely posed as wives of soldiers while some legitimate wives drew relief from one ward and the mother or sister of the same soldier drew relief in another ward. Some applicants used certificates of enlistment of deserters and others used certificates of men who had joined two regiments and then were rejected by both. There were also recipients who sent their windfall to Ireland. And although fraud may not have been intended, sometimes two wives of the same man applied for relief. At any rate, almost twelve thousand persons received relief from the Union Defense Committee in 1861.[5]

The plight of the needy in wartime served as a perfect opportunity for plunder by the Common Council. In August 1861, the council called a special meeting supposedly to help indigent families of volunteers and slipped through a motion by Alderman Terence Farley, a shady politician who was under indictment, to appoint twenty-two street opening commissioners. The vague or nonexistent duties of the unnecessary commissioners reputedly cost the city a quarter of a million dollars.

The economy had not yet reacted to the inflationary influences of the war, and unemployment remained high during the summer. The St. Nicholas was one of many hotels that reduced rates. Its American plan dropped from $2.50 to $2.00 a day. The Workingman's Union called on the mayor to create jobs by giving out work on public buildings. Many stitchers and sewing girls who had lost their jobs before the war had not yet been rehired. Some made small wages doing part-time sewing for the army, but others were tempted by vice and crime. The unemployment problem was so grave that a suggestion was made that the city's poor be transported to the West, where they could find jobs. It was not an extreme idea. The Children's Aid Society made a practice of shipping poverty-stricken children to the West.[6]

Ripples of dissatisfaction also appeared among women of greater means who paid taxes on their property but could not vote. A Mrs. Dall produced a book, *Woman's Rights under the Law*, that discussed such questions in moderate language and attracted favorable comment from males. *Harper's Weekly* sympathetically asked why a capable woman could not vote whereas a recent immigrant, ignorant of government, could vote on the disposition of her taxes. "Let any intelligent man ask himself why his mother should not vote," the article read, "and the man drunk at the corner grocery should, and the answer would be amusing to hear."[7] Although no immediate action was taken, some sentiment arose that taxation and true representation must eventually go together.

While many suffered and some were ready to give their lives for their country, others were looking for ways to make a profit. Despite the depression, imaginative and often rapacious minds saw the commercial opportunities of war and began to conjure up moneymaking schemes. Activity increased on the stock exchange, and the trading day from ten in the morning until four in the afternoon was insufficient for some members to complete their business. The board, disturbed because business was carried on in the street after the closing hour, asked its members to refrain from this practice as much as practicable.[8]

Marshall O. Roberts, a former associate of Cornelius Vanderbilt, bought the ship *Empire City* at auction for $12,000 and chartered it to the government. By the end of the war he had made about $1 million in charter contracts.[9] John Develin and Charles Stetson, the operators of the Astor House, who were friends of Thurlow Weed, bought the ship *Cataline* for $18,000 and rented it to the government for $10,000 a month at the start of the war. Weed was never implicated in the transaction, but his name did appear on some notes related to the *Cataline*. Develin and Stetson swore that this was merely a friendly accommodation, but Weed had his fingers in many financial pies and it would not have been out of character if he had shared in this particular deal. He took advantage of inside information and political friends to become an agent for state and national governments in purchasing ships and arranging contracts for uniforms, muskets, and other war materials. When Congress passed an act in July 1861 which permitted the president to license trade in cotton with rebel states, Weed was quick to recognize the value of a product in short supply. This strange trade, so helpful to the South, outraged Union generals and lined Weed's pockets.[10] Weed worked quietly and smoothly and was never averse to crossing party lines for the sake of business. And he had sufficient prestige to make demands on officials at the highest levels of government. He did not hesitate to ask Mayor Fernando Wood to call on him. "I would come to the Mayor's office," he explained, "if it would not make too much talk."[11]

Twenty-five-year-old Jay Gould was not yet an industrial giant, but he was already showing his skill as a trader. A partner in a Wall Street brokerage firm, Smith, Gould, and Martin, he was ever anxious for a pool operation or stock maneuver based on advance information about the result of a battle. Exclusive news was a precious asset for speculators.[12]

Aristocratic J. Pierpont Morgan was another young financier starting a career in downtown New York. He rented a small office at 50 Exchange Place and became involved in an unsavory sale of obsolete weapons to the government soon after Fort Sumter. Two associates, Simon

Stevens and Arthur Eastman, received a cash advance from Morgan to buy five thousand carbines that had been condemned by the army four years before as unserviceable and dangerous. The two men paid $3.50 each for the guns and sold them to General John C. Frémont, commanding officer of Union troops at St. Louis, for $22. Frémont refused to pay almost $110,000 when he learned that tests proved the weapons' worthlessness.

The War Department, after investigation, paid Eastman and Stevens $55,550, but the gun dealers were not satisfied and sued the government in the Federal Court of Claims for the remaining amount. The court held that Frémont had entered into a contract and said that "by arrangement between Stevens and one J. Pierpont Morgan, the voucher for the first 2500 carbines delivered was to be made out in the name of Morgan which was done." Morgan may not have known the condition of the guns when he entered into the agreement, but he could not have remained ignorant of the fraud during and after the trial. Nevertheless, he remained silent and collected his money. The court's decision served as a precedent for later "deadhorse claims" to be paid to shady contractors who did business with the government throughout the war.[13]

Secretary of the Navy Gideon Welles ignored Cornelius Vanderbilt's offer of help as an experienced shipping man in the early days of the war and instead named his brother-in-law George D. Morgan and William Aspinwall, respected New York merchants, as agents for chartering and buying ships. Morgan apparently did a conscientious job in negotiating the best possible deals with tough shipowners, but he also made a handsome commission of $70,000 between August and December 1861. Senator John P. Hale, a member of the Naval Affairs Committee, condemned Morgan's activities and demanded a return of the money pending the determination of a reasonable payment. *Frank Leslie's Illustrated Newspaper* called Morgan's commission a "swindle" and also demanded that he return the money to the government. The paper went to the extreme of printing a drawing of a poor widow of a soldier, who it claimed was dying because she had not received his pay as a result of Morgan's depletion of the treasury. Another drawing showed Morgan's luxurious dining room. Morgan was not impressed. He kept his money.[14]

Later in the war, William Aspinwall returned $25,000 to the government in connection with a deal in which he was involved and received much public praise for his altruism. It was a small amount to pay to protect his reputation. He was one of the richest men in the city and a few years before had been estimated to be worth the handsome sum of $4 million.[15]

Not all businessmen in the city were self-serving. Many of their products and services were desperately needed to fight the war, and they filled a large void. John Englis, for example, a highly reputable ship-builder, launched the *Unadilla* in the brief span of fifty-eight days. The first gunboat delivered to the navy after Fort Sumter delighted Gideon Welles because the builder completed it twelve days ahead of the contract deadline. Abram Hewitt of Cooper, Hewitt and Company, worked at fever pitch to meet the demands of the War Department for mortar beds and gun carriages. His company was the first in the United States to produce iron deck beams for war vessels and could supply the navy with a reasonable quantity at short notice. He also risked time and money to learn how to manufacture gun barrel iron so the Union could be independent of foreign production. For the first time, an American company fabricated a product equal to the best British iron.[16]

Although new business opportunities were evident everywhere, Hewitt learned that the problems of doing business multiplied. Costs jumped alarmingly, and he found it difficult to meet current payments because debts owed his company in the North as well as the South were almost impossible to collect. The only solution he saw was to cut wages. In May, Hewitt received a tempting invitation to increase his profits when the Richmond, Fredericksburg, and Potomac Railroad Company in Virginia sought telegraph wire and instruments to construct a telegraph line on its roads from Aquia Creek to Richmond. The railroad officials claimed that their request was merely to meet operational needs and had no military significance, but Hewitt was not taken in and dutifully advised the War Department.[17]

By the fall of 1861, business activity increased generally and war prosperity began to emerge. Bankers learned to their surprise that the war had not stopped production. Although imports into the city declined for the first nine months of 1861, exports increased. Retailers did a brisk business, too. Sales volume pleased Rowland Macy, and he continued to expand his stock, adding Zouave jackets, capes, fancy soaps, perfumes, and toilet extracts. Gradually, Macy's was becoming a department store.[18]

On Broadway, entertainment receipts revived. Late in September fashionable people in the city attended the festive opening of Lester Wallack's new theater at Broadway and Thirteenth Street. The theatrical manager had leased the northeast corner from William B. Astor for the sizable rent of $8,000 a year for the first ten years and built the most elegant theater in the city with imposing lobbies and lounges. Some of the actors in his excellent stock company received as much as $100 a week. Wallack opened with a three-act play, *The New President.* The patrons paid one dollar for orchestra seats or seven dollars for a private box seating seven. Seats in the family circle were a more reasonable twenty-five cents. Through the winter Wallack presented a series of comedies on Monday nights starting with *She Stoops to Conquer,* which became a great success. These were Wallack's golden days.

Wallack's old theater, renamed the Broadway Music Hall, presented a "drama of intense interest," *The Battle of Bull Run.* A few months later, the theater was renamed again as Mary Provost's Theater, and a brilliant actor from a brilliant theatrical family, John Wilkes Booth, played Richard III. He created a sensation, and thrilled audiences applauded him enthusiastically.

P. T. Barnum attracted a wider audience. He built an elaborate plumbing system to pump water from New York bay to two tanks in his museum, where he exhibited two white whales and later a hippopotamus, "the greatest behemoth of the Scriptures." The construction cost thousands of dollars with a gratuity of an extra thousand to an aldermanic "ring" for the privilege. At the end of the year Barnum offered a new drama, *Odena, or the Spirit of the Waters.* The fairy story's popularity was probably increased by the exotic nymphs in flowered gauze.

Soon New Yorkers even made fun of the Battle of Bull Run. Bryant's Minstrels, well established in the city, presented a burlesque of the battle without upsetting anyone. Dan Bryant played Uncle Abe.[19]

The theater was not the only source of entertainment on Broadway. Business picked up in concert halls and saloons, too. Charley White's New Place, one door west of Broadway on Grand Street, advertised, "Who Complains of Hard Times?" and offered a free "lunch" every night from eleven to one in the morning. "Free and easy" halls also abounded. The Gaieties at 616 Broadway advertised "pretty waiter girls" in an atmosphere "more like a drawing room than a concert hall."

The Alhambra Assembly Rooms nearby held a concert and ball every evening with "splendid music and beautiful young lady dancers." The Eagle Concert Saloon at 650 Broadway, trying to match its competitors, advertised "the handsomest Young Lady Waiter Girls in the City."[20]

The concert saloons shocked many citizens as "obscene dens," which they considered worse than any scandalous doings during the Restoration or Regency periods in England. Yet they thrived under laws that were inadequate to police them. Owners made big profits, and scantily dressed "artistes" reportedly made enormous salaries. The halls offered minstrels, comics, and singers, but it was the waiter girls with their rouged cheeks, jet earrings, and suggestive mannerisms that attracted the customers who came to leer. Attempts to regulate their behavior by increasing license fees had no effect, and "police descents" were worthless. The saloons continued to attract eager patrons with their gaslight transparencies, cartoons, and large vermilion posters. The *Herald*, accused of being the "only sheet vile enough to lend itself to such uses," felt no guilt about carrying ads about the "pretty waiter girls." Soon a grand jury would be called to look into these disreputable halls.[21]

Even on the Bowery the war created new opportunities to make money. One small-time hustler with a slightly distorted idea of military training promoted his shooting gallery. He advertised that his "accomplished professors" would give "free" instruction to possible recruits.[22]

The moral tone of the city appeared to be in decline, and the *Herald* was often considered an accessory to the fact. The spicy newspaper's "Personals" column attracted avid readers and severe critics. Critics said that it was a trap "laid by gamblers, debauchees, profligate vagabonds." A typical notice read: "If the young lady who, on Monday afternoon, at about four o'clock, took a Sixth Avenue small car at the corner of Varick and Water Streets, and left it at the corner of Waverly Place, and wore a black and white check dress, trimmed in front and below with black silk, edged with crimson, fur cape and muff and black bonnet with green velvet behind, desires to become acquainted with one who admires her very much, she will address a few lines to— —"[23] Criticism of the "Personals" increased, but the paper's circulation did not suffer and the column was one of the most popular features of the *Herald*.

The new money that circulated in the city seemed to signal the lower moral standards. Money never precluded morality, but money and immorality made good companions. Money meant more freedom for entertainment of all sorts, but perhaps most of the apparent decline could be attributed to greater public display. As in all wars, ironically, there was a pleasurable side. Men and women found an easy excuse to let down barriers. But war could also interrupt entertainment and bring people up short.

6
Maritime Affairs

A large crowd gathered at the United States Circuit Court in October 1861 to hear the trial of the *Savannah* crew argued by some of the best lawyers in the country. The prosecutor, District Attorney E. Delafield Smith, had retained William Evarts to conduct the government's case. Samuel Blatchford and Ethan Allen were also on the prosecutor's staff.

Among seven defense lawyers were Daniel Lord and James T. Brady. Lord, a Yale graduate, was a classmate of the father of one of the crew of the *Savannah*. James Brady, a popular and successful Irish lawyer, specialized in criminal cases and had saved a small army of men from the gallows. His charming courtroom manner bewitched both juries and spectators. Algernon Sullivan joined the defense staff after spending two months in Fort Lafayette on unfounded charges of disloyalty.

The crew was indicted under the Federal Act of 1790, which called for the death penalty for piracy and robbery on the high seas. The men appeared before the court well dressed and calm. No one questioned the facts of the case. A letter of marque signed by Jefferson Davis had been found on board the *Savannah*. The question was whether the facts constituted piracy. Did their acting under a commission from the Confederate president absolve the prisoners from allegiance to the United States? The arguments were complex and revolved around the right of states to secede or revolt and the fundamental meaning of the federal government.

Brady, performing at his best, claimed that the crew acted in good faith and sought to capture prizes under the rule of law. The French and English recognized the Confederacy as a belligerent, and he said that Abraham Lincoln had recognized the right of revolution in 1848. War was an actuality, and the privateersmen, four of whom had never been citizens of the United States, had the right to use force without condemnation as pirates.

Evarts's presentation of the government side was long and probably too scholarly for the jury. The great lawyer did not do himself justice. He had a quick wit , crystal-clear voice, and natural good humor, but he was ponderous and overly intellectual. For all his brilliance, he had a habit of using too many convoluted sentences. He spoke for almost two days, and much of what he had to say seemed to go over the heads of the jurors. Evarts insisted that the motive of the crew was robbery at sea for personal gain and did not accept the right of secession or revolution as a defense. The United States did not recognize the belligerent rights of the Confederacy, he said, and the *Savannah*'s crew could not hide behind their commission. The law of 1790 denied that rebellion could be used as a plea against piracy.

The jurors deliberated from 3:30 P.M. until 11:00 A.M. the next day and then announced that they disagreed. Eight members favored conviction. Four jurors, apparently believing that the death penalty was too harsh or that Jefferson Davis might retaliate as he threatened, voted for acquittal. Despite Lincoln's charge that the crew members were pirates, there was no public storm or protest over the indecisiveness of the hung jury. A second trial was anticipated, but it never took place. Other events attracted attention, and the *Savannah* case faded away. In the next year the crew members were quietly exchanged for Union prisoners.[1]

While jurors pondered the fate of the *Savannah*'s crew, a contingent of Confederate soldiers landed unexpectedly on Governor's Island. They were a disheveled lot of prisoners of war who were shipped to the post for confinement. They were poorly clothed, sick from the sea voyage, and suffering from exposure. Shortly after their arrival, Henry Bellows heard rumors of their mistreatment and paid a visit to the island as president of the Sanitary Commission to investigate conditions.

Bellows found that the Union officers had not been prepared for the sudden arrivals and the prisoners had spent a few nights in cramped quarters. As soon as possible, food, medicine, and blankets had been furnished, and each man had his own bed in spacious casemates. Bellows wandered among the prisoners and gave them a chance to air their grievances. But the southerners made no complaints except to wish they had not been brought north. The men were homesick, and the cool fall weather probably deepened their sadness. The Union surgeon on Governor's Island was not impressed by the southerners' personal hygiene. He told Bellows that he had seen only one prisoner use a toothbrush. The men were sluggish as well as unclean and had to be forced outside for fresh air and recreation. Bellows left the island satisfied that the Confederates were well cared for and hoping that Union prisoners received care half as good.[2]

Other Confederate prisoners were held on David's Island in Long Island Sound. Algernon Sullivan's wife, a native Virginian, and other women originally from the South set up a soup kitchen for the prisoners with the permission of the government.[3]

Before the end of the year, another maritime event stirred New Yorkers more than the *Savannah* case. It was the seizure of two Confederate emissaries on the high seas by Captain Charles Wilkes, commander of the USS *San Jacinto*. The southerners on board the British merchant ship *Trent* were James Mason of Virginia and John Slidell, a native of New York, former member of the exclusive Union Club, and uncle by marriage of August Belmont. Slidell now resided in Louisiana. The two men were bound for London on a diplomatic mission. Wilkes took the envoys to Boston, where they were confined as political prisoners at Fort Warren.

The public was unconcerned about the niceties of international law, and Wilkes immediately became a popular hero. Even the lawyer Joseph Choate was overjoyed by the dramatic act. He wrote to his mother, "The capture of Mason & Slidell and the glorious onslaught upon South Carolina have elated the whole world about us and one feels as if he had come into a new country and among a new people in the last few days, everybody is so elated and happy." The absence of military victories made the *Trent* affair all the more welcome. And the Irish in the city were happy about an event that irritated the English. The Board of Aldermen, aware of their constituency, regarded the incident "with the liveliest emotions of gratification."[4]

The *Herald* had already suggested that the North and South should reconcile their differences and fight Canada. Bennett believed that a foreign war would bring domestic peace. The annexation of Canada was said to be a favorite idea of Secretary of State Seward, and it was also believed that Spain had designs on Dominica and Mexico. "Linking all these things together," the *Herald* wrote, "we are free to say that our recent proposition for an armistice with the South, and a compromise, including a warlike coalition for the employment of our Northern and Southern armies against England and Spain, in Canada and Mexico, does not appear to be an impossibility . . . and what better way can there be for a settlement of our domestic troubles than a warlike union for the expansion of our territories and our power, North and South, against our European rivals and enemies, constantly intriguing for our destruction and the control of this continent?" Now, as tension increased over the *Trent,* the newspaper claimed that the idea of a war with Great Britain alarmed no one.[5]

To say that war with Great Britain alarmed no one was a stretch of James Gordon Bennett's wild imagination. There was a strong sense of indignation in the city against British insolence, but the mercantile interests had a deadly fear of such a war. The threat was too real. It was more of a probability than a possibility. Parke Godwin believed that the British intended to make war. "Just now," he wrote Bigelow, "a foreign war would be disastrous, but two months hence, when we shall have got the whip hand of the rebellion as we surely shall, we shall be more prepared." Like so many others, he did not have the slightest conception what was in store for the remainder of the Civil War. James Bowen, more sensible than Godwin, knew that the United States was fully occupied with the rebellion and to start a war with the British would be madness. "Nevertheless," he wrote Bigelow, "the feeling against Great Britain is of intense hatred, and the conclusion of the whole matter is that we must give up the traitors, put down the rebellion, increase our navy, perfect the discipline of 600,000 men in the field, and then fight Great Britain. This is the present sentiment—what it will be when our debt is 900 millions with the certainty of its increase to 2000 million if we fight her, time will determine."[6]

Beneath the popular acclamation for Wilkes, questions arose about the propriety of the seizure and the effect it would have on the delicate relations between the United States and Great Britain. The act was reminiscent of British impressment in the War of 1812, and the United States had never recognized the right of search on the high seas. The incident made the stock market especially nervous. Headlines in the moderate *Times* were enough to frighten anyone. They read, "Great Preparations for War," "Arms and Artillery shipped to Canada," and "An Immediate Conflict Anticipated." Sober-minded men asked what was to be gained by such a rash act. Time cooled tempers, but belief in an imminent clash with the British remained. It was recognized that in the event of war with England, New York, "the radiating center of commerce, wealth, and intelligence," would be very vulnerable to hostile attack. The city was accessible from the sea, and the work was already under way to increase harbor defenses. Guns had been mounted at Fort Schuyler, Battery Hudson, Fort Richmond, and Sandy Hook. Governor Morgan bought thousands of cubic feet of pine lumber to serve as floating obstructions in the Narrows, and there was talk of setting up other fortifications at such places as Coney Island. But the costs were astronomical, and there was doubt that a large force could be stopped.[7]

Despite any misgivings, the city proceeded with a reception for Captain Wilkes. The New-York Historical Society made him an honorary member, and the Common Council officially received him at City Hall. Wood presided in the Governor's Room and, unworried about international ramifications, said that Wilkes had distinguished himself as a statesman as well as a naval commander. The tall, gentlemanly Wilkes sincerely replied that he did not expect such honors. For the time, at least, Wilkes served as a needed hero. "Imperial Photographs" taken of him in full uniform went on sale at Gurney's Gallery on Broadway.[8]

Before long, however, nervousness increased in the city. Reports of British troops sailing for Canada made the city more sensitive to the likelihood of war with Great Britain. Prices of imports rose and businessmen received instructions from overseas not to send goods on American ships because of the possibility of international war.

In the last days of Wood's administration, the mayor wrote a letter to the Common Council about his concern for the critical condition of the city's defenses. The letter was probably intended to cover his tracks as he left office. He mentioned that as early as 1856 he had advised of the importance of security from hostile attacks. Now he wanted the Common Council immediately to apply to the proper department in the federal government for help in defending the city. He had previously shown no sense of urgency on the subject, yet now he could not envision a better target for an enemy attack. In the event of war with England, he pictured an immense steam fleet sailing from Bermuda and Halifax for an amphibious landing on the south shore of Long Island. In a few hours they could possess the heights opposite New York and dominate the city.

He reminded council members that this was a British plan in 1812 and that during the Revolution their army had successfully executed such an invasion at Gravesend Bay.[9]

The tension throughout the city caused the New York press to reconsider its position and to write about the need for conciliation with Great Britain. The editors were undoubtedly influenced by pressure from Wall Street. In mid-December prices on the stock exchange declined as much as 7 percent. Investors' confidence reached a new low, and this was no time to fight a second war. Bankers and other businessmen used their influence with the government to calm the situation. P. T. Barnum offered his lecture hall for a prayer meeting to help keep the peace with England. Once again, practical minds sought peace, and this time they succeeded. Even the *Herald* stopped calling England a "toothless old lion." Perhaps Bennett realized that he had gone too far. When Lincoln's Christmas cabinet meeting found a way to ease the embarrassment and release Mason and Slidell, the city, and especially Wall Streeters, breathed easier.[10]

The timing of the *Trent* affair was terrible for New York bankers, who had planned to lend the third installment of $50 million to the government and then cover it with a loan in Europe if the rate of exchange was favorable. That door was now closed, and the bankers advanced their loan to the government without any prospects for their own relief. Their specie was turned over to the government, which made matters worse by disbursing it to other parts of the country to cover government debts. One observer said, "Our commercial supremacy is therefore passing away as a consequence of our patriotism."[11]

The country's financial worries were far from over. National credit declined, banks were ineffective in selling sufficient government securities, depositors withdrew their money, and specie dwindled. By the first of December, Chase had received only $197 million of the $400 million he had asked for to fight the war, which was becoming more costly every day.[12] Fear of national bankruptcy loomed, and on December 28, New York bankers met at Cisco's office. After a six-hour night conference, it was concluded that the government's financial policy gave them no alternative but to suspend specie payments as Cisco had predicted. It was a reluctant decision, and they realized that the path led to limitless debt and irredeemable paper currency. Some of the bankers felt that they had been compelled to take the step by Chase, whom they regarded as an ambitious second-rate lawyer rather than a practical business-man.[13]

Although someone said that even the Christmas trees "cast a shadow," the dark financial picture had a brighter side. Employment improved with the demand for war materials, and almshouses and the Association for Improving the Condition of the Poor showed a sharp drop in relief cases. The Confederacy's hope for a revolt of the hungry masses in New York City was a vanishing dream.[14]

7
Mayoral Election

The arrival of autumn renewed interest in local politics. Jimmy Lynch, one of the leaders in the artillery battery of the Eighth New York Militia, who had turned their backs on the Battle of Bull Run, ran for sheriff in November 1861. It was one of the most lucrative offices in town. Although the *Tribune* and *Herald* called Lynch a coward, he had the backing of Fernando Wood and the *Irish-American* and won the election easily. The city was unconcerned that the new sheriff lacked both character and heroism.[1]

In the race for mayor, which took place in December, Mozart Hall supported Fernando Wood for reelection, Tammany Hall favored C. Godfrey Gunther, a rich fur merchant, and the Republicans combined with the Taxpayers Union and the Rentpayers Association to name George Opdyke as their candidate. The two Democratic organizations did not hesitate to abuse each other with exaggerated claims and counterclaims, and both damned the Republican nominee. The Woods were disgusted with Tammany because it would not unite with Mozart Hall to win votes presumably for themselves. They accused Tammany of supporting Lincoln and charged that their former friends were fraternizing with "abolitionists of all shades."[2] The claim was nonsense. Tammany-backed Gunther was as bitterly opposed to the war as the Woods.

The Republican candidate, testy fifty-six-year-old Opdyke, a dignified figure with well-groomed mustache and long sideburns, was a man of wide interests, intellectually as well as politically and commercially. He began his business career in the city as a clothing manufacturer and later imported dry goods. He then turned to banking, and his firm, George Opdyke & Company, which he had established about twenty years before, prospered. In the past few years he had devoted much of his time to politics. He served in the state legislature, and as a delegate to the Republican National Convention in 1860 helped nominate Abraham Lincoln. George Templeton Strong may not have been too far off the mark when he described Opdyke as a "pushing, intriguing man, fond of power and position."[3]

The mayoralty election took on national significance as Wood was accused of being sympathetic to traitors. Treasonous or not, Wood received the endorsement of the *Herald, Express,* and *Journal of Commerce.* And Gunther's interest in the peace movement strengthened rather than weakened his candidacy against both Wood and Opdyke. The Republican Opdyke was denounced as an abolitionist. Police Judge Thompson said he would as soon see Mason and Slidell elected as "the miserable Abolitionist Opdyke." Detractors charged with an element of truth, that Opdyke was involved with antislavery fanatics, war profiteers, and Wall Street speculators.[4]

Wood presented himself as a conservative candidate opposed to abolition. Although he said it was a citizen's duty to support the government, he took full advantage of his constitutional rights to blast the Lincoln administration. In a rabid speech at the Volks Garten he said the Republicans wanted to free slaves so they could compete with white workingmen in the North: "They are in favor of war as long as slavery exists on this continent and they will prosecute it as long as a drop of southern blood is to be shed and so long as they themselves are removed from the scene of danger. They will get Irishmen and Germans to fill up the regiments and go forth to defend the country under the idea that they will themselves remain at home to divide the plunder that is to be distributed." Wood's violent outburst so infuriated United States Marshal Robert Murray that he asked Seward for instructions to arrest Wood. And Weed's friend John Develin wrote Seward, "If you do not arrest and imprison him for his traitorous sentiments so openly and boldly expressed I can only say that you will make a mistake which by and by you will have cause to regret." But nothing happened to Wood, and the flurry passed.[5]

Wood was aware that his outspoken criticism of the administration might bring its wrath down upon him. In an attempt to cover himself and waylay opposition, he had the nerve to write Secretary of State Seward that he was apprehensive about government interference to prevent his reelection. Seward's son and assistant, Frederick, responded for his father. "He directs me to say in reply that the Administration, so far as he knows, does not, in any way interfere in the popular elections, and that it affords him much pleasure to be assured of your support of the Union, which in the present alarming crisis, is the cause of the country itself."[6]

But Wood's support of the Union was suspect in many quarters. Even the *World* wrote disparagingly of Wood's character and claimed that every secret sympathizer with the rebellion would rejoice at his election.[7] Nevertheless, the electorate was restless, uncertain, and depressed by the war and susceptible to Wood's charges. The national administration stumbled from one blunder to another and tested the patience of the most loyal citizens. Its leaders appeared no less than corrupt and incompetent. The levelheaded Morgan Dix wrote, "If I said what I think of our Rulers I should be in danger of Fort Lafayette." He shared the view with others that Lincoln was only a "shadow" and that "Seward" is *ipso facto* President; & he is drunk every day or opiumized." One of Dix's parishioners went further. He was sure that the end was near. The rebels would soon take Washington, and the northern and western states would find a new capital in the West.[8] It was a volatile time.

The three-cornered race made the outcome doubtful. Trivia, as in most campaigns, took on ridiculous proportions. An accusation that Opdyke had not contributed to the Irish Brigade assumed gigantic importance. Such a lapse could cost innumerable votes, and Opdyke hastened to state publicly that he had given as much as Wood.

Although the *Irish-American* newspaper supported the mayor for reelection, Wood's organization lost some of its usual strength with the Irish. And many Germans switched to Gunther. Continual reports of Wood's corrupt practices finally appeared to hurt him. One allegation claimed that Wood had awarded a five-year street-cleaning contract for $279,000 a year when another bidder offered to do the work for $84,000 less. To make matters worse, Benjamin Wood had a quarter interest in the winning contract.[9]

Tuesday, December 3, was election day. Crowds gathered at each of the party headquarters, and through the evening each group alternated between optimism and pessimism. The latest news in this close race created either groans or cheers in the smoke-filled rooms. About eight o'clock in the evening, Opdyke showed up at his headquarters at 618 Broadway. The rooms and stairways were so choked with people that someone gave an alarm that the building was unsafe and the first

George Opdyke, the Republican mayor of a Democratic stronghold, 1862–63. (Courtesy of the New-York Historical Society)

floor was giving way. Panic ensued, and some suffered bruises and torn coats in the rush to escape, but the building remained upright. By ten o'clock Opdyke seemed to be the winner as the result of the split Democratic vote, and the crowd evaporated.[10] He had barely squeaked to victory by beating Gunther with little more than six hundred votes and Wood by about twelve hundred votes. A Republican Unionist would now lead a Democratic stronghold. Tammany Hall rejoiced at Wood's defeat, but the early returns had favored Gunther and Tammany had expected better. Certainly there was no reason to be pleased with Opdyke. The question remained, How could a Republican mayor be effective in a Democratic city?

Henry Bellows, always optimistic, regarded Opdyke's election as an augury of national strength. Nothing could have been less true. The victory was simply a quirk of local politics.

David Turnure was among those citizens who considered Opdyke's candidacy "offensive to every man's sense of decency," and he had favored Wood as the best man to beat him. Now he deplored the Republican's election at a time when abolition proposals were rife in Congress. He thought Opdyke's election would be looked upon "as an endorsement by the conservative city of New York of emancipation doctrines and tend to confirm them [the South] in their hostility to the North."[11]

Wood's defeat delighted the *World,* and the paper announced that the lame-duck mayor could never recover politically from the blow. The newspaper attributed his fall to "utter want of common honesty." Wood was inventive, energetic, daring, and a splendid executive, but "his very associates in political intrigues could not trust him."[12] The analysis of Wood's talents and integrity may have been correct. The conclusion was incorrect. Wood's political life was not over. He would be heard from again.

8

Despair

A dullness permeated the city in the first week of 1862. The usual New Year's calls were fewer and even the ice melted in Central Park to spoil the skating. No dramatic Union victories inspired the people, and there was profound doubt about the strength of the nation to sustain the war. All in all, things were not good and nothing dispelled the spread of bleak forebodings. Immediately after the suspension of specie payments at the end of the last year, there was not enough money in circulation for either government or business to function for very long. In the previous month, cash reserves of New York banks had fallen to a low point of little more than $29 million, which was less than half the amount on hand at the start of 1861. The war debt had already reached $600 million, and there was no hope of raising money abroad. The stock market opened weak and reflected general indecision. Insurance companies feared attacks by privateers on merchant shipping and shipowners transferred their registries to foreign nations. Strained relations with England still worried city leaders, and recruiting slowed to a trickle. It was not a happy picture.[1]

In his inaugural address the new mayor referred to the defenseless city, saying it was all-important to make the harbor "impenetrable" and "impregnable." Mayor Opdyke thought no foreign attack on America could be successful without the capture of New York City. He wanted the federal government to hurry up and complete the harbor fortifications. More heavy-caliber guns were needed and more troops to man them. Governor Morgan shared the mayor's concern and had taken some steps to strengthen the harbor, but he had not received much help from the federal government. He wrote Thurlow Weed, "The government talk about doing it, and promise pretty well, but thus far they have accomplished really nothing." Morgan was sure that sooner or later there

would be war with England and there was a real possibility that iron-
plated ships could steam up the Narrows and shell Union Square.[2]

The tone of the Republican mayor was quite different from that of
his predecessor, Fernando Wood. Opdyke looked at the ambivalent attitudes in the city and stressed its patriotic contribution to the war and
spirit of unity. More than sixty thousand volunteers had left the city to
defend the Union, and he said that more than a $100 million had been
loaned to the federal government. Loyalty to the Union was the overriding sentiment that he saw in his new realm.

Yet Opdyke was also concerned about the effect of the war on commerce, which was the city's "paramount interest." Since his administration had not been responsible for earlier business conditions, he ignored
the phases of the economy that were improving, especially employment,
and concentrated on the dark side. He did not mind mentioning that
many mercantile houses had suspended payments and others had gone
into liquidation. Every segment of business, he claimed, suffered from
the war and the tax rate was climbing. In the past twenty-five years it had
risen from 44/100 of 1 percent to a hefty 2 percent, and although the
poor did not pay taxes, they were hurt by higher rents and higher prices.
The implication was clear that this was the result of a long line of incompetent and wasteful Democrats. Opdyke saw a need to retrench and stop
unnecessary extravagance in municipal affairs before high taxes forced
businesses to move out of the city. He also wanted the federal government to reimburse the city for the $1 million it had advanced to the
Union Defense Committee for equipping troops. It was a futile request.
The city would still look for the reimbursement from the federal government as late as 1929 without success. The mayor also wanted the state to
reimburse the city for money appropriated by the Common Council for
relief of families of volunteers. Opdyke, the businessman, wanted to put
the city on a businesslike basis.[3]

When the Board of Trustees of the Fire Department presented its
annual report for the previous year, there was no spirit of unity. Although the trustees lamented the "gallant" Ellsworth and defended the
behavior of the Fire Zouaves, they showed little sympathy for the war
and no echo of Opdyke's patriotic views. "It is with sorrow," they declared, "that we have at this time to record the existence of an unnatural
war, produced by ambitious and selfish demagogues."[4]

Opinions shifted with the latest bit of news, true or false. Misinformation and misinterpretation played as important a role as truth. In February, spirits rose with word of General Ulysses S. Grant's capture of Fort Donelson, and it seemed that this might be the death blow to the rebellion. In this mood, Washington's birthday became an excuse for an excessive display of patriotism. At the Battery, a hundred guns fired salutes, Trinity Church bells chimed, and a military parade marched through heavy mud and slush created by a February thaw. Washington's Farewell Address was read throughout the city, and in the evening extra illumination in many houses made a pretty picture. In the next few days, to reinforce the sense of optimism, newsboys ran through the streets crying, "Extra!" Supposedly, Manassas had been captured.

At the Century Club, where the town's intellectuals gathered to talk, play billiards, and drink their St. Croix and Jamaica rum punch, at least one member was ready to celebrate. He bet Alfred Jones a bucket of champagne that federal troops would be in Richmond in the first week of March. Jones was skeptical but accepted the wager with a cheerful willingness to lose.[5] But hopes quickly faded, and soon a new alarm stirred the city indicating a major reverse.

Secretary of War Stanton telegraphed Governor Morgan on March 9 about havoc inflicted by the ironclad *Merrimac* off Hampton Roads, Virginia. The day before, the Confederate ship, renamed *Virginia*, had sunk two Union ships, the *Cumberland* and *Congress*. Visions of widespread destruction of East Coast ports filled imaginative minds. New York Harbor seemed more vulnerable than ever. The Bank of New York hurriedly subscribed $15,000 for the defense of the city. The governor ordered volunteer regiments into harbor forts, militia went on standby duty, and troops on Governor's Island went on alert and carried out gun drills twice a day. Morgan took a special train from Albany to be on hand for the emergency.[6]

Henry B. Renwick, a well-known engineer and architect, received a confidential telegram from Assistant Secretary of War P. H. Watson which included a suggestion from Stanton that Renwick and Abram Hewitt form an action committee to meet the *Merrimac* threat in New York. The telegram read, "You will bear in mind that every hour's delay to destroy the Merrimac may result in incalculable damage to the United States." Renwick and Hewitt immediately met at Mayor Opdyke's house with others to discuss the problem. They decided that the most effective defense was to sink loaded coal barges in the Narrows, and they started preparations at once. They placed their main hope, however, in a new ironclad. Hewitt knew more about this unusual ship than most people because he had supplied special iron rails to Griswold and Winslow, who were partners with John Ericsson and C. S. Bushnell in the construction of the vessel.[7]

In recent days, New Yorkers had ignored this strange-looking craft that had sailed in their harbor. It was called the *Monitor* and had been launched at Green Point on the other side of the East River. The first truly ironclad ship built in America had made two disappointing trial runs in the surrounding waters. Cornelius Delamater in the city had provided the engines, boiler, and machinery, and there were problems. On the first trial the cutoff valves would not admit steam to the cylinders properly. On the second trial the steering apparatus was defective. Navy and merchant marine officers predicted failure for this oddity that looked more like a coffin than a ship. But the defects were corrected, and the *Monitor* left New York under tow of a small tug bound for Hampton Roads on March 6. On board was a volunteer crew of fifty-eight officers and men.[8] Two hours after the *Monitor* left New York, orders arrived from Washington for the captain, Lieutenant John L. Worden, to proceed to the Potomac instead of Hampton Roads. Fortunately, Worden was unaware of the orders.

Although the engagement between the *Monitor* and *Merrimac* was, like most battles, something of a stalemate, the *Monitor* stopped the advance of the Confederate ship up the coast. Nevertheless, fears of a future attack remained. Mayor Opdyke, reflecting the insecurity in the city, told the Common Council that the slight damage the ironclads had inflicted on each other with their heavy projectiles showed that it was possible for such a ship to enter the harbor.[9]

Secretary of War Stanton, apparently unconcerned about butting into naval affairs, turned to Cornelius Vanderbilt for help. Concerned observers assumed that the *Merrimac* would come out again, and conventional minds in Washington believed that Vanderbilt's large, fast steamship called the *Vanderbilt* could offer the best defense. On March 15, Vanderbilt received a telegram from a War Department official that read, "The Secretary of War directs me to ask you for what sum will you contract to destroy the Merrimac or prevent her from coming out from Norfolk — you to sink or destroy her if she gets out? Answer by telegraph, as there is no time to be lost."[10]

Vanderbilt, a big, blustering man with a high forehead and a shrewd mind, wasted no time. He took a train to Washington at once and conferred with Stanton and Lincoln. When Lincoln asked if he could stop the *Merrimac*, Vanderbilt confidently answered that his chances for success were probably nine out of ten. He intended to cover the ship's machinery with five hundred bales of cotton, raise the steam, and ram the *Merrimac* with every ounce of power. Vanderbilt would not accept money for his ship and hurriedly prepared for action. On March 23, he arrived at Fortress Monroe ready to do battle, but it was probably fortunate for the magnate that the *Merrimac* never came out again. Experts believed that the *Vanderbilt's* paddle wheels could have been easily destroyed and the ship would have been helpless. Vanderbilt expected to lend his ship for the emergency, but the arrangements were vague, and Lincoln, Stanton, and Welles thought it was a gift to the government. For several months the ship served as a transport, and in July Lincoln suggested to Congress that "some suitable acknowledgment be made." About a year and a half later, Congress passed a resolution of thanks. Privately, Vanderbilt claimed that he did not appreciate the gesture. "Congress be damned," he said, "I never gave that ship to Congress. When the government was in great straits for a suitable vessel of war, I offered to give the ship if they did not buy it; however Mr. Lincoln and Mr. Welles think it was a gift, and I suppose I shall have to let her go." But such talk was done only among intimates, and he was probably pleased when he received a gold medal from the government for his patriotism. Vanderbilt did not lose money working for the government. He chartered some of his ships for healthy fees even though they were usually less exhorbitant than those charged by other shipowners.[11]

Vanderbilt did not give the appearance of being an efficient or patriotic businessman when Stanton named him a government agent to buy ships for a movement of military forces to New Orleans later in the year. He blamed his poor performance on his lieutenant, T. J. Southard, but the responsibility was Vanderbilt's and at best he appeared to be a careless buyer. Senator James Grimes of Iowa, a member of a later investigating committee, discovered that Vanderbilt had bought the *Niagara*, whose planks ripped out in a calm sea. The rotten beams were incapable of holding a nail. Grimes also claimed that Vanderbilt had chartered ships at unnecessarily exhorbitant rates. According to a congressional report, he had agreed to pay $900 a day for the first thirty days for the

Eastern Queen and $800 a day for the remaining days whereas the government had previously chartered the ship for $500 a day. He paid $250 a day for the *Quinebang,* which the government had previously chartered for $130 a day. And there were other similar cases. No Excuses could explain away Vanderbilt's slipshod and embarrassing transactions.[12]

Oddly, during these difficult days, the full shipbuilding resources of the city were not put fully to use to supply the Union navy. The renowned William Webb refitted many steam vessels for the war, but his major effort went into building two large ironclad frigates, the *Re d'Italia* and the *Re Di Portogallo,* for the Sardinian navy. When the *Re d'Italia* slipped into the water at the end of 1863, the Sardinian agents were delighted with the ship's performance. Expert admirers considered the thirty-two-gun warship an outstanding example of naval architecture. Two eight-hundred-horsepower engines gave promise of a speed of twelve knots, which was believed to be greater than any other ironclad then constructed. And it was probably the first ironclad to cross the Atlantic. Yet apparently no one complained that the ship should have gone into the service of the Union navy.[13]

Soon after the *Merrimac* threat passed, word arrived of trouble near Shiloh. Good military news was impossible to sustain. The excitable Horace Greeley shouted in his high voice, "Battle yesterday at Pittsburg Landing, rebels whipped us of course. Our soldiers are being driven into the Tennessee today. Our generals are drunk. Buell ought to be shot, and Grant ought to be hung." And his opinion of McClellan was no more flattering. He did not hesitate to express his lack of confidence in the "Young Napoleon" and went so far as to say that General George B. McClellan did not march on Richmond because he might kill some of his potential supporters for the next presidential election.[14]

George Dow, an inveterate letter writer, half-humorously concluded that it would be a good idea for the president to send the abolitionist Wendell Phillips and a few others of his ilk to the Confederacy to present their lectures. He thought this would cause so much commotion among the rebels that the Union could take Richmond without any trouble.[15]

A short time later, a business firm in the city exhibited extraordinary optimism in sharp contrast to the pervasive pessimism. By the end of April, Admiral David Farragut took New Orleans, and Carter, Hale and Company at 2 Maiden Lane, sent a young employee, Augustus K.

Sloan, to the newly occupied city to collect the company's outstanding debts. Not surprisingly, Sloan did not collect a penny, but he would not forget the trip. On the voyage south, his ship hit a rock near the Bahamas and he was marooned on an island for four weeks.[16]

Shrewder and greedier businessmen did not take off on such quixotic missions. They remained at home to speculate in gold. The price of gold rose with each military defeat. Each increase in the value of gold reflected doubts about the government's ability to stand behind the irredeemable paper money. The first issue of $150 million in this new paper currency came out in February, and other issues followed. Many sincere businessmen regarded gold speculators as nothing less than traitors, but the depreciation of greenbacks and the overwhelming opinion that the United States was on the brink of financial disaster only stimulated their activities. Although the Stock and Exchange Board abolished dealing in gold, a gold exchange soon evolved outside of its jurisdiction and about half of the Stock and Exchange Board members participated. Early in 1862 an Open Board of Stock Brokers started operation in a dark basement at 23 William Street with few restrictions. Many of the operators were curbstone brokers who cast aside any pretense of gentility and rudely blocked the streets to the annoyance of nearby brokerage houses.[17]

Profiteers and speculators were an important part of city life, but moneymaking did not capture everyone's heart and mind. The city was too large and too diverse for greed alone to rule. One sign of unselfishness was the increasing number of women who volunteered as nurses in the city hospitals. Many of them were fashionable ladies who a short time before would have disdained such work. Now, they "walked the wards," did the messy jobs, and surprised themselves with their lack of squeamishness. Other ladies gathered in parlors throughout the city to roll bandages and scrape old sheets into lint that could make pads to stop the flow of blood.

In the absence of government action, voluntarism was accepted without question. Government had always remained remote from the problems of individual welfare, and citizens willingly stepped in to fill the gap. Yet the volunteers were not always sufficient or well organized. There were times when detachments of wounded or sick soldiers arrived in the city weak, hungry, and thirsty and no preparation had been made for them. In the spring, Dr. Satterlee, the surgical and medical purveyor for the army, set up part of the Park Barracks for the wounded, and a selected group of physicians and medical students provided care. Funds came from the New York Surgical Aid Association, which solicited contributions from private citizens. New Englanders took over a building on Broadway to care for their disabled soldiers who were bound for home.[18]

The urgent appeals of the Sanitary Commission for supplies reached the ears of schoolchildren, who wanted to do their part. Ward School 45 at Twenty-fourth Street between Seventh and Eighth avenues provided one example of their interest and generosity. The principal told the pupils that they could ask their parents for contributions but warned not to press them if they objected. The children's campaign succeeded in collecting five wagonloads of necessities for the commission.

Not everyone cooperated with the Sanitary Commission as well as did the children of Ward School 45. According to George Templeton Strong, the treasurer, Secretary of War Cameron and General McClellan continually disappointed members of the executive committee by failing to keep their promises. Lincoln and Cameron's successor, Stanton, seemed no better. General Montgomery Meigs, the quartermaster general, was the one man with whom they were satisfied because he had some needed hospitals erected. The commission had been so unsuccessful in its requests for reforms of the Medical Bureau that the leading members were on the verge of resigning. But they never did so, and eventually they began to see some progress.[19]

The city was home to some of the finest medical institutions in the country, and their services were badly needed. Unfortunately, demands on them increased as their staffs decreased. To help care for the thousands of new patients, an army hospital was under construction at Governor's Island and soon another would be built at Fort Schuyler with thirty-four wards, each in a long, low building and containing fifty or more beds. Other hospitals such as St. Luke's, St. Vincent's, and the Jews' Hospital, as well as New York and Bellevue, extended their medical services for the military.

The Jews' Hospital had been established a few years before on West Twenty-eighth Street to provide medical care for members of that faith. The policy was honored in the breach more often than not, and immediately after the outbreak of war, the directors of the hospital passed a resolution promising to care for soldiers wounded in the service of their country. As the war went on, the directors further broadened their outlook, and eventually they formally announced that no distinction would be made concerning "either the nationality or the religious belief of the sufferer." The hospital, now known as Mount Sinai, still carries out that policy set in wartime.[20]

Confusion over the responsibility of federal, state, and local governments in various areas was constant, and the care of sick and wounded soldiers became an increasingly important aspect of this broad problem. Opinions varied about what role each level of government should play, but in the absence of precedent, the city assumed the burden for many activities that would later be regarded as federal functions. The arrival of hundreds of disabled soldiers in the city each week prompted the national affairs committee of the Board of Aldermen to recommend founding and supporting a soldiers' hospital near the northern boundary of Central Park. Mayor Opdyke recognized the need for such a facility, but he thought it should be the responsibility of federal and state governments. He thought it was more urgent and a proper function for the city to care for families of volunteers.

Despite Opdyke's reservations, Alderman Farley and others arranged for the Sisters of Charity of St. Joseph's Hospital to take over the buildings of Mount St. Vincent Academy in Central Park, where they cared in the saintliest ways for soldiers with amputations. Sometimes patients of another religion found these women in funereal black habits frightening only to learn that they gave them the gentlest attention. While serving as a visiting surgeon at St. Joseph's, Dr. Stephen Smith of Bellevue developed a new surgical technique in amputations that helped to elminate pain and sores when a patient was fitted with a wooden leg.[21]

In anticipation of medical problems that would be created by the war, Dr. Smith prepared *A Handbook of Operative Surgery,* which became a standard text. Another valuable medical book, *Military Medical and Surgical Essays,* was published by the Sanitary Commission. Most of the essays were written by senior members of Bellevue, who were among the most renowned in the world of medicine. W. H. Van Buren, a humane and progressive physician, wrote "rules for preserving the Health of the Soldier." Austin Flint wrote about pneumonia, Stephen Smith discussed amputations, and the elderly and distinguished Valentine Mott contributed essays titled "Pain and Anaesthesia" and "Haemorrhage from Wounds, and the Best Means of Arresting it."[22]

Another well-established medical institution responded to the need for aid. The College of Physicians and Surgeons, located in a four-story building at Fourth Avenue and Twenty-third Street, appointed Dr. William Detmold as professor of military surgery and hygiene. Throughout the war he offered a course of lectures for students who wished to prepare for military service. The modern facility, built only a few years before, included an anatomical amphitheater that could seat more then three hundred spectators. To receive a medical degree from so well regarded an institution as the College of Physicians and Surgeons, a student had to complete two full courses of lectures, write a thesis, study under the direction of a regular physician for three years, be of good moral character, and be twenty-one years of age.[23]

Sharp disputes were occurring in medical science that resulted in rapid changes. One of the great battles in the medical world concerned the tendency of blood to produce inflammation. The established practice when inflammation existed was to let blood. Pneumonia, among the forms of inflammation, was believed to be located in this way. But bleeding was now almost out of fashion. One prominent doctor said he had not bled twice in fifteen years, and another said he had bled only once in nine years.[24]

Dr. William Hammond, an eminent neurologist, who became the new surgeon general, said that vivisection had shed light on "how the circulation of the blood affected the tissues, & that the drawing off blood, was found to have no effect upon the inflamed part." The new treatment for pneumonia, introduced by a Dr. Todd, author of the respected *Todd's Clinical Lectures on Nervous Disorders,* included the use of stimulants, beef tea and brandy. Dr. Hammond told Henry Bellows that if he were confined to one medicine it would be brandy. Another doctor involved in the friendly dinner conversation disagreed. He chose opium because he considered it both a stimulant and a sedative.[25]

As the war progressed, dysentery became an increasing problem. Dr. Van Buren believed that the best treatment for this scourge was to "evacuate the bowels with castor oil, & afterwards give opium in some form at regular intervals. Absolute rest, beef tea & cream ... flannel bandages across the belly; starch & laudanum injections & stimulus as required."[26]

Although New York medical men were in the forefront of their profession, conditions at hospitals were hardly ideal. There was little interest in cleanliness and almost no knowledge of antiseptics. Bellevue, for all its distinction, was no exception. When Dr. James R. Wood, a highly respected surgeon, operated, he wore a black silk gown buttoned tightly around the neck and wrists and a boutonniere. He was aided by a house surgeon, who wore an old coat and kept waxed silk ligatures in the buttohole of his left lapel. Dr. Wood had an elaborate collection of highly polished instruments with deeply ridged ivory handles. If an instrument did not satisfy the doctor, he would angrily throw it on the floor, a practice not confined to the Civil War period. Dr. Mann Silver watched Dr. Wood operate in the amphitheater and said, "The anesthetic, ether, was given by the junior assistant from a cone made with a towel and folded newspaper, with a wad of absorbent cotton within. No special preparation of the surgeon, assistants, patient, instruments or dressings was made for the operation."[27]

Bellevue organized a new ward for soldiers and made a conscientious effort to improve hospital administration. A new warden reduced the number of rampant rats that were known to attack pauper babies and posted a searcher at the entrace to prevent visitors from bringing alcoholic beverages to the patients. The smells from the "commodious" dissecting rooms, however, were overpowering. And a serious attempt during the war to improve treatment by subdividing medical services with a specialist in charge of each was rejected by a committee that studied the proposal. The time was not right for such a drastic change, and the committee failed to see the advantages of specialization.[28]

The shortage of professional staff made the maintenance of any standards an uphill battle. Senior doctors such as Franklin H. Hamilton and J. W. Gouley left for the army, W. H. Van Buren devoted his time to the Sanitary Commission, and Stephen Smith, as a member of the Emergency Corps of Surgeons of New York City, was frequently called away for special duty at hospitals in the South near combat areas. The junior medical staff was even more depleted. At the start of the war, almost all of the young doctors resigned to join the service, leaving the few who remained in a demoralized state. It was especially difficult to find young men to tend to the wards, and interns often served as house physicians and surgeons. Young Titus Coan, later a contract surgeon for the army and then a naval surgeon, served as house surgeon in the early days of the war. In addition to his regular duties, he cared for sixty or seventy mothers in the Lying-in Department, where there was about thirty births a month. Medical students were another burden for him because their training occurred at the bedside, and he also had to help visiting doctors at clinical lectures. Despite the work, Coan considered Bellevue the "ideal place for learning medicine."[29]

Bellevue, on the East River at the foot of Twenty-third Street, one of the oldest hospitals in the country, was accustomed to emergencies. It was established in colonial days as the New-York Almshouse with an infirmary and had only two requirements for admission — illness and indigence. During a yellow fever epidemic in 1795, a temporary hospital was set up on Belle Vue Farm, and eventually the attractive Kips Bay Farm and Rose Hill Farm with their orchards of plums, peaches, pears, and apples were added to the property. Teaching of students had begun at the hospital in the eighteenth century, but by a timely coincidence the medical college at Bellevue opened its doors the same month the Civil War began. In 1860, the Commissioners of Public Charities and Corrections requested an examination of the institutions under their jurisdiction, and a subcommittee headed by Dr. Isaac Taylor suggested establishment of a college for the education of young men independent of a clinical hospital. Working together they could become one of the largest schools and hospitals in the nation. The commissioners accepted the idea, and on April 11, 1861, the day before Fort Sumter was fired on, construction began on a college building on the hospital property. Classes began the same month, and the war determined some of the curriculum just as it did at the College of Physicians and Surgeons. Bellevue proudly and competitively announced that it was the first to establish a professorship in military surgery and stressed that Dr. Hamilton had been on active service since the start of the war and had every opportunity for becoming "practically familiar" with the duties of a military surgeon. As the war went on, such courses became increasingly important for medical students who hoped to enter military service because the Army Medical Corps made them a requirement for candidates. Dr. Hamilton, also a professor of fractures and dislocations wrote the first complete treatise on fractures in English and systematized the treatment. He may also have been the first advocate of skin grafting.[30]

A number of respected surgeons from New York City joined Union troops at Yorktown to lend temporary assistance. McClellan had landed an army of one hundred thousand men on the Virginia peninsula in May with the aim of advancing to Richmond. Mrs. McClellan, who lived in the city, assured her friend Maria Daly that the war would be over by the fourth of July. Mrs. McClellan never had any doubts about her husband's brilliance or that he was a man of destiny. She had told Henry Bellows that she had made a great sacrifice in giving up her husband to the country. Bellows, undoubtedly thinking of himself, felt that other wives could make the same complaint and their husbands did not have the general's "honors & emoluments."[31]

Bellows received an urgent telegram requesting nurses to help on the peninsula. Some women from his church immediately volunteered, and within a day he rounded up five surgeons, ten dressers, thirty-two male nurses, ten female servants, and eight "ladies." He was surprised when his wife offered to join the group. Eliza Bellows, a kindly woman, was perpetually ill, and he had not thought her a likely candidate. She admitted that she was not born to be a heroine and the horrors of war unnerved her, but she believed she had two important qualifications. The sight of wounds did not overcome her and she could live for a long time with little food and water. Her offer delighted Bellows, and he encouraged her on the general principles that "extra exertions in the self-sacrificing way, always pays, & that *moral tonics* are invaluable to nervous constitutions."[32]

Off the Virginia shore, the *Daniel Webster,* an old ship that the army had given to the Sanitary Commission, served as a transport. Frederick Olmsted was on board with surgeons, medical students who worked as dressers, male nurses, and four of the New York women who wanted to be part of the action. They were the energetic Georgeanna Woolsey and her sister Eliza, Christine Griffen, and Mrs. David Lane. Nearby, on board the *Wilson Small,* were Eliza Bellows and Eleanor Strong. The determined women on both ships worked day and night in the galley and cared for the sick and wounded who came on board dirty, wet, shivering, and hungry. The most common ailment was typhoid fever.[33]

Mrs. Bellows withstood the strain and looked upon the experience as a "time of glorious privilege." She wrote from the *Wilson Small,* however, that these sentiments were not shared by the Irish servant girls, who, she claimed, did less work than anyone. Within two weeks, Mrs. Bellows's wartime adventure was over and she was back in New York. Her husband said she looked "capitally well," but despite his continual worry about her he considered her time away "rather too short." Nevertheless, she would not forget the exhilarating episode, and Bellows found that she had become much more sympathetic to his work.[34]

Not all the heroines were in the field. The *Ocean Queen* brought hundreds of men to New York from the Virginia peninsula suffering from the "virulent fever." They were sent to the north building of the city hospital, which rapidly filled up. Each morning Jane Woolsey went into the fever wards taking oranges, jelly, and papers to them. Men who seemed scarcely sick one day were often dead when she returned the next day. Each day five or six men died. Not every volunteer was as brave as the Woolseys.[35] Maria Daly went to the hospital one day with the best intentions and heard there was a need for someone to read to the sick and write letters for them. She found that she would have to go among typhoid patients, however, and that quickly dampened her ardor. She decided instead to visit the Park Barracks and devote one day a week to the Woman's Central Association of Relief at Cooper Institute.[36]

While sick soldiers jammed the hospitals, doctors at New York Hospital struck for an increase in salary. Since house doctors usually received extremely poor pay, they probably had good reason to complain, but their tactics misfired. They wrote an "impudent" letter to the Board of Trustees and requested an immediate answer. The strike was settled when the trustees replied that they could pack up and leave.[37]

While Union troops faced frustration on the peninsula, the black people of the city found cause for celebration. Congress had abolished slavery in the District of Columbia. It was a big step forward in their struggle for freedom, and they met at Cooper Institute to express their thanks, prayed together at Shiloh Church, and held a joyous ball at the Metropolitan Hall on Prince Street.[38] In a year filled with disappointment, this was one of the happier and more positive events, but it attracted little attention from the white population.

When McClellan, after a slow start, defeated the Confederates at Williamsburg and captured Norfolk, others in the city thought they had something to celebrate, too. The editors of the *Herald* and *Tribune* once again deluded themselves and concluded that the war was almost over. Their illusions rapidly faded. Most newspapers now printed such major news on the front page. Only the *Evening Post* and some minor papers persisted in publishing important stories in the center spread opposite the editorials. The front pages reflected an emotional roller coaster from one battle to the next. Bad news followed good news in July, when newsboys sold extras telling of the Union defeat at the Seven Days' Battle. Mothers and fathers of soldiers gathered near newspaper offices hoping for the best and fearing the worst. The lists of killed and wounded grew longer and longer.[39]

At first glance, everyone in the crowded streets seemed as unconcerned as in "the most halcyon hour of peace." Then in an instant the illusion could be destroyed by the sudden sight of a young man in uniform with both legs shot away or a pale-faced soldier suffering from fever. Still, most scars of war were invisible to passersby in the street. Those who suffered tragedy often hid their anguish. For Francis Lieber, the war had turned into a nightmare. Yet he courageously tried to keep up a pretense of cheerfulness. The Columbia professor, envied as a "man of influence" in the administration, received the devastating news that his son Hamilton had lost an arm in battle for the Union cause. Soon, more tragic news arrived. His son Oscar was killed fighting in the Confederate army. "This is a house of sorrow," he wrote Alexander Bache. A third son, Guido, served in the infantry with the Eleventh Regulars of the Union army, and fear of seeing his name in the "dread catalogues" was a constant strain. Lieber and his wife read the casualty lists with "drained and feverish eyes."[40]

Talk of a quick victory was no longer heard. Stories that the rebels could be conquered easily because they had no money or ammunition disappeared, and no reports circulated in the streets that the end of the war was near. There had been too many false reports that the back of the rebellion had been broken. Respect for the fighting ability of the rebels increased, and a realization dawned that the Confederates believed their cause was sacred.

On the fourth of July, Nelson Waterbury, the grand sachem of Tammany hall, publicly declared that the war could be ended if Lincoln "set his foot firmly upon abolitionism and crush[ed] it to pieces." Union soldiers could then fight "unembarrassed," and victory would be achieved.[41] Such recommendations from the speaker's podium were usually greeted with enthusiasm by the audience.

McClellan's failure to take Richmond in 1862 made critics still more conspicuous in the city. Military defeat allowed them to declare that the war had been a mistake from the start. They were sure that victory was impossible and that the Confederacy would soon win recognition from European nations. The most ardent government backers had to admit that the war was not going well and were on the defensive in their conversations. Such despondency spread throughout the city that

DESPAIR 131

Union supporters held a public meeting in Union Square for the express purpose of bolstering spirits. Mayor Opdyke declared that he went to the meeting to renew his vows on the altar of patriotism. He also sent a message to the Common Council to "seek out, discover, and bring to punishment every disloyal person; and let us call on all the loyal to stand together." But the Common Council was never quick to act on the mayor's words, and this was no exception. The councilmen had their own doubts about the war.[42]

The critical voices that fed the prevalent despair came from many directions, and their ideas, theories, and convictions were often vastly different. Some were Peace Democrats, some were War Democrats, some were Republicans, and some were simply disloyal, but they all agreed that the war was poorly led and worthless to pursue. Unanimity in support of war was not an American tradition; a substantial minority of citizens had opposed every war since the American Revolution. New York City was a base for British troops and a loyalist stronghold throughout much of the War for Independence. The War of 1812 had stirred vociferous opposition from northeastern merchants, and the Mexican War had roused fierce opposition, especially from antislavery advocates. So the dissenters, in keeping with their heritage, followed a well-worn path.

Lincoln found little comfort when he looked for help from the premier city of the nation. The crosscurrents of opinion that flowed through the streets, offices, and clubhouses added to his burden. The bankers gave begrudging assistance, the press preferred to criticize, and local politicians found ready reasons to resist the administration. A solid phalanx of presidential support was missing.

Maria Daly, a devoted Democrat as well as a devoted Unionist, was mystified by the ascendancy of Abraham Lincoln. He did not provide the leadership the nation needed. "Can our countrymen be so blind, so stupid," she wrote, "as to again place a clod, though an honest one, in the presidential chair?" It was only 1862, and she was worried about the next presidential election. Her opinion of Lincoln was so low that she said she would not willingly sit at the same table with him or his wife.[43]

Samuel Morse looked upon the hated war as a simple case of mathematics. Courage or righteousness had no relationship to victory. He wrote his sister-in-law, "If one part equals 3 and the other 9, it does not require much knowledge of mathematics to decide which part will overcome the force of the other. Now this is the case here just now. Two thirds of the physical and material force of the country are at the North, and on this account *military* success, other things being equal, must be on the side of the North."[44]

Morse's analysis and assurance of northern superiority was as clearheaded as it was disdainful of the war, but his words were written before recent Union defeats. By July his depression reached new depths. He saw the conflict between rabid abolitionists and rabid secessionists creating overwhelming hatred. "I see no hope of union," he wrote. "If there was a corner of the world where I could hide myself, and I could consult the welfare of my family, I would sacrifice all my interests here and go at once. I have no heart to write or do anything. Without a country: Without a country!"[45]

August Belmont, unlike Morse, had no interest in hiding from the world, but he, too, was discouraged by events. Military disasters did not frighten him as much as the apathy and distrust he found everywhere, especially among men he respected who were unquestionably loyal to the Union. As Democratic national chairman, he was as critical of Lincoln as ever, and he did not believe the president had called up enough men. "Where we would have found last winter ten men eager to enlist . . . we will scarcely now find one, so deep is the gloom and distrust." The martial spirit had certainly waned, but Belmont's remarks were inconsistent because he thought the land war was a mistake. If he had been president, he said, he would have ordered fifty iron gunboats, regardless of cost, and taken possession of every southern port.[46]

Belmont hoped for a negotiated peace with the South, and this was a commonly held view. He thought Weed and Seymour could try to find out if the South would listen to reason and moderation. Belmont, however, had his critics. George Strong looked upon him as a baiter and thought he deserved "hanging as an ally of the rebellion."[47] Thurlow Weed's clever mind was in a depressed state, too. He saw military and political perils everywhere, and he was hardly a symbol of iron will and determination. Yet he realized that reverses provided a favorable season for the troublemakers. "Recent disasters," he wrote, "bring your 'Jim Brook's' and 'Bill Duers' to the surface croaking."[48]

Weed was right. Congressman James Brooks, Judge William Duer, a son of a president of Columbia College, Fernando Wood, and others of their coterie were making much more noise these days. They were much more extreme than their fellow Democrat August Belmont, and in a mass meeting at Cooper Institute in July they flung out a rash of provocative statements. Duer said that if traitors were to be hanged in accordance with their guilt, Charles Sumner, the rabidly antislavery senator from Massachusetts, should follow Jefferson Davis to the gallows. Wood joined in the denunciation of abolition and secession, reaffirmed the principles of the Crittenden Compromise of the year before, and charged that the New York Emancipation League was an attack on the Union. The former mayor was picking up political steam. He anxiously awaited the congressional elections in the fall to stage his comeback with the rising demands for peace.[49]

At another time, these charges might have been hooted down. At the moment they did not seem so incredible, and there were many receptive listeners. And how could they be blamed when some of the staunchest government supporters had grave doubts about the war. William Evarts was only one of many. He had always been generous in backing Lincoln, but privately he now questioned whether the president had the experience and skill to manage the crisis. Originally, like many New Yorkers, he was a Seward man. Now he wished the secretary of state would take charge. He told Seward that the people chafed, Congress was leaderless and filled with malcontents, and the cabinet had no fixed purpose. Evarts wanted Seward to lead a new and revitalized cabinet.[50]

Throughout the summer the continued threat of a foreign war created further anxiety. McClellan thought such a war was probable, and through an intermediary he urged James Gordon Bennett to stress the need for coastal defense and home guards to man forts and repel invasion. McClellan's defensive psychology fit in with idle discussion in the city about installing a thousand guns in the harbor. Such talk was nonsense. Much more modest objectives were difficult to accomplish. Mayor Opdyke told the Common Council that the rebels were energetically producing ironclad ships and it was necessary to build floating batteries or rams as auxiliaries to the forts in the harbor. He suggested appropriating $1 million for this purpose even though he regarded it as a violation of the city charter. The extreme urgency, he believed, warranted such action, but nothing happened.[51]

William Webb had submitted plans to the government for harbor defense and construction of war vessels, and now he went to Washington with a letter of introduction to President Lincoln from C. H. Marshall, a

large shipowner.[52] By July, Webb signed a contract to build an ironclad
shot-proof steam screw ship of war with a ram for $1,125,000. A naval
committee had disapproved Webb's plan, but Secretary of the Navy
Welles had such confidence in the master builder he overruled the committee. Nevertheless, the new project did not ease the tension. Work on
the ship moved slowly, and although it may have been Webb's greatest
achievement, the ship was not completed until the war was over. It was
called the *Dunderberg*, 378 feet long and 73 feet in width, with five-inch
iron plating and a speed of fifteen knots. In 1867, the French government bought the ship for $3 million.[53]

The man most directly responsible for strengthening the fortifications in the harbor was Colonel Richard Delafield of the U.S. Corps of
Engineers, and the governor worked closely with him. Morgan believed
that the federal government had done little in this direction, but any reasonable man had to admit that there were higher priorities. Delafield was
a conscientious, intelligent officer who made vast improvements under
trying conditions. During the first two years of the war, more was done
to modernize the defenses than in any previous period since the founding of the republic. But there was still much to be done.

Protection from attack by sea presented a complex strategic, engi-
neering, and intellectual problem to challenge the best military minds.
A naval force could approach the city in two ways: from Long Island
Sound, which led into the East River, or from Sandy Hook into the Narrows, the approach used by the British fleet in its invasion of New York
in 1776.

An attack from the sound seemed more likely because the islands
between New London and Long Island gave the enemy an advantageous
cover for a rendezvous. The most distant point from the city where batteries could command the channel was at Fort Schuyler, located on a narrow tongue of land called Throgs Neck. It was built with heavy granite
blocks similar to those at Fort Sumter and had two casemated and one
barbette tier of guns that faced every point of the channel. On the land
side there was a bastioned front with a ditch and casemated defenses.
The land front was calculated to resist a siege of at least twenty-five days
without aid or reinforcements, assuming that a suitable garrison and
munitions were on hand. "No hostile force can ever reduce it," said
Delafield, "so long as we are true to ourselves in supplying it with the necessary armament ordnance stores, other needful supplies and garri-

son."[54] The problem was that although this important post had been constructed several years before, it was not fully armed on either the land or water fronts and was not garrisoned with enough men to fire the guns presently in the battery. And this was the best position to defend the East River, New York City, the Navy Yard, and Brooklyn.

The Fort Schuyler area was so highly regarded as a defense point that the opposite shore was being fortified with casemated batteries. Here, too, however, the work was incomplete. Nevertheless, when these forts were finished, Delafield envisioned the bed of the channel covered with torpedoes operated with "the electric wire, the fruits of American science and genius, and discoveries of Franklin—Fulton—and Morse." He also wanted "moveable power," a shot-proof steam vessel with heavy guns that would cooperate with shore batteries and have a prow that could puncture ships below the waterline. It was a good plan, but it remained only a plan.[55]

The second line of enemy approach, from Sandy Hook, Staten Island, and the Narrows, also presented a multitude of problems. Extensive casemated works were under construction at Sandy Hook, and some of the sixty or seventy guns they were ready to receive had been mounted. Still, the fortification was not in a defensible condition. It was open in the rear, and there was no garrison to man the existing guns. Another two years were needed to complete the works, and an enemy could occupy Sandy Hook and blockade commerce before it was finished.

Two old forts on this line of approach to the Narrows were Hamilton and Lafayette on the Long Island shore. They were partially armed, but their armament was not reliable against modern ships and they were waiting for guns of increased caliber. Fort Lafayette, of course, served another purpose as the notorious holding pen for arbitrarily arrested dissenters.

On the opposite side of the Narrows, on the heights of Staten Island, Fort Richmond was armed with rifled and smoothbore guns but lacked sufficient powder, shot, and shells. Fort Tompkins was under construction and would not be useful for another year. There was also Battery Hudson at the Narrows, a remodeled work, which was being fitted with 64-, 124-, and 350-pound projectiles and rifle projectiles of 100, 150, and 250 pounds. A garrison of New York volunteers was stationed there undergoing instruction as artillerists. Delafield recommended a combination of chains and rafts across the Narrows, an idea that appealed to Opdyke and Morgan. Study groups examined the problem, and all agreed on the principle, but none of the experts could agree on how it could be done efficiently.

If an enemy penetrated these outer defenses there were still additional forts in the inner harbor—batteries at Governor's Island, Bedloe's Island, Ellis Island, and Castle Clinton, often known as Castle Garden. Fort Columbus, one of the oldest fortifications in the country, was located in the center of Governor's Island with ancient guns that were not strong enough to cope with modern firepower. Castle Williams and South Battery were also on the island, but the caliber of their guns was too small and no effort had been made to adapt them to heavier guns.

Although the total strength of the harbor forts was greater than ever before, Delafield was the first to admit that not enough had been done to satisfy the public. Every fort was inadequate. While Governor Morgan looked to Delafield for help from the federal government, Delafield, on behalf of the federal government, looked for help from the state. Delafield hoped the state could supply funds for guns and munitions, shot-proof steam batteries, submarine defenses, and channel barriers. Neither Morgan nor Delafield could satisfy the wants of the other, but under the circumstances, both men worked well together and shared mutual respect. They wanted to be ready for any "eventful moment."[56]

Farragut's successful passage up the Mississippi, despite heavy gunfire from Forts St. Philip and Jackson, that led to the occupation of New Orleans increased fears that ordinary forts of masonry were outmoded and could not withstand rifled cannon. In addition, the range of casemated guns in the forts was narrow and their aim was uncertain. *Harper's Weekly* reported that the first gunboat that laid off the levee virtually captured New Orleans. Such reports created a new awareness that a single warship in the North or East River could do the same.

After the clash between the *Monitor* and *Merrimac*, Abram Hewitt had gone to England to learn more about the manufacture of iron plate. While there, he discussed the problem of permanent fortifications with army and navy officers. The prevalent belief overseas, he wrote the secretary of war, was that forts of the future must be covered with iron but that there was no need to construct them on such an extensive scale as the old stone structures.[57]

Theodore Timby, inventor of the ironclad revolving tower, suggested that a cordon of revolving towers and chains be placed in the harbor. Each tower would be a hundred feet in diameter with sixty guns in two tiers that could revolve once a minute under steam power. This system would be constructed at the Narrows. The huge chains, stretched from fort to fort, were to be attached to windlasses and operated by a steam engine. The chains would lie on the bottom until the enemy approached and then drawn up. A series of "torpedoes," actually mines, was to be affixed to the chains so they could be raised directly under a vessel detained by the chains and discharged by a galvanic battery. Defenders of this expensive proposal argued that an enemy warship could cause more costly destruction in the city in one hour. The plan may have been feasible, but the city would have remained vulnerable to attack from Long Island Sound, and the project never went beyond the drawing board.[58]

The anticipation of an invasion of New York Harbor did not seem exaggerated at the time, and a new series of events that increased the strain with England made it more credible. The *Alabama,* built and launched in Liverpool, began its successful reign as a Confederate raider of commercial ships and struck at the pocketbooks of New York businessmen. In the fall of 1862, Captain Raphael Semmes of the *Alabama* audaciously sent a message to the New York Chamber of Commerce via the captain of an old brig, *Baron de Castine,* that he would soon be off New York. The daring Semmes hoped to raid the city, but his dreams vanished when he found that he was short of coal. Master's Mate Fullam wrote in his diary, "We were startled and annoyed to find that only four day's coal were on board. To astonish the enemy in New York harbor, to destroy their vessels in their own water, had been the darling wish of all on board."[59]

Other Confederate raiders preyed on Union ships and tormented merchants and insurance carriers, who cried for action from Washington. Extra insurance premiums to cover war risks rose to 4 percent of the insured value in 1862 and climbed steadily throughout most of the war. Soon the New York Chamber of Commerce informed Secretary of the Navy Welles that "the war premium alone on American vessels carrying neutral cargoes exceeds the whole freight in neutral ships." Shipowners frequently paid the extra insurance rates for their shippers and reduced their charges for freight to keep their customers. Despite these incentives, shipping cargo on safer neutral ships became increasingly attractive.[60]

The Chamber of Commerce in New York demanded that the federal government do something. But once again, the government seemed helpless. In the coming months the *Alabama* became an elusive phantom as it roamed the seas creating havoc from Galveston to Singapore. The frequency of sinkings by marauders led Mayor Opdyke, who was always sympathetic to the problems of businessmen, to ask Congress to pass an act to grant authority to issue letters of marque.[61] The challenge to free commerce had to be met by extreme measures, and he and members of the National War Committee of the Citizens of New York saw privateering as the answer. The Confederate outlaws had to be pursued and liberal rewards offered for their capture. If licensed piracy was necessary to accomplish the deed, so be it. Many of these same men of substance had undoubtedly been outraged by privateering in the past. Now the shoe was on the other foot.

Opdyke's unusual request disturbed Senator Sumner, who tried to bring New Yorkers to their senses. He told John A. Stevens, Jr., president of the New York Chamber of Commerce, who favored the plan, that it was impractical. He believed that sea rovers with letters of marque overtaking neutral ships and searching could cause more evil than good and bring on the condemnation of civilization: "You would not threaten a whole street to catch a few robbers." Sumner sensibly suggested that private persons who wanted to battle Confederate raiders could turn their ships over to the Union navy and let them be commissioned.[62] Congress did not approve the letter of marque scheme, but it clearly exhibited the near panic among commercial interests that the *Alabama* and other marauders had instigated.

Many American shipowners, threatened with bankruptcy, transferred their vessels to foreign flags, and the United States merchant fleet never recovered from the blow. One report indicated that in 1860 two-thirds of the commerce in the port of New York was American, and in 1863 three-fourths of the commerce was foreign. By 1864, the New York *World* claimed that 608 American ships had transferred to the British flag since 1860 and about 300 ships had transferred to other foreign flags.

Meanwhile, the Confederates had reinforced Richmond and Lincoln needed more soldiers. It was suggested military training be initiated in the city's public schools for boys twelve years of age. Newspaper advertisements that read, "A good price will be paid for ten men to complete a regiment now in the field," and other ads attempting to form new regiments, did not produce the desired results.[63]

At a meeting of the Woman's Central Association of Relief, a Mrs. Kirkland proposed that manufacturers and merchants send their young male employees to war and employ young women in their place.[64] She hoped that such a movement might spread throughout the country. The association appointed a committee to support the idea, but no organized movement developed.

In the drive to raise more troops, Lincoln gave Seward a letter to take to New York City to show influential men. The president wanted a hundred thousand men as quickly as possible so that McClellan could take Richmond and substantially end the war. Lincoln did not want to leave any doubts about his determination to see the war through and used his strongest language. "I expect to maintain this contest," he wrote, "until successful, or till I die, or am conquered, or my term expires, or Congress or the country forsake me. I would publicly appeal to the country for this new force, were it not that I fear a general panic and stampede would follow, so hard is it to have a thing understood as it really is." Armed with this letter, Seward quietly met in New York with Governor Morgan, Governor Andrew Curtin of Pennsylvania, and other interested officials. They decided that an extra incentive was needed to gain the necessary manpower, and Seward telegraphed Stanton for authority to promise recruits an advance of $25 dollars of a $100 bounty. Stanton authorized the advance, and Seward replied, "Let the President make the order. . . . No one proposes less than 200,000; make it 300,000 if you wish. They say it may be 500,000 if the President desires." On July 12, newspapers made the call for men appear to be a voluntary request by eighteen governors of loyal states to the president. Lincoln called for three hundred thousand men. Seward did his work well, but the extra men did not bring an immediate victory.[65]

The war was moving too slowly, and Abby Woolsey was one of those who tired of McClellan's caution. She wrote to Georgeanna that his policy was too expensive and was ruining the country. And she saw signs of financial disaster at first hand. "We are bankrupt already," she said, "Stewart and Lord & Taylor began yesterday to give change to their customers in postage stamps. ... Aspinwalls and Uncle E. blue as indigo. Don't know what to do about our property and their own too."[66]

The sticky postage stamps circulated throughout the city in large numbers and were a nuisance. Anyone who received the stamps worried about their value because they wore out after much handling and could easily be counterfeited. Everyone tried to pass them off to someone else as quickly as possible before they were left with them and took a loss. The Post Office opposed the use of postage stamps as currency, but the government did not furnish the city enough small change. A five or ten cent coin was a rare sight. The Board of Aldermen proposed that the Corporation of the City of New York enter the currency business to issue small notes of five, ten, twenty-five, and fifty cents to end the circulation of stamps. Eventually, however, the practice ceased. The federal government supplied more currency, which was bolstered by "shinplasters" produced by private firms and some of the adjoining towns and villages.[67]

The postage stamps were merely a minor irritation and hardly a financial disaster. The very comfortable Woolseys did not feel any economic hardships from the war, but the poor in the city, especially the poor families of volunteers, continued to suffer. The Common Council established a half-million-dollar fund to help needy families of volunteers at a rate not to exceed $12 a month, including an allowance of $1.50 for each child under fourteen years of age. The payment centers attracted crowds looking for relief only to be turned away until their situation could be investigated by a politically appointed "Visitor."[68]

Other problems persisted in the city. Although some citizens expressed satisfaction that the moral fiber of the citizens had not deteriorated to the degree predicted by clergymen at the start of the war, disorderliness did not disappear. Dram shops closed on Sundays, and there were fewer arrests for drunkenness on the Sabbath. Theaters also closed on Sunday, and stronger legal measures were under way to suppress concert saloons. Criminal cases on the court calendars were down sharply from the previous year. Yet this appearance of virtue was illusory. Illegal liquor shops were on the increase, and concert saloons with their half-dressed women in the windows proved to be difficult to shut down. A brisk business in pornographic books went on with soldiers and sailors, and Mayor Opdyke admitted that it was almost impossible to stop.[69] And police raids on houses of ill repute brought no lasting results.

Late one Saturday night, police trapped eighty-six men and women in a house on James Street. They were locked up for the night and taken before a judge in the morning. All the male customers were discharged, and the females were fined five dollars each. It was a routine procedure and routine discrimination against women.

Two well-known madams, Irene McCready and Josephine Woods, maintained an establishiment on Eighth Street near Broadway and were accustomed to interference by police in the Fifteenth Precinct. It was a minor hindrance that had no permanent influence on their trade. Before the war was over, a police census indicated that the city contained 599 houses of prostitution, 2,123 prostitutes, and 72 concert saloons with bad reputations.[70]

During 1862, the state legislature passed a law to close down concert saloons. The police, in compliance with the new law, swept through the city to stop the sale of alcohol by "waitresses." Their vigilance shut the doors of several establishments, but some resisted. The "444" was as crowded as ever even though the girls stopped selling liquor. A bar, conveniently located next door, did a booming business. The saloon ran an ad that said, "Despite all efforts of Bigotry and Fanaticism to destroy its existence—We cannot be crushed." The management of the Melodeon piously announced that it could not prevent the patronage of female guests. The proprietor of the Gaieties, who had previously run an artists' model studio that had been closed by the police, advertised, "We still live-beautiful danseuses, charming lady vocalists, attractive ballet troupe." But he no longer mentioned waiter girls. Soon he decided to offer all his attractions free, including waiter girls, "whose welfare and interest have excited the attention of the New York Legislature." The free offerings supposedly transformed the concert saloon from a theater into a restaurant and blocked legal proceedings.[71]

Although statistics are untrustworthy, it is probable that by the end of the year almost a tenth of the population was arrested for one reason or another. Virtuous or sinful, the atmosphere in the city was changing. These were signs of the times and the war was at least partly responsible. George William Curtis wrote in *Harper's Monthly Magazine* that New York City had lost "much of its old town character" and was "every year more a metropolis."[72] And in 1862 it was a despondent metropolis.

9

Emancipation

Hiram Barney, the collector of the Port of New York, received a letter in July 1862 from one of Lincoln's cabinet members, probably Chase, who wrote that as the war clouds grew blacker there was only one way to draw the lightning: "Make an act of emancipation the conducting rod." Barney, a longtime antislavery man, agreed. He was a strong Lincoln supporter who was sure that the president was the most popular man in the country. But he also believed that the nation had been fighting to conciliate and that "the country can be saved only by a change in the medicine and treatment."[1]

Lincoln, much more aware of the complexities of emancipation, knew that it would not be a magical cure-all. He struggled with the many delicate ramifications and tried not to offend the four slave states in the Union. Lincoln knew, too, that emancipation could affect recruiting and the forthcoming election. He had already sent a special message to Congress suggesting compensated emancipation and had received endorsements from the *Herald* and *World* as well as the *Times, Tribune,* and *Evening Post.* But more was needed than newspaper support. The proposal was not well regarded in Congress and bogged down. The *Times* believed the expense of the president's plan was the reason for its failure.

Lincoln wrote to Raymond, editor of the *Times,* on March 9, 1862, and asked him to reconsider the question of expense. A little arithmetic proved his case: "Have you noticed the facts that less than one-half day's cost of this war would pay for all the slaves in Delaware, at four hundred dollars per head?" The cost of eighty-seven days of war, according to the president, would pay for all the slaves in Delaware, Maryland, Kentucky, Missouri, and the District of Columbia.[2] The argument impressed Raymond, and he immediately advised his office to back the president without qualification. Still, the plan made no headway.

Although strong feelings existed on both sides of the slavery issue, attitudes were changing in the city. In February, the captain of a slave ship, Nathaniel Gordon, was executed in New York City. Not long before, James Roosevelt, the United States district attorney, had believed that punishment by death for the importation of slaves was unenforceable. Now all efforts to save Gordon on technical grounds were quickly swept away and the condemned man even failed to escape the gallows by attempting to poison himself with strychnine.[3] Henry Bellows noticed a rapid change in public opinion and concluded that God was protracting the war to shorten the life of slavery.[4]

Peter Cooper was one of those who had almost imperceptibly changed his views during the past year. He had been a firm believer in compromise and the necessity to protect southern rights. Now, he declared that slavery was "our national sin." He wrote to his friend Nahum Capen of a story Dr. Bellows had recently told about a prominent lawyer in Philadelphia who feared that the country had not suffered enough in the revolutionary war. The lawyer thought it would have been better to have suffered longer or left those states out of the Union that would not agree to fix a definite date for the end of slavery. Cooper had decided that the sin of slavery doomed the nation to "long years of retribution."[5] Still, tempers flared over slavery. On the fourth of July, posters appeared around the city addressed "To the People," asking for vengeance upon Horace Greeley and Henry Ward Beecher, who were considered to have caused McClellan's reverses. The announcement, signed "By many Union Men," called for a public meeting in the City Park that afternoon. But few people showed up because antislavery men tore down the posters.[6]

Diversity of opinion continued to make the city a contradiction filled with intricacies. Certainly Samuel Barlow and Horace Greeley manifested a peculiar contrast. Barlow, the hardheaded man of business, Democrat, antiabolitionist, and fainthearted Unionist, came from a different mold than Greeley, the erratic, eccentric Republican, who was becoming more adamantly abolitionist every day. But the two men shared one common goal. The war distressed them, both desperately wanted peace, and they were ready to grasp at almost any straw in the hope of ending hostilities. But their thought processes were so different that they might as well have lived in two separate worlds.

During this hot summer, Samuel Barlow alarmed his friend and cohort August Belmont because he appeared to be teetering on the brink of treason. Barlow, who had made many indiscreet and "slashing" remarks about the government, was vacationing at New London, Connecticut. Belmont wrote to Barlow in a jesting manner that scarcely hid his concern: "I am sorry to say that you feel more attached by your old secesh friends than by Union men like myself—I am told they congregate at New London, trying their evil influences upon foreign diplomatists & hoping for good news from Stonewall Jackson. ... Seriously speaking I think you make a mistake by associating your name with Corcoran, Day & other men of that stamp, who are disloyal & unreservedly express their sympathy with the Rebels. I tell you this as a friend because I know that you do not share their treasonable views & I trust you will take my advice as kindly as it is given."[7] This would not be the last time that a friend worried about Barlow's sympathies.

Barlow deceived himself. He believed that he came by his strong states'-rights and antiabolition views honestly as an old-time Jeffersonian. But those were merely wistful sentiments that did not match the actuality of his day-to-day life, which was heavily involved in the new industrial world. He was a shrewd lawyer and moneymaker, especially in railroads, and some of his agents carried on activities during the war that could be considered trading with the enemy. He was ready to end the war at any time and refused to admit that the Confederates would never give up their independence.[8] Compromise had become a way of life for Samuel Barlow. As a lawyer he had made a practice of settling disputes out of court through negotiation, and he believed the war could be settled the same way. *Negotiation, compromise, and settlement* were three key words in his vocabulary.

Horace Greeley by contrast, was impatient over the war and became increasingly irritable and outspoken against slavery. His failure as a military analyst turned him more and more to stress the need for emancipation. After many mental gyrations, the pacifist and moralist had reluctantly accepted the immoral war to serve the moral cause of abolishing slavery. In so doing, he symbolized the torment of so many who were caught between two immoral conditions, war and slavery. Yet his anguish and inconsistencies made him an ineffectual supporter of the administration. His support increased with Union victories and decreased with Union defeats, when his help was most needed.

Greeley let off steam in a message to the *Tribune* published under the headline "The Prayer of Twenty Millions" in which he expressed his disappointment in Lincoln's policy. He accused the president of not executing the law, especially in connection with the emancipation provision of the Confiscation Act recently passed by Congress. It said that slaves of anyone who supported the rebellion were free. Greeley thought the president was unduly influenced by certain "fossil politicians" from the border states and that timid counsels were perilous. There was entirely too much deference to slavery: "On the face of this wide earth, Mr. President, there is not one disinterested, determined, intelligent champion of the Union cause who does not feel that all attempts to put down the Rebellion and at the same time uphold its inciting cause are preposterous and futile."[9]

Lincoln answered Greeley's letter promptly. Ignoring the "dictatorial tone" and errors of fact in Greeley's statement, he concentrated on his own policy. The president did not want anyone to have any doubts about where he stood. "I would save the Union," he wrote. "I would save it the shortest way under the Constitution. ... If I could save the Union without freeing *any* slave I would do it; and if I could save it by freeing some and leaving others alone I would also do that." But he added a personal wish that "all men every where could be free." Greeley published Lincoln's letter in the *Tribune* on August 25 with a long, surly reply of his own. The publisher claimed that he had never doubted Lincoln's desire to "reestablish the now derided authority." He only intended, he said, to raise the question, "Do you propose to do this by recognizing, obeying, and enforcing the laws, or by ignoring, disregarding, and in effect denying them?"[10]

Greeley misjudged Lincoln, and he became merely another thorn in the president's side. The publisher, however, was regaining influence with the public that he had lost after Bull Run. The *Tribune*'s circulation climbed again, mainly because its correspondents in the field, such as George Smalley and Sam Wilkeson provided excellent war coverage. Nevertheless, Greeley's prodding did not budge the president. Lincoln knew that he needed a military victory before he proclaimed emancipation, and victory was elusive. In the meantime, James Gordon Bennett feared that his competitor's ranting would produce a "deteriorated hybrid race."[11]

Henry Bellows, unlike Greeley and others who favored emancipation, did not believe that it would alter the course of the war. He had been too close to the battlefield and seen too much misery to believe that there was an easy way to attain peace. He knew that the Union had been "outgeneraled" and that southern hatred of the North combined with desire for independence could not be overcome by any proclamation. "Were we to declare Emancipation tomorrow," he wrote, "it would not do either good or harm." He had arrived at the conclusion that the war could be ended only through military power. The time had come to "get mad." Though this was a sad and dreadful necessity, he saw no alternative. "You might as well compromise & make treaties with rattle-snakes & wild cats."[12]

William Cullen Bryant wanted emancipation as much as Greeley and military power as much as Bellows. He was another of the city's Republican newspapermen who raged against Lincoln. During the winter, Bryant boarded in a townhouse on Fourth Avenue, but in summer he frequently commuted to his home in Roslyn, Long Island, by steamer. He liked the *Jesse Hoyt,* which left Peck's Slip every afternoon at 3:45 and arrived in Roslyn two and a half hours later. Although he may have been less rude in his dealings with the president, at times his words were sharper than Greeley's. Bryant was unhappy with the men around Lincoln, partly because he had not recommended them. The editor was not shy about urging the appointment of his friends to office or expressing bitter disappointment when they were not accepted.

At the start of the war, Bryant recognized the need for time to make military preparations, and after the fiasco at Bull Run he ridiculed Greeley as a newspaper "general." By the summer of 1862, Bryant was beginning to think that newspapermen could run the war as well as generals. He tired of McClellan's delays and wanted him removed. Perhaps Bryant was right in believing that McClellan's mind was on his political prospects rather than fighting a war. In August, Bryant wrote, "A deep lethargy appears to have fallen upon the officers of our government, civil and military, from which they must be aroused, or it will prove the sleep of death."[13] During this same month, Bryant and a rich friend, probably Dr. Charles King, called on Lincoln and speculated on the dire consequences if the war was not prosecuted more vigorously.

One of Bryant's friends told him that even if his criticism of Lincoln was justified it "must be a dash of cold water upon our recruiting."

Yet Bryant remained as certain of his own righteousness as he was of Lincoln's indecision. He continued to write cutting editorials about the ineffective president. Soon Bryant's despondency led him to charge that the administration's irresolute course was "little short of madness."[14] Lincoln must have wondered about his Republican "supporters," and they had private doubts about the president. George Strong, who devoted most of his time to the Sanitary Commission, was ready to admit that Lincoln was unequal to his place. He confided to his diary that Lincoln's only special gift was his "fertility of smutty stories."[15]

Political support for the administration was not always good business. Rabbi Samuel Isaacs, one of the founders of the Jews' Hospital, was the editor of the *Jewish Messenger*. When he gave wholehearted support to the government, he found that he lost valuable readers with southern sympathies. He knew that the paper depended on paid subscribers, and he firmly believed that Judaism needed such an organ. But, he wrote, "We want much more truth and loyalty, and for them we are ready, if we must, to sacrifice all other considerations."[16]

Although the city was full of critics of the administration, there were always those ready to help. When the second Battle of Bull Run turned into another miserable defeat in August 1862, Secretary of War Stanton telegraphed the mayor for medical help. The mayor gave the message to Dr. Elisha Harris, who immediately rounded up thirty surgeons who set aside their own practice and left for the South on the evening train.[17]

While the latest military defeat was fresh in people's minds during that hot, muggy month, news that Lincoln had ordered a draft hit the city and brought on a rash of nervous anxiety. It was the last thing anyone wanted to hear. The order, based on the Militia Act of 1862, recognized that the militia "shall include all able-bodied male citizens between the ages of eighteen and forty-five." But it was not a true national draft. It depended on state quotas that could be filled by volunteers, and its administration was left to the states. Nonetheless, enrollment, the first step, was about to start in the city. The judge advocate-general hired 120 clerks to draw up lists of eligible men.[18]

Joseph Choate wrote to his wife that the draft "creates some excitement and not a little squirming." He recognized that the government was entitled to "our services and to our lives if need be, and I know that both you and I would bear it with brave hearts if duty should require me to go in person." He thought the commotion over the draft was absurd "among certain cowardly people who claim an exemption from the draft, and they have made most foolish endeavors to escape their liability, but gradually the general mind has got used to the idea." Despite Choate's brave-sounding words, Union reversals did not stimulate him to volunteer his own services. Although there were many exceptions, the "comfortable" classes did not intend to serve in the army. And Choate was comfortable.

One hot, humid day in the latter part of August, Mayor Opdyke urged businessmen to close their shops and offices at three o'clock and attend a recruiting meeting in Central Park. Choate had no intention of complying with the mayor's request. He did not see how standing under the broiling sun listening to "some Irish orator" could help fill the ranks of the Union army. Nonetheless, he felt qualms of conscience over his contented sense of success with his career and marriage. He wrote to his wife, who was in the country for the summer, that they ought almost to reproach themselves for their "unalloyed joy" during such a dreadful time. They should do more for the war effort, he said, and "in some way or other sacrifice a little of our abundance to the great cause to which we are as sincerely devoted as the warmest patriots about us." But his devotion to the cause was limited. He suggested that when his wife returned, she might help "some poor family who have given their father— or only support to the war. . . . We must struggle against selfishness in our great love—and don't you think it does tend slightly that way?"[19]

Many foreign-born residents saw the draft as synonymous with slavery and decided to go home. When a war bulletin announced that if any person who was liable for the draft attempted to leave the country, he could be arrested for disloyalty without the benefit of habeas corpus, the anxiety of some turned to panic. The War Department appointed John Kennedy, the superintendent of the Metropolitan Police, as a special provost marshal, and Joseph Choate thought virtual martial law existed. He said New York City had a provost marshal "who seems by the general orders of Mr. Stanton to be invested with full power to capture anybody and clap him into any prison that may suit his fancy."[20]

Canada became a refuge for many draft dodgers, and others frantically took passage for Europe. The scheduled departure of the transatlantic steamship *Etna* caused pandemonium. Women and children laden with luggage and suffering from the intense heat crowded on the dock while men of the family rushed around looking for a way to board the ship without being caught. The main gangplank was the only entry into the ship, and the police were stationed there to inspect passports. Some passengers on board slipped their legitimate passports to friends on the dock, but the ruse was discovered. Two men disguised themselves as crew members without success, and others found that bribery did not work. One Irishman slipped by, but the frustrated people on the dock told the police and he was dragged off.[21]

The unhappy incidents over the draft were unnecessary. The draft was postponed, but the uncertainty continued. Some found a haven in the city militia, which exempted members from the draft because they were subject to special calls of service. Eventually, this escape was blocked. Irish aliens who wished to evade the army had the humiliating experience of asking the British consul for a certificate which stated that they demanded the protection of the British government.

After the first flush of enthusiasm at the outset of the war, the volunteer system proved insufficient. Advertisements emphasized additional incentives to volunteer, and yet the demand for more men was endless. Spinola's Empire Brigade offered a ninety-dollar bounty and relief tickets for families. The Fourth Senatorial District Regiment advertised, "Secure the bounty and avoid the draft." The Sixty-sixth Regiment offered promotion from the ranks, relief for families from the city, and "before leaving the state—$129; on joining regiment in field $13; at expiration of enlistment, $75." The New York State Battery offered $142 immediately and made duty sound painless. "Choose light artillery for easy service," its ad read. "No musket drill. No long marches, can march or ride — No knapsacks or heavy loads to carry — No trenches to dig." The Common Council appropriated money for a fifty-dollar bounty for every volunteer and did its best to make the payment easily and quickly. When a man passed the mustering office, he could go to City Hall, show his certificate, and receive his money at once. Still, recruits were hard to come by.[22] The bounties served as a stimulus, but they created a new brand of thief, the bounty jumper, who enlisted and then usually asked for a pass for a few days to handle family matters and disappeared. Some men enlisted from two to six times and were never arrested. They were merely reported as "missing."

Occasionally hecklers obstructed recruiting efforts. Gangs gathered around recruiting stations to dissuade men from enlisting by describing dreadful wounds and poor treatment in the army. Such incidents were numerous enough to prompt Mayor Opdyke to ask

Superintendent Kennedy to detail an officer at each recruiting station.[23] One obstructionist denounced the government to a small crowd near recruiters until someone suggested ducking him in the park fountain. Then he quickly vanished. Even appeals for recruits took strange twists. Lieutenant Charles Frothingham wanted men for Spinola's Brigade "to put down the wicked rebellion which has been brought about by such men as Wendell Phillips, Horace Greeley, Henry Ward Beecher and a host of other abolition traitors."[24]

Despite the need for troops, blacks were still not admitted into the service. In July 1862, Congress passed a bill introduced by Senator Preston King of New York to accept "persons of African descent for the purpose of constructing entrenchments, or performing camp service, or any war service for which they may be found competent." Equal pay for equal work was nonexistent, and such service was a poor beginning for the eventual enlistment of blacks. The concern seemed prevalent that the use of black soldiers would change the nature of the war and make it a war for abolition. Archbishop Hughes had already warned Secretary of War Cameron that Catholics would fight to support the government and the Constitution but not to abolish slavery; "indeed they will turn away in disgust from the discharge of what would otherwise be a patriotic duty." John Mullaly, editor of the *Metropolitan Record*, criticized congressional attempts to allow blacks to join the Union army, announcing that "white men are not willing to become the tools of sectional agitators."[25]

The shortage of soldiers was a continual worry for Mayor Opdyke, and their color would have mattered the least to him. He received unsettling information in September that there was reason to expect rebel ironclads originating in Europe to enter New York Harbor, and he knew the forts were undermanned and that the men on duty were so inexperienced they were scarcely serviceable. His conferences with General Harvey Brown, in command of harbor fortifications, General Charles Sandford of the National Guard, and Governor Morgan only underlined the need for more men and arms, and his requests for help from Washington usually failed to elicit even a reply. Frustrated, Opdyke wrote to Secretary of War Stanton apologizing for bringing up the matter "when the enemy is at your door" but emphasizing that the safety of New York City was at stake. Opdyke received a negative reply from General in Chief Henry Halleck: "At present time not possible to send troops to

New York. Every available man must be in the field against the enemy."
Opdyke appealed to the president but realized he would get little help.
By the end of the year, the Common Council, always anxious to spend
money and with some genuine concern, expressed its intention to improve the defense of the city, but there was more talk than action.²⁶

Recruiting received a slight boost when Michael Corcoran returned in an exchange of prisoners. His arrival attracted almost as much
attention as any event in the war. The commanding officer of the Sixty-
ninth Regiment was now a brigadier general and had become the idol of
the Irish in New York. At the suggestion of Archbishop Hughes, he had
been promoted during his captivity by the rebels after Bull Run to make
up for real or imagined neglect of his regiment. Hughes wrote Seward
that a slight was worse than a blow and that Corcoran's promotion would
heal a wound of Irish-Americans' "'amour propre.'" It was difficult to
ignore this skillful manipulator, and he got his way.²⁷

Corcoran had kept up his spirits during his imprisonment in Virginia and wrote plucky letters home that never wavered from upholding
the Union cause. When he showed up at the Battery, Mayor Opdyke did
not miss the political opportunity. He was on hand with an enthusiastic
crowd to greet this popular immigrant who had risen from the ranks as
a private. The hero intended to organize a new Irish brigade. He said
there was no inducement strong enough to keep him from the battlefield, "not even fee simple of Broadway." His arrival was a grand excuse
for a triumphant parade to Union Square with American and Irish flags
flying. Joseph Choate wrote that "green crinoline sweeps the city" and
the kitchen help for miles around had emptied into the streets to welcome their hero. Corcoran stood in his carriage bowing to admiring
crowds to his right and left, who were impressed by his humility and dignity. Even Choate could not repress his enthusiasm for the joyous day.
Touched by the good feeling, he said, "the occasion belongs to us all."²⁸

During Corcoran's absence as a prisoner of war, Governor Morgan
had commissioned him as a harbormaster so his family could receive the
income from that position. No political gesture was too good for the
Irish of New York City. But Corcoran declined the office and money, and
as a gesture of their esteem, the harbormasters presented him with a
magnificent sword at the Astor House. It was fine American steel, etched
in gilt. The scabbard was ornamented in silver with gold bands of oak
leaves and laurel. The guard represented a spread eagle and was con-

CORCORAN LEGION

FIFTH REGIMENT.

COL. WILLIAM McEVILY

A FEW GOOD MEN ARE WANTED

TO FILL UP CAPT. WM. L. MONEGAN'S COMPANY.

This is a splendid opportunity for young men to join a Crack Regiment. You will have good officers, who will pay every attention to your welfare.

All Promotions will be made from the Ranks!

Relief Tickets will be immediately issued to Families of Volunteers.

The highest Bounties will be paid, and good Quarters, Rations and Uniforms furnished.

This Regiment is quartered at STATEN ISLAND, in a position highly favorable to the health and good condition of the men.

THOSE WISHING TO JOIN CAN APPLY TO

Lieuts. MICHAEL McDONALD, and DANIEL H. McDONNELL, Recruiting Officers.

No. 52 FIRST AVE., COR. OF THIRD ST.

BAKER & GODWIN, Printers. Printing House Square, opposite City Hall, N. Y.

The recruiting poster of the proud Irish-American Corcoran Legion looked for "a few good men." (Courtesy of the New-York Historical Society) nected with the top of the grip by silver chain. It also had a Russia leather belt. The beautiful gift cost the harbormasters $250.

The need for recruits remained despite Corcoran's help, and Mayor Opdyke's disappointment resulted in one of the most unusual activities in the city during the war. If there were those in the city who could be accused of disloyalty or disinterest in the war during these depressing dog days of August, there were also those who were eager to fight harder. One of the oddest manifestations of this eagerness was the formation of the National War Committee of the Citizens of New York.

On August 25, 1862, a call went out for citizens to assemble at City Hall. The announcement said that the time for discussion was over and the hour for action had arrived. The purpose of the meeting was precisely spelled out and did not appear to be unusual. The first goal was to fill up veteran regiments of New York volunteers; second, to make full response to the state call for new regiments; and third, to organize and fill up Corcoran's new brigade before the end of the month. To accomplish all this, the committee needed resolute hearts, strong arms, and financial means.[29]

The mass meeting at City Hall Park resulted in the creation of the National War Committee of the Citizens of New York, chaired by Mayor Opdyke and assisted by a long list of distinguished citizens who had been elected to help. Unfortunately, these men were named to the committee without their authorization, and before long several of them, including A. T. Stewart, Cornelius Vanderbilt, and Peter Cooper, declined the honor. Moses Grinnell was very direct in his request to withdraw his name. He told Opdyke that from what he had heard, the committee's proceedings were incompatible with the announced purpose and its actions would embarrass the government.[30]

There were misgivings about the true purpose of the committee from the start, perhaps colored by lingering memories of the inefficiencies of the Union Defense Committee. It presumed to speak for the entire community, which was clearly impossible, and many people believed it had had assumed responsibilities and powers that were unwarranted. Doubts about its declared motives and suspicions about the members' undeclared motives were soon whispered around town.

Despite the undercurrent of criticism, George Opdyke, John A. Stevens, Jr., Charles Gould, and other staunch members of the committee met in rooms at the Chamber of Commerce to make up for the lack of vigor in prosecuting the war. As news of Union reversals reached them, they sincerely intended to increase efficiency in the conduct of the war. One of their first tasks was to raise money for recruiting, and they particularly sought support from monied people and corporations, "inasmuch as property in the loyal states is valueless should the rebellion succeed." Special efforts were to be made to recruit men for the Corcoran Legion, and there was little criticism of this objective.[31]

August Belmont gave the committee a thousand dollars for recruiting accompanied by a public letter stating that he would hold the members personally liable for its disbursement. Suspicions about the committee still persisted. The members felt offended by Belmont, whom they believed had impugned their good faith, and they indignantly returned the money. Opdyke wrote to Belmont, "If the committee is abused, it is abused by those who either ignorantly err, or wish the nation to be defenceless at the feet of treason."[32]

Nevertheless, as time went on, the committee seemed less concerned with its limited goals and looked to wider horizons. Its members firmly believed that there was a need for greater central direction of the war effort. The administration's slipshod methods in fighting the war cried out for precise direction. Scarcely anyone could disagree. Every report from Washington seemed to confirm the disarray, and Opdyke and company, confident of their managerial abilities, were certain that they could correct the horrendous inefficiencies. They intended to pull the management of the war together for the entire country, not simply New York City or even New York State. The word *national* in the committee's name took on added significance. There appeared to be political implications in taking their work beyond the city because Opdyke, David Dudley Field, and prominent members of the committee were Radical Republicans.

Young John A. Stevens, who shared their views, had seen the war as an opportunity to extend his personal influence, but his attempts to make friends among public men in Washington so that he might gain a "satisfactory position" had failed.[33] Frustrated but still ambitious, he found in the National War Committee a way to pursue the war vigorously and at the same time achieve greater personal recognition.

One of the early moves of the committee that attracted adverse attention was its invitation to General Frémont to raise fifty thousand men. John C. Frémont, an idol of many Radicals, agreed to accept the invitation if the government gave its sanction. But Secretary of War Stanton quickly objected in a brusque telegram to Opdyke. The governor, he said, had the assignment to raise volunteers, and there was no reason to interfere with his efforts. Any authorization for high-ranking military officers to raise an army corps would only produce disorganization.[34] Since the committee's purpose was to improve the management of the war, this must have come as a shock. The matter was dropped, but the committee moved on to more presumptuous exertions.

The National War Committee now appointed subcommittees to confer with governors to step up efforts in forwarding recruits. For that purpose, David Dudley Field went to Ohio and Illinois, and William Orton went to Indiana. They determined how many soldiers had already left each state and investigated the difficulties encountered in transportation and supplying uniforms, equipment, and arms.[35]

The aim of the committee's study was to centralize and systematize efforts. A major recommendation it made was that a uniform manpower depot system be established throughout the United States so there would always be a reserve to replenish regiments in the field. This idea had merit as an attempt to resolve the chaotic conditions caused by decentralization, but this self-appointed private group, hindered by all the defects of voluntarism, was not the agency to make such reforms. A condensed version of the subcommittee reports was sent to the president and secretary of war where it rested.

The members of the committee, unconcerned by their lack of military experience, went on to explore new inventions, the state militia, and the forts in the harbor. They were quick to complain to the governor about the conditions they found and advised Admiral Hiram Paulding that he should always have one or more steamers in the harbor. They also took up the question of an ambulance corps and army hospital arrangements. Their study convinced them that ambulance drivers were a brutal, criminal, and worthless lot. On this issue they not only invaded the jurisdiction of the Army Medical Bureau but appeared to compete with the Sanitary Commission. They were so busy with these wide-ranging functions that they forgot about helping recruit for the Corcoran Legion. General Corcoran found it necessary to remind the committee that it had not paid the promised bounty to many of the new recruits.

Undaunted, the committee members directed their energy to a specific military operation. William Alexander, representing a group of Union men in western Texas, came to the city discouraged and almost hopeless in his cause to relieve that section of the country from the Confederates. He laid his case before the National War Committee, and its members were immediately intrigued. Another investigation by a subcommittee was undertaken and concluded that loyal people in western Texas would flock to the Union if they could be assured of federal assistance. The National War Committee advised the president of the urgency in sending a military force to retake western Texas and restore it to the Union. The committee had a plan of operation drawn up by General George Stoneman whereby five thousand men would take possession of the mouth of the Rio Grande and control both banks up to Brownsville with the consent of the French government. This action was expected to complete the blockade and have the extra advantage of forestalling French occupation of the area.[36]

The hyperactivity of the National War Committee with its attendant failures and frustrations led to its eventual demise. It was a misguided venture that went far beyond its original purpose and led to more wasted effort instead of increased efficiency. Its leaders took too much upon themselves and lacked the competence and authority to improve the prosecution of the war. They only added confusion and distrust.

Meanwhile, discipline among the troops encamped in the city remained a problem, and their outrageous behavior did not help recruiting. The Vosburgh Chasseurs at Camp Scroggs on Harlem Road in the vicinity of 106th Street received orders to depart before they collected their back pay. Some wives and children had showed up to take part of the pay and were rightfully disappointed. Many of the men drank too much and began burning tents, tearing down fences, and starting fires in the messhouse and guardhouse. The regiment had been in the process of organizing for eight months with little progress, and conditions in the camp were so chaotic that the officers were as discouraged as the men. Finally, the outbreak was quelled by separating the companies. One company marched all the way to Madison Square, given dinner, and put up at the Park Barracks.[37]

While the Vosburgh Chasseurs made trouble, the city awaited news of General Robert E. Lee's invasion of Maryland. The summer military campaigns had given relief to Richmond while Washington was under threat of siege. There was little confidence that Lee could be stopped. On September 15, a *Times* editorial called on Lincoln to strengthen his cabinet: "His Cabinet secretaries have been mere clerks. ... He needs a new Cabinet."[38]

During this same month, Hiram Barney, a son-in-law of Lewis Tappan, an early abolitionist, was in Washington when John Hay called on him at the Willard Hotel and told him the president wanted to see him. The two men had known each other for many years and Lincoln was fond of Barney so the request did not seem unusual. The port collector met Lincoln at the War Department, and the president said, "I am glad to see you. I want to have a private talk with you." According to Barney, they went into an inner office, and Lincoln said, "Now that we are alone and not liable to be disturbed I have something to show you which I think will interest you." He took a paper from his pocket and read the first draft of the Emancipation Proclamation. Lincoln said confidentially, "You must not talk about this thing for no human being but yourself has seen it." The president asked Barney what he thought about the statement. Barney was pleased but suggested that the president wait until matters were in better shape before he made it public.[39] Lincoln, who probably held the same view, appeared to take Barney's advice. But they did not have to wait long.

Suddenly, the war situation looked better. Headlines read, "Glorious News," "The Rebels in Full Flight toward the Potomac." The news was of the Battle of Antietam, and this time it really looked like the beginning of the end. McClellan's dispatches were vague, but the Confederates appeared to be on the run. McClellan had stopped Lee's advance into Maryland, but later the battle was called a "defeat for both armies." Still, grasping for any appearance of military success, northern leaders preferred to interpret the outcome as a victory. Wall Street speculators, however, retained an air of skepticism. In the boardroom of the Stock Exchange large transactions in United States securities and railway bonds took place, but gold remained firm, indicating a lack of faith in the news.

Victory or not, the battle had been bloody, and casualties were high on both sides. The lists of killed and wounded were reported in the press by regiment, company, and type of wound such as arm, shoulder, breast, or head. The lists horrified readers, and some believed that this grisly news discouraged recruiting. The rebels, they said, withheld their casualty lists and did not make the same mistake. Another reminder of the reality of war particularly affected those who had not yet been touched by the gruesomeness. Brady's Gallery on Broadway placed a little placard at the door which read, "The Dead of Antietam." Men and women climbed the studio stairs to see the photographic exhibition of dreadful scenes and spoke in hushed tones of their terrible distinctiveness.

During the battle, the Sanitary Commission sent twenty-five wagonloads of stimulants, condensed food, and medicine to the front in addition to supplying eighty military hospitals. Gossipmongers ignored these strenuous efforts, however, and spread rumors throughout the city that soldiers had to buy many of these articles from the Sanitary Commission. Henry Bellows, disturbed by the accusations, wrote a public letter from the commission's office at 498 Broadway denouncing the false stories. No supplies were ever sold to soldiers by the commission, and Bellows declared that its books, methods, and returns were always open for inspection.[40]

Despite the unpleasant aspects of the "victory" at Antietam, Lincoln announced his Emancipation Proclamation. The Board of Aldermen had energetically opposed such a statement. In an attempt to block the president, the board had passed a series of resolutions condemning any proposed proclamation of emancipation. Mayor Opdyke joyfully vetoed the resolutions and informed the Board of Aldermen that its measures would be antagonistic to the president's newly established policy.[41]

Although Lincoln's announcement created mixed feelings in the city, the *Times* said that the need for the proclamation was "indisputable." Archbishop Hughes, however, opposed the proclamation and was willing to join some Protestant clergymen in a public letter of disapproval. The idea collapsed when some of the fainthearted feared it might be imprudent to speak openly. Samuel Morse saw the proclamation as a bitter pill and another reason to think the president was a weak and vacillating politician.[42] George Dow was typical of many ordinary citizens in the city who held more moderate views. He was not an abolitionist, and he did not believe white soldiers were ready to accept blacks into the army or that they were needed to win the war. Still, he was not willing to let slavery stand in the way of victory. To him, the war had made slavery a dying institution.[43]

Weed had tried to use his influence to prevent Lincoln from issuing the proclamation and regarded it as "idle fulmination." He believed that a policy of abolition would hinder recruiting. "It is beginning to be feared," he wrote Bigelow, "that ultra abolitionists have been and are willing to see the Union divided. The Tribune ... squints that way yesterday. There are others who would be willing to serve as President of a Northern republic. ... The Radicals are organizing for U.S. Senator. Many want Field or Opdyke (or rather F & O want the place), though they may unite on Wadsworth."[44]

David Turnure did not minimize the significance of the proclamation. He considered it the most important paper ever issued in this or any other country. But such thinking was not a compliment. Lincoln's announcement was a "gross unqualified usurpation of power." It defied the Constitution and laws that had existed for eighty years and been sustained by the Supreme Court. In his view, there was no constitutional authority for the Emancipation Proclamation, which upheld states that had passed personal liberty bills. Worse still, it sundered the intention of the Constitution and the Union. "The blood freezes in the veins," he wrote, "when we contemplate the horrors which may follow in its train & words fail to express the cold blooded atrocious villainy which it exhibits."[45]

It was already evident to Turnure that the black population was creeping northward, especially in localities adjoining border states when slaves were emancipated in the District of Columbia. Soon they would interfere with white labor and create difficulties that would become a burden to society. The advocates of freedom and equality for blacks in Congress were wicked fanatics who would cause more dilemmas for the country. And he did not think emancipation was beneficial for blacks. Turnure was convinced that they were poor creatures who were "the victims of hypocrisy and mistaken philanthropy."[46]

Bryant of the *Evening Post*, in contrast, was pleased, and the emotional Greeley gave his heartiest approval at first and later expressed reservations that the Proclamation had not gone far enough. The *Herald* was unhappy but restrained its criticism, and the *World* complained about the "crazy radicals." The *Express* accused Lincoln of giving in to foul fanatics. The only group in the city that was unanimous about the proclamation was the blacks. They rejoiced and crowded into the hall at Cooper Union to celebrate another major step toward the freedom of their race. Fearing a disturbance, they charged an admission fee to discourage attendance of proslavery troublemakers.

Judge Charles Daly's disgust for the administration rose higher in response to Lincoln's new policy, coming on top of talk about raising black troops, which he was sure would slow down regular recruiting.

Daly, born in Ireland, was positive that the Irish would not fight for blacks. Some abolitionists, he heard, had told the Irish that soon they would have "good, faithful colored servants, and that these Irish will then have to go back to their poorhouses." Besides, the Irish believed that abolitionists hated both Irish and Catholics and wanted to kill them off by placing them in front of the battle.[47]

The Irish judge's views did not differ much from those of the *Irish-American*. The newspaper considered Lincoln's proclamation illegal and ineffective under the Constitution and charged that it gave the South an incentive to fight even more desperately. "In fact," the newspaper claimed, "the document is no more or no less than Mr. Lincoln's formal surrender to the abolition policy of the Radicals."[48]

Frank Leslie's Illustrated Newspaper was another publication that was displeased with emancipation. Leslie, an English emigrant, had established a string of magazines during the past few years, and at the start of the war he tried to maintain a neutral position to protect his wide circulation in the South. His straddling was impossible to keep up, and he gradually increased his support for the North, but he showed little sympathy for slaves, who he said were "sensual, gluttonous, thievish, and hopelessly lazy."[49]

The *World* was one of the most severe critics of the Emancipation Proclamation. The newspaper had been taken over by its bright and witty twenty-seven-year-old night editor, Manton Marble, the previous April. Barely keeping the paper alive, he shrewdly gained financial backing in September from Samuel Barlow, August Belmont, Samuel Tilden, and other rich Democrats, including, briefly, Fernando Wood. Marble, originally a conservative Republican, conveniently shifted his political views by degrees as he picked up financial sponsors. Soon the *World* became one of the most influential papers in the city and consistently attacked the administration. The young editor looked upon his job as the same as that of a statesman except that his judgment had to be quicker and he did not have the luxury of remaining quiet at opportune times because his paper came out every day. He established a friendly relationship with McClellan, and his correspondents did their best to present the general in a favorable light. Encouraged by McClellan, Marble blasted Secretary of War Stanton at every opportunity during the spring and summer.[50]

McClellan's friend Major General Fitz John Porter was always ready to add fuel to the fire against the administration. And he was willing to use the pages of the *World*. He wrote spitefully, indiscreetly, and probably dishonestly to the editor that "the Proclamation was ridiculed in the army—causing disgust, discontent, and expressions of disloyalty." He claimed that those who fought the battles were tired of war and wanted the Union restored.[51]

Lincoln noticed that stocks declined on Wall Street after his preliminary announcement of the proclamation. In a letter to Vice-President Hannibal Hamlin, he indicated that the stock market was down and that army enlistments were slow. "The North responds to the proclamation sufficiently in breath," he wrote, "but breath alone kills no rebels."[52] He may have had a point, but all measurements and forecasts of public opinion had their faults. Lincoln knew as well as anyone that his announcement would give him political troubles and it would not be an asset in the forthcoming election. Another part of Lincoln's plan to solve the slavery problem also met with skepticism. The proclamation called for continued interest in voluntary colonization of blacks on this continent or "elsewhere." Earlier in 1862 Lincoln had proposed such a project in Central America to black leaders who showed little enthusiasm for the suggestion. Now James Bowen considered Lincoln's scheme for colonization absurd and "either a piece of charlatanism or the statesmanship of a backwoods lawyer, but disgraceful to the administration. . . . I think it was to allay the fears of Irish laborers among us that labor would be reduced at so early a day by an irruption of the blacks."[53]

Lincoln and his party faced other handicaps, too. The suspension of habeas corpus and a large number of arbitrary arrests in the city combined with indecisive military results would certainly work against him at the polls. George Strong was convinced that arbitrary arrests were a bigger detriment to his party than the Emancipation Proclamation. Locking men up for months without legal authority gave the Democrats a genuine issue against the government. The issue was a gift to the Democrats because the arbitrary arrests were of little value. The catch-as-catch-can methods against suspects lacked any procedural standards, and the arrests had no influence on the course of the war. Fear of imprisonment in Fort Lafayette did not curtail free expression in New York City. Declamations against the war, the administration, and the Union were commonplace, and many citizens roaming the streets made statements that were as seditious as those uttered by men who were clamped behind bars.

During these difficult days, the Roman Catholic Archbishop Hughes made a semiofficial government-paid trip to Europe to improve international understanding. His Grace, initially with Thurlow Weed, visited England, France, Italy, and Ireland. In France, the target of his mission, the cleric met with Napoleon III and Empress Eugenie for an hour and a quarter and emphasized the mutual interests of the United States and Europe. The archbishop told the emperor that he represented the whole country, not just one section, and spoke for peace and humanity. Hughes apparently enjoyed his travels and hoped to extend his tour to St. Petersburg and other far-off places at an additional cost to the government of $10,000, but Lincoln and Seward did not accept his offer.

Hughes's diplomatic journey did not escape criticism from members of his church, who thought he had strayed from his calling. The *Catholic Mirror,* published in Baltimore, referred to the archbishop as the "champion of desolation, blood and fraticide," and Hughes admitted that some regarded his remarks on returning home as "a war blast in favor of spilling blood." Even Pope Pius IX appeared to offer a slight rebuke to Hughes by reminding him to pray for peace with other American bishops. Nevertheless, at home, Aldermen Terence Farley, Francis Boole, William Walsh, and John Brady called at the Hughes residence to present an elegant copy of congratulatory resolutions for his mission and to extend the hospitality of the city on behalf of the Common Council. Despite the kind resolutions, the archbishop made no great claims for his trip. His only objectives, he said, were to carry a message of peace and to correct European minds about conditions in America. He did not find it an easy task as some may have believed, and he was disappointed that his accomplishments were less than desired. He returned home with the definite opinion that there was no love for the United States abroad and that the war provided a pretext for foreign nations to combine against Americans.[54]

The Common Council's extravagant gesture may have reflected a new sense of prosperity in the city. The war may not have been going well, but the war economy started to thrive. Profiteers began to enjoy their profits. Trade in the port was far better than anyone had expected.

Exports for the past year were very heavy, and imports, especially sugar, tea, and coffee, were strong. Customs revenue ranged from $100,000 to $250,000 a day. The stock market was active, and the speed of telegraph communications had made the exchange a center for financial transactions for the entire country, not simply the city. Volume on the exchange reached fifty thousand shares a day and sometimes more. City bounties also placed money in circulation. It was estimated that each regiment formed in the city received bounties from the municipal government which amounted to anywhere from $150,000 to $250,000.[55]

Inflation contributed to this prosperity and was painfully evident to homeowners. Earlier in the year, coal sold for $4.50 a ton. In September, as winter approached, the price went to $7.50 with warnings that it might go to $10 or $12 a ton in the next thirty days. Everyone who owned a home breathed easier when the bin was filled with fuel and they could live in comfort through the cold months. But heating a house was taking a much larger portion of a person's earnings. Inflation was also evident in restaurant meals. The price of a meal was much more expensive and the portions were smaller.

Workingmen and women suffered the most from inflation because wages did not rise as much as prices. Journeymen house painters wanted an increase from 17.5¢ an hour. Journeymen coppersmiths received $1.75 a day or less and demanded $2.00. Hackmen looked for an increase of $2.00 to raise their weekly wages to $9.00. Boss bakers, sign painters, boatbuilders, and journeymen shipjoiners also wanted more money. A rash of brief strikes took place, and some employers met the demands but others did not. There was little uniformity in employers' accepting or denying demands even within the same trade. Irish laborers who worked for the Manhattan Gas Company at the foot of 14th Street and the East River went out on strike for higher wages. After a few days they refused to return to work unless a number of discharged workers got their jobs back. The management solved the dispute by firing all the Irish strikers and hiring German workers in their place.[56]

Nevertheless, money was freer. The end of summer brought the new fashions for the coming season, and women crowded the stores on Broadway to see the latest textiles and styles. Husbands were known to "give wives $50 to pitch in." Milliners presented new French bonnets that were smaller and simpler in decoration. Fine straw trimmed with velvet and plumes were considered "distingué" for fall wear. Demand was strong for expensive cashmere shawls and rich silks. Clan plaids, such as Rob Roy and Royal Stuart, were popular with women of "cultivated taste," but plain colors dominated dress. A shirt and skirt of drab merino with rows of scarlet woolen braid and a scarlet cashmere jacket with plaid, cut buttons was very fashionable. The skirts were worn full and long behind. Sleeves were puffed and loose at the wrists. Wreaths were in favor for a headdress, and hair was raised in puffs or waves from the side to the front of the face.[57] Frank Leslie's *Gazette of Fashion* devoted less attention to the war and more to style because the editor believed readers were weary of the war. "We turn, almost with feverish delight," the magazine said, "to something that will occupy our thoughts to the exclusion of the woeful images of the wounded, the dead and dying on the field."[58]

The new prosperity did not stop the shipment of thirty impoverished children to the West. The Children's Aid Society organized the group and included several young girls from the Girls' Lodging House on Canal Street.[59] And prosperity did not stop the pain of war for the families of the killed and wounded.

The approach of fall also stirred the political camps again. The Democrats in the state nominated Horatio Seymour for governor, and his most stalwart followers were in the city. Seymour was a tall, lean, dignified man in his Prince Albert coat and patent leather boots. He gracefully expounded his conservative political views, which disdained both abolitionists and southern extremists. Before the war he had favored the Crittenden Compromise, and he was willing to wait for slavery to die a natural death because of the flood of cheap immigrant labor. He opposed the Emancipation Proclamation and did not want the federal government to interfere with slavery. He did not care for Lincoln's strong hand, especially in the suspension of habeas corpus, and questioned the constitutionality of the president's actions. Seymour also had serious doubts, in the early part of the war at least, that the South could be conquered, and if elected he hoped to use his influence to end the war as quickly as possible.[60]

The Republicans, at Greeley's urging, chose General James Wadsworth of Geneseo as their candidate for governor. He was a rich landowner who opposed slavery and seemed too radical to attract moderate voters. The *Herald*, favoring Seymour, claimed that Wadsworth's nomination was a sign that the radicals had taken over the Republican party.

The moderate Weed probably agreed. He was not pleased with the candidate, and he tried to keep Wadsworth out of the city during the campaign because he believed his presence emphasized the unpopular antislavery issue.[61]

Unlike Weed, Greeley did not hesitate to promote the antislavery issue in the city. In a large campaign meeting for Wadsworth at Continental Hall at Thirty-fourth Street and Eighth Avenue, the editor declared that the issues were now the Union and slavery. He said he had not met three men since Lincoln announced the Emancipation Proclamation who were not happy. This was obviously untrue unless he had been hiding in a closet. Antiemancipation had become a popular rallying point for the Democrats. In an optimistic and expansive mood, and often a victim of his own impulses, Greeley flatly predicted that the country would be free and united by spring and the South would make peace before January.[62]

Greeley had many misgivings about the president, but he tried to ingratiate himself with Lincoln. Greeley wanted his friend Schuyler Colfax to pass the word to Lincoln that he was anxious to strengthen him in the country. "If, then, he should desire the public to be enlightened in any particular direction, or wish Congress to be pressed in favor of Confiscation, or any other measure, I will endeavor so far as I can, to defer to his judgment."[63] Lincoln saw human nature work in many peculiar ways. If he received this message, he must have recognized it as one more peculiarity.

During the campaign, Mrs. Lincoln visited the city on another shopping spree with her young son Tad, but she listened to critics too. She wrote a frank letter to her husband saying that "McClellan & his slowness are ... vehemently discussed. ... Many say they would almost worship you, if you would put a fighting General, in the place of McClellan." She added that she had had two suits made to order for Tad for twenty-six dollars.[64]

Some sections of the city greeted Wadsworth warmly despite Weed's trepidations. German-Americans held a large meeting at Cooper Institute under the chairmanship of Professor Francis Lieber and enthusiastically endorsed the Emancipation Proclamation. A day or two later, Seymour criticized his political enemies for calling him a traitor. The *Times* virtuously responded that it had never done so but had simply charged him with "giving aid and comfort to traitors." The newspaper said that his election would be "hailed with bonfires and illuminations at the Rebel Capital, as a substantial victory of their allies and confederates in the loyal states."[65]

August Belmont was especially sensitive to charges that Democrats were suspected of sympathizing with secession, let alone treason. He wrote to Barlow that the party had to grasp every opportunity to "clear their skirts" from these suspicions. He believed that anything that could be done to erase that image would help "more than all the money you may be able to collect in New York." But Barlow, as Belmont well knew, had aroused as much suspicion about his sympathies as anyone in the city. Perhaps that was Belmont's underlying message.[66]

Samuel Tilden held many views in common with Seymour and suggested that the candidate emphasize support for the Union while making all possible concessions to the South. Seymour followed Tilden's advice and publicly declared, "We will give you everything that local self-government demands; everything . . . but to dissolve the federal bond between these states." The Democrats were the "let-alone" party, he said, the Republicans the "meddling" party. Seymour had become the spokesman for property rights, states' rights, and civil rights for whites.[67]

The city preferred Seymour's words to Wadsworth's. When the votes were counted it was evident that New York City voters made the difference in the results. Seymour won election by 10,752 votes. The city made up for an upstate deficit by giving him 31,309 over Wadsworth. Seymour had another advantage in the city. Although conservatives had won a philosophical victory, the mechanics of practical politics were at work, too. Local Democrats had seethed over their loss of patronage after their defeat in the previous election. This time they temporarily forgot their factional feuds and united to gain office.

The members of Tammany Hall and Mozart Hall may have detested each other, but they detested the loss of jobs more. As practical men they had held their own peace conference before the election. For the time being, Tammany made no attacks on the loyalty of Mozart. Smith Ely spoke for Tammany, and at his side was the clear-thinking William Tweed. Fernando Wood did the talking for Mozart Hall. Sharp disagreements followed, but finally the politicians ironed out their knotty problems and came up with a deal satisfactory to both groups. Mozart Hall was to have a surrogate and Tammany Hall a supervisor, the state assembly nominations were divided, and each side received three congressional districts.[68]

Fernando Wood immediately took rooms in the Metropolitan Hotel so he could qualify as a candidate for Congress in the Fifth District. His brother Benjamin ran for Congress in the Fourth District, and both were successful. Judge Daly, once a friend of the former mayor, was shocked when he learned that the Democrats had nominated "those two scamps, Fernando Wood and his foolish, unprincipled brother."[69] Daly had not forgiven the Woods for proposing that the city secede from the Union.

Fernando Wood ran against Captain John Duffy, a member of the popular Sixty-ninth Regiment. The captain was a Democrat supported by Jeffersonian Democratic, Republican Union, and People's Union conventions. He spared no words in condemning Wood as a traitor, secessionist, and politician with an insatiable appetite for power. Duffy said there was only one issue, the choice between loyalty and treason. If that was the fundamental decision for the voters of the Fifth District, they showed precisely where they stood.[70]

As returns arrived at Mozart Hall on election night, the faithful reached new heights of exuberance. They applauded each favorable report, and Judge Dean declaimed, "Abolitionism at North and Secessionism at South would be buried in one grave." And they would not hear of any more men incarcerated without a hearing. Later, the former mayor appeared, and cries went up, "Fernando forever."[71]

Wood claimed that the election portended a great constitutional change. The president, he said, had received all the men and money he had asked for and yet the administration remained "fanatical, imbecile, and corrupt." Now the Union could be returned to a conservative course. He thought he could see hope for peace. At least, he saw the possibility that southerners would lay down their arms to allow a convention to be held to settle their differences in a way that would be constitutional and just for every section of the country.[72] Such talk appealed to voters, and the election of Seymour and the irrepressible Wood brothers was certainly a signal of the city's dissatisfaction with the national administration and the war.

When the returns rushed into the *Tribune* office were so contrary to the wishes of its publisher, some of the newsboys could not resist running into the street shouting that they had an extra that Horace Greeley had committed suicide.[73] One victorious Republican who supported the Emancipation Proclamation was Henry Raymond of the *Times*. He was elected to the state assembly. The *Herald* regarded his triumph as a "disgrace to the city." Yet the ambitious Raymond was free with his criticism of Lincoln. After the election his paper faintly praised the president for his "kindheartedness," "concern for fair play," and "placidity of temper," but blamed the widespread failure at the polls on lack of confidence in his leadership. "Quick, sharp, summary dealings don't suit him at all. He is all the while haunted with the fear of doing some injustice, and is ever easy to accept explanations. The very first necessity of war is extreme vigor, and yet every impulse of our constitutional Commander-in-Chief has been to get rid of it." Raymond believed that those who voted on the side of the administration had done so in spite of its poor management of the war.[74]

The election was a bitter pill for a minority in the city. Henry Bellows blamed the results on impatience and considerable indifference among the people. Some, he believed, were tired of the "crab-like pace of the war" and others did not appear to have any sense of right and wrong.[75]

Wall Streeters had placed bets on the election ranging from a hundred to five thousand dollars. Most of the bets were at even money. Now that the election was over, the stock market remained steady and the political results did not seem to cause a ripple in its activity. The repudiation of the president in New York did not upset the speculators in the least.[76]

Lord Lyons, the British minister to the United States, arrived in New York shortly after the election, and fashionable society figures immediately vied with one another to entertain him in their elegant drawing rooms. His hosts and their friends had gained considerable assurance with the election of Seymour and spoke openly to the diplomat about their desire for peace. Although they did not go so far as to say that they would accept southern independence, Lord Lyons astutely realized that would be the consequence of their wishes. He wrote Earl Russell, "At the bottom I thought I perceived a desire to put an end to the war even at the risk of losing the Southern States altogether; but it was plain it was not thought prudent to avow the desire."[77] The British diplomat received the impression from his conversations with these stylish acquaintances that they believed the election results would force the president to reduce his war aims and seek reconciliation with the South. He had heard some expressions of hope for an armistice followed by a constitutional convention. Others saw the possibility of peace through foreign mediation.

The Connecticut Copperhead Thomas Seymour visited the city soon after the election and was delighted to see the joy expressed over the results.[78] August Belmont thought the election was clear evidence that most northerners were not abolitionists and were willing to make constitutional concessions for the sake of peace.[79] Samuel Barlow was another who was overjoyed at the election of Horatio Seymour. He was sure that Seymour's defeat would have destroyed all hope of reunion. He wanted Seymour to pay a quiet visit to the president to allay misleading advice that he received from radicals. "You occupy today a position of power and influence second to that of no man in the Country," he wrote Seymour, "and it is vitally important that this influence should be felt before it is too late to save anything from the wreck which a persistence in the past policy of the Govt. will render inevitable." Barlow did not think the cabinet could make a vigorous war or a satisfactory peace. "One & perhaps both must be accomplished in the next six months as European interference is now very probable." Barlow, undoubtedly thinking of the next presidential election, also hoped that Seymour would visit McClellan, in whom he had the utmost confidence. The tide was turning for the Democrats, and Barlow could almost see McClellan in the White House.[80]

Fernando Wood, ecstatic over his election to Congress, was full of urgent news. He told Mayor Opdyke that a reliable source had told him that the southern states would send representatives to the next Congress if they received a full and general amnesty. He asked Opdyke to pass the information to his friends in the administration. He saw himself in a leading role as a peace missionary and wanted permission from the government to correspond with Confederate authorities. Opdyke said that several senators from New England were in the city and he would get in touch with them and then advise Wood.

Opdyke's reply was probably an excuse to escape from a slippery situation with Wood. At any rate, the mayor never saw the senators. The disappointed Wood then took it upon himself to write directly to Lincoln. With total lack of humility he wrote,

> As an humble, but loyal citizen . . . I ask your immediate attention to this subject . . . I suggest that gentlemen whose former social & political relations with the leaders of the southern revolt may be allowed to hold unofficial correspondence with them on this subject. . . . Your Inaugural address . . . pointed out the prophetic vision . . .

that after a bloody and terrible struggle "the still small voice of reason" would intervene and settle the controversy.... Has not the time
arrived when to quote your own language we should "cease fighting"
—at least long enough to ascertain whether the "identical questions"
about which we began the fight may not be amicably & honorably
adjusted, and "the terms of intercourse" be once more established?
It is to this end I address you.

Lincoln replied courteously, confidentially, and bluntly that he suspected
Wood's information was groundless. He believed that Wood's story
meant the same as cessation of hostilities, and in that event full and general amnesty would certainly follow. "My belief," he wrote Wood, "is that
they already know it, and when they choose, if ever, they can communi-
cate with me unequivocally. Nor do I think it proper now to suspend military operations to try any experiment of negotiations." Nonetheless,
Lincoln would receive any exact information from Wood with "great
pleasure." Lincoln's letter was not what Wood had hoped to receive. His
ambition for a major role in peacemaking was frustrated, and he showed
his pique. A few days later, he wrote Lincoln that his answer "filled me
with profound regret. It declines what I had conceived to be an innocent
effort to ascertain the foundation for information in my possession of a
desire in the South to return to the Union."[81]

Wood's behavior belied sincerity, and his integrity was always in
question so that any skeptic could doubt that his desire for peace was
anything more than a personal political maneuver. Yet at times Wood
had shown considerable courage, or possibly unmitigated gall, in taking
positions that supported peace efforts, and his consistency in that direction never faltered. Perhaps his Quaker heritage carried more weight
with his inner soul than even he realized. Yet if Quaker heritage had any
meaning for him, why was he so callous about slavery? For the moment,
however, his great weakness was refusing to admit that wishing for peace
did not make it so.

Opponents of the president believed by November that they had
found the perfect candidate when Lincoln replaced McClellan with Am-
brose E. Burnside. McClellan left the service and joined his wife, who
had been living temporarily with the Barlows in their home at 1 Madison
Avenue. Samuel Barlow hoped to become a president maker. As a pre-
lude, to show his esteem for the general, Barlow instigated a fund-raising movement to buy McClellan a house in Manhattan. August Belmont

was also close at hand. The Belmonts were often seen with the McClellans at the opera, theater, and even a masquerade ball. Ironically, a military man had become the darling of Democrats searching for peace.[82]

While schemes to achieve peace were bandied about, Surgeon McDougall, the military medical director in New York, faced a more immediate problem. The city's hospitals were jammed with soldiers, partly because of the continual flow of regiments into the city from upstate and New England. Each regiment brought cases of measles, mumps, syphilis, and a variety of other diseases. Now one more battle, this time at Fredericksburg, had turned into defeat and Surgeon McDougall expected another thousand sick and wounded to arrive during the bitter cold days of December. As an emergency measure to ease the strain, he hired the steamship *Thomas P. Way* to serve as a processing station for the new arrivals before they were distributed among the city's hospitals.

McClellan paid a solemn visit to Bellevue, where there were three hundred wounded. Dr. Coan said that he shook every soldier's hand and often inquired, "What's the matter with you my man?" And he asked about the pain. Coan described McClellan as solidly built, about five feet seven inches tall, who gave an impression of great physical strength and a powerful jaw. Life in the outdoors had given him a coarse complexion, and his dark hair was sprinkled with gray even though he had a red moustache. The doctor said that he hardly smiled and did not have the youthful air his pictures presented. Coan did not think he was too tactful and did not regard him as great, a genius, or a coming man. "I trust," he wrote, "that he may never have our armies committed to his leadership again."[83]

For days after Fredericksburg, newspaper columns were filled with lists of killed and wounded. The names of officers and men cut across all segments of society and ethnic groups. Yet a glance at the casualties for the 105th New York Regiment left little doubt that Irish-Americans had taken a heavy blow: "Thomas McGuire, Co. A, leg amp; Jas Dolan, Co. C, shoulder; J. McMahan, Co. H, breast, severe; D. Finn, Co. H, abdomen; M. Riley, Co. C, groin; Sgt. McManus, Co. H, leg, severe; H. Mcilainy, Co. I, forehead, severe." The ranks of the Sixty-ninth were also seriously depleted. It was a strange war. The Irish, so sympathetic to the South, were among the harshest critics of the war and abolition, but the casualties they suffered were a tragic contradiction to their frequently expressed sentiments.

Some New Yorkers, feeling the effect of the bloodshed, came up with ideas to end the war that were more farfetched than anything Fernando Wood had proposed. James Gordon Bennett and his *Herald* put forth one of these peace plans. Bennett hoped the country could be united by fighting common foreign foes. There was Canada to take from Great Britain, Mexico from France, and Cuba from Spain. "We have been cutting each other's throats for the profit and amusement of the monarchs and aristocracy of Europe." He thought the North and South were fighting over abstractions that should have been prevented by statesmanship, conciliation, and compromise. Fighting foreign foes made sense to Bennett, but few agreed with him.[84]

The definition of a Peace Democrat was always imprecise and sometimes meaningless, and not all advocates of mediation to end the war were Peace Democrats. The erratic Horace Greeley, depressed by Burnside's bloody defeat at Fredericksburg, also talked of negotiating for peace. He even approached Clement Vallandigham, the leading Copperhead in the North, about possibilities for peace. When Greeley met Henry Raymond on a train bound for Albany one day, he told him of his latest whim. Raymond was shocked and considered his conversation an act of treason. Greeley said, "You'll see that I drive Lincoln into it."[85]

Greeley's new theme was peace without victory. Foreign mediation struck him as the way to accomplish that goal, and he behaved like a self-appointed secretary of state. He was either unaware of or ignored the Logan Act, a statute on the books for sixty years, which forbade American citizens from negotiating with foreign governments. Distressed beyond fear of punishment, he turned to Henri Mercier, the French minister to the United States, in the hope of gaining the aid of Louis Napoleon. But Seward was not about to be usurped by a journalist, and he let Mercier know that mediation was not possible, thereby bursting Greeley's latest bubble.[86] The tragic war seemed endless with no easy way out. Hoping for peace did not achieve peace.

The Christmas season was sad, but New Yorkers tried to make sure that soldiers, the destitute, and orphans received a good dinner. The 223 children at the Colored Orphan Asylum at the corner of Fifth Avenue and Forty-third Street thoroughly enjoyed a fine feast that was supplied by friends and neighbors. The well-run institution provided for "whole orphans" and parents of "half orphans" paid fifty cents a week for their support. When a boy reached the age of twelve, he was hired out until he was twenty-one, when he received a hundred dollars in cash. The girls hired out when they were twelve and received fifty dollars when they were nineteen.[87] The children did not feel sorry for themselves. They appreciated their good home, and for them Christmas 1862 was a time of joy.

10
Loyalty

A select group of concerned citizens met in the select surroundings of Delmonico's to save the republic. They were certain the nation was on the brink of bankruptcy. The same faces had been together many times before to confer and commiserate over the national trial. Each had talent, each considered himself a Unionist, and each was shocked by the constitutional transgressions of Abraham Lincoln. Belmont the successful financier, Tilden the able lawyer, Barlow the man of parts, Brooks the publisher, and Seymour the intellectual politician were all convinced that their superior minds perceived a better way to run the country. On this February day in 1863 their purpose was to organize a society to educate the people.

The serious discussion of these earnest men produced the Society for the Diffusion of Political Knowledge, a propaganda agency. Belmont wanted to set the record straight about loyal conservative Democrats, and Tilden wanted to condemn arbitrary arrests and the absence of habeas corpus. Morse was honored with the presidency, and rich supporters assured him that funds would be plentiful.[1] Peace with honor and abandonment of abolition were Morse's aims, and he immediately attacked the "fanaticism of the hour." Sensitive to charges of disloyalty, he asked a fundamental question, "What is disloyalty?" Then he gave his answer. The word seared the minds of conscientious Americans who opposed the war and instilled a defensive need to explain their position. Morse told his audience there was no doubt that the foundation of the American system of government rested with the sovereignty of the people. The new society would appeal to that supreme power. He meant to use a citizen's right of free discussion to seek help for the cause of peace at the ballot box. Such action, he knew, was not treason, conspiracy, or resistance. It could not be disloyal to appeal to the power of the people.[2]

Morse knew that he had raised a penetrating and troubling question for a democracy and that it would be difficult, if not impossible, for anyone to respond without considerable hedging.

Nevertheless, there was never a shortage of opinions. Newspapers quickly took sides, but the debate that followed centered more on the new organization than on the question Morse had asked. The *Times* called the meeting "surreptitious" and the participants disloyal Copperheads, but the gathering was certainly not secret. The *World*, as expected, defended its friends, and the *Evening Post* considered Tilden's remarks revolutionary intrigue intended to eliminate Lincoln.

Tilden replied to the *Evening Post* that he had no revolutionary intent, but he reemphasized his low opinion of the administration. He compared the government's actions with "the voyage of a ship with a false compass." Lincoln, in Tilden's opinion, was a political hack whose experience was largely confined to county conventions and Springfield lobbyists. His harsh criticism sounded profound, as he always did, and appeared to touch the heart of the matter without offering any solution.[3]

The opposition did not stand still in this public relations battle. On February 14, Charles King, John A. Stevens, Jr., and others formed the Loyal Publication Society. They were distressed by the "enemies of the government and the advocates of a disgraceful Peace" who circulated journals and documents of a disloyal character. They rallied their forces to counteract this pernicious influence certain in the knowledge that they were on the side of right. The time had arrived to give true direction to public opinion. Their stated purpose was to distribute "journals and documents of unquestionable and unconditional loyalty" throughout the country. The indefatigable Francis Lieber became chairman of the publications committee and diligently went to work. Nationalism was a major theme in the society's pamphlets, and one of its main objectives was to sway soldiers away from the disloyalists by providing "our troops with some nutriment more healthy than the World, Express, or Herald."[4]

Greeley, with his unique perspective, moved along his own path in search of peace while these propagandists sniped at each other. He appeared to be cultivating his relations with the extreme Copperhead Clement Vallandigham, who wrote to him, "Evidently you & I have mistaken each other for some time in the past." Vallandigham convinced himself that he was a true Unionist, and he had previously thought of Greeley as a Disunionist. "Now," he wrote, "if all you ask is the old status quo with no new concessions, only new guarantees of said status — we shall agree at last."[5]

James White warned Greeley that making friends with Vallandigham was suicidal: "Let us put down traitors at home as well as down South by force." But White had little to worry about. This was simply one more of Greeley's brief, impractical sojourns.[6] Still, Greeley's bewilderment and frustration showed the extreme positions he was ready to explore to end hostilities. He never had the slightest doubt about his own devotion to the Union, but loyalty, to a large degree, is a subjective matter. Others may well have believed he was flirting with disloyalty.

Loyalty was a sore subject for both Copperheads and Unionists. Its qualities were difficult to define neatly. Faith in the Union, faith in the Constitution, faith in states' rights, faith in the people, all were subject to endless interpretations. The strong-minded, certain of their convictions, sharply disagreed over large and small points while others, less intellectually inclined, shook their heads in confusion. Conflicting concepts of the nation affected the depth of fervor for the Union. There was much loud talk about the "Union as it was, and the Constitution as it is," but the terms for establishing an enduring Union had always been uncertain. Was it a nation that demanded allegiance to states first and the federal government second? Was it a nation with or without slavery? Loyalty was supposed to remain constant. Instead, it was fragile and inconstant, changing with moods and events.

When southern sympathizers flirted with disloyalty, they took pains to explain that their devotion was the essence of democracy. They echoed Thomas Jefferson's phrases about the infallibility of the people, the right to speak up against the government, and the right to revolt. The Unionists, or at least the branch that supported the administration, took pride in their loyalty but diluted their democratic principles by supporting a government right or wrong. They closed their eyes to constitutional lapses.

Joseph Thompson, the Congregational minister at the Broadway Tabernacle, claimed that the people's right of revolution ceased when a free popular government was established. Francis Lieber rationalized that American colonists fought the British to gain their liberty yet the southern cause was to uphold slavery. Explanations on both sides were illogical, incomplete, and unsatisfying, raising more questions than they answered.

Henry Bellows preached a sermon titled "Unconditional Loyalty," in which he said that criticism of the head of government in a time of crisis was criminal. According to Bellows, Lincoln's cause was the "sacred cause of government itself," and Lincoln was responsible only to God. Yet loyalty remained a matter of opinion. Before the war was over, some of Bellows's fellow members at the Union League Club whispered doubts about his loyalty in their smoking and reading rooms. In a later sermon, Bellows tried to check partisan extravagance and give a charitable interpretation to the "views and motives of a great and dangerous opposition." Bellows believed that his own loyalty was beyond question, but he found to his dismay that his remarks did not sit well with some ultra Republicans who had forgotten that he was the author of the phrase "Unconditional Loyalty."[7]

Some city residents were beginning to think that those who preached loudly about loyalty meant loyalty to the administration or the Republican party, not to the nation or Constitution. As the war continued, a new suspicion or accusation arose that the federal administration had been "abolitionized" and that loyalty was now equated with abolition. David Turnure, a literate and studious observer, said he and others had been told that Abraham Lincoln was a conservative, not an abolitionist. Now he was disillusioned because he realized that he had been deceived—Lincoln really was an abolitionist. Turnure resented the implication that he should give the administration "unhesitating feality to and unquestioning endorsement of all their acts." He thought the nation was sinking under an accumulating weight of debt and infamy, and he felt contempt for his countrymen, who were blinded by passion that was leading to irretrievable ruin. Every day arbitrary and unconstitutional acts were committed "under the sacred mantle of patriotism." He was tired of the "immaculate patriots." Why should he give blind obedience to a policy that his intuition and judgment told him was destructive? Why should he be excommunicated from the body politic as a traitor?[8]

Despite the dissension that often made New York City seem to be a center of disruption, the reality of fighting the war went on. Mayor Opdyke stated in his annual message that the city had contributed about $300 million in taxes, gratuities, and loans to the government since the start of the war and had supplied more than eighty thousand volunteers.[9] And the city Chamber of Commerce loyally stood by the government, reaffirming its allegiance with a series of resolutions and trying to bolster public opinion by denouncing "a feeling of impatience and despondency that is unworthy of a brave people."[10] The difficulty with the resolutions was that they underlined the pervasive doubts in the city about moral obligations.

Other loyal citizens had plans to organize and provided a perfect illustration of the divided opinion in the city. Some members of the Sanitary Commission, disgusted with the election of Horatio Seymour as governor, thought of forming a club to support the war and democracy. They wanted a place to meet where they could share their convictions. The Union Club at Fifth Avenue and Twenty-first Street should have qualified as a comfortable meeting place, but the fashionable club had refused to expel Judah P. Benjamin, a Confederate cabinet member. He had been allowed to resign respectably, and that was too much for dedicated Unionists.[11]

Professor Wolcott Gibbs, Henry Bellows, George Templeton Strong, and other members of the executive committee of the Sanitary Commission envisioned their proposed club as a way to strengthen respect for the Union. It was to be political but not partisan. An early prospectus referred to the organization as the National Club because it meant to cultivate devotion to national rather than sectional interests. Frederick Law Olmsted hoped the membership would consist of "clever" literary, artistic, and professional men, who would form a "true American aristocracy." Aristocratic or democratic, the club took shape. The annual dues were twenty-five dollars, and soon the new Union League Club found rooms at the corner of Broadway and Seventeenth Street, where the members had an excellent view of public happenings in Union Square.

The formation of a gentlemen's club in the midst of a bloody war was not a momentous occasion. Nonetheless, it gathered together some of the serious-minded leaders in the city who strongly supported the war effort and generally held broad views about equal rights. One of the Union League Club's early ambitions was to recruit a black regiment. Although the twelve thousand or so blacks in the city represented only about 1.5 percent of the total population, sensible and just citizens believed they should be enlisted in the Union army. The club's request for permission from Governor Seymour to found a black regiment, however, was rebuffed with the excuse that he had no power to give approval.

Racial prejudice was still strong, and many white soldiers ⸀
it would be degrading to fight alongside a black man. The *World* sa
practice would be "unjust in every way to the white soldier to put hiɪ
a level with the black." Corporal Felix Brannigan of the Seventy-fouɪ
New York wrote, "We think we are too superior." Not long before, ⸀
writer to the *Times* claimed that "one negro regiment, in the present temper of things, put on equality with those who have the past year fought
and suffered, will withdraw an amount of life and energy in our army
equal to disbanding ten of the best regiments we can now raise." Governor Seymour was aware of these sentiments and he was not a man to
break down social barriers.[12]

Differences between the mayor and the Common Council exem-
plified the variety of opinions in the city even more sharply than did editorials, propaganda agencies, or social clubs. The controversial case of
Major General Fitz John Porter, a resident of the city, pointed up these
differences. Porter had been court-martialed after the Second Battle of
Bull Run for failure to act and disobedience of orders. The court found
Porter guilty, and he was dismissed from the service. The merits of this
celebrated case would be discussed, challenged, and reviewed for the
next twenty years. Porter, a good friend of McClellan's, was at least weak
in his intentions and lacked agressiveness on that day of battle.

Porter had close ties with the city as shown in his vicious antiadministration correspondence with Manton Marble, and the Common Council members considered him a friend in distress who shared their views.
The council members, hardly great military minds, resented the accusations of Porter's cowardice and planned to put the War Department in
its place. They recognized that this was an excellent opportunity for
them to use a military personality to exhibit their opposition to the conduct of the war. In the process, they raised the debate over the limits of
loyalty. This was an odd activity for municipal representatives, but the
temptation was too great to let pass.

The aldermen and councilmen adopted a resolution expressing regret and alarm over the dismissal of their "fellow citizen and townsman,"
whom they declared was "the personification of all that was brave, loyal,
and patriotic." The Common Council affirmed its right to examine and
criticize civil and military tribunals. The councilmen seemed to take
pleasure in making a political issue out of a military issue by claiming
that Porter's trial was unfair and that there was a "system of persecu-

tion" at work against the "conservative element in our armies," which was shown, they said, by replacing General McClellan and suspending General Don Carlos Buell as well as dismissing General Porter. Such discrimination could not be allowed to continue because it would "end in the ruin of the country and the disruption of the Government." The council extended its sympathy to General Porter and invited him to visit the city. The Governor's Room at City Hall would be set aside for his use so he could witness the regard and esteem of the citizenry as "one of the most intrepid, courageous, skillful, zealous, loyal and patriotic commanders of the Army of the Potomac, the findings of a partial and prejudicial court-martial to the contrary notwithstanding." This resolution, as was customary, was forwarded to the mayor for his approval. The mayor frequently disagreed with the council, rejecting requests to spend money and disapproving resolutions, usually with courtesy and tact. He returned this resolution without approval accompanied by some of his most strenuous language. He considered the council's condemnation of the United States government as revolutionary and calculated to undermine the foundations of the republic. The resolution, he said, lacked respect for constitutional authorities. Opdyke believed Porter had received a fair trial. He saw no need for a eulogy. "To tender him municipal honors," he wrote, "would place this loyal city in a false position, and could not fail, I am convinced, to shock the patriotic sentiments of a vast majority of its people." The ceremonial occasion was blocked, but the opposing viewpoints remained unchanged.[13]

The tension in the city was relieved by an event that fascinated citizens of all political opinions. It was the forthcoming marriage of twenty-five-year-old Charles Stratton, thirty-two inches tall, better known as General Tom Thumb, to twenty-two-year-old Lavinia Warren. The dainty thirty-inch-tall Lavinia set up residence at the Fifth Avenue Hotel, where she received a multitude of famous visitors. The Vanderbilts and Astors and Generals McClellan and Burnside were among those who called on the bride-to-be. P. T. Barnum's hand was in all the wedding preparations, and he basked in reflected glory as the eventful day approached. The showman, a strong Lincoln supporter, knew that the happy occasion could only increase the receipts at his American Museum. Lavinia's appearance at the museum as the smallest woman alive some days brought in more than three thousand dollars. Her photograph sold well, and her "cartes de visite" brought another three hundred dollars a day. Barnum had not arranged the wedding that caused this attention. It was a true love affair, but Barnum was ready to enjoy the benefits.

When inquiries were made about the use of the chapel at Trinity Church, the stern rector, Morgan Dix, wanted no part of the show. As someone who knew him said, "Ah, you can see by his face that he is determined to keep the devil down." Barnum claimed that the couple had applied to Bishop Potter to perform the nuptial ceremony and obtained his consent, but "some of the most squeamish of his clergy was brought to bear upon the bishop, and he rescinded his engagement." The Reverend Thomas Taylor of Grace Church on Broadway courageously risked looking foolish, one of life's worst dreads, and agreed to perform the ritual with the assistance of the Reverend Junius Wiley of St. John's Church in Bridgeport, minister of the bride's family.

The event took on national proportions far beyond the triviality that might have been associated with the marriage of two show people. Wedding presents arrived from all over the country. President and Mrs. Lincoln sent a beautiful set of China screens. Mrs. August Belmont sent silver chaste charms, and Mrs. Cornelius Vanderbilt presented a finely crafted coral and gold brooch, earrings, and studs. The two thousand wedding invitations became prized possessions, and there were offers to buy them for as much as sixty dollars each.

The wedding took place on February 10, 1863, with Commodore George Washington Nutt, twenty-nine inches tall, as best man. The church was packed, and crowds jammed the streets for a look at the bride and groom. A platform had been built in front of the chancel so that the congregation could see the ceremony. But as the newlyweds marched up the aisle, only those at the ends of the pews could see the little couple. The bride wore white satin, lace, and a long train. Her hair was rolled "a la Eugenie," and she was a perfect beauty. The groom and best man wore full dress suits.

Sometime after the wedding, an agitated pewholder who had not been admitted to the ceremony wrote a complaining letter to the Reverend Taylor with a snide remark about the "mountebanks." The minister was not in awe of his parishioner. He replied, "If the marriage of Charles S. Stratton and Lavinia Warren is to be regarded as a pageant, then it was the most beautiful pageant it has ever been my privilege to witness. If on the contrary, it is rather to be thought of as a solemn ceremony, then

it was a touchingly solemn as a wedding can possibly be rendered. . . .
Surely, there was never a gathering of so many hundreds of our best people, when everybody appeared so delighted with everything; surely it is
no light thing to call forth so much innocent joy in so few moments of
passing time; surely it is no light thing, thus to smooth the roughness and
sweeten the acerbities which mar our happiness as we advance upon the
wearing journey of life." No one could have made a better response.[14]
The sensitive rector understood that the people hungered for a reason
to be joyous.

Tom and Lavinia provided a pleasant diversion, but only too soon
the reality of war and the clashes of opinion returned. McClellan was in
the city and freely expressed his many resentments against the administration. He visited Samuel Barlow's office regularly and could always
count on a sympathetic ear. McClellan's friend Fitz John Porter was often
present discussing his own grievances. McClellan, full of venom, spewed
abuse against Lincoln, Stanton, and Halleck. When Hiram Barney
heard of these meetings, he wondered if McClellan had not violated military discipline, which would make him subject to dismissal from the service or disgrace.[15]

Early in March, Congress passed a national conscription law that
was a new cause for controversy. It was a much stronger measure than
the Militia Act of the previous year. Alien declarants as well as male citizens between the ages of twenty and forty-five were to constitute the national forces. To enact the law, the federal government overrode state
governments and organized boards of enrollment and provost marshals.
Draftees were allowed to provide substitutes or buy an exemption for
three hundred dollars. Immediately workingmen in the city castigated
the law that favored the rich and penalized the poor.

The Mozart Hall General Committee realized that the draft was a
choice target, denounced it as grossly unconstitutional, and declared
that "people everywhere should be awakened to the infamous distinctions which it makes between rich and poor." Fernando Wood was at this
meeting, and he was equally aware of the opportunities the draft offered for agitation. He added his own words about the subject of loyalty.
"Loyalty," he said, "is a monarchical derivative. What means it? The King
can do no wrong. No loyalty for me." As far as he was concerned, there
were only two political parties, one for the government and the other
against it. He did not think there was any such thing as a War Democrat.

The Mozart Hall committee arranged for a mass meeting to be held a few days later. Everyone was invited to attend who was "opposed to the conscription act, opposed to war for the negro ... [and] in favor of the rights of the poor." Fernando Wood took center stage at this gathering and imaginatively pictured two revolutions, "one at the South, with the sword, and the other at the North by executive and legislative usurpations." Following the speakers, resolutions were put forth and passed. One asked the New York courts to uphold the writ of habeas corpus and preserve freedom of speech and press. Another declared, "This administration cannot conquer the South if they would—and would not if they could ... we favor peace and conciliation as the only mode left to restore the Union."[16] There was no evidence in this meeting of the much-needed stamina to carry on the war.

Some New York City volunteers had their own ideas about loyalty and military service. The Hawkins Zouaves was one of the earliest regiments formed in the city. Now its term of service had almost expired, and the men looked forward to leaving the war behind them. They were stationed at Fort Nansemond, Virginia, which Confederate troops overlooked from a nearby hill. General James Longstreet had laid siege to the fort, and shellfire and sharpshooters forced the Zouaves to keep under cover all the time.

When General Dix heard of the regiment's intention to leave, he pleaded with the men to remain in the army a little longer. He called their position a "post of honor." The general's message was read to the regiment, and the men voted whether to leave or stay. They unanimously turned down the honor of serving any longer. Colonel Rush Hawkins did not mince words when he wrote to General Dix, who was the commanding officer of the Department of Virginia. Hawkins and his men felt they had given as much as their country could demand. "Our contract has been fulfilled to the letter." Hawkins had a good argument. His regiment had continually faced the enemy, had changed camp twenty-nine times, and spent five months on the sands of Hatteras. In two years, four hundred of his men had been killed or wounded. "We asked no bounty ... we love our country ... but we feel that others who have remained in the background should step forward to the front.... The 'post of honor' is not new to us. We have had it before and paid for it dearly.... Individual courage and bravery have all gone for naught. The imbecility of many high commanding officers in the field has cast a damning blight and disgrace over the graves of our brave countrymen." Their sacrifices were meaningless to them and did not provide a sense of pride. Weariness dimmed any romantic ideals they may have once held about patriotism.

The disillusioned colonel and his men were not detained. They were mustered out under General Orders No. 27 "with the heartfelt satisfaction of having done their duty." On May 6, 1863 the Hawkins Zouaves arrived in New York on the steamer *Kennebec* and marched up Broadway to the applause of onlookers. Their desire to leave the army was understandable, but it did not help the manpower shortage that the War Department struggled to solve.[17]

The following month, another well-known regiment returned home on the transport *Cahawba* from New Orleans. It was Billy Wilson's Boys, the Sixth Regiment New York State Volunteers. They landed at Pier 1 and immediately paraded to the Park Barracks at City Hall. Memories of this rowdy gang lingered, but it was reported that they looked well, hearty, and neat. It seemed necessary to explain that "none of the returning regiments were more orderly in their deportment on their arrival here." Detachments of the regiment had taken part in a variety of skirmishes, and their most important engagement was repelling the enemy at Santa Rosa Island near Pensacola. The day after reaching home, the men marched up Broadway to Union Square, accompanied by their regimental goat, and back to City Hall, where they were reviewed by the Common Council and entertained at dinner in the City Assembly Rooms. Alderman Farley complimented the men on their service, and Wilson responded with allusions to the daring performance of his regiment. As he talked, however, his men gathered around him and were so noisy that their leader's words were drowned out. Apparently the war had not completely repressed them.

Edward Pollard, editor of the *Richmond Examiner*, had a different version of Billy Wilson's valor. Pollard was hardly a disinterested observer, but he wrote that select Confederate troops landed on Santa Rosa in the dark of night and drove off the "notorious regiment of New York bullies, with their colonel flying at their head." He charged the New Yorkers with revolting acts of brutality and claimed that eleven of thirteen dead Confederates recovered on the field were shot through the head even though they had suffered body wounds. "This fact," wrote

Pollard, "admits of but one inference." But this story, true or false, was not known in New York when Billy Wilson and his boys received their heroes' welcome.[18]

The politicians may have taken pride in the city's soldiers, but there was little reason for pride in the city streets. Garbage and ashes piled high in the gutters and smells were nauseating. The city inspector was aware of the health hazards, but the private contractor responsible for street cleaning claimed the city owed him money. He refused to clean the streets and prevented anyone else from doing the job. Street cleaning had always been inefficient and unwieldy because contractors turned over much of the work to subcontractors, and it was difficult to pin down responsibility. One editorial complained that the "ways of the municipality are inscrutable." Although no epidemic broke out, there were 140 more deaths in the city through May than in the previous year and there was good cause to fear the spread of disease.[19]

A plague of a different sort was caused by the increasing number of army deserters who found refuge in the city. Many found havens with friends, and General John Wool issued an order calling on private citizens to turn them in. In late February, twenty-eight deserters were arrested and a small riot erupted when sympathetic citizens tried to rescue them from the hands of the law. A barracks was set up on Broome Street to hold deserters for trial or return them to their units. Some of the men were bounty jumpers, others were merely stragglers. In an effort to bring strays back to the fold, the army allowed them to return without punishment by the first of April. The only penalty was to forfeit pay for the period of absence.[20]

Although some deserters were treated leniently, others suffered terribly. A barracks on Park Row, used as a way station for soldiers in transit through the city, contained one room for deserters and other military offenders. It was fifteen feet wide by twenty feet long and was called the "Pen." Lewis Sayre, a medical doctor associated with Bellevue, found sixty-one men confined there one day, but the officer in charge told him that as many as seventy-seven had been held at one time and some remained for three or four months. The horrified doctor reported on January 13, 1864, to Mayor Gunther that there was no place for the men to sit or sleep except on the filthy floor, "not even straw to cover the floor as a hog or horse would have." Forty-five men usually slept in the room at night packed together on their sides. The others were taken outside and chained to trees until the forty-five had some sleep and then they switched positions.

Lice and vermin covered the men, and the stench was beyond belief. A guard took one man at a time to the latrine in the park while the others waited regardless of normal necessity or dysentery or diarrhea. Occasionally, the room was hosed down, but the drains were insufficient and the water only forced refuse such as potato skins, bones, and pork skins into a corner. The men were fed through bars and ate with their dirty fingers because knives and forks were not permitted. Dr. Sayre called the Pen an outrage on humanity and wrote that if the general government "treat their soldiers worse than wild beasts, in God's name let them take them away from the city . . . do not permit the city any longer to be disgraced by allowing them to occupy its grounds, and on them practice such horrid barbarities."[21] These inconsistencies in the treatment of soldiers were maddening. Leniency that amounted to dereliction of duty was countered by severity that amounted to inhumanity. Standards, rules, and regulations appeared to be in a state of collapse.

About this same time, George Templeton Strong heard that General Joseph Hooker had prohibited circulation of the *World, Express,* and other "disloyal" and "Dirt Eating papers" in the Army of the Rappahanock. Lawyer Strong wrote in his diary, "Good for Hooker, I dare say it's unconstitutional, but I know of nothing so unconstitutional as armed rebellion against the Constitution." He had no objection to suppressing the sale of "traitorous demoralizing newspapers" in army camps if it helped put an end to the war. To him it was the lesser of two unconstitutional alternatives.[22]

Soon, however, the Copperheads in the city had a reason to complain that was more important than the temporary suppression of newspapers. On May 6, General Burnside arrested Vallandigham for violating General Order No. 38, which stated that in the Department of Ohio, "the habit of declaring sympathies for the enemy (would) be no longer tolerated." A few days before, Vallandigham had said in a speech at Mount Vernon, Ohio, that the war could end by negotiation or French mediation and that the administration was unnecessarily prolonging the fighting. He also said that the war was not being fought to preserve the Union but to free the blacks and enslave whites. These sentiments were almost the same as those Vallandigham had expressed at a meet-

into the city. He called for a large, organized force of state troops to work with the army now facing the enemy in the Susquehanna Valley, and he pleaded with the governor to use existing law by instituting an immediate draft. Such an idea could not have been well received by Seymour, who opposed the draft with all the intellectual force he could command. Delafield also wanted to use the thousands of veterans whose two-year and nine-month service had expired. The War Department offered a bounty of upwards of four hundred dollars, and these men would make excellent soldiers. Delafield was full of ideas, but he probably did not expect Seymour to accept his suggestions.[31]

Colonel Delafield had been an official member of Governor Morgan's staff as well as a United States Army officer, and Morgan had frequently consulted him on defense matters. Seymour, however, ignored Delafield so thoroughly that before this emergency he had requested that his name be dropped from the Governor's staff, although he remained willing to provide any information Seymour needed. Since Seymour had previously resisted requests to increase defense forces, his order for thirty regiments of militia could be interpreted as a grudging move or an expression of panic in a crisis.[32]

Responsible authorities were suddenly taking a second look at their jurisdictions and taking pains to go on record that they were in command of the situation. General Wool wrote to Governor Seymour about the defense "of this great Emporium." He told Seymour that the federal government could scarcely exist a day if anything happened to the city "from which a large proportion of the supplies for the Army and Navy have been obtained, and at least ninety (90) percent of the money borrowed by the Government to carry on the war." He wanted the governor to know that he had been increasing his defense efforts, especially to mount large, long-range ten- and fifteen-inch-caliber guns and men to man them. But, he did not have more than 450 effective men to garrison nine forts and batteries in the harbor. He urged the governor to continue to construct permanent defenses, but he believed the best immediate defenses were ironclads, gunboats, and obstructions in the channel.[33]

Opdyke said the invasion of Pennsylvania should serve as a warning to the city. He anticipated trouble from both inside and outside the city and sought help from any quarter. Opdyke considered the rebel navy a threat, and he sought artillerists for the forts from General Sandford to replace those who had been sent to the front. He also urged General Wool, commanding the Department of the East, not to take any more men from the garrisons. "The importance of this city to the nation," he wrote, "demands that it should not be left at the mercy of the rebel navy."[34]

A few days before, General Wool had asked Colonel Delafield to examine the defenses on Governor's Island. On June 19, Delafield, who had been working hard to strengthen the harbor fortifications, gave Wool a discouraging report. Much of Delafield's work had been nullified by an influx of families of soldiers and bureaucrats. The quarters at Fort Columbus were turned over to schoolmasters, laundresses, and children. Even worse, the hospital built on the island blocked the gunfire of Fort Columbus on the channel and land fronts it was designed to command. Utterly depressed, he wrote that it was suicidal to build forts to defend the channels leading to the city and navy yard at a cost of millions and then obstruct them. The only solution was to demolish several structures. Working at cross purposes was a common ailment that had reached a new high on Governor's Island.[35]

Opdyke was also disturbed because the navy had withdrawn its warships from the navy yard and had left the city unprotected. He wrote to Secretary of the Navy Gideon Welles of his concern, and the ironclad monitor *Passaic* was assigned to defend the harbor.

The Common Council could even claim to have made every effort to defend the city. After years of neglect, the council had requested $1 million for harbor defense earlier in the year, but the state legislature stalled in passing the appropriation. John Stevens, president of the Bank of Commerce, had attended a meeting of the Harbor Defense Committee in March. He found that the mayor had little control over the aldermen, who were inclined "to do things in their own fashion." After an evening of inaction, he concluded that the proposed $1 million would do little good. Nevertheless, he recognized that the harbor was exposed and vulnerable.[36]

The Board of Councilmen used the emergency to boost the career of unemployed General McClellan by passing a resolution that began, "Whereas, the rebels have ruthlessly dared to invade the loyal territory of the United States with the infamous intention of seizing and destroying with fire and sword the property and lives of our people," and continued that because General McClellan was not on active service and his character as a patriot, man, and soldier was well known and highly esteemed, the administration was requested to place the general "in the position which the present crisis demands for the safety of the Republic."[37] The resolution was sent to the Board of Aldermen for concurrence, but the crisis was at hand and the president had other plans for a new commander.

Suspense over an imminent battle in Pennsylvania turned the stock market dull and gold speculators feverish. In mid-June, wild and depressing rumors spread throughout Wall Street and gold advanced 1.5 percent. Horace Greeley, never steady in time of crisis, trembled with fear that "Bull Run strategy should result in another Bull Run defeat. If so, where are we?" The *Times* reminded its readers that only the previous month Fernando Wood had said that "the hand of God is uplifted against us, and that we cannot conquer the South." Now an editorial referring to Wood said, "There is not a more brazen piece of humanity than he — [and he] would not dare to repeat that talk, Foolhardy as he is."[38] The war was at the city's doorstep, and once again its mood shifted.

The brief renewal of national ardor in the city was a perfect time for the appearance of Miss Major Pauline Cushman at P. T. Barnum's museum. She was billed as a "Union Spy and Scout" and recounted her experiences in the "Secret Service of the United States." Although her story was undoubtedly embellished and her rank of major was honorary, there was an element of truth in her adventures. The raven-haired beauty, an ambitious professional actress, was appearing in Nashville in *The Married Rake* when she was "banished" to the South as a "sympathizer" with the blessing of Colonel William Truesdail, in charge of the police for the Union Army of the Cumberland. He assigned Cushman to collect information in General Braxton Bragg's Confederate command. Whether she picked up any worthwhile information is a moot question. Luckily, the advance of Union troops rescued her just as she was discovered by the Confederates. She made her way to New York and remained at Barnum's for several weeks, where she cast a spell over her audiences.[39]

Along with the news of triumph at Gettysburg in early July came the long lists of killed and wounded that were published day after day. Hundreds of soldiers poured into the New York hospitals. At Fort Schuyler, 618 men arrived from Gettysburg on July 12. All but two or three of the arrivals were wounded, and simply dressing their wounds was an enormous job. A few days before, Titus Coan had signed a contract to serve as a private physician for three months at the army hospital, and he was overwhelmed with work. Three days later, another 300 men arrived directly from the battlefield.[40]

One of the more prominent casualties at Gettysburg was the politician Daniel Sickles, commanding officer of the III Corps. A shell shattered his leg and it was amputated. It was a paradoxical fate for a man who had once hoped New York City would secede from the Union. Some people called Sickles a hero at Gettysburg, but he was always controversial and even his performance on that sad day was disputed. On the second day of the engagement, Sickles, impulsive in war as in politics and private life, ignored his orders from General George G. Meade to hold the position at two hills, Little Round Top and Big Round Top, and moved to a forward position. The Confederate General James Longstreet, tore into Sickles's line and placed the entire Union force in jeopardy. Sickles's men were overwhelmed in Longstreet's onslaught and had to be rescued by one of General Winfield Scott Hancock's divisions.

The final outcome at Gettysburg was decisive, and news of Grant's victory at Vicksburg was equally welcome. The price of gold dropped, and moneylenders, ever impressionable, boasted a new confidence that was reflected throughout Wall Street. Once again, loyalty showed will-o'-the-wisp qualities. Success on the battlefield momentarily made allegiance to the Union a popular ideal. At last the North appeared to be gaining the upper hand in the long struggle. And again, for a brief period, New Yorkers were ready to believe that the end of the war was near. A joyous Maria Daly wrote, "Now if Lincoln had but the sense to publish a general amnesty and annul his emancipation act, we might have a united nation."[41] Her views were not uncommon in the city. The victories at Gettysburg and Vicksburg were well received, but they fell short of the desire for an immediate ceasefire.

11
Riot

The victory at Gettysburg gave the city a bona fide reason to celebrate. But the celebration turned to ashes when, a few days later, a new
crisis enveloped New York. The provost marshal's department had completed enrollment of potential draftees. It had been a difficult process in
a city with so many transients and evaders. False names, false residences,
and false statements created inexplicable and disproportionate lists
from one ward to another. But the job was over, and the government was
ready to set the draft in motion despite the strong undercurrent of
resistance.

Just then, Mayor Opdyke received a request from Colonel Frank
Howe for protection of the Fifty-fifth Massachusetts (Colored) Regiment
when it arrived in the city. The request was reasonable but offensive. Opdyke informed Howe that he would see if General Sandford's thin militia
forces could provide an escort. He also advised the colonel to seek help
from the police commissioners, who were not under his control, to protect the regiment from insults. Opdyke knew that the passage of these
troops through the city could cause a nasty disturbance, but he told
Howe, "I cannot see how any loyal citizen can find it in his heart to do
otherwise than welcome the addition of their forces to the national service, lessening as it will the coming draft upon the white population."[1]
Fortunately, the Massachusetts soldiers passed through the city without
incident. The hoodlums who might have caused trouble were too occupied with the coming draft.

July 11 was set for the start of the draft for unmarried men between the ages of eighteen and forty-five and married men between
eighteen and thirty. For weeks the draft had been a subject that created
grumbles, fears, and threats among the populace. The Mozart Hall
Committee had drawn up resolutions charging that a draft subverted

states' rights and that the president should be advised not to enforce such a law until its constitutionality was decided.[2]

The *Metropolitan Record*, no longer known as the "Official Organ of the Most Rev. Archbishop of New York," now called itself "A Catholic Family Paper," and its tone had become more strident after Lincoln announced the Emancipation Proclamation. The draft was the last straw for its editor, John Mullaly. In March, an article appeared under the title "The United States Converted into a Military Despotism — the Conscription Act the Last Deadly Blow." By the following month, Mullaly was willing to give up the war. "Which do we prefer — to let the South go, or to lose our own liberties in an attempt to force it unwillingly into the union with us." He foresaw the need for an occupation army of a million men to subject the southern states. "For our part we must say that we prefer liberty to Union on such terms" and ended heroically, "if that be treason make the most of it."[3]

The reaction of the *Metropolitan Record* may have been expected, but the language of several other newspapers was equally harsh. The shift in the purpose of the war disturbed the *Journal of Commerce*, usually mild in its criticism of the administration. It had become a war for abolition, the paper said, and the men who sought to pursue hostilities with conscription until slavery was eliminated were "neither more nor less than murderers." Newspapers that supported the administration tried to present the scheduled call in the best light but gave the impression of overselling. Antiadministration papers took bitter delight in finding an issue that caused so much popular antagonism. The *Daily News* called the draft "an outrage to all decency and fairness" and claimed that the aim was to "kill off Democrats and stuff the ballot-boxes with bogus soldier votes." Benjamin Wood, never at a loss for making extreme and unfounded statements, said, "One out of about two and a half of our citizens are destined to be brought over into Messrs. Lincoln and Company's charnel house." He emphasized that the draft did not touch the rich man, who was left to his "luxurious repose." In the latter remark he was correct. But he roused racial prejudice by charging that the draft "would compel the white laborer to leave his family destitute and unprotected while he goes forth to free the negro, who, being free, will compete with him in labor." The old cry was always effective. Wood suggested that the time had come for laborers to hold a mass meeting to express their views on the subject.[4]

Any gathering of unhappy workingmen during these tense days could easily ignite a disturbance. Since the start of the war, workingmen had become steadily more sensitive about their grievances and some expressed themselves vociferously. On the docks violence had frequently broken out during the past few months and heightened the fear of trouble over the draft. Longshoremen did not work steadily, often only three or four days a week, for pay as low as $1.50 a day. Frustrated in attempts to gain higher wages, they spent too much spare time in saloons on West and South streets, and their belligerence increased with their alcoholic intake. Fights between whites and blacks who were regarded as strikebreakers were not uncommon, but a police captain in the area said the cause was usually rum rather than reason. Nonetheless, there were many ugly scenes. In the spring of 1863, the Metropolitan Police barely saved two blacks from lynching.

In June, about 3,000 longshoremen stopped work and demanded a raise of twenty-five cents an hour during the regular day and fifty cents for overtime. The need to load ships to meet the demands of war did not impress the strikers. The government had to bring 150 deserters from prison on Governor's Island and 65 convalescents from Bedloe's Island to load army transports scheduled to depart with ammunition and supplies. To prevent violence, regular army troops with fixed bayonets and hundreds of police guarded them. Although many strikers soon agreed to an increase to two dollars a day and twenty-five cents for overtime, the truce was uneasy and racial resentment persisted.

There was also a report that three carloads of former slaves had been brought from the South as strikebreakers. Although the story may not have been true, it inflamed the much trumpeted fear that black labor would drive out whites when abolition was a reality. Earlier in the year, iron and shipbuilding workers had held a mass meeting at Tammany Hall to protest importation of foreign workers and southern blacks.

Frank Leslie's Illustrated Newspaper claimed that the draft law converted the republic into "one grand military dictatorship," and the more extreme Roman Catholic *Freeman's Journal* charged that the draft made a despot of Abraham Lincoln, a "deluded and almost delirious fanatic." The antiadministration *World* had urged strong prosecution of the war but did not see any inconsistency when it called the draft "an oligarchic conspiracy plotting a vast scheme of military servitude."[5]

Fear of trouble when the draft began pervaded the city. George

Templeton Strong wrote, "That soulless politician, Seymour, will make mischief if he dare. So will F'nandy Wood, Brooks, Marble, and other reptiles."[6] Strong's assessment of these men may have been harsh, but certainly they had no love for conscription. Governor Seymour believed the draft was unconstitutional and on July 11 sent his adjutant general to Washington to urge its suspension.

The draft stirred the embittered Fitz John Porter to write Manton Marble that some people "high in power are more knaves than fools." He continued, a little more prescient than even he realized, "when you hear federal guns are used in New York City & harbor you will conclude that despotism is & has been the aim of some parties." He ended his letter, "Hope you wont be drafted."[7]

Critics complained vehemently about the weakest element in the conscription act. It provided the right to pay three hundred dollars for a substitute, which clearly favored prosperous people and hurt the poor. The act would probably not have passed Congress without this provision, but the complaints about favoritism were justified and strengthened the enemies of the draft.

The president and high-ranking members of the War Department considered placing a military force in the city during the call, but they decided that to do so would alarm the people. In the event, all troops were urgently needed in Pennsylvania.

The mood in New York City in summertime could be especially volatile. Men and women, trying to catch a breath of fresh air, spent hours sitting on doorsteps and curbstones with little to do. Business slowed down in July and August, and when unemployed men had time on their hands their grievances magnified and violence often broke out. Yet when the first draft call was made on Saturday, July 11, a hot, muggy day, all was quiet. The Ninth District Office at 677 Third Avenue opened at nine in the morning, and Provost Marshal Charles E. Jenkins began to pull names from a large wheel. In the next few hours more than twelve hundred names were called. A curious crowd gathered outside, but when the business ended at four o'clock the crowd left without any disturbance.[8]

The luck of the draw, however, worked against lasting peace and quiet. The call to service of several men from Black Joke Engine Company, Number 33, created an issue because firemen were exempt from duty in the militia and believed they should also be excused from the draft. During the remainder of the weekend, disgruntled groups collected in taverns to voice their feelings and consume alcohol, which contributed to a buildup of their captious spirits.

Riots have deep and complex causes, but the initial outburst usually occurs like spontaneous combustion. This time, violence began on Monday, when the provost marshal continued the draft call. The mob did not need an excuse for pouring out a tidal wave of emotion. Unruly clusters of wrought-up people thoughtlessly and criminally started a commotion, and their wild behavior spread contagiously to others. The mob, full of bravado, roamed the streets looking for and finding trouble. Those unfortunates, rich or poor, white or black, who crossed their paths were in danger of their lives.

On this same morning, the Board of Aldermen was summoned to meet at City Hall. Alderman Farley wanted the board to request the corporation counsel to test the constitutionality of the draft. The meeting came to nothing because too few members showed up to make a quorum.

Provost Marshal Jenkins had barely begun the draft on Monday morning when a hose cart from the Black Joke Engine Company, loaded with stones, appeared on the scene. Firemen threw stones through the window and then entered the office, spilled turpentine on the floor, and set the building on fire. Nearby houses started to burn, and when a deputy provost marshal pleaded with the rowdies to put out the fire he was beaten up.

Mayor Opdyke had warned government officials to expect trouble, and now he frantically followed up his messages with reports of an organized riot. He asked Seymour for military aid from adjoining counties and did not learn until later that the governor was on vacation. His second telegram, sent at 3:40 P.M., went to the governor at New Brunswick, New Jersey. It read, "The riot threatens to be serious. A block of buildings has been burned — I think it best you should come to the city at once." He also sent a dispatch to Stanton and requested Admiral Paulding at the New York Navy Yard in Brooklyn to send the marines. The busy mayor also issued a proclamation warning all those engaged in the riot to desist at once and return to their homes and jobs, but it had no influence on the mobsters.[9] George Strong and Wolcott Gibbs urged the mayor to declare martial law. According to Strong, Opdyke said that was General Wool's business, Wool said it was Opdyke's business, and no one issued the order.

The riot spread. Telegraph wires were out, and hoodlums cried out, "Down with the rich." This became a reason to invade and ransack private homes. Young men and boys shouted madly in the confusion. Some cheered Jefferson Davis, and one man was knocked down because he said he was for the Union. Neither the police nor the Invalid Corps had the strength to stop the havoc. Police Superintendent John Kennedy left police headquarters on Mulberry Street and went into the streets to appraise the situation. He was so severely beaten that Commissioner Thomas Acton had to serve in his place. Eventually, Acton and Brevet Brigadier General Harvey Brown, in charge of the federal forts in the harbor, would rally their slim forces and defend the city. In the next few days they received little sleep and little help.

Colonel Henry O'Brien, commanding officer of the Eleventh Regiment of New York State Volunteers, was trapped in a circle of fiends who killed him, fired pistol shots into his head after he died, and dragged him through the streets by a cord around his neck. Two priests later discovered the body and took it to the "dead-house" at Bellevue.[10]

A wild horde, made up mainly of Irish, rushed to the Colored Orphan Asylum on Fifth Avenue between Forty-third and Forty-fourth streets. Hundreds of rioters ran through the four-story building stealing anything in sight. Women and children stood beneath the windows and caught bundles of bedding and clothing that men tossed to them. Trunks of crockery, carpeting, and furniture were moved out in the mad fury. The mob was not satisfied with simple robbery. Some, bent on destruction, carried axes, and others cried, "Burn the niggers nest." Soon a fire started. Volunteer firemen, in contrast to the behavior of the hoodlum firemen, bravely tried to put out the fire but were foiled when the mob chopped the hoses.[11] Luckily, the orphans had time to escape out the back of the building and were taken to the Twentieth Precinct. More than two hundred children remained at the station house for the next three nights, where priests brought them food. Later they were taken to Blackwell's Island for safety. People of all walks of life were suddenly threatened by a war within a war at their doorsteps. Morgan Dix lived at a rectory at 50 Varick Street in a poor neighborhood. Nearby St. John's Chapel had a Sunday school for black children, and a large num-

The disgraceful burning of the Colored Orphan Asylum on Fifth Avenue between Forty-third and Forty-fourth streets during the draft riot, July 1863. (Courtesy of the New-York Historical Society)

ber of black people lived at St. John's Lane and York Street. A servant told Dix that she had seen a black man hanging from a tree on Clarkson Street and men and women setting the body on fire. Dix was skeptical and thought it must have been an effigy, but later he learned the story was true. During the night, houses behind the rectory were sacked and Dix set up a watch to protect the church.[12]

Joseph Choate had packed his trunk and was ready to leave for Salem when the riot altered his plans. The riot in the Twenty-second Ward was led by the ward's alderman, and during the night the sky was red with flames. Although his neighborhood on Twenty-first Street was quiet, he took four blacks into his house for protection. "All this," he wrote his mother, "is the natural fruits of the doctrines of Seymour, Wood, and Vallandigham." The next day, friends of Choate, the Gibbons family, lost almost everything. Two of the daughters were at home when a gang led by two men on horseback arrived at their gate with sabers drawn. A report had gone around that the Gibbonses were related to Horace Greeley, and that was sufficient reason for the mob to pillage the house. The girls escaped to a neighbor's home while the crowd stole furniture, books, pictures, china, and beds. The house was then set on fire, but neighbors were able to extinguish it. One of the neighbors, however, was killed in a scuffle while he was helping fight the fire. The father of the Gibbons girls was not at home and that probably saved his life. Choate happened to be in the neighborhood about the time the gang finished destroying the Gibbons home. He found the girls two doors from their home, and they were so glad to see him they almost swooned in his arms. He led them over a dozen adjoining rooftops, found a carriage, and took them to his house. On Seventh Avenue, about a half-dozen blocks from Choate's home, three blacks were hanged and their bodies subjected to horrible barbarities after they had been killed. One of the black men was twenty-three-year-old Abraham Franklin, who lived nearby.[13] Mobsters overwrought by the draft law who sought vengeance by harming black people were exhibiting a particularly senseless aspect of the riot. Blacks were subject to the draft, and few could afford to pay for a substitute if called.

The doorstep of Charles Woolsey's house on Tenth Street was covered with black ashes, and he heard that the gashouse on Twenty-third Street had been blown up. It was rumored that the powder mill on Twenty-eighth Street would be blown up, and he invited friends who lived near the mill to stay with him.

The Jews' Hospital on Twenty-eighth Street was in the middle of much of the rioting. The staff was kept busy tending to wounds, and the hospital took on the appearance of a casualty aid station at the front. The same was true of Bellevue.[14]

Two days later, Woolsey left the city for Astoria, and while driving there heard gunfire in Harlem. His wife, Harriet, in a note to Abby Woolsey wrote, "Uncle E. is perfectly indignant and in a state of suppressed rage at the Irish, but he agrees with Aunt E. in not allowing a word said against them at table, or within reach of any servant's ears." Joe Howland, Eliza Woolsey's husband, was on a bus jammed with toughs and was addressed by one: "Your're a fancy looking sort of a chap; what would you pay for a substitute?" Howland had been wounded at Gaines Mill in the Peninsula campaign, and he replied, "I don't need a substitute, I went myself." They talked about the army and concluded that they had met before. The slightly tipsy tough turned to his companions and said, "Take good care o' this gen'lman, he's a partic'lar frien' o' mine."[15]

George Blunt, a prominent citizen who was pilot commissioner and author of *Blunt's Coast Pilot,* found a black man hanged from a lamppost in front of his house. A placard on the chest of the dead man read, "We will be back for you tomorrow." According to his grandson, Blunt went to the newspapers and asked them to print an announcement that he would be glad to receive the rioters and had a Colt revolving rifle and two Colt revolvers with which to entertain them. The rioters did not return.[16]

A drunk in the basement of St. Luke's Hospital shouted, "Turn out by six o'clock or we'll burn you in your beds." At about the same time, an injured rioter was brought into the hospital for care. Reverend Dr. Muhlenberg, founder of the hospital, courageously went outside and told a mob that the doors were open to everyone, "Would they threaten this house with fire and storm?" The answer came back, "No, no," and another incident was averted. But disorganized bands of troublemakers continued to wander through the streets. Herman Melville, a native New Yorker, wrote, "The Town is taken by its rats — ship rats and rats of the wharves."[17]

At Forty-fourth Street near Lexington Avenue, other rioters, looking for alcohol, wrecked the Bull's Head Hotel.[18] Similar scenes occurred all over the city, and anyone who sold liquor was an automatic target for looters. No one was safe because the aimless mobs forgot all reason. They shouted, "Down with the rich," and attacked the poor. They shouted, "Down with the niggers," and attacked whites. Two Protestant missions in an impoverished neighborhood were destroyed without cause. Railroad tracks were torn up, telegraph poles were torn down, and paving stones dug up to throw through windows.

The draft had become an excuse for running wild. Brooks Brothers lost thousands of dollars worth of merchandise, and Lord and Taylor employees had to use guns to defend their store at the corner of Grand and Chrystie streets. Then whorehouses were discovered as a rich source of ready cash and became another target. A greater threat to the city was an attack on the armory at Twenty-first Street and Second Avenue. Police guarded the armory for awhile, killing several mobsters. Eventually, however, the police withdrew and the mob walked off with guns and started another blaze.

Rioters looking for men to join their ranks seized Alfred Jones at the depot of the Sixth Avenue Railroad and dragged him into the street. "I promenaded arm in arm with a drunken Irishman," he said, "and was let go upon making a 'speech against the draft'—with the word & matter of the draft entirely left out. They said I was all right & left me after shaking hands generally."[19]

Windows were broken at the *Tribune* office, and some furniture was destroyed in the counting room. Greeley refused to protect his building with arms, but some *Times* employees went to the aid of their competitor. The next day, the *Times* proudly reported the noble deed in its columns. On Tuesday night, the *Times* turned on the gas jets and brightly illuminated the office, partly in honor of Grant's victory at Vicksburg and partly to throw light on the *Tribune* office, which was allegedly threatened by midnight prowlers. The *Daily News,* unscathed by rioters, declared in an editorial that it had warned of insurgence as a consequence of the draft. It was clear to the editor that black people were reaping the results of abolitionist activities, which had created "understandable resentment" against them.[20]

The white marble subtreasury building at the corner of Nassau and Wall Street, patterned after the Parthenon with its portico of eight Grecian columns thirty-two feet high and more than five and a half feet in diameter, seemed to be a sure target for trouble and Cisco, the assistant treasurer, took no chances. Guns were distributed to employees, hand grenades and bottles of vitriol were placed at the windows, and a guard of green soldiers surrounded the building. Mounted pickets stood by through the night, mainly for communicating with the customhouse, and a gunboat was anchored at the foot of Wall Street. Cisco shrewdly sent out agents all over the city to watch the rioters so he might have advance notice of an attack on the treasury. A mob marched down Greenwich Street and was thought to be headed for Wall Street, but the threat faded away. George Strong called on Cisco on the fifteenth and found him "serene and bland." The police superintendent had thought earlier that Cisco might go into "spasms" if he heard unsettling news.[21]

Army and navy officials grimly told Hiram Barney that they could not help him defend the customhouse. He arranged his own defenses on the first day of the riot and was keenly aware of many vulnerable points that could not be protected. He spent an anxious night expecting a disturbance, but the hours passed quietly. The next day he strengthened his defenses and felt more confident. Strong, a self-appointed patrolman, called on Barney, too, and found him "flaccid and tremulous."[22]

The jewelers on Maiden Lane locked their safes, closed their doors, and appointed a vigilance committee. The treasures of Maiden Lane might have attracted looters, but again reason did not rule. An intimidating crowd moved west on Barclay Street and left the jewelers undisturbed.[23]

Governor Seymour was on vacation at Long Branch, New Jersey, when the uprising began, and he arrived in the city on the fourteenth. He conferred with the mayor and General Wool at the St. Nicholas Hotel but saw no need to declare martial law. He issued a proclamation asking the citizens to go home and stop the violence. That same day he addressed a peaceful crowd at City Hall and opened his remarks by addressing them as "My friends." It was a harmless introduction, and certainly Seymour intended to reduce the tension. Yet the *Evening Post* and *Tribune* magnified them out of all proportion as a concession to the mob.

Later, Seymour issued a second proclamation which declared the city and county in a state of insurrection and warned of legal penalties if state authorities were resisted. Seymour also met with Colonel Robert Nugent, the acting provost marshal general in New York City, and insisted on the suspension of the draft, but his demand was academic because the rioters had already stopped the draft.

Henry Bellows returned from the battlefield at Gettysburg, where he had been supervising the work of the Sanitary Commission with the wounded. He found a reign of terror in the city and wondered what good victories in the field accomplished when mobs ruled the city streets. He thought the shameful behavior in the city was a greater disgrace than a military defeat.[24]

Neighbors in exclusive Stuyvesant Square decided the time had come to defend themselves and formally organized the Stuyvesant Square Home Guard. They received an order from the mayor for one hundred muskets or carbines from the police department, but the carbines they received were useless. Members of the Home Guard were told to provide themselves with revolvers, policemen's whistles, and dark caps with a white star for identification. In the event of trouble, a guardsman was to whistle three times. If the minutes of the Home Guard are any indication, these rich residents of the city were left unharmed and by the time they had fully organized the danger had passed.[25]

Proclamations had no influence on mobs, which continued to roam the city for three days. On Wednesday morning, the fifteenth, the *Herald* published a letter from Archbishop Hughes calling for peace in the city despite Greeley's "assault upon the Irish." At about this time, one example of an assault upon a citizen by the Irish was given in a sworn statement by Ellen Parker. She complained that five Irishmen, Patrick O'Neill, Patrick Kiernan, Barney Fagan, Frederick Hammers, and Micheal Dunn, entered the back door of her house on the corner of Fifth Avenue and Sixty-first Street and terrified her by looking for a "damned Orangeman" and threatening to cut him into four quarters if they found him.[26]

The major contribution of the Board of Aldermen and Board of Councilmen that day was to express their animosity against the draft by adopting a resolution stating that it was injurious to the city. The working classes were needed for the city industries, they said, and the draft was likely to produce a "popular outbreak of most serious consequences." In the interest of "justice, humanity, and economy," they called for the appropriation of $2.5 million to aid draftees and their families.[27] The resolution was obviously meant to appeal to the mob, but it was a strange statement to make in the midst of an already serious outbreak.

By evening, the Sixty-fifth Regiment of the New York National Guard arrived, and early Thursday morning the Seventh Regiment appeared. Their presence made a deeper impression on the rioters than proclamations or resolutions. The riot began to wane as the Twenty-sixth Michigan Volunteers, 152d New York Volunteers, and Seventy-fourth Regiment of New York National Guard also showed up. Secretary of War Stanton notified Opdyke that five regiments were under orders to return to New York because Lee's army had been "broken." Late in the day, horsecars began to run again, a sure sign of a more normal life. Still, fear remained in the brooding city that the riot might erupt again over some slight provocation.

The 152d New York Volunteers set up camp at Stuyvesant Square, and soon they had their own grievances. Their rations were supplied by a private contractor, and they complained that they repeatedly received rotten food. The pork was wormy, and the maggots in the soup had to be skimmed off. Neighbors took pity on them and supplemented their rations.[28]

Slowly the emergency wound down and order returned to the city, but the riot had given the Confederacy a brief moment of hope. The *Richmond Dispatch* wrote, "The red battle flag now waves in New York over streets wet with the gore of Lincoln's hated minions." But there was no enduring benefit for the South. New York City went back to normal, complaining about the administration and the war.

As the riot quieted, Archbishop Hughes extended an invitation on placards around town to the men of New York to meet at his house on Friday, July 17. Ironically, the archbishop had previously favored conscription as the only fair way to provide for the nation's manpower needs. A draft could apply to rich and poor alike. He had seen his congregation decrease as the number of poor widows and orphans increased. Hundreds gathered outside his residence as he addressed the crowd in his purple robes. It was a rambling speech, undoubtedly intended, like Seymour's, to calm the situation, and yet it was unsatisfying. He began, "They call you rioters. I cannot see a rioter's face among you ... I address you as your father ... no doubt there are some real grievances, but still I think there are many imaginary ones." He praised Ireland, made no accusations against the rioters, and assured everyone that they had a right to defend their homes. But "as Irishmen and Catholics" they had no cause to complain about the government. He advised them to go home and keep out of danger.[29] By the time the archbishop finished his speech, his listeners were confused. They did not realize that he was a sick man and did not have long to live. In any event, his remarks were anticlimactic. The worst of the riot was over.

Joseph Choate thought that the archbishop "behaved like the Devil," nor was Governor Seymour much better. Choate did not expect the courts to punish the rioters because "they are all in the hands of the Irish." Maria Daly may have reflected a wider sentiment. She regretted the "cruelties" but was not unhappy with the possibility that the blacks might have been taught a lesson. Since the war began, she said, "they have been so insolent as to be unbearable."[30]

Although the prevalence of the Irish among the rioters was unquestioned, law-abiding Irish in the city were chagrined. The dichotomy among the Irish was absurd. Irish rioters were put down by Irish police and soldiers. Irish priests risked their lives to protect and feed the blacks during the worst days. Paulists patrolled the streets to cool raging tempers. Father Treanor of Transfiguration prevented a lynching of blacks, Father McMahan of St. John the Evangelist talked a mob out of destroying Columbia College, and Father Quarter deflected other troublemakers from burning down a house. A. F. Warburton, an Irish-American, abhorred the burning of the Colored Orphan Asylum and wrote, "My blood has tingled with shame." Patrick Keady, president of the New York Practical House Painters Association, sent a letter to members of the union, most of whom were Irish. "I do not for a moment," he wrote "suppose that any of you took part in the late riots. You are too well aware of your own interests to do that ... disgraceful scenes [by] thieving rascals of this and adjacent cities, who have never done a day's work in their lives."[31]

The Roman Catholic *New York Tablet* decried the participation of all rioters, especially the Irish. "There is no denying it! ... Shame! Shame on such Irishmen, they are a disgrace to the country from which they came." The *Tablet* considered itself the only loyal Catholic newspaper in the city and with good reason. The extreme *Metropolitan Record,* according to the *Tablet,* "is openly disloyal and would much better suit the neighborhood of Richmond than New York." Most "respectable" Catholics had stopped reading the *Metropolitan Record,* and Archbishop Hughes, once closely associated with the paper, had given up writing articles for it. Oddly, the *Tablet,* with a much larger circulation than the *Record,* did not receive the patronage of the city. The *Metropolitan Record* was one of the newspapers granted the financial plum of publishing notices of the city corporation, not the *Tablet.*[32]

Although many workingmen may not have been involved, the riot did indicate discontent among the working classes. The poor man's sense of injustice mingled with racial hatred, partisan politics, criminality, anxiety for peace, disillusion with Lincoln's administration, and mob furor. They were frustrated and confused with their lives that knew little except the miseries of poverty, and the draft threat made them even more fearful of the future. The draft became their excuse to vent their emotions and excuse their barbaric behavior. In ignorance, they victimized others without realizing that they victimized themselves.

Rumors, and later legends, magnified the casualties of the riot until the count reached a thousand or more deaths. The most authoritative estimates place the total number of deaths at 119, including all doubtful reports. As may have been expected, the Irish suffered the greatest losses. In one list of death certificates for rioters, 52 of 82 had Irish names. In addition, 178 soldiers and police and 128 civilians were wounded. Although less ghastly than the wild casualty figures that were rumored around the city, this was still the worst riot ever to occur in the United States. The cost to the country and city was about $1.5 million in damages and claims. Even more significant, this episode, unlike most American riots, was directed against the government as well as the rich and blacks.[33]

A. T. Stewart sent Mayor Opdyke $5,000 for a relief fund for police, firemen, and soldiers who were wounded in the riot and for families of those killed. Leonard Jerome sent $1,000. Members of the New York Stock Exchange forwarded another $5,000 for the fund, and there were many other contributions. Rewards were also offered by the city for the discovery, arrest, and conviction of the murderers.[34]

Sympathy extended to the black people, too. At the end of the riot there were hordes of homeless blacks. One estimate claimed that more than three thousand had no place to live in the city and others sought refuge in the surrounding countryside. Hundreds had gone into hiding on Long Island and in the woods along the Harlem River. Some had gone to Hoboken to escape the wrath of the rioters. A Committee of Merchants for the Relief of Colored People Suffering from the Late Riots in the City of New York immediately went to work to relieve conditions. It collected $40,779 and with the help of black clergymen investigated individual needs and doled out the money. The aim of the committee was to go beyond the emergency and create conditions whereby blacks could support themselves without being molested. Its report noted that black people had seldom depended on charity in the past and had always been generous in helping those in distress. The committee was sensitive to the difficulties blacks would have in resuming normal lives. Many were still harassed in the streets and others lost their jobs because employers feared their presence would cause trouble. Some railroad cars that had previously accepted black passengers now refused them rides. Quietly, the committee successfully used its influence with the railroad companies to return to their previous practice and also helped find jobs for the unemployed.

During August 1863, the committee assisted six thousand blacks. Most of the male recipients were laborers and longshoremen, drivers for cartmen, and waiters. But there were also 11 ministers, 8 carpenters, 2 engravers, 3 music teachers, and a physician. Most of the female recipients were "day's work women," but there were also 163 seamstresses, 4 teachers, 13 nurses, and 1 artist.[35]

Despite fears about hiring blacks, a number of commercial firms expressed the intention of employing them in the future. Some businessmen believed the practice could alleviate costly work stoppages. *Harper's Weekly* commented, "Employers who heretofore preferred Irishmen to negroes are now going to take into consideration the riotous propensities of the former, and for the sake of their business — to which interruption is loss and possible ruin — at all events to dilute their operative force with enough colored men to rescue themselves against the chance of another Irish riot." But these were ideas that quickly faded.[36]

Although hundreds and probably thousands of men, women, and children engaged in unlawful behavior during the outbreak, the chief instigators may not have exceeded three hundred. Yet few of the rioters were brought to justice. The district attorney in Manhattan was "Elegant Oakey" Hall, once a Republican, who had been elected to the position with the endorsement of Mozart Hall. He had attended Harvard and graduated from New York University. It was said that August Belmont brought him into the Democratic fold. His father had been in the wholesale grocery business in New Orleans, and the son had shown considerable sympathy for the South and slavery. He regarded the Democratic party as a "refuge from fanaticism which threatened to engulf the Union." He also had a taste for literary life and wrote skits that were produced at the Olympic Theater. At a trial in the Court of General Sessions, Hall said that he loathed the conscription law as much as anyone, but the law had to be upheld and the mob suppressed. Some of the rioters whom he brought to trial soon after the event received severe sentences, but they were exceptions. Almost 450 men and women were arrested, but only 81 were brought to trial and only 67 of that number were convicted, mostly with short sentences.[37]

Dealers in lethal weapons were treated with surprising leniency after the riot. Late in July, Mayor Opdyke learned that Sidney Roberts of 80 Broadway was selling hand grenades indiscriminately, and it was feared that they might have been bought for use in a future outbreak. Opdyke simply wrote Roberts a letter requesting that he sell only to those who were "assuredly loyal." That, he explained, was the policy of other dealers in grenades, and he hoped Roberts would do the same.[38]

The draft remained a problem to be resolved. Early in August, Governor Seymour wrote to the president protesting the high quota assigned to the city and requesting that the draft be suspended. Manton Marble wrote to the president expressing his concern about the constitutionality of the draft and his belief that the law should have been tested in the courts. He admitted that government troops had quelled the riot "without usurping more than necessary local authority," but he agreed with Seymour that the draft should be postponed until a decision of the courts could be announced to the people, whom he was certain would abide by a judicial decision. It was best, he said, to work "within Democratic ideals." The Board of Aldermen also had constitutional concerns about the conscription act and proposed an ordinance to relieve the city of its "unequal operation." The mayor rejected the proposal with the comment that it was "common to characterize all distasteful laws as unconstitutional." The questionable constitutionality of the conscription act may have been the best argument of its opponents, but the man in the White House was not impressed.[39]

John A. Stevens, Jr., was alarmed that the government even listened to pleas for a change in the draft. Any alteration in the plan, he said, would be a "virtual admission of the right of the mob." He reminded Chase that a "compromising disposition" in 1861 had ended in disaster and the same attitude could bring another disaster. He did not think the draft had much to do with the recent riot, which he thought was inspired by hatred for Negroes and a desire to plunder instigated by rebel sympathizers and the friends of Governor Seymour. If the new draft call produced another riot, it would be the Republicans in the city who would be in danger of losing their lives and property. But Stevens was assured that the Republicans had only one opinion: "Let the draft go on. If the Govt. be not maintained what warranty have we of life or limb."[40]

Lincoln had no intention of stopping the draft. He wrote to Seymour that he could not consent to such action because "time is too important." He did not object to abiding by a decision of the Supreme Court on the constitutionality of the draft law, and he would be glad to facilitate such a case. But he could not wait while it was sought. "We are contending," he said, "with an enemy who, as I understand it, drives every able bodied man he can reach, into his ranks, very much as a butcher drives bullocks into a slaughter pen. No time is wasted, no argument is used. This produces an army which will soon turn upon our now victorious soldiers already in the field, if they shall not be sustained by recruits."[41]

Despite Seymour's complaints about the draft and the high quota for New York City, the federal government set another day for the call to commence. Lincoln reduced the number of draftees and agreed to a commission to study the draft in New York, but on August 19, 1863, the draft began again.

About two weeks after the riot was quelled, General Dix replaced the aging General Wool, whom some believed had not done enough during the riot. Wool had been criticized for doing too much on his own authority at the outbreak of the war. His selection to replace Wool, however, was as much political as military. He was a good choice because he was a prominent Democrat as well as an able man who loyally supported the government. Dix, a firm leader, issued orders to his troops to use live ammunition and "not only to disperse the mob, but to follow them up, and so deal with them that the same persons should never be assembled again." Dix warned the citizenry of New York shortly before the new call that any disturbance of the peace would be met with prompt and vigorous measures. He did not want any misunderstanding. The draft law, he said, was founded on the principle that every citizen who enjoys the protection of the government is liable to be summoned in time of danger to take up arms in the common defense. Permission to furnish a substitute or buy exemption was simply to provide for hardship cases.[42]

Dix was especially apprehensive because he thought that Governor Seymour might try to block the draft and provoke a clash between the state and federal governments. He was convinced that opposition to the draft was simply a subterfuge for giving aid to the Confederates. Dix did not intend his words to be idle. He telegraphed the provost marshal general in Washington on August[12] that he ought to have ten thousand troops in the city when the draft resumed. "That there is widespread disaffection in this city," he wired, "and that the opposition to the draft has been greatly increased by Governor Seymour's letters cannot be doubted."[43]

Dix was not alone in anticipating trouble. Harriet Seaver, for one, agreed. She lived in an Irish neighborhood, and she said "their [the Irish] looks and actions" since the riot filled her with horror. Even the children were "vipers." She cleaned and loaded an old pistol and decided to remain at home and defend herself.[44]

When the critical day arrived, Dix wisely kept his troops in the background, and the draft proceeded. Nevertheless, the entire police force was under special orders, and soldiers were evident at the Battery and Madison Square. Navy ships stood by in both rivers and the upper bay in the event of an emergency. At 185 Sixth Avenue, office of the provost marshal of the Sixth District, the wheel, a wooden box with an axle mounted on a frame, turned, and a confirmed blind man drew the names of conscripts. There was no disturbance. The law of the land prevailed over the mob and August 19 passed quietly. "The gorilla appeared to have gone out of town," wrote *Harper's Weekly*.

The Common Council had tried to ease the pain for conscripts by passing a resolution on July 15 while the riot was in full force. The councilmen were not concerned with vigorous pursuit of the war. Their objective was to appease a violent population and protect their own political hides. The resolution called for an appropriation of $2.5 million "to relieve the City of New York from the unequal operation of the conscription." The comptroller was to pay $300 for each person drafted who was found unable to pay, and any drafted person who agreed to serve three years would receive $300. Mayor Opdyke, however, rejected the resolution as too vague.

Before the new draft call commenced in August, the Common Council passed another expensive measure appropriating $3 million for the payment of $300 commutation money for a poor man with a dependent family. The draftee could serve in the army and give the money to his family or buy a substitute. This popular move was intended to take the sting out of the draft, and it was believed that the mayor would give his approval. Instead, Opdyke waited until the call had started in an orderly manner and then vetoed the proposed ordinance.

The mayor's veto message declared that disbursing $3 million without auditing provisions was too unwieldy. The loosely written ordinance, he said, could be interpreted to permit any indigent person, with or without a family, to stay at home without anyone taking his place. According to Opdyke, it "would virtually render the draft a nullity in this city" and gladden the hearts of those trying to destroy the Union. He asked, "What would be thought of a Common Council which should seriously propose to pay all fines assessed upon non-attending jurors?" He thought the principle was the same, and he saw no reason why the poor should be exempt from serving in a war that was waged in the interest of poor men. Besides, the tax burden in the city was already too heavy.

Opdyke's arguments might have been more persuasive if his son had not provided a perfect example of favoritism for the rich and discrimination against the poor. His name was called for the draft, and he quickly paid the commutation fee. The next man called, Timothy O'Hara, could not afford $300 for exemption, and he quickly ended up in the army. It was a blatant example of unfairness.

Opdyke tried to show some sympathy for the masses by suggesting a compromise. He said there were two legitimate purposes for appropriating money from the city treasury in connection with the draft: to procure substitutes for those who served in the fire and police departments and the city militia and to provide for destitute families of those who served in the army. The mayor was willing to accept an ordinance to meet these situations. The Common Council, however, was in no mood to compromise. The councilmen and aldermen met immediately and pledged to pass the $3 million ordinance over the mayor's veto at the expiration of the necessary lapse of ten days. The Common Council was not worried about sham indigents, runaway substitutes, plundering the city treasury, or destroying the draft.

Meanwhile, in a surprise move, the Board of Supervisors, a body primarily concerned with tax appraisals, concluded that the Common Council and mayor would never agree and passed its own ordinance appropriating $2 million for the exemption of firemen, policemen, and city militia. Certain cases of indigents with dependent families would also be exempt. The mayor, comptroller, and supervisors William Tweed and Orison Blunt were to serve as a committee to hear cases and carry out the provisions of the ordinance. This measure was acceptable to Opdyke because it was similar to his own suggestions.

The unusual move by the Board of Supervisors caught the Common Council off guard, but amid much bluster and denunciation, the council passed its $3 million ordinance over the mayor's veto and charged that the Board of Supervisors had no right to pass its competing ordinance. The corporation counsel supported this view by giving his opinion that the only board of relief was the Common Council. But it did not matter. The ordinance never went into effect.

The *Times* called the overriding veto by the Common Council a "ludicrous farce," which merely passed a defunct ordinance to carry out the council's previous pledge to a populace that hated the draft. An editorial asked why it was more difficult for New Yorkers to bear arms than citizens in other parts of the country. The *Times* answered its own question by saying that New York City was distinctive because of the mob action and because there were more rich to levy taxes on to pay the bill than elsewhere.

As the days passed, the tempest over the competing ordinances faded and the Board of Supervisors set up ward auxiliary committees to hear cases appealing for exemption. The mayor and Board of Supervisors placed a want ad for ten thousand substitutes, "To Whom three hundred dollars will be paid by the County Substitute and Relief Committee." All those interested were to apply immediately at 71 and 73 Duane Street.[45]

The Common Council members appeared to be content with having displayed their intent, made a public show of their disgust for the draft, and spoken for the poor of the city. They could claim that as men of good faith they had done their best to fulfill their pledge to the people. The draft was never strictly administered, and certificates for exemption from duty for physical disability were generously distributed. A "poor general constitution" or a "severe cough" could often get one exempted from service. A Dr. Thomas Brinsmade said that exemptions issued for a large number of diseases was greater than generally known. The provost marshal in New York City called almost eighty thousand men, but only twenty-three hundred went directly into the army. The others were exempted, commutated, or bought substitutes.[46] Soon avoiding the draft became an organized business. Thompkins and Company, located at 645 Broadway, advertised that the "New York Draft Assurance Association will this week, for $10, guarantee an undrafted party exemption from the draft. For $25 we will furnish any drafted party with an acceptable substitute. At these rates we simply take the risks of an ordinary life insurance company."[47]

In September, the Common Council, still showing an antimilitary attitude, passed a resolution to clear troops out of the Battery and other city parks. Opdyke vetoed the resolution. He said the troops could prevent "a repetition of the scenes of arson, pillage, and murder" that took place in July. Fears of another riot lingered, but the struggle to earn a living occupied most people's minds and helped suppress the unpleasant memories.[48]

12
Living

The violence of the riot hurt the poor more than the rich and may be interpreted as demonstrating that self-destruction was an inherent part of poverty. But the poor of the city had to fight other enemies in addition to themselves, and one of the worst was inflation. A list of taxable incomes for 1863 portrays the lopsided economic situation. The upper 1 percent of income earners consisted of only about sixteen hundred families who made about 61 percent of the income of the city. This inequity existed even though the war provided employment opportunities for the poor. And a sharp reduction in immigration stemmed competition in the labor market. Potential immigrants feared involvement in the American war, and as a result fewer aliens arrived in 1861 and 1862 than in any year since 1847. But wages did not keep pace with prices, and workingmen and women and their families suffered. It was estimated that in July 1863 retail prices rose 43 percent from 1860 but wages were up only 12 percent.

Since the start of the war, food prices had doubled and tripled. In 1861, lamb cost ten cents a pound and rose to twenty-three cents by 1863; mutton went from six to eight to thirteen to fifteen cents; and beef rose from eight to ten to fifteen to eighteen cents. Coffee jumped to fifty cents a pound from a low of ten cents, and sugar climbed from five to twenty cents. To make matters worse, quality went down as prices went up. Wheat was often impure, loaves of bread were smaller, and coffee was often adulterated.

The cost of housing also went up. Rents rose 15 to 20 percent, coal went up more than 30 percent, and wood 20 percent. The war brought home building to a near standstill, and the poor were crowded into thousands of dark, ill-ventilated, unhealthy tenements. Mark Twain reported to a San Francisco newspaper that a city inspector claimed that more than half a million New Yorkers lived in fifteen thousand tenements and some built for eight families "swarmed with two or three hundred persons." These struggling masses had no time to think of war on a grand scale or such abstractions as courage, honor, and duty. Each day they stubbornly fought their own private wars to survive in the squalid surroundings that rarely provided an escape to a better way of life.[1]

The cellar population grew to alarming proportions. Captain Lord of the Sanitary Police made a survey that indicated that more than twenty-two thousand people lived in cellars. He also found four thousand tenements that had no fire escapes and about the same number that were badly ventilated. An estimated twenty thousand squatters lived in deplorable conditions. In the worst areas, plumbing was almost nonexistent. Much of the city lacked sewers, and trenches dug a foot or so into the ground in the backyards served as toilets. Waste water and slops were thrown into the gutter. Cholera among infants swept through the slums in the summer and smallpox in the winter. Typhoid and typhus were persistent threats in the poor downtown wards near the East River and in the neighborhood of East Thirty-second and Thirty-third streets between First and Second avenues. The lax street cleaning by politically assigned contractors was a perpetual problem, and the accumulation of filth contributed to the spread of sickness. Hospitals were crowded with patients with contagious diseases. Six young physicians at Bellevue contracted typhus and died and several staff members became seriously ill. As the mortality rate climbed, the city inspector reported that the city had never been so vile.[2]

The few housing regulations in the city were generally ignored without penalty, and major landlords such as William Astor found it worthwhile to remain on friendly terms with Tammany Hall and the city administration. Astor had not approved of Fernando Wood, but he always found it good business to meet the mayor at least halfway. During the war, Astor was happy with the high returns on his investments and did not think the condition of the poor was his responsibility.

The shortage of housing raised rents for the middle class and rich, too. Homes located between Fourteenth and Twenty-third streets on Madison or Fifth avenues brought rentals of $2,000 to $5,000 a year. Before the war, the same houses rented for $1,000 to $3,000. A block or two one way or the other in New York City could make a big difference in rent. The up-and-coming Joseph Choate leased a house for five years at

93 West Twenty-first Street between Sixth and Seventh avenues for $700 a year. He said it was neither fine nor fashionable, but it was comfortable. Steadily on the rise, he produced a substantial income. "It is comfortable to have a comfortable income," he wrote his wife. But he was not pleased when he paid an income tax of $550, which he thought was "a little too heavy."[3]

Clothing was another big expense. Even the relatively well-to-do hesitated to buy clothes. Edmund Stedman, a Wall Street operator, wrote, "Today, with great difficulty, I pay $50 for my new overcoat. Three years ago 'twould have cost $25. So much for war prices, high tariff, reign of shoddy."[4] Professors at New York University were among the many in the middle class who were hurt by inflation. They claimed that no similar institution paid such low salaries to its faculty and appealed to the university council for an increase to $2,000 a year.[5]

The busy garment industry, flushed with military contracts, created more jobs for women. But discrimination against women was an accepted practice that few questioned. Women normally received half the wages men did for the same work. Sewing girls working on underwear were paid as little as seventeen cents for a twelve-hour day. Girls making cotton shirts received twenty-four cents a day but had to supply their own thread. A "baster" of cavalry pantaloons made thirty-two cents a day, and a woman, working fourteen hours, received sixty-eight cents for making a boy's suit. Two linen coats could be made in a long day for twenty cents each. Sewing bindings of books was more profitable. Women performing that job were paid one of the highest wages, seventy-five cents a day. Some women could have made more money in domestic service, but they looked upon the work as an indignity that placed them on the same level with Irish and blacks.[6] The pathetic need of women for money was often evident in the want ad columns. It was not unusual to see an ad such as the one placed by a "respectable married woman" who "has a good fresh breast of milk" and wanted to serve as a wet nurse.[7]

Discontented working women tried to improve their conditions by holding a mass meeting with the backing of a number of workingmen's unions in the city. It resulted in the formation of the Working Women's Protective Union late in 1863. In the following year the union ran a placement bureau, which found jobs for thirty-six hundred women. Despite miserable pay, one of the chief grievances of women was nonpayment for work, and the association sought legal help. One of its strongest supporters was Judge Daly.[8] An exception in the depressing picture for female employment was Margaret Getchell, who worked for R. H. Macy. A former schoolteacher from Nantucket, she went to work for Macy as a cashier, and he soon promoted her to bookkeeper. She was tactful as well as having a good head for numbers and gained the respect of everyone. Her talent as an executive and merchandiser impressed the hardworking Macy, who increasingly relied on her. In time, she became superintendent of the store. It was not unusual for women to work in retail stores, especially with the shortage of manpower during the war. But it was unusual for a woman to hold such a responsible position. Macy, unlike many employers, had always been quick to hire women. Although he did not pay any more than was necessary, he was friendly by nature and could be kind and generous in specific instances. Normal store hours were a grueling ten hours, six days a week, and no one worked harder than Macy, who was usually at the store late into the night.[9] Retail clerks, male or female, were not well paid as a rule. Charles Rogers, one of A. T. Stewart's "nice young men," received a promotion from the fine white goods department to embroideries, which pleased him, except for his annual salary of $500, which did not make him particularly happy. Nevertheless, a wage of $300 a year for such work was not unusual.[10]

Labor organizations multiplied rapidly in the city, even though sentiment against unions for men as well as women was strong. The Chamber of Commerce tried to destroy the molders' and machinists' unions and employers' associations organized during the summer of 1863 and fostered blacklists of trade unionists and lockouts.[11]

Despite the problems of the poor, improved employment helped many lower-income people open savings accounts and start a nest egg. The Bank for Savings in the City of New York was one of many banks that opened thousands of new accounts during the war for laboring-class persons. Many of the accounts held small amounts, but the average size of deposits increased.[12]

Some workmen, especially skilled workmen, saw sharp rises in their pay. According to John Roach, who built the engines for William Webb's *Dunderberg*, wages of machinists climbed rapidly from $3.50 to $4.50 a day in August 1862 to $4.00 to $5.75 a day in November and $5.00 to $6.50 in December. Government shipyards paid high wages to attract employees, and private shipyards, to the irritation of their owners, had to meet government offers. Increased payroll costs plus the rise in the cost of metal from $20 a ton in 1862 to $80 a ton in 1864 forced William Webb to petition Congress for relief in his contract to build the *Dunderberg* and contributed to the delay in construction. He claimed that the price of some materials rose 100 percent to 150 percent between 1862 and 1864.[13]

Mayor Opdyke, taking credit for a partial return of prosperity, emphasized the increase in employment and in imports and exports and the ready sale of real estate at higher prices during his administration. The city treasury also accounted for more money in circulation. Opdyke repeatedly vetoed spendthrift measures from the Common Council in his efforts to retrench, but he fought a continuing and often losing battle. About half a million dollars had been paid in bounties to volunteers during 1862 and more than $1.2 million for relief to soldiers' families. The latter expenditure, in excess of Opdyke's recommendation, was controlled by the Common Council, which did not please him. He correctly considered the councilmen's political supervision inexpedient if not fraudulent, but he did not use his veto in that case because he considered the purpose worthy.[14]

Despite the suffering of the poor, new rich arose and the old rich got richer. The contrasts were as sharp as ever. Hamilton Fish, despondent during the difficult years of the war, was especially depressed at seeing people make money through political contacts and outright corruption. The value of real and personal property increased, and in 1863 A. T. Stewart paid income tax on an annual income of $1,843,637. William Astor and Cornelius Vanderbilt were almost in the same class. Aggressive money-makers, some honest, some dishonest, some loyal, some disloyal, found business opportunities as never before. The *New York Independent* estimated that several hundred men in the city were worth $1 million and some were worth $20 million. Twenty years before, the paper said, there were not five men in the United States with as much as $5 million.[15]

Military victories and defeats created a topsy-turvy stock market. Actions on the exchange reflected the fortunes of war and made advance information a valuable asset. J. P. Morgan installed the first private telegraph wire in his office, and his operator was a friend of Grant's telegrapher, who often supplied the latest word on military movements.[16] Wall Street speculators thrived on uncertainty, and each day brought new excitement. Railroad securities were especially active. The New

York Central stock rose from 87 to 130 between January 1862 and January 1863. The record of the Erie Railroad was more striking. Earnings jumped from $5 million in 1860 to $10 million in 1863, and the stock price vaulted from 17 to 126½. In August, the *Herald* estimated that railroad securities had increased in market value within the past year at least $500 million. The rush to buy and sell stock fattened brokers' profits. Major brokerage firms frequently made $5,000 a day in commissions.[17]

E. A. Pollard, editor of the *Richmond Examiner,* wrote bitterly that the war in the North was in many respects "nothing more than an immense money job ... it enriched the commercial centres of the North, and by artificial stimulation preserved such cities as New York from decay." If he had spent a day on Wall Street watching the trading, he might have been doubly convinced of the truth of his accusation.[18]

A visitor to the Gold Room, amazed by what he saw, wrote, "Men leaped upon chairs, waved their hands, or clenched their fists; shrieked, shouted; the bulls whistled 'Dixie,' and the bears sung 'John Brown;' the crowd swayed feverishly from door to door, and as the fury mounted to white heat, and the tide of gold fluctuated up and down in rapid sequence, brokers seemed animated with the impulses of demons, hand-to-hand combats took place, and bystanders, peering through the smoke and dust, could liken the wild turmoil only to the revel of maniacs." The rise and fall of gold prices could make anyone excited. In April 1862, the price of gold was 100½. By the end of January 1863, it was 160, and in March it was about 139. And greater fluctuations were still to come.[19]

When the Philadelphia financier Jay Cooke came to town to promote the sale of war bonds, speculators were irritated. He seemed entirely too patriotic to them. In turn, Cooke looked upon gold speculators as the nearest thing to traitors.

The sense that a quick fortune was within easy reach increased the gambling fever and attracted new people to Wall Street. Never before had the market appealed to so many. Strange new economic forces were at work, and the desire to make a killing could not be resisted. The veteran investor Henry Clews did not think women had the capacity for finance and considered them financial parasites. Nonetheless, many housewives dared to enter this new world. Some of the so-called crinoline of Wall Street pledged their diamonds for margin and astounded their husbands with their success. Women did not engage in the noisy melee on Wall Street. Frequently they sat in carriages nearby or in back offices, where they issued their instructions to brokers. A ladies board was said to have set up in one of the Broadway hotels.

The Fifth Avenue Hotel was a busy place after hours for buying and selling stocks. The board of the stock exchange was distressed by this outside activity and tried to prohibit its members from this or other evening exchanges. Its resolution to that effect failed to pass, however, and it had to be satisfied with requesting members not to participate in these gatherings.[20] The New York Stock Exchange was not only an exclusive club, it was a very profitable one. The board took great pains to limit membership so that profits would not be spread too thin. Competition from the other exchanges sprouting up in the city was unwelcome. Stocks and bonds were as much a subject of conversation as the most recent news from the battlefront. Tips were exchanged and opinions given with and without knowledge. By 1863, the Stock and Exchange Board was officially known as the New York Stock Exchange, but it did not merge with its major rival, the Open Board of Stock Brokers, until after the war.

From time to time the board of the New York Stock Exchange put aside business matters and offered resolutions to donate money to charity. The Sanitary Commission, the Christian Commission, the "Military Kitchen" at Fort Schuyler, and the Colored Orphan Asylum were among the recipients of its beneficence. Henry Bellows, who was in a position to know, said that the chief philanthropists in the city were the active businessmen, not the idle rich.[21]

Not all speculators were outwardly emotional in their approach to profit making. Young Jay Gould, quiet and somewhat shy, kept his thoughts to himself as his penetrating black eyes searched for every advantage. He cautiously made a trade or formed a pool, and in time his shrewdness paid off. Before the war ended, he joined forces with the bold Jim Fisk and the cadaverous, shifty Daniel Drew, and with their holdings in the Erie Railroad started to do battle with the great Cornelius Vanderbilt and the New York Central.[22]

In the self-seeking atmosphere of Wall Street, the secretary of the treasury had difficulty raising money for the increasingly expensive war and looked to his friend Jay Cooke for assistance. Chase appointed Cooke as an agent for selling "Five-Twenties," twenty-year bonds that paid 6 percent interest in gold. This apparent favoritism for Cooke annoyed Assistant Treasurer Cisco and New York financiers, who thought that advice should be sought from Philadelphia only after New York, the premier financial center, had taken a position. But Chase had not received the vigorous aid he needed when he solicited offers in New York. He was either ignored or demands were made for a considerable discount below par. Chase realized that he had to seek buyers in all parts of the country in an aggressive campaign, and the Treasury Department was not geared for such action.

After a meeting with Chase, Henry Cooke wrote to his brother about the sensitive New York financiers, who felt they were mistreated by the secretary of the treasury: "The fact is I am convinced that they kicked up something of a 'row' because instead of going to them directly he [Chase] went to them through a third person [Cooke]. They are as bad as our generals in the field. They would rather the public interests should suffer than that their petty pride should be rubbed by a fancied slight." Cooke created confidence in government bonds throughout the country and accepted enormous responsibility. As the sole subscription agent for the sale, he became known as the financier of the Civil War. He organized subagencies throughout the United States, and much of his success could be attributed to positive salesmanship and advertising in newspapers. Cooke's agents in New York, however, used their own names and did not like to admit that the loan came to them through Philadelphia. His leading New York agents were Fisk and Hatch; Livermore, Clews and Company; and Vermilye and Company. The Cookes' assessment of the attitude of New York financiers seemed accurate. In May 1863, the *New York World* criticized Chase for giving "to this house [Jay Cooke] a monopoly of the five-twenty funding business instead of doing the business by accredited assistant treasurers in the different states." The Cookes had their own interests to serve, but they stepped into a void and performed a real service for their country. Even Cisco had to admit that Cooke's commission of 3/8 of 1 percent was low and the risk was high.[23]

Wall Street was not the only place in the city where men and women scrambled for riches. War contracts brought prosperity to machine shops that produced iron forgings, castings, and marine engines. Phelps, Dodge & Company on Clift Street made money in metal and held large acreages of timber, iron, and coal. Insurance companies accumulated large sums of money, which were invested in a variety of ways. Mutual Life of New York doubled the number of policies it held during the war. The success of insurance companies did not come solely from soldiers going to war. Much of their income came from marine insurance, accident insurance, which was new, and fire insurance. Atlantic Mutual announced a dividend of 40 percent in one war year, and dividends of other companies ran from 6 to 20 percent.

Trade through New York Harbor also continued to do well with heavy increases in agricultural exports. Petroleum was also becoming an important export item. In 1863, almost half a million barrels of petroleum left New York. Some exports, however, looked suspicious.[24] In 1863, the navy reported that a shipload of army wagons, critically needed by the Confederacy, had been cleared by the New York customhouse for shipment to Matamoros, Mexico. Suddenly, trade through Matamoros had awakened. In 1863, seventy-two ships arrived in the Mexican port from New York. And, of course, trade between Matamoros and the Confederacy jumped.[25]

An increase in both imports and exports between New York and Nassau also became evident. By 1862, trade rose between these two points more than $400,000 over 1860. A large part of the goods arriving in New York from Nassau obviously came from the Confederacy. At the same time, shipments from Great Britain reached New York for transfer to Nassau, where they were transferred again to blockade runners. Hiram Barney, collector of the port, was fully aware that even "noncontraband" shipments were suspicious. He reported one cargo of "sulphate of quinine in quantities of one thousand ounces, chloroform by the hundred pounds, surgical instruments by the dozen cases, cotton cards by the hundred dozen, and uniforms or clothing for the army."[26]

In 1862, Congress had authorized the secretary of the treasury to block the clearance of ships that might end up, directly or indirectly, in Confederate ports. To carry out the act, Barney required a bond from the master or shipowner equal to the value of the cargo as a guarantee that the cargo would actually arrive at the given destination. New York was the only port that called for such a bond for cargoes to Nassau, and shipowners voiced strong complaints about this interference even though the trade continued.

Money was important to New Yorkers. They enjoyed making it, but they also enjoyed spending it, especially on gala occasions. Hotels and boardinghouses were full of young men in uniform, many with oak leaves or eagles on their shoulders, and they wanted a good time. Although many in the city never believed that soldiers were welcomed as warmly as in Boston or Philadelphia, New York had never been so lively, and young ladies of good and not so good social standing kept busy entertaining them.

In September 1863, an unexpected opportunity for extravagant partying arrived. A fleet of Russian warships sailed into the harbor in an apparent show of friendship for the United States. Americans believed that Russia would be a good ally if England or France caused more trouble. Official records later revealed that the Russians feared a war with France and Great Britain over their treatment of the Poles and wanted their ships out of ice-clogged British-controlled waters for the winter.[27]

The city wined and dined the Russian commander, Admiral Lisovski, and his officers and men. The Russians, undoubtedly to their amazement, became a popular craze. The convivial Common Council wasted no time offering the hospitality of the city. A delegation from the council took a boat to Admiral Lisovski's flagship riding in the harbor to present their welcome and escort him to City Hall. The Russians greeted the delegation with a twenty-one-gun salute and their best rendition of "Yankee Doodle."

Andre Fremont, an urbane alderman, read resolutions thanking the Russians for their courtesies to the United States, particularly "during the present unfortunate difficulties," and tendering hospitality. The resolutions, engrossed on silk with a roller, tassels, and a case, were given to Lisovski. The admiral expressed his appreciation and broke out bumpers of champagne. He toasted the president of the United States, and Alderman Fremont, rising to the diplomatic occasion, toasted the emperor of Russia. The fall day was magnificent, and the entire First Division of the National Guard joined the procession to City Hall, where Mayor Opdyke welcomed the Russians with a speech. Even the streets were clean, or cleaner, for the occasion.

A banquet at the Astor House for three hundred persons was said to have cost $10,000, but the peak of extravagance was a municipal affair at the Academy of Music attended by the mayor and a large assortment of city dignitaries. Photographs of Russian and American officers recently taken at Brady's gallery on Broadway lined the walls, and the auditorium for dancing was decorated with "groves of oranges and citrons" and "bowers of myrtle and jessamine." The guests indulged in a wide variety of delicacies that ranged from pigeon flavored with champagne to pies of fat goose liver Perigord. Among the numerous pastries and pies for dessert was charlotte russe. It was estimated that 12,000 oysters, 12 huge salmon weighing thirty pounds each, 1,200 game birds, 250 turkeys, 1,000 pounds of tenderloin, and 3,500 bottles of wine were consumed.

David Farragut, the Union's greatest naval hero, a native Tennessean, now made New York City his residence. He helped entertain the glamorous visitors, but he seemed lost in the crowd. Edwin Godkin, a British journalist, noticed the modest and unassuming officer standing unobtrusively in a corner. He was a small man in a plain uniform that appeared shabby compared with the splendor of the Russians. He talked quietly, and Godkin thought he was pensive and shy.

Some in the city, perhaps a little more astute or skeptical, were not pleased with the fuss over the Russians. Henry Bellows was aware of Russian hostility to England and guessed that they were glad to escape the frozen waters of the Baltic. But more important, he did not consider Russians "natural allies." Despite the American inclination to scrap with the British, he believed the United States had much more in common with Great Britain. Continued irritation of the British could lead to war, which he was sure would be popular, but he believed it would be against American interests. Yet the modest, kind, and courteous behavior of these visitors, who spoke very good English, impressed Bellows.[28]

The hospitality extended to the well-behaved Russians was not always consistent. As Russian sailors wandered about the city streets sightseeing, they were often taken advantage of by greedy merchants. Some Broadway stores demanded Russian gold coins for articles worth half the price in greenbacks. Like other crazes, the interest in the Russians was a passing fancy. New Yorkers finally had their fill of the "feast of flags" and "feast of trumpets." Some citizens felt guilty when they read that the ladies of the city who attended the Russian ball reputedly wore a million dollars worth of diamonds. Such display seemed sinful when Union soldiers were dying on the battlefield or starving in southern prisoner of war camps.[29] Before leaving, however, the Russian officers of the fleet showed their gratitude by collecting $4,760 to provide fuel for New York City's poor.[30]

Despite the turbulence of war and city life, a life of the mind also

existed in the city, and some intellectuals found time and sufficient soli-
tude to carry on their work. Richard G. White, a lawyer and music critic,
wrote a satire about Copperheads called *New Gospel of Peace* and produced the first major edition of Shakespeare. Professor John W. Draper
of New York University published his *History of the Intellectual Develop-
ment of Europe,* which attracted considerable attention, favorable and un-
favorable. The book emphasized faith in science and rejected superna-
tural ideas. Draper also lectured at the New-York Historical Society
during the war, and his talks became the basis of a book, *Thoughts on the
Future Civil Policy of the United States,* which concentrated on climate, immigration, and politics.

Francis Lieber, notwithstanding his multitude of assignments,
completed *Instructions for the Government of Armies of the United States in the
Field,* which was a humane step forward in international law. Lieber cod-
ified, or at least attempted to codify, proper conduct for an army at war.
The task was gigantic, and he faced such difficult questions as the treatment of prisoners, status of enemy property, looting, surrender, and the
rights of civilian populations. His code became General Order No. 100
of the Union army, and in time other nations adopted it.

Even the draft riot had intellectual consequences. Charles Loring
Brace, a social service worker, published *The Races of the Old World* in
1863. He had studied racial theories for some time, but the riot had disgusted him so much that he decided to attack "narrow prejudices" and
wrongheaded ideas about race. Influenced by Charles Darwin, he held
the view that biology indicated a unified origin, and he argued that the
human race had existed "hundreds of thousands of years before any of
the received dates of Creation" and started a controversy that attracted
a wide readership.[31]

Yet the city ignored its most talented author and native son. Herman Melville returned to New York in 1863 and took a house on East
Twenty-sixth Street, where he lived in obscurity. *Moby Dick,* written some
years before the war, was neither a critical nor a popular success, and
nothing he had written since had received substantial recognition. He
was now forty-four years old, his work was in a tailspin, and the little
prose and poetry that he produced did not match his earlier efforts. After the war, he worked as an unknown customs inspector. In 1891, almost thirty years later, he completed *Billy Budd,* but he died that year and

the novel was not published until 1924. The city did not always show kind, balanced, or necessarily wise judgment and acclaim for its inhabitants and visitors.

The controversial baiter Benjamin Wood published one of the most unusual wartime works. During these busy days, he was the only politician in the country to write a novel, which surely indicated his excess energy. It was called *Fort Lafayette: or Love or Secession,* and considering that the author was a man capable of bias that teetered on treason, the book appeared to be a fairly objective presentation. Although the novel may not have been great literature, no one could deny that it conveyed a profound message. And the author, despite his rascality, appeared as a serious, sincere, and almost evenhanded thinker. Wood created four major characters to represent varying viewpoints about the North and South. The southerners, Oriana Weems and her brother Beverly, were firm believers in states' rights and the consent of the governed. They bitterly resented the Union's "power of coercion." A third character, Harold Hare, was a northern nationalist, who minimized the importance of states' rights and regarded southerners as traitors. He had no doubt that the government had the "power to sustain itself" and that it was necessary to destroy the Confederacy. The fourth character, Arthur Wayne, served as the voice of moderation. He did not see any excuse to let the "horrors of war" run rampant. Wayne undoubtedly represented Wood. While the others saw war as a normal and expected part of life, Wayne argued that life was "too sacred" and with "God's help I shall not shed human blood." Although he was not a pacifist, he did not believe that the state had the right to destroy life, the "masterpiece of God," or to justify murder for the sake of the nation's survival. Wood pictured Wayne as an opponent of emotionalism and simplistic answers to complex problems, who wanted reason, applied Christianity, and compromise to prevail.[32]. The problem was how to achieve peace, and Wood's ideas were not workable because they were beyond human capability. Wood, like Samuel Barlow, deluded himself by believing that peace could be obtained through a reciprocal agreement. He refused to recognize the obstacle that peace seekers with human frailties could not overcome. Jefferson Davis and the Confederacy might recognize that slavery was a dying institution and give it up, but the South would not surrender its one remaining war goal, independence. And Abraham Lincoln and the Union were not going to grant that wish.

Humans had not reached the state of perfection that Wood required to accomplish his purpose. Nevertheless, his book was thought-provoking, idealistic, and farsighted. He understood the consequences of war. But Wood's curious book did not appear to change anyone's opinions. The war continued.

13

A New Mayor

L ocal politics held the spotlight in the fall of 1863. The mayoralty election was to be held in December, and the discussion of candidates, always a favorite subject, began early. Opdyke had no desire to run for reelection, and politicians wrangled about possible tickets over their steaks, wine, and cigars. The war had severely jarred party organizations in the city, and individuals often found that their current opinions and their old affiliations were at odds.

Democrats accused Republicans of starting the war, and Republicans accused Democrats of inciting the recent riot. James Gordon Bennett made the crude statement that the Republicans suffered with the "niggerheads" and the Democrats with the "copperheads." Such claims and counterclaims were, of course, oversimplifications. Intelligent citizens hoped for serious discussion of the issues, but in the end they would have to settle for the results that emerged from the local machinations. New factions had to be established because Democrats were torn over the war and Republicans were torn over the Lincoln administration.

This was also a gubernatorial election year, and the two overlapping campaigns competed for the electorate's interest. At a mass meeting at Cooper Institute Governor Seymour presented his view of the position of the Democratic party. He was running for reelection against Republican Reuben Fenton. Seymour declared, "We say most clearly that we are the party for stopping the war at the earliest possible period. ... Whatever other men may do we will contend for the Union as it was and we will have it. We will contend for the constitution as our fathers framed it."[1] But many Democrats searched for other alternatives. The election for governor took place in November, and when the votes were counted Fenton won by a majority of about thirty thousand. The state had become disillusioned with Seymour, and Republicans were pleased to see that the "disloyal" Democratic vote in the city was greatly reduced, probably a reaction against the draft riot. It seemed reasonable to assume that the new mayor, even if a Democrat, would give strong support to the war. But those who searched for a trend in the state election that might continue in the city election were deceived.

Municipal affairs disgusted most of the upper economic and social classes of the city, who were sure they received little in return for their high taxes and were victims of corrupt scoundrels elected to office by ignorant immigrants. *Harper's Weekly* called the popular system of government in the city a "ludicrous failure" and stated, "The most miserable and ignorant of other countries are shot into New York like rubbish: they become the willing slaves of the word Democracy; they are led by the demagogues who depend upon their votes for success; they are flattered by the capitalists who fear their excesses, and hope to purchase safety by the spell of 'fellow-Democrats.' " As a result, substantial citizens were overborne by those with no political principles or native attachments.[2]

In an effort to improve the tone of local politics, John Jacob Astor, Jr., and R. B. Roosevelt, representing a committee of merchants and citizens of New York, sought a meeting with President Lincoln to discuss "important business." A movement was under way to nominate General Dix, a Democrat, for mayor, and this was obviously the reason for their request. On November 8, Lincoln replied that he would be happy to meet with the committee. The next day, however, Lincoln wrote privately to Astor and others that it was beyond his province to interfere with New York City politics, but he would not place any restraint on Dix if he received the nomination.[3] Dix immediately settled the matter by telling Lincoln that he felt he could be more useful in the army and removed his name from consideration.

The campaign to name Dix as a mayoralty candidate continued briefly when some Democrats and Republicans met at a Union convention at Twenty-third Street and Broadway. But the effort failed, and the Unionists ended by nominating a Republican, Orison Blunt, a conservative Lincoln supporter, who was considered an honest and efficient member of the Board of Supervisors. Factional feuds marked other nominations. The increasingly influential William Tweed threw his weight behind his friend the reputedly corrupt Francis I. A. Boole, who had served as an alderman and was now city inspector. The Irish were somewhat disenchanted with Boole because he had recently made too many kind remarks about black people. Nevertheless, Boole received the backing of both Tammany and Mozart Halls.[4]

Tweed was becoming an important political presence in the city. He was a natural leader. Overweight and almost six feet tall, he was always ready with a smile, a strong handshake, and a willingness to do a favor. He was surprisingly abstemious in his habits and was known as a man who stood by his friends. During the war Tweed was ubiquitous as a member of the Board of Supervisors, a fire commissioner, and a deputy street commissioner. The latter job involved control of streets, wharves, and piers but had nothing to do with street cleaning. He was a man on the move with a bright future.[5]

Another faction called McKeon Democracy, supposedly a reform group under the leadership of a prominent lawyer, John McKeon, named the rich fur merchant C. Godfrey Gunther, who had failed once before as a candidate for mayor. The round-faced, forty-two-year-old Gunther, born on Liberty Street, wore chin whiskers with a clean-shaven upper lip, a style that may have been influenced by his earlier attendance at the Moravian Institute in Nazareth, Pennsylvania. He was a firm believer in states' rights and as a consequence was sympathetic to the South and slavery, which made him attractive to antiwar Democrats. In May, he had been chairman of the Vallandigham protest meeting, and he was a founder of the Anti-Abolition State Rights Association. Although he had been closely associated with Tammany and once served as its sachem, he ran as an independent with the support of "Jefferson Democracy."[6] His hatred of the war was, if anything, deeper than that of the most devoted followers of Fernando Wood in Mozart Hall and made him a curious candidate for a nation in the midst of a desperate struggle. Gunther was socially outgoing and had enjoyed serving as a volunteer fireman and playing politics. He had a strong following among German-Americans, who assumed he was German. His father, however, was a French Alsatian. His mother married Christian Gunther, a German, after his father died, and Gunther adopted his wife's three children, who took his name. Since Gunther was generally believed to have been a friend of the rioters, his chances of winning the election were considered "microscopic." The *Herald* saw no need to expand the damage of the New York mobs by electing him.[7]

Boole, the favorite, must have had misgivings about the campaign. He took the unprecedented step of showing up at a meeting of black voters at the Metropolitan Assembly Rooms. He informed his audience that there was no question that he would be elected but still solicited their support. He went further by pledging his word of honor to try to abolish the practice of driving black people out of the cars of the Eighth Avenue Railroad and to protect them from violence. He willingly went on record as a friend of the "colored." A few months before, no Democrat in the city would have dared risk his reputation by making such a remark.[8]

Once again, however, this was a three-cornered race, and anything could happen. When the ballots were counted in the December election, Gunther, the underdog, won by a plurality of about 6,500 votes, a slap in the face for Tweed, Tammany, and Mozart Hall. It was also a confirmation of the antiwar sentiment in the city. As in the past, the Democrats had trouble uniting their party, but unlike the previous mayoralty election, a Democrat had overcome the split. The Republican, Orison Blunt, a poor third, received only 19,383 votes.

Whatever the reasons he was elected, Gunther was an odd choice for mayor at this critical time. The war still had a long way to go, and the leader of the largest and most powerful city in the United States was totally opposed to its continuation. Gunther's abhorrence for war went beyond city politics. He was probably a genuine pacifist. His opposition was a matter of principle that appeared to be closely connected with his religious beliefs. During his administration, he would be called many derogatory names for his "peculiar views": a "Jeff Davis muddlehead," a "satellite of Jeff Davis and a red mouthed traitor," and probably worse. He remained unfazed by the criticism and claimed that he was not a secessionist, though he never altered his views. He was sure that the South would return to the Union when convinced that the North would abide by decisions of the Supreme Court and "stand by the Constitution."[9]

In his inaugural address Gunther spent more time expressing concern about the small amount of revenue derived from the sale of manure from the city streets than about the "calamitous war," which he barely mentioned. He announced that he would sedulously abstain from "exciting topics of political discussion" and confine his official remarks to municipal affairs. He claimed the right, however, "to the enjoyment of my opinion on all these questions," and his detestation of the war would never be a secret. Unwittingly or not, the citizens of the city of New York had elected a man of principle, but they were strange principles for a politician of a nation at war.[10]

C. Godfrey Gunther, the peace-loving mayor of New York City, 1864–65. (Courtesy of the New-York Historical Society)

14
Political Embarrassments

L incoln Clubs sprouted up throughout the city early in 1864 in anticipation of the coming presidential campaign. Many influential Republicans in the city thought these efforts were a step in the wrong direction because Lincoln was a hopeless candidate. They wanted a winner with a decisive personality who could end the war and abolish slavery.

Horace Greeley was one of these staunch Republicans who had given up on Lincoln. Inconsistency was the only consistent element in Greeley's makeup, but he was convinced that there were better alternatives to the incumbent president, who drifted and lacked "signal ability." For awhile he liked Chase, but his ardor for the Ohioan cooled as he considered John C. Frémont, Benjamin F. Butler of Massachusetts, and even Ulysses Grant. Other Radical Republicans, usually regarded as more stable than Greeley, were just as anxious to discard Lincoln and joined in the search for a dynamic leader. Among these dissidents were former mayor Opdyke, William Cullen Bryant, and Parke Godwin of the *Evening Post,* Theodore Tilton of the *Independent,* and the hardworking lawyer David Dudley Field.[1]

John A. Stevens, Jr., a member of this coterie, gave every appearance of laying groundwork for the nomination of Chase and kept in close touch with the secretary of the treasury and his friends. He told Chase that it was easy for Lincoln's friends to say, " 'no politics only put down the rebellion,' " but in his opinion a little more politics was needed.[2] The time had come for New York to redeem itself for the disastrous election of Seymour in 1862.

Even within this close group of New York dissidents there were jealousies and personal relations that required delicate handling. Stevens knew the value of Greeley in helping him advance his political plans, but he also knew Greeley's weaknesses. The editor was good on

235

broad policy, Stevens told a Chase friend, but he was not a man for detail
or executive management. He was also indiscreet and a poor judge of
men, "the prey of political sharpers and innocent as a lamb."[3] Nonetheless, Stevens knew that the *Tribune* was important if he wished to succeed, and Greeley was the *Tribune*.

Intense political maneuvering between radicals and conservatives
within the Republican party at the start of the year centered on patronage in the city. The conservative Thurlow Weed met John Nicolay, Lincoln's secretary, at the Astor House in March and told him frankly that
a change should be made in the customhouse. Weed, now a permanent
resident in the city, was hardly an objective observer. The collector's job
was a political plum that he would gladly grab for one of his followers.
Hiram Barney, the collector of the port, was a Radical Republican, who
had no use for Weed or Seward and considered the latter "a coward and
a small minow politician." One of Barney's many benefits in his well-paid
post was the privilege of selling labor contracts to haul goods from docks
to storehouses, unpack boxes, and sample incoming merchandise. Barney assigned the contract to his own firm without fear of conflict-of-in-
terest charges. It was a traditional practice, but even he admitted that the
government could save $37,000 by doing the work itself.[4] Weed thought
Barney, a friend of Chase, a weak manager plagued by four deputies
who continually intrigued against Lincoln. Weed said the deputies fired
subordinates simply because they took an active part in primaries for the
president's reelection.

More embarrassing to Barney were the financial irregularities uncovered in the customhouse. No one questioned Barney's integrity, but
the exposure of scandalous transactions in his office hurt him. The
House Committee on Public Expenditures aired charges of misconduct
in the supposed shipment of contraband goods and mismanagement of
business affairs. Testimony told of deception, bribery, and inefficient
methods, but the committee did not make any judgment about the alleged illegalities. Nevertheless, the House reported that there had been
"oversights, deficiencies, discrepancies [and] imperfections," as well as a
possible conflict of interest by the deputy collector of the port.[5]

Although Barney reported to Lincoln that he was mortified by
learning that he had placed confidence in unworthy persons, he wondered if it was possible to avoid such incidents when jobs were filled by
political influence. He had been plagued by office seekers who contin-

ually pressured him, and he was reaching a state of exhaustion. Despite difficulties, he genuinely believed that the customhouse was more efficiently managed than at any time in the past. But he was willing to resign whenever Lincoln wished. Barney has usually been identified with Chase but was actually Lincoln's choice for the job, and the president retained faith in the collector. Lincoln did not immediately replace him.[6]

Lincoln complicated matters by trying to keep all factions in New York happy. He appointed John T. Hogeboom as appraiser at large in the New York customhouse on the recommendation of Chase. This appointment distressed Edwin Morgan, now a United States senator, who was always closely associated with city affairs. He knew nothing of the decision until it came before the Senate. Morgan told Weed, "The President rather appoint Chase's friends than to say no." Although Morgan tried to put on the best public face, he told Weed that the appointment of one of the president's "most active and malignant enemies left him quite powerless."[7]

The able, ambitious Chase, anxious for the presidency yet declaring his loyalty to Lincoln, jealously continued to see that his Radical Republican friends received appointments in New York. Each appointment further irritated the conservatives, who had other plans and ambitions. The ill will between Weed the conservative and Opdyke the radical deepened. Opdyke wrote to James Hamilton, "Mr. Weed is growing desperate in malignity and falsehood as he sees the political sceptre in this state passing from his hands." Opdyke considered Weed's remarks against himself and family slanderous and waited for an opportunity to show up Weed's "true character."[8] Yet Opdyke was deceiving himself or trying to deceive others, in the belief that Weed was losing political power.

The Democrats, divided by issues of war and peace, also sought a strong presidential candidate. They had serious issues to present to the electorate such as arbitrary arrests, individual liberty, and compromise with the South. These were popular themes, but Democratic drive was diluted by the fear of overstepping the bounds of criticism into treason. Fernando Wood, always walking a fine line between loyalty and treason, intended to make himself heard at the state and national conventions as the leader of the peace men. He had already opened the year in Congress with an amendment to an enrollment bill, which called for an exemption from the draft for those who did not believe in its humanity, necessity, or eventual success until an effort was made to end the war by negotiation.[9] The house rejected this amendment, but he had made his point. August Belmont and other conservative Democrats hoped to unify their party by avoiding Wood's extremism. But the year was young for both Democrats and Republicans.

Politicians joined hands one day and cut each other up the next day in their struggle for power. Unity was their favorite goal yet they scrapped and divided public opinion. They envisioned unity as agreement with their ideas whatever they might be. John A. Stevens, Jr., said there would be no divisions if men of honor and integrity, not "chuffling politicians," led a "United" party. But who were the men of honor and integrity? Who were the "chuffling politicians?"[10] Not everyone agreed with Stevens's choices.

Factions of all shades were jealous of what appeared to be the South's singleness of purpose. In the name of unity, Peter Cooper, formerly a Democrat, Francis Lieber, and other Republicans pleaded with the national executive committee of their party to postpone the national convention scheduled for June. They argued that unified support for their candidate was essential, but they believed that unanimity was impossible at that time.[11] Although they signed their letter as friends of the government and supporters of the administration, many party members who favored delay in nominating a candidate really meant that they wanted time to find someone to replace Lincoln.

Some Democratic and Republican workingmen in New York showed a greater sense of unity than party politicians by forming a bipartisan association to support the Union, the New-York Workingmen's Democratic-Republican Association. On March 21, 1864, Lincoln wrote to advise the association about unity and capitalism in America. He warned the tempestuous workingmen against prejudice and hostility among themselves and reminded them that "the most notable feature of a disturbance in your city last summer, was the hanging of some working people by other working people." He also told them not to war on property. "Property is the fruit of labor—property is desirable—is a positive good in the world. That some should be rich, shows that others may become rich, and hence is just encouragement to industry and enterprize. Let not him who is homeless pull down the house of another; but let him labor diligently and build one for himself, thus by example assuring that his own shall be safe from violence when built."[12]

THE TWENTIETH UNITED STATES COLORED TROOPS RECEIVING THEIR COLORS ON UNION SQUARE, MARCH 5, 1864.—[SEE PAGE 187.]

Twentieth U.S. Colored Troops receiving colors at Union Square, March 5, 1864. (Courtesy of the New-York Historical Society)

A few other superficial signs of unity and good feeling appeared in the city that crossed class and racial lines and gave some hope. In the city where mobs had hanged black men to lampposts and burned the Colored Orphan Asylum, another event took place which at least momentarily encouraged a spirit of harmony. Crowds packed the sidewalks and cheered the departure of the first black New York regiment. The troops received a gift of colors at the Union League Club and proudly marched down Broadway. The parade seemed to symbolize a new era of understanding between the races as spectators applauded and waved handkerchiefs. Many blacks watched the procession with tears in their eyes and believed that a new world was beginning for them. Even Maria

Daly, who said she preferred the commonest white to any black, had to admit that she was moved as she watched the impressive ceremony.[13]

Although the parade of black troops was a heartwarming experience for many onlookers, the affair had an uglier side. When the War Department gave permission to raise the troops, Governor Seymour refused to help. George Bliss, a member of the Union League Club, who was active in black recruiting and eventually raised the Twentieth, Twenty-sixth, and Thirty-first New York regiments, wrote to the governor asking for his support and did not receive a reply. And when preparations were made for the new troops to march down Broadway, the social Seventh Regiment refused to lend its band. An officer turned down one request by saying that he would be damned if his men marched in front of "niggers." Racial prejudice existed among some Union League members who became annoyed when a black chaplain received an invitation to speak at the club.[14]

A few newspaper critics also made snide remarks on this happy day. The *Herald* commented that the presentation of colors was made as "an emblem of love and honor from the daughters of this great metropolis to her brave champions," which act the newspaper thought was excessive. "This is a pretty fair start for miscegenation. Why, the phrase 'love and honor' needs only the little word 'obey' to become the equivalent of a marriage ceremony." The *Metropolitan Record*, never a friend of blacks, registered even greater disgust at the sight of a black regiment on parade. In an article titled "New York Disgraced," John Mullaly saw this display as sad proof "of the degeneracy of our Government." And his blood tingled with indignation when he saw fellow whites give "by voice and gesture, their approbation of this infamous parody of patriotism." But his views were not surprising. His paper had previously upheld slavery for theological reasons.[15]

In the next few months, the widow of a black soldier would be removed from an Eighth Avenue streetcar in keeping with the policy of segregation, although the Union League Club defended her rights. When the club prepared to take the case to court, the Eighth Avenue line gave up its policy of discrimination and the Sixth Avenue line followed suit.[16]

Other New Yorkers cast aside factionalism and worked together in a state of near frenzy to make the forthcoming Metropolitan Fair to aid the Sanitary Commission a success. "New York," wrote Harriet Woolsey, "is really in a disgusting state of fashionable excitement; nothing is talked, or thought of, or dreamed of, but the big Metropolitan Fair!" All the Woolsey women joined in the excitement. The mother of the family knew that she had to keep her mind occupied. She dreaded picking up the newspaper each day in fear that she might see the name of her son Charley on the casualty list. Abby busily made a handsome silk flag and "tidy-covers" edged with lace. Mary painted little wooden articles for sale. Harriet enjoyed the fuss and sensibly laughed at the petty rivalries and jealousies that developed in the name of charity. Kate Hunt, a friend of the Woolseys, spent a thousand dollars for some Parisian pieces for the fair. Mrs. Parker had thousand-dollar tea sets to offer, Mrs. Schemerhorn provided elegant watches, and, Harriet said, "Mrs. Somebody-else, the beautiful jewelry sent from Rome." George Templeton Strong noticed that this noble work did not necessarily produce sweetness. "All the committees are at swords' points," he wrote in his diary. "The quantity of gossip, intrigue, and personal pique that grows out of the Fair and its hundreds of committees is stupendous and terrible." Yet, as Henry Bellows said, the enterprise stirred up "the latent patriotism of this vast metropolis, & of binding together its fragmentary & disjointed population."[17]

The city erected a huge building for the extravaganza at Sixth Avenue and Fourteenth Street called the Palace Garden and a barrackslike building known as Union Square on Seventeenth Street that ran from Broadway to Fourth Avenue and housed the music hall, children's department, and colonial "Knickerbocker Kitchen." Gifts flowed into the city from all over the country, and a receiving station was set up at Great Jones Street.

Mayor Gunther recommended that the fair's opening day be observed as a holiday. His proclamation sounded almost apologetic. Always anxious to let people know that he did not approve of the war, he explained that during this "unhappy strife, in which our once peaceful States are involved," there were good Samaritans working to allay the pain.[18]

The opening ceremonies on April 4, 1864, started with a gigantic parade of about ten thousand troops led by the erect and energetic General Dix and General Charles Sandford, head of the New York militia. Robert Anderson, the hero of Fort Sumter, now a major general, was on hand to review the procession, and Joseph Choate, gaining a reputation

THE KNICKERBOCKER KITCHEN—A SPECIAL OBJECT OF INTEREST IN THE METROPOLITAN SANITARY FAIR

The Knickerbocker Kitchen was a favorite attraction at the Metropolitan Fair to aid the Sanitary Commission. (Courtesy of the New-York Historical Society)

as an eloquent speaker and able lawyer, made the main address. His musical speaking voice and an "Army Hymn" by Oliver Wendell Holmes, sung by choirs from several churches in the city, stirred the listeners. In the next three weeks, about thirty thousand people visited the fair to see industrial and agricultural products, a picture gallery with six hundred paintings, a curiosity shop, and an Indian department. The picture gallery in the main hall included Emanuel Leutze's *Washington Crossing the Delaware,* Frederick E. Church's, *Heart of the Andes,* Albert Bierstadt's, *Rocky Mountains,* Daniel Huntington's, *Mercy's Dream,* and Régis Gignoux's *Indian Summer.* The showing was so popular that there was talk of establishing a permanent art gallery in the city. Among the

donations for sale were a James Fenimore Cooper manuscript and a
bowie knife that allegedly belonged to James Bowie, who had fought to
the end at the Alamo. Morgan Dix, fascinated by the fair, described it as
a marvel of "taste, luxury, and splendour."[19]

A luxurious restaurant could seat a thousand people. And at the
Knickerbocker Kitchen, women dressed in colonial costume sold waf-
fles, coffee, and trinkets. Maria Daly turned down an invitation to work
there because she did not want to dress up in a fancy outfit and pour tea
for the rabble.[20] The rabble, however, were few in number because admission to the exhibits cost $2. A billiard tournament cost an additional
dollar.

In the department of arms and trophies, two beautiful swords donated by Tiffany were on display. They were to be given to the most popular army and navy officers. Popularity was to be determined by ballot,
and each vote cost one dollar. The voting for naval officer drew little interest, but that for the army officer attracted much attention and apparently reflected intensity of feeling. The connivance of Grant supporters
gave the impression that McClellan was the leading contender. When
August Belmont and Samuel Barlow visited the fair, they added a thousand votes with a donation of a thousand dollars to give McClellan a
healthy majority. They did not know that the Union League Club and
other Grant backers had conspired to hold back their ballots until the last
moment. To the surprise of many, General Grant trounced General
McClellan by about fifteen thousand votes. Whatever the results, the
idea was a brilliant money-maker that raised $45,855.

As an adjunct to the fair, the rich William Aspinwall opened his
house at University Place and Tenth Street for viewers to see his works
of art, which were reputed to be the largest collection of old masters in
the United States. The eminent artists represented were staggering.
Among them were Leonardo da Vinci, Rembrandt, Van Dyke, Rubens,
and Sir Joshua Reynolds. August Belmont also opened his home for a
less impressive showing of modern European paintings that included
Meissonier and Rosa Bonheur.

Another side event for the benefit of the fair was dramatic per-
formances at Leonard Jerome's private theater on Twenty-sixth Street.
Tickets sold for five dollars each and attracted only the affluent of New
York society. Isabel Rogers played the Duchess in *The Follies of a Night*,
and Mrs. George Templeton Strong was Mlle. Duval, her lady-in-wait-

ing. It was an elegant evening. Hard work, excitement, and rivalry made the fair a huge success. Most important, the sensation of the year was a financial boon to the Sanitary Commission. The net proceeds were reported to be over a million dollars.[21]

While thousands crowded into the Metropolitan Fair to support the Sanitary Commission and show their faith in the Union, gold speculators continued to capitalize on military setbacks. The price of gold climbed, and when it approached 175 many people thought there would be financial disaster if the price went beyond that figure. As fear increased, so did the number of gold speculators. McClellan's father-in-law, General R. B. Marcy, advised him to sell his railroad stocks and buy gold.[22]

Jay Cooke, always skeptical of the motives of New York financiers, spoke to Chase about the destructive actions of the gold speculators. Gold reached 170, and there was now talk that its price would rocket to 500 and the Chase greenbacks would be as worthless as Confederate "shinplasters." Cooke wanted to teach the speculators a lesson. He was certain he could bring the price of gold down to a workable level by selling $6 or $7 million of gold stored in the New York subtreasury. In mid-April, Chase arrived in New York and conferred with Cisco and Cooke about the plan. Chase was nervous about the idea, but by then gold was about 188, far beyond the anticipated danger point, and it seemed imperative that something be done. Chase courageously gave Cooke approval to proceed with the scheme under the utmost secrecy and then left for Washington.

Cooke worked confidentially with David Crawford of Clark, Dodge and Company. On the first day they sold only $2 million of gold so that no suspicions were aroused. Purchases required greenbacks or checks marked "good," which required greenbacks. Cooke aimed to bring the price down to about 180 on the first day, but it dropped to 174. The next day, Cooke sold more gold. The price dropped sharply, and confidence in gold dropped. Some firms known as Copperhead firms suspended operation. Banks demanded greenbacks from the gold buyers, and the greenbacks rose in value. By then Wall Street was rife with rumors. The story spread that the substreasury was ready to sell $20 million in gold to break up the conspirators who were trying to destroy the government's credit. By April 21, Cooke had sold about $7 million worth of gold, and he had shown the power of the government in the financial world. The price of gold fell to about 160. Cooke may have wanted to push the speculators further, but Chase said that as secretary of the treasury he lacked the authority to go on. On April 22, Cooke wrote to Chase that he had the impression "that no one here heartily loved their country better than their pocketbooks." Cooke's experiment was noble, but it had only a temporary effect. Soon the price of gold took off again and reached phenomenal new heights. In July, as Jubal Early drove through Maryland, the price touched 285, the highest quotation of the war.[23]

A serious but lesser problem was the depreciation of gold coin in circulation. The practice of filing off some of the gold or clipping coins and filling them with a baser metal became so widespread that the Board of Gold Dealers requested the Bank of New York to set up a gold department to examine gold coins and certify their value. Within three months more than $41 million in coin was examined by passing the coins through a series of sieves and isolating suspicious pieces for separate weighing and testing.[24]

The securities market fluctuated sharply through April. So-called panics were frequently short-lived, but investors could be severely hurt. On April 15, Edmund Stedman wrote, "Panic in stocks this morning. Took all my courage to support myself and friends in holding on to stocks. Made a rally at noon. Went home after a ticklish day, feeling that the crisis had passed." But on the fourteenth, Stedman was one hour late for work and found that prices were up and he could have turned a handsome profit if he had been on time. In the afternoon, stocks declined rapidly and he began to sell at a loss. The next day, the panic continued and many of Stedman's friends suffered badly. April 18 was worse. It was called "Blue Monday." On that day, subscriptions were fairly heavy for government "ten-forty" bonds, which were issued to raise $75 million. They ran for a period of not less than ten or more than forty years at 6 percent interest. At the same time, there were heavy payments for duties at the customhouse and calling in of loans. Banks contracted their notes, increasing the stringency in the money market. In a hectic day, some brokers went by the board, margins were wiped out, and contracts violated. Emotions ran high, curses filled the air, and some fistfights started. Nevertheless, by April 22, confidence returned to the

Wall Street on a quiet day in 1864. (Courtesy of the New-York Historical Society)

Street until the next crisis came along. The ups and downs of the stock market did not prevent Stedman from buying the house of his dreams at 184 East Tenth Street a few days later. He believed he had a real bargain at $9,000 and paid $20 down.[25]

Relative calm on the exchange during May led members to believe that the new stability was the result of improved communications from the War Department, which cut down sensational rumors that had affected public sentiment. The board of the New York Stock Exchange passed a resolution of thanks to Secretary of War Stanton.[26]

General Grant might not have received such a strong popular vote if the Metropolitan Fair had been held in May or June. He was then fighting in the Wilderness and at Cold Harbor, Virginia, where his casualties were counted in the tens of thousands. Appeals went out in the city for more linen and cotton rags, "thoroughly clean and sweet," for the

Medical Bureau and Sanitary Commission. Grant appeared to be brutal and reckless, and Lincoln's conduct of the war seemed endless and aimless. Plans to replace him in the White House made more sense than ever. The people, tired of war, listened more intently to politicians calling for an end to the butchery.

Thurlow Weed thought this was a good time to head off McClellan. He wrote the general's close friend Samuel Barlow urging that McClellan write a letter to the president so that Lincoln might restore him to command or even look with favor on McClellan's nomination for president. The two kingmakers had ulterior motives. Weed certainly knew that restoration of McClellan to a military career might eliminate him as a presidential contender. Barlow replied to Weed somewhat disingenuously that McClellan had no political aspirations and had never been influenced by political considerations when he was in command. Barlow insisted that although McClellan avoided politics, he regarded the Radical Republicans, his prime opponents, bitterly and Democrats, who befriended him, kindly. That was undoubtedly true, but while Barlow denied McClellan's political interests he inconsistently reemphasized the general's political beliefs. Barlow referred to McClellan's Harrison Landing letter to the president in July 1862 during the Peninsular Campaign, which had given the appearance of offering political advice. In that letter the general opposed arbitrary arrests, confiscation of property, and "forcible abolition of slavery." Barlow claimed that McClellan had no reason to change these views and he could see no grounds for McClellan to write to the president now. He closed his letter by reaffirming McClellan's belief in prosecuting the war with vigor. If nothing else, Barlow blocked Weed's maneuver.[27]

On May 11, a new draft call was scheduled to begin. Less than a thousand men were needed to fill the quota, but Mayor Gunther pleaded for a postponement from General Dix. About eight thousand stevedores were on strike, and large numbers of street cleaners were unemployed until their employers settled on a new contract with the city. Gunther feared that a draft call with so many men idle could cause another riot. Charles Halpine, a writer, said the bounty thieves and brokers alone would cause a riot. For the time being, the mayor had his way, and soon volunteers filled the quota.[28]

The city's problems and political fencing were overshadowed by the indecisive slugging match between Grant and Lee. The return of a New York regiment to the city gave clear evidence of the scars of war. It was an old city militia regiment, the Scottish Seventy-ninth, that had volunteered as a body of about a thousand men at the start of the war. Its original term of enlistment was two years, and the men agreed to remain in service an additional year. The regiment had seen heavy action in some of the major battles of the war—Bull Run, Antietam, Fredericksburg, and the Wilderness—and had paid a high price. Only 120 or 130 original members of the regiment were left to receive the welcome of Mayor Gunther and the Common Council.[29]

The war brought out the best and worst impulses in people. The men of the Seventy-ninth had bravely gone to their deaths. Joseph Howard, an able newspaperman and drama critic, conceived a hoax to rig the stock market. He convincingly wrote a "Presidential proclamation" calling for another four hundred thousand men for the army and for a day of public humiliation and prayer. The editor at the *World* and the foreman of the printing room at the *Journal of Commerce*, both antiadministration papers, innocently published the depressing proclamation in good faith. Immediately, speculators in the Gold Room profited when the price of gold went up a few percentage points to 184. The *Herald* was almost caught in the deception too, but the trick was discovered before its papers were distributed.

The night editor at the *Times* was more alert. About three-thirty in the morning, he received the proclamation, allegedly from the Associated Press. It looked like the usual AP copy, but the handwriting was different and his suspicions were aroused. When the editor checked around the office, he learned that the story had not come in an AP envelope and the delivery boy had left at once. The editor sent the manuscript to the AP office with an inquiry about its origin. A reply soon came back: "The 'Proclamation' is false as hell and not promulgated through this office. The handwriting is not familiar." When he heard about the incident, Secretary of War Stanton speedily obtained an executive order from the president to stop publication of the papers that had "wickedly and traitorously" published the proclamation and to arrest the owners and editors of the *World* and *Journal of Commerce*. General Dix was to hold the persons arrested in close custody until they were brought to trial before a military commission. He was also to "take possession by military force of the printing establishments."[30]

As soon as the papers realized their error, they offered substantial rewards for information about the perpetrator through the pages of the

Times. Nevertheless, General Dix carried out the executive order even though he knew that Stanton had taken too extreme a position. Soldiers entered the newspaper offices, stopped the presses, arrested the men they found at work, and arbitrarily held them under guard. The seizure on May 18 could not have been more untimely for Manton Marble of the *World.* He planned to be married the next day and was forced to postpone his wedding.

Dix advised Stanton almost immediately that his investigation indicated that the proclamation had been calculated to deceive. Fingers were pointed at Samuel Barlow, but he was innocent. Two days later, Dix told Stanton that the culprit, Joseph Howard, had been arrested and sent to Fort Lafayette for three months on charges of treasonably attempting to give aid and comfort to the enemy. Howard, a city editor for the *Brooklyn Daily Eagle,* had not expected such a harsh reaction. He frankly admitted that his sole purpose in the hoax was to make a quick profit by buying gold one day and selling it on the rise early the next day. Francis A. Mallison, a reporter for the *Eagle,* had helped Howard, and he, too, was sent to Fort Lafayette. Later, Howard would excuse his hoax as a burlesque of the long string of proclamations that had come out of Washington. Howard had consulted a Mr. Kent, a partner in the reputable brokerage firm of Kent and Clark, about the effect such a proclamation would have on the market before he undertook the scheme. He showed Kent a draft of a proclamation, which he claimed he had received through secret channels in Washington, with the assurance that it was about to be issued. Kent later recognized the similarity with the bogus proclamation that was published and informed General Dix.

The New York Stock Exchange, a sensitive enclave, was skittish about any association with the hoax or charges of disloyalty. The board defensively announced that several applications for membership in the exchange had been rejected in the past few days on the supposition of disloyalty. The applicant most recently rejected had even been vouched for by one of the oldest members of the board. It was extremely difficult to attain membership in the New York Stock Exchange, and some qualified candidates must have believed that it would be easier to enter the gates of heaven.

The hoax also created some rumbles around town about the necessity to control gold speculation. The financial correspondent for the *Times* had not previously supported legislation to regulate supply and demand of gold. Now he believed that the city was scandalized by gold gambling and urged passage of Senator John Sherman's bill to suppress traffic in gold. The next month, Congress passed a "gold bill," which supposedly prohibited speculative trading in gold futures. Penalties of fine and imprisonment were imposed on anyone who contracted for a later delivery of gold unless he held gold of the same amount when the contract was executed. But government regulation caused more confusion, and the act was quickly repealed.

The *Journal of Commerce,* anxious to cover its embarrassment over the hoax, adopted a noble pose without vindictiveness. The editors wrote, "It is not we that have been harmed so much as he [the President] who so fiercely struck at us. We are grieved for him. He has withdrawn his grasp and we are again free. And now for the private wrong done us, we find it in our hearts to forgive him." The *World,* less magnanimous, complained about the shock on the public mind. "Do not imagine, Sir, that the Governor of this State has forgotten to do his duty; don't imagine that the people of this City or State or country have ceased to love their liberties, or do not know how to protect their rights."[31]

Stanton had countermanded the executive order the day after it was issued, but the damage was done. In New York, General Dix faced a barrage of criticism. Governor Seymour was alert to this perfect opportunity to take a popular stand on freedom of the press and individual liberty. He instructed Oakey Hall, the district attorney, to present the facts of the army raid on the press to a grand jury. The president accepted responsibility for his order, but that did not stop the governor's proceedings or prevent the possibility of General Dix ending up in jail for carrying out his instructions. Secretary of the Navy Gideon Welles, a newspaperman himself, despised the *World* and *Journal of Commerce,* but even he did not believe the seizure of the newspaper offices could be defended. And rival newspapers such as the *Tribune* and *Herald* forgot their bitter feuds with the *World* and rallied to support the paper against the common enemy that might infringe upon their cherished constitutional rights. The grand jury, however, refused indictment, which infuriated Seymour. He told Hall the jury had not done its duty and accused Marble of being unwilling to help the district attorney.[32]

Manton Marble thought Seymour's indignation came a little late. The Governor had not shown any interst in the case in the beginning. The incident illustrated the strains behind the scenes within the Democratic party that were not evident to the public. Publicly Marble had given Seymour's administration "Unwavering support," but privately he resented Seymour's ineffectiveness in stopping arbitrary arrests. Men, he said, had been kidnapped from New York City streets and other cities in the state "almost daily since Gov. Seymour went into office. What hindrance has he even interposed. What protest has he ever uttered." Now, the governor complained that Marble had not looked to him for help and charged that he had not cooperated with the district attorney. "Why Mr. Cassidy," Marble wrote to his friend at the *Atlas-Argus* office in Albany, "when I was being driven down to Gen. Dix's office, it did not so much as occur to me to look to Albany for help. Help for other men unlawfully dealt with had not been in the habit of coming from that quarter. ... I know of nothing to distinguish my arrest or the suppression of the World from many other arbitrary & illegal acts which for two years had been peaceably & without protest suffered to be accomplished." In addition, Marble claimed Seymour's imputation that he had not helped Oakey Hall with the facts was false. He said he had been in constant touch with the district attorney since the event took place.[33] But the matter was closed even though there was no doubt that Lincoln had strained the Constitution in this brief crisis.

Another scoundrel, Theodore Allen, charged with swindling recruits out of their bounty money at Lafayette Hall on Broadway, caused a few tense moments when United States detectives under General Dix and city policemen attempted to arrest him at Mercer and Spring streets. He drew a gun, which luckily misfired, and then some of his friends tried to rescue him from the law. They appeared ready to shoot it out when other detectives and police arrived and held them off. It was another situation when police could not count on the backing of the citizenry.[34]

The federal detective force was out for bigger game than bounty swindlers. T. J. Barnett begged Samuel Barlow not to make so many indiscreet remarks. Although Barnett did not expect Barlow to be arrested immediately, he knew it was under contemplation. "Certainly no gentleman believes you treasonable," he wrote Barlow. "But gentlemen are not alone concerned; there is an army of blood suckers who think that such men are fair game." Barlow joked about being a "suspect," but it was not a laughing matter. Who could tell where loyalty ended and disloyalty began? Barnett had faith in Barlow's loyalty but doubted his judgment when he insisted that an "entente cordiale" could be restored between the North and South. Barnett told Barlow that railing generalities did as much good as baying at the moon.[35]

An incident at Pier 13 on the North River raised suspicions of traffic in contraband. Five cases of rifled muskets were found on the dock alongside the steamer *Mexico* bound for Havana. Customhouse officials detained the ship, but the captain vigorously denied that he had any intention of taking the cargo aboard. Illicit trade between New York and foreign ports accessible to the Confederacy thrived throughout the war with little interference. General E. R. S. Canby at New Orleans reported to General Halleck that arms, munitions, and other scarce supplies were unloaded at Matamoros for transfer to Texas. Sometimes rifle barrels were hidden in crates of crockery and pistols in boxes of soap. Other times no effort was made to conceal the military items.

A large number of patriotic women, ready to make sacrifices, gathered at a meeting of the Women's Patriotic Association for Diminishing the Use of Imported Luxuries at Cooper Institute. Their purpose was to discuss ways to check waste during the war. The audience, however, was disillusioned by the appearance of an elegantly dressed committee on stage and speeches by men who did not seem interested in carrying sacrifice too far. An uproar broke out over a resolution regarding the purchase of imported goods. The women in the audience felt they had been "humbugged" and wanted a stronger pledge to buy no more goods than "possible." The committee was more interested in the appearance of action against waste than the reality and probably worried about the effect on business. The leaders simply wanted to make a statement suggesting that people not buy more imported goods than they could "conveniently do without." The committee overrode the majority in the audience and caused such a disturbance that police ordered the women out of the hall. "A Loyal Woman" wrote an indignant letter to the *Times* saying, "We want to sacrifice ourselves for our dying brothers on the field. ... To come to an economy meeting in robed silk dresses and carriages was rather ridiculous."[36]

During this same month, a radical fragment of the Republican party unalterably opposed to the renomination of Abraham Lincoln held a convention in Cleveland, Ohio. B. Gratz Brown of Missouri and the abolitionist Wendell Phillips were prime movers at this convention. Horace Greeley, despite his many bitter words against Lincoln, was noticeably absent. He may have been erratic, but he was too shrewd to join this splinter group. He and his friends intended to control the Republican party. Yet Greeley had covered his bet by publicly announcing his high regard for Frémont at an earlier meeting in New York that had kicked off the "pathfinders' " campaign.

John Cochrane, a changeable politician from New York City who had veered from antiabolitionist to abolitionist, Democrat to Republican, and conservative to radical, denounced the Lincoln administration in a major speech at Cleveland. John Frémont received the nomination for president and Cochrane was rewarded with second place on the ticket. Although his chances of success were almost nonexistent, Frémont planned to run a serious race. Thurlow Weed considered it "slimy intrigue."[37] Nonetheless, it demonstrated the prevalence of anti-Lincoln sentiment.

A few days later, some Radicals held a meeting in New York City in hope of catapulting Grant into the presidency despite his lack of interest and recent frustrations on the battlefield. The announced purpose of the meeting was to laud Grant for his services, and Lincoln raised no objections. Instead, he sent a letter joining in the praise of Grant and thereby played into the hands of the Radicals. The meeting fizzled, and Lincoln, in control of the regular organization, received the nomination at the Republican convention on June 7 at Baltimore with amazing ease.

Mrs. Dix said that her husband, General Dix, had been asked to be a candidate for vice-president and had declined. It is not known who asked him. His candidacy may simply have been mentioned in conversation among politicians, but Dix ardently supported the Union and would have been a good candidate. Henry Raymond, no more prescient than anyone else, favored replacing Vice-President Hannibal Hamlin with the Democrat Andrew Johnson of Tennessee to give the ticket a truer Union flavor. He helped to accomplish the deed, which supposedly added strength to the slate for the coming campaign. But Lincoln's renomination was a long way from reelection, and many Republicans in New York City remained dissatisfied with their candidate.

Manton Marble's *World* took pleasure in criticizing the Republican candidates, describing them as "mere plebeians." One Lincoln supporter in the city took heart from the *World*'s nasty remarks. He considered abuse from Marble to be "as honorable as the Victoria Cross or the Order of the Garter."[38]

Although nothing seemed to go right for the administration, one victory pleased businessmen, especially insurance carriers. In the past two years the Confederate raider *Alabama* had captured sixty-two merchant ships. Its skillful captain, Raphael Semmes, escaped detection time and again and was becoming a legendary figure. Finally, he met his match on June 19, 1864, when John Winslow, captain of the cruiser *Kearsage,* cornered Semmes off Cherbourg and sank the *Alabama.* Insurance men breathed easier, and the Chamber of Commerce in New York was so pleased with Winslow and his men it raised a purse of $25,000, which was distributed somewhat unevenly. Winslow received $10,000, the officers of the *Kearsage* $10,000, and the crew $5,000.[39]

The sinking of the *Alabama,* however, did not solve Lincoln's political problems. Patronage continued to be a particularly thorny subject in the city. The efficient John J. Cisco, assistant treasurer, announced that he planned to retire by the end of June. He had served three administrations and was ready for a rest. Lincoln let it be known that he was anxious to avoid a dispute over filling this important post, and at first Chase and Senator Morgan appeared to cooperate. Unfortunately, the two able candidates they agreed upon for the job turned down the appointment. Then Chase, on his own, put forth the name of Maunsell B. Field, a man of high social standing with literary interests who was coauthor of a romantic novel. Chase opponents charged that Field was not respected by either politicians or financiers. Field, however, was hardly a novice in the financial world. He had served as an assistant to Cisco for many years and was now assistant secretary of the treasury. Nonetheless, Senator Morgan objected to his appointment and offered three well-regarded New Yorkers, R. M. Blatchford, Dudley S. Gregory, and Thomas Hillhouse, for consideration. Chase believed one of these men might be suitable in peacetime but not under the pressures of war. One man, he told Lincoln, was over seventy and another over sixty. Chase ignored Morgan and presented Field's name to the president. Lincoln advised Chase that he could not appoint Field because he was not acceptable to Morgan and asked him to select one of the three the senator had suggested.

Lincoln frankly admitted his political problems in New York to Chase: "Much as I personally like Mr. Barney, it has been a great burden to me to retain him in his place when nearly all our friends in New-York, were directly or indirectly, urging his removal. Then the appointment of Judge Hogeboom to be general Appraiser brought me to and has ever since kept me at, the verge of open revolt. Now, the appointment of Mr. Field would precipitate me in it.... Strained as I already am at this point I do not think I can make this appointment in the direction of still greater strain." Lincoln later told Field that the Republican party in New York was divided into two factions and he could not afford to quarrel with either of them. "By accident, rather than by design of mine," he said, "the radicals have got possession of the most important Federal offices in New York.... Had I, under the circumstances, consented to your appointment, it would have been another radical triumph and I couldn't afford one." Chase still intended to have his way. As a first step, he asked Cisco to withdraw his resignation temporarily. Cisco relieved the situation by agreeing to remain in office another three months. Then Chase, in a huff, replied to Lincoln, "I cannot help feeling that my position here is not altogether agreeable to you; and it is certainly too full of embarrassment and difficulty and painful responsibility to allow in me the least desire to retain it." Chase enclosed a letter of resignation, but it was not the first time he had made such an offer. This time, possibly to Chase's surprise, the president accepted the resignation. Lincoln's skill with words was well illustrated in his acceptance of Chase's resignation: "Of all I have said in commendation of your ability and fidelity, I have nothing to unsay; and yet you and I have reached a point of mutual embarrassment in our official relation which it seems can not be overcome, or longer sustained, consistently with the public service."[40]

It was unfortunate that Chase's ego competed with his enormous ability. He had made a great contribution to the war effort under the most trying circumstances. He had made tough decisions and had made a primitive banking system work when there was every reason to believe it would collapse. Now, as he left office, one of his most valuable plans was coming to fruition.

From the start of Chase's service as secretary of the treasury, he had recognized the weaknesses of the existing banking system in fighting a war. In actuality, there was no system. Banks issued unregulated notes, frequently suspended specie payments, and too often failed. Bank notes were printed on all kinds of paper and presented a variety of appearances. By 1863, sixteen hundred state banks issued about twelve thousand different kinds of bank notes. And bank notes issued in one state usually were not accepted by another. There were no regulations to prevent a bank from issuing notes far beyond its capital stock. Jay Cooke claimed that some banks issued eighteen to twenty times the amount of their capital stock in notes and the only security was the good faith of the institution. It was estimated that $50 million a year was lost by people who were victims of bank failures, counterfeits, altered notes, and the cost of exchange between different areas.

As early as 1862, Chase recommended the organization of national banking associations supervised by the federal government to issue bank notes backed by federally guaranteed bonds. The plan could help clear the confusion and fluctuations of state bank notes. George Opdyke, a businessman at heart, was mayor of New York City at the time. He wrote to Chase that his proposal was admirable and superior to any state paper that had ever emanated from the Treasury Department. "It is clear in statement," he said, "sound in theory, logical in argument, and most comprehensive in its grasp."[41]

Opdyke's appraisal of Chase's plan may have been correct, but it was not met with enthusiasm by Congress or New York City bankers. A defective law based on the proposal passed in 1863, but it was replaced with a more effective law on June 3, 1864, which permitted the creation of banking associations with national charters controlled by a comptroller of currency in the Treasury Department. Under this system, each bank had to buy United States bonds to be deposited in the federal treasury worth not less than $30,000 or less than one-third of its capital. The new currency was called national bank notes. The comptroller issued the notes to the national banks, and they were equal to 90 percent of the United States bonds received.

This law did not meet automatic acceptance by bankers. Uniformity and safety did not have universal appeal. Some foresaw the dangers of presidential favoritism similar to the problems associated with the "pet bank" system in Andrew Jackson's day. Others imagined a Hamiltonian Bank of the United States. Probably more important, large New York City banks did not make much profit from note issues and did not believe they had much to gain from the new system. The Metropolitan, Bank of Commerce, and American Exchange were among the city banks that spoke out in opposition.

The new plan eventually attracted New York bankers by an arrangement for the redeposit of reserves from smaller rural banks that created central reserve banks in the city, which were given 40 percent of the resources of the system and guaranteed control of the national money market. Fears about the law evaporated, and the Republicans had shrewdly strengthened their ties with business.

The first person to establish a national bank in New York City was John Thompson, publisher of the *Thompson Bank Note Detector*. His First National Bank of New York, in the basement of a building on the corner of Wall Street and Broadway, began with a capital of $100,000. Soon after, a Second National Bank appeared under the Fifth Avenue Hotel with $200,000 capital, followed by the Third National Bank with $300,000 capital. Eventually, with the help of Jay Cooke, the Fourth National Bank of New York was organized with capitalization of $5 million. George Opdyke, no longer mayor, was elected president.

Although some banks did not care to serve bankers, the First National Bank of New York quickly recognized the benefits of the new act. It had a large number of correspondents across the country, and more than half of their deposits were from other banks. Under the new Banking Act, the national banks throughout the United States could count their deposits at a national bank in New York as a part of their required reserve.[42] The new system took time to establish, and it never became a panacea for all financial woes, but it was a big step in building stability for which Chase deserved much of the credit. In mid-1864, however, dreams of reaching the White House seized Salmon Chase.

Embarrassing political situations in New York City multiplied for Lincoln during this election year. One of the most awkward incidents for him was the arrest for fraud of Isaac Henderson, the navy agent at New York. Henderson, a prominent Methodist and part owner of the *Evening Post*, was a member of one of the city's most sanctimonious circles that included his partners, William Cullen Bryant and Parke Godwin.

Secretary of the Navy Welles had no doubt that Henderson was guilty of making commissions from companies selling products to the Navy Yard. He was also aware that the case involved his old friend Bryant and the *Evening Post*, which had been highly critical of the administration. The ramifications were plentiful and opened old sores between the conservative and radical Republicans. Bryant had attacked the conservative Thurlow Weed for years. Now it was Weed's turn to take the offensive and charge that Henderson's arms were "shoulder deep in the federal treasury."[43]

Since Welles knew he was disturbing a hornet's nest, he informed Lincoln of the case before it became public. Lincoln asked Welles if he was certain of Henderson's guilt and offered no objection. The accusations were based on a deposition by a merchant, Joseph L. Savage, who stated that he received less than the total amount when he submitted vouchers to the navy agent and the difference went to Henderson.

The same day the news of Henderson's arrest appeared in the press, a letter from Henderson was simultaneously printed in the *Times*. He claimed that he had been wrongly accused of paying too much for materials and cited examples. The navy agent admitted, for instance, that he had paid $25 a barrel for pitch when it was charged that the proper price was $2.50 a barrel and $3.50 for a gallon of turpentine for which it was claimed that he should have paid $1.35. Henderson, in his defense, said that at the time he bought these products he paid the going price.

The *Evening Post* portrayed Henderson as a model of rectitude and an innocent victim of a political vendetta. Bryant wrote to Lincoln through Welles reaffirming Henderson's "spotless" reputation and asked the president to give him his job back. Bryant added, "What makes these severe proceedings still more unkind is that Mr. Henderson has always zealously supported your administration, that he has used all his influence in its favor, and that he desired and approved your second nomination." The editor's impertinence and implication were obvious, but Lincoln took the trouble to reply, "Whether Mr. Henderson was a supporter of my second nomination I neither knew, or enquired, or even thought of." He closed by writing, "While the subject is up may I ask whether the Evening Post has not assailed me for supposed too lenient dealing with persons charged of fraud & crime? and that in cases of which the Post could know but little of the facts? I shall certainly deal as leniently with Mr. Henderson as I have felt my duty to deal with others, notwithstanding any newspaper assaults."[44]

The righteous Bryant continued to support Henderson in the pages of the *Evening Post* and classified the case as one more "arbitrary arrest." He was confident that eventually Henderson would prove his innocence. In a hearing before a United States commissioner, the government claimed that the deductions from Savage's bill represented the extortion of a 7 percent commission. Edwards Pierrepont, Henderson's lawyer, attacked Savage's integrity and said that the $2,000 Henderson had received from the merchant was actually interest on a loan made to him. Pierrepont tried to obtain a dismissal, but the commissioner held

Henderson for trial. The case, however, did not go to trial until after the war. In May 1865, the United States Circuit Court judge ruled that the evidence was insufficient to support the charge and a jury returned a verdict of not guilty.[45]

Henderson was legally exonerated, but later doubts cropped up about his innocence. His partner Parke Godwin, disillusioned over internal affairs of the *Evening Post,* stated that Henderson's private bank account showed "very large transactions which are believed to correspond singularly with the entries in the books of the contractors implicated with him." Later, Henderson was involved in a messy business affair when he misappropriated newspaper funds and wrongfully made charges of $200,000 against the account of his loyal friend Bryant. Only a pledge of Henderson's stock as security avoided a criminal trial.[46] But all of that was in the future and did not lighten the intricate and prickly political problems in the city during the forthcoming presidential campaign.

During the summer of 1864, Parke Godwin was among those who joined Greeley and others in an effort to force Lincoln to withdraw as the party's nominee. Greeley envisioned a Democratic victory even though the Democrats had not yet nominated a candidate. He believed that another Republican candidate might give the party a chance to turn the tide. John Jay was sympathetic to this idea and thought it would be wise to confront Lincoln with the so-called facts in the hope that he might withdraw.

The division between the two wings of the Republican party was so sharply drawn that some Democrats believed they could persuade the radicals to join them against Lincoln in the coming election. Amasa Parker, aware that politics made strange bedfellows, wrote to Tilden, "Those who compose that branch [Radicals] are now entirely *out* with Mr. Lincoln."[47] He thought the time had come to make overtures to them and suggested that Tilden talk to Bryant. Although nothing came of the scheme, it was an indication of the strong sentiment for a coalition to beat Lincoln.

The cabal consisting of George Opdyke, Theodore Tilton, and David Dudley Field was among the city leaders who set out to overturn Lincoln's nomination. John Austin Stevens, Jr., secretary of the Chamber of Commerce and son of the president of the Bank of Commerce, was another active member of the movement. Stevens's actions enraged some people, who said he had transformed the Chamber of Commerce from a business organization into a political machine.[48] The charge had some justification because Stevens devoted a large part of his time to political rather than commercial affairs. He was certain that Lincoln could not be reelected and would have been delighted with the nomination of Chase, with whom he had developed a close relationship. But now Ben Butler was the man on whom he pinned his hopes. He said that if the Democrats did not nominate a loyal man, "We may yet nail to the mast the flag of old Ben Butler and fight out the fight." He corresponded diligently with people around the country who shared similar views, and Edgar Conkling of Cincinnati bolstered his opinion by telling him, "I will guarantee your success with Butler if you get Lincoln to resign."[49]

Men such as Greeley, Opdyke, Field, and Stevens who strove to split the Republican party continued to argue that a new candidate was needed to achieve unity. A new candidate would inspire confidence and infuse life into the party. Lincoln's nomination was a misfortune and premature. Times had changed. Another four years with Lincoln as president would be a disaster. One plan to accomplish their purpose was to hold a convention in Cincinnati, and Stevens got a large number of signatures for a convention call. All radicals, however, did not agree with these tactics. Francis Lieber, for one, refused to sign a petition asking Lincoln to withdraw. Although a call for a new convention went out privately with the hope that it would gain support of the loyal governors, the plan made no headway.

Reluctantly, the radicals who had plotted to ditch Lincoln realized they had no alternative and supported the regular party ticket. Opdyke frankly admitted that his exertions for a new candidate had failed and that the plan had to be abandoned. Later, Chase wrote to the stubborn Stevens that he hoped the young man had carried out his intention to disconnect himself from any activity "unfriendly to the Union nominations at Baltimore and that you will come out zealously in their support."[50]

Some of the dissidents changed their colors so quickly that doubts were raised about their motives. Greeley's sudden turnabout startled Alford Erbe, who wrote John A. Stevens, Jr., "There is room for a suspicion that Mr. Greeley and perhaps others have acted insincerely from the start . . . to make a strong show of opposition and thereby make privately the best bargain they could."⁵¹ Such tactics were not new to politics, and Erbe may have been right. Greeley was always more devious than his apparent air of innocence indicated. But no one could deny that quick changes were characteristic of Greeley. Erbe, however, knew that nothing further could be done, and he was deeply disappointed.

The arrival of summer reminded New Yorkers of the first anniversary of the riot. Mayor Gunther conferred with General Sandford about the safety of the city. Gunther had never exhibited any love for the military, but he did not want the city's forces reduced. Sandford reassured the mayor, but that was not enough for Gunther, who wanted public credit for protection of the city. For the record, he sent Sandford a letter the day after their meeting that was obviously intended for citywide readership. He wrote that for the great center of commerce "we should not by any action of our own, place those great interests in jeopardy by their withdrawing our military protection. ... I entertain grave apprehensions that their withdrawal from the city, at a time when the depreciation of our currency is bearing heavily on the mass of our population, might tempt the lawless and evil disposed to avail themselves of what would seem to them a favorable opportunity for arson and plunder." The letter, published in the press, irritated Sandford, and he answerd by repeating the assurances he had already given the mayor. He added that he did not appreciate publication of the mayor's letter, which might unnecessarily excite fears. Gunther blamed the publication on his copyist, but he did not seem overly concerned. He had carried out his ploy.⁵²

General Dix was also concerned about the safety of the city. Grant's lack of success in Virginia had cost tens of thousands of casualties, and Dix received urgent demands for troops for the front. He quietly conferred with the police and concluded that the withdrawal of forces from New York might invite a new outbreak. His son Morgan noted in his diary, "Thus we appear, after the lapse of a year's time, to be thrown back into the same mortifying, humiliating, & very critical position which we stood last July. What can be more discouraging?" Depression and anxiety increased when General Dix received telegraph messages that the Confederates were about to take Baltimore. He heard that the railroad and telegraph lines were cut between Baltimore and Philadelphia and that rebels were capturing trains full of passengers between the two points. Confirmation of reports was difficult, and a breakdown in telegraph lines between New York and Washington made the situation even more grave. After a couple of days of anxious waiting, word arrived that the alarm was unfounded.[53]

Fernando Wood muddied the waters during these tense days by saying that the defense of the capital was the sole reason he had raised the Mozart Regiment, the Fortieth New York. Now he believed the regiment was being "prostituted" for other purposes, and he wanted an immediate peace. This did not sit well with either the colonel of the regiment, Thomas Egan, or his men, who countered that Wood had not really raised the regiment in the first place. Egan explained that he had organized the Fortieth New York as the "Constitution Guard" with funds he and his friends had furnished. But the regiment could enter the federal service only by authorization of the Union Defense Committee, and at the time Mayor Wood had the right to nominate a regiment for the one remaining opening. Under the circumstances, Egan accepted the name Mozart Regiment bitterly. But he deprecated "pretensions to our paternity as a regiment of Fernando Wood." Egan wrote to M. F. Odell, "I speak the true sentiments of every member of the 40th New York when I repudiate all cries of 'Peace, Peace!' on any other terms than those of absolute surrender by every armed rebel." The officers and men of the Fortieth went further by publishing unanimous resolutions repudiating Wood. But Wood was a difficult man to embarrass, and his cries for peace continued.[54]

Greeley was beside himself during these hot and humid days, and he seemed to become more volatile every day. Although he still supported the war, he was horrified and despondent over the high casualties. In July, Greeley received a letter from a friend, William Jewett, which was written at Niagara Falls and presented visions of peace. "I am authorized to state to you," Jewett wrote, "for our use only, not the public, that two ambassadors of Davis & Co. are now in Canada, with full powers for a peace." He urged Greeley to go to Cataract House for a private interview that would lead to peace terms. At the same time, Samuel Tilden received an invitation from a Jewett associate, George N. Sanders, in Canada asking him to meet with Clement C. Clay and Jacob Thompson, representatives from the South. Tilden was assured that all the difficulties of the war could be adjusted with honor. But Tilden appears to have wisely ignored the letter. Jewett was not the most substantial person to pin hopes on, but Greeley forwarded his letter to Lincoln saying, "I venture to remind you that our bleeding, bankrupt, almost dying country also longs for peace; shudders at the prospect of fresh conscriptions, of further wholesale devastations, and of new rivers of human blood." He also told Lincoln, probably correctly, that there was a widespread conviction that the government was not anxious for peace and that that perception would do much harm in the coming election. Greeley believed that he had a workable plan to attain peace and reunion. It required aboliton of slavery with $400 million compensation to the slaveowners, amnesty for all political offenses, representation of slave states in proportion to population, and a national convention to settle outstanding disputes. "I do not say that a just peace is now attainable," he told Lincoln, "though I do believe it to be so. But I do say, that a frank offer by you to the insurgents of terms which the impartial say ought to be accepted, will, at the worst, prove an immense and sorely needed advantage to the national cause; it may save us from a northern insurrection."[55]

Lincoln did not need to be reminded of the horrors of war or the desire for peace. Greeley's letter was presumptuous, but Lincoln had an answer. The president replied that he would issue safe-conduct for any person from the Confederacy who bore terms offering unconditional restoration of the Union and the abandonment of slavery. He also assigned Greeley the task of meeting the commissioners and escorting them to Washington. Lincoln, weary of Greeley's carping, reportedly said to Senator James Harlan of Iowa, "I just thought I would let him go up and crack that nut for himself."[56]

Greeley did not want the assignment. It was easy to criticize but hazardous to accept responsibility for such a delicate diplomatic mission. Lincoln knew the pitfalls that Greeley faced when he wrote, "I not only intend a sincere effort for peace, but I intend that you shall be a personal witness that it is made." It was Greeley's turn to act, not write. Reluctantly, Greeley left for Niagara Falls, met Jewett, and soon found that the "ambassadors" were not accredited representatives of the Confederacy. Greeley was forced to advise Lincoln that neither Jacob Thompson nor James Holcombe of Mississippi, another southern agent, nor Clement Clay had worthwhile credentials. Nevertheless, he added that if given safe-conduct to Washington and then to Richmond, they would gain the necessary authority. Greeley's chastening experience altered his tone a little as he tried to protect his exposed position. "I am of course," he wrote, "other than sanguine that a Peace can now be made."[57]

Lincoln played his hand to the full and went further than he ever had before in emphasizing the abolition of slavery as necessary in any peace plan. On July 16, 1864, Lincoln wrote, "To Whom It May Concern: Any proposition which embraces the restoration of peace, the integrity of the whole Union, and the abandonment of slavery, and which comes by and with an authority that can control the armies now at War against the United States, will be received and considered by the Executive Government of the United States, and will be met by liberal terms on other substantial and collateral points, and the bearer or bearers thereof shall have safe-conduct both ways." Lincoln's statement about slavery aroused criticism among northerners who thought it too extreme. Later in the month, Charles Dana, assistant secretary of war and former managing editor of the *Tribune,* told Henry Raymond that if the president had left slavery out of his letter he would have done himself and his party great injury. "As you are very well aware," he wrote, "he is more or less under suspicion of a want of earnestness upon this supreme question and if in such a communication he had omitted all reference to it, people would have taken for granted that he was willing to sacrifice his emancipation proclamation, and let the Southern States come back with their old powers."[58]

John Hay, the president's secretary, delivered Lincoln's note to Greeley at Niagara Falls. Hay met the men with whom Greeley had been conferring and was not impressed by their appearance and character. Nonetheless, Hay, by direction of the president, offered safe-conduct to Clement Clay, James Holcombe, George Sanders, and Jacob Thompson to Washington in the company of Greeley.[59] The sham of the southerners' mission soon became obvious. Holcombe replied to Greeley through Jewett, who released a copy to the Associated Press. "We feel confident," Holcombe wrote, "that you must share our profound regret that the spirit which dictated the first step toward peace had not continued to animate the councils of your President." The "rude withdrawal of a courteous overture for negotiation" was not understood, Holcombe claimed, and the South could not accept Lincoln's advance terms of peace.[60]

The public letter placed Lincoln in a bad light and was made worse by Greeley's silence. The *Evening Post, Times,* and *Herald* took pleasure in attacking Greeley for attempting to negotiate with the Confederacy. Bennett called Greeley a "nincompoop without genius." Yet it was Lincoln who had to take responsibility. William Evarts, a rare city leader who was outspoken in his support of Lincoln, wrote to the Union Club at Yale, "The struggling boat's crew that goes for an immediate cessation of hostilities with the rapids above Niagara, may resume them, but it will be at the bottom of the Fall."[61]

Greeley deserved to be the laughingstock. Still, Lincoln was falsely portrayed to the public. More than one person had concluded long ago that Greeley was more dangerous to his friends than to his enemies. The incident increased interest in New York City in the movement that was under way to replace Lincoln as the Republican presidential candidate. Greeley's failure as a peace negotiator did not stop him from continuing to place the blame on Lincoln for what he himself had failed to achieve. On August 8, Greeley accused Lincoln of being misled when he did not let Alexander Stephens, the vice-president of the Confederacy, go to Washington on a peace mission the previous year. "And the day after the news of Vicksburg's surrender you should have sent to Richmond, if necessary, proffering terms of pacification, and begging the Rebel chiefs no longer to prosecute this murderous fray."[62]

Lincoln's patience with Greeley was wearing thin, but he tried to respond to the editor's misunderstanding about Stephens. The Confederate vice-president had intended to go to Washington in the name of the "Confederate States" in a ship of the "Confederate States Navy." He made no pretense of making a peace proposal then or later. It was a good explanation for Greeley and probably a waste of the president's time.[63]

Henry Raymond wanted to expose the Niagara Falls episode, which he regarded as "tomfoolery" by publishing the entire correspondence between Lincoln and Greeley in the *Times*. Lincoln was willing except that he wanted the deletion of some of Greeley's depressing remarks about the state of the country such as the "bleeding, bankrupt, almost dying," which he believed could harm public morale. Greeley escaped having the correspondence exposed because he objected to any deletions. Lincoln resignedly wrote to Raymond that he had decided it was better for him to submit for the time to the consequences of the false position "than to subject the country to the consequences of publishing these discouraging and injurious parts." Publicly Greeley won the day, but Lincoln lost any remnant of faith he may have had in the editor of the *Tribune*. "Sometimes," Lincoln said, "when far gone, we found the leather so rotten the stitches would not hold. Greeley is so rotten that nothing can be done with him. He is not truthful; the stitches all wear out."[64] Greeley's country boy air of innocence, honesty, and simplicity was really a coating of a complex, deceitful, and ambitious character. Still, Greeley was right that the people desperately wanted peace.

Nothing seemed to go right for the faction-ridden Republican party. While Republican hopes plummeted, McClellan's strength grew in the city. The previous fall, the Common Council had shown its affection for the general by passing a resolution signed by the mayor that sang his praises. And in August 1864, a rally supporting McClellan for president brought out an immense, enthusiastic crowd. It may have been the largest public gathering ever assembled in the city. McClellan was clearly the favorite, although whether he would receive the nomination at the Democratic convention in Chicago was still a question.

Raymond, as chairman of the Republican party, received only bad news from his state chairmen. The Niagara Falls affair had added to his troubles, and he wondered if Lincoln had been wise in so emphatically calling for the abandonment of slavery as a part of any peace plan. In a somber mood, Raymond reflected a widespread attitude in the city when he wrote to Simon Cameron of the general desire of the people for a change, their belief that the war had languished under Lincoln, "and that he cannot or will not give us peace." He almost sounded like Greeley when he was depressed. Yet he recognized that the people would reject a peace that brought disunion: "I fear that the desire for peace, aided by the impression or suspicion even that Mr. Lincoln is fighting not for the Union but for the abolition of slavery, and by the draft, the tax, the lack of victories, the discontent with the Cabinet and the other influences that are swelling the tide of hostility to the Administration will overbear it and give control of everything to the Opposition." It was hardly a positive outlook for a national chairman to take.[65]

Raymond met members of the national executive committee of the party at the Astor House and received confirmation of his worst fears. Raymond wrote to Lincoln proposing that Lincoln appoint a commission to make a peace offer to Jefferson Davis "on the sole condition of acknowledging the supremacy of the Constitution, all other questions to be settled in a convention of the people of the United States." Raymond understandably wanted to show the electorate some genuine movement toward peace. It was a last gasp to achieve success at the polls. Lincoln was not interested in any more attempts at peace conferences, but he was willing to let Raymond go to Richmond for another try. The cabinet, however, objected, believing that it would do more harm than good, and the proposal faded away.[66]

Mayor Gunther did not lose an opportunity to speak in favor of peace. President Lincoln had proclaimed August 24 as a day of fasting, humiliation, and prayer, and the mayor added his own pronouncement. He urged that the ministers, "who have inculcated the doctrines of war and blood so much at variance with the teachings of their Divine Master . . . involve the mercy of Heaven to hasten the relief of our suffering people by turning the hearts of those in authority into the blessed ways of Peace."[67] There was no reason to doubt the sincerity of Gunther's longing for peace or his disgust with the easy acceptance of war by some clergymen. His irritation with the hypocrisy of war was one of his most appealing characteristics. But neither he nor anyone else offered a workable plan for peace.

By now, Lincoln thought his reelection was improbable. He had even gone so far as to dangle the possibility of a prestigious post, perhaps minister to France, as an enticement for James Gordon Bennett to ease his criticism. But the publisher was not tempted. Lincoln heard gloomy predictions from almost every quarter, and the transmitters of bad news never spared him. Thurlow Weed, recognized as a great political seer, met Lincoln early in August and told him that his reelection was an impossibility.[68]

The doomsayers spoke with certainty. Greeley wrote to Opdyke, "Mr. Lincoln is already beaten. He cannot be elected. And we must have another ticket to save us from overthrow."[69] He was still ready to support Grant, Butler, or Sherman for president and Farragut for vice-president. Bryant commented to his wife that Lincoln had lost ground since his nomination. All anyone could do was hope. The experts had analyzed the situation and were certain of the outcome.[70]

As party chairman Raymond faced practical as well as theorectical problems. He needed money for the campaign and was surprised to meet resistance from Secretary of the Navy Welles when he sought funds from a traditional source. In August, Gideon Welles walked into the president's office while Raymond was conferring with Lincoln. Welles had low opinions of most of the president's political associates, and Raymond was no exception. He considered Raymond "a political vagabond" and a humble henchman of Weed and Seward. While the two men were in his presence, Lincoln decided it was a good time to discuss Raymond's fund-raising complaints. Raymond told Welles that he was not pleased with the naval constructor at the Brooklyn Navy Yard, who blocked the collection of party assessments from the workers. Raymond said such collections were customarily made during previous administrations, but Welles remained unsympathetic. The secretary realized that "parties did strange things in New York," but he believed the practice was "inexcusable and indefensible." Welles remained adamant even when Abram Wakeman, the New York postmaster, pressed the subject later in the month. Raymond had expected 5 percent of the men's annual wages, but he had to proceed without the help of the Navy Department. It was one more defeat for the national chairman in a campaign that seemed hopeless. Welles, working off his wrath in his diary, later wrote that in party matters Raymond had neither honesty nor principle. "Money and office, not argument and reason, are the means which he would use. This fellow, trained in the vicious New York school of politics ... is spending much of his time in Washington working upon the President secretly, trying to poison his mind and induce him to take steps that would forever injure him." New Yorkers, whatever their political shade, were not to be trusted.[71]

15
Presidential Election

The embarrassing efforts at negotiating peace, patronage disputes, and military frustrations divided the Republicans and buoyed the spirits of the Democrats, who expected victory in November. Backed by Barlow and Belmont, McClellan's nomination seemed more certain every day. For most of the past year, the general lived at the house on West Thirty-first Street that had been given to him by friends. The city was filled with admirers who were certain that McClellan, the best general in the Union army, had been needlessly cast aside by Lincoln. Now, he might well be the next president of the United States. The city government emphasized its admiration for him by authorizing the street commissioner, an odd choice, to spend $1,000 for a portrait of the general.

Francis P. Blair, Lincoln's friend, supporter, and father of Montgomery Blair, the postmaster general, went to New York City in the hope of waylaying McClellan's candidacy. He saw James Gordon Bennett, by no means a Lincoln supporter, who analyzed the problem in his practical fashion. The publisher advised Blair, "Tell him [Lincoln] to restore McClellan to the army and he will carry the election by default." Then Blair, on his own authority and initiative, spent two hours with McClellan hoping to discourage him from accepting the nomination at the upcoming Chicago convention. He told McClellan that if nominated he would be defeated and that it would be wiser to inspire northern Democrats by requesting Lincoln to reassign him to a military post. The general listened courteously, thanked Blair for his suggestions, and remained noncommittal while disclaiming interest in the White House.1

The month of August 1864 was so depressing for the Republicans that the Democrats had good reason to dream of glory. Fernando Wood planned to dominate the national convention. At the start of the year he had said "that the National Democracy was unqualifiedly opposed to the further prosecution of the war of emancipation and extermination now being waged against the seceded States, and will continue to demand negotiation, reconciliation, and peace." Wood intended to pursue these principles in the selection of a candidate and the writing of a platform. Early in August, Wood's friends at Mozart Hall unanimously passed a resolution that they would not vote for any man for president who favored further prosecution of the war.[2]

The more moderate August Belmont sounded no less harsh when he addressed the Chicago convention. "Four years of misrule," he said, "by a sectional, fanatical, and corrupt party have brought our country to the very verge of ruin." Four more years of Lincoln would bring "utter disintegration of our whole political and social system amidst bloodshed and anarchy."[3]

Although the words of the war and peace factions of the Democratic party were strident and excessive, no one in the convention demanded peace without reunion. The peace men, led by Vallandigham, drafted the platform, which called for hostilities to cease "at the earliest possible moment." Much was made of the peace plank. It did not renounce the Union although it gave the impression of extremism. Its call for a peace was unattainable for the simple reason that the Confederacy, insisting on independence, would not cooperate. Still, the platform led to false interpretations of disloyalty and was a detriment to the Democratic candidate.

Although the Wood brothers preferred another candidate, McClellan easily won the nomination. Fernando Wood's influence within the Democratic party was clearly on the wane. Noah Brooks, a Washington correspondent, said that according to Lincoln, Fernando Wood had told the president, "We Peace Democrats are the only Democrats; all others are bastards and imposters, there is no such thing as a War Democrat for that is a contradiction in terms." Wood did not expect the Democrats to win the election. But when peace arrived, he believed the Democrats would work with southerners and regain their "rightful ascendancy." Wood never counted himself out, and he undoubtedly expected to take part in that ascendancy.[4]

Governor Seymour was chairman of the notification committee, and he wrote the letter advising McClellan of his selection as the Democratic presidential candidate at the St. Nicholas Hotel in New York City. When McClellan responded with his letter of acceptance, which was written with the help of Barlow, he disowned the peace plank in the platform. Such a declamation was an absolute necessity if he wished to retain a large body of followers within the Democratic party. Despite the sharp differences in personality, political issues, and conduct of the war, McClellan joined Lincoln in pronouncing his faith in the Union.[5]

New York City greeted McClellan's nomination with wild enthusiasm. Tammany Hall decorated and lighted its building and arranged for a big ratification meeting in City Hall Park. At the meeting, enthusiastic Tammanyites attacked "the imbecility of the administration of Abraham Lincoln," which had "forfeited the confidence of the loyal States" by its unconstitutional behavior and attempting to raise the executive branch of government over the legislative and judicial.[6] *Imbecility* was a favorite word of politicians and newspapermen in this day, and they wore it threadbare in their accusations against Lincoln and his administration. "Little Mac's" stock was on the rise as jubilant Democrats ignited bonfires around the city.

Two weeks later, fifty or sixty disgruntled peace men, unwilling to support McClellan, met at the St. Nicholas Hotel to select another candidate. Benjamin Wood and James McMaster of the *Freeman's Journal* were anxious to lend their influence, but the group failed to name anyone and the effort collapsed. No alternative was left except to vote for McClellan.[7]

At the end of the dismal month, Lincoln sent his secretary John Nicolay to see Hiram Barney, the New York port collector. The time had come to ease the political strain by asking Barney to resign. Nicolay told Barney that the president wanted to express his kind personal regards and continued friendship. It was a gracious gesture under difficult circumstances. Lincoln admitted, however, that it would relieve him of political embarrassment if Barney resigned. Barney, acting as a true gentleman, cheerfully complied with the president's request. Actually, he had written a draft letter of resignation in June and had intended to send it to Chase's successor as secretary of the treasury, William Fessenden. When he immediately submitted his formal resignation, Weed won another political scuffle.[8] The new appointee for this lucrative post was Weed's good friend Simeon Draper. The removal of Barney and the success of Weed incensed William Cullen Bryant, who wrote John Murray Forbes, a Boston financier, "I am so utterly disgusted with Lincoln's behavior that I cannot muster respectful terms in which to write him."[9]

Crowds in New York City show their strong support for George McClellan in the 1864 presidential campaign. (Courtesy of the New-York Historical Society)

Also in August the Confederates dealt a demoralizing blow to New York City. The Confederate steamer *Tallahassee* audaciously captured two Sandy Hook pilot boats off New York Harbor, bringing the war close to home. The rebel ship laid in wait for outbound vessels and in less than two weeks, according to official records, destroyed or damaged more than thirty ships. Some estimates ran as high as fifty-four ships destroyed, and insurance men shivered over the consequences. Many ships, ready to depart, waited impatiently in the harbor for the threat to pass. Finally, the *Tallahassee* sailed for Nova Scotia.

Yet the city may have been fortunate not to have suffered greater damage. John Taylor Wood, a grandson of President Zachary Taylor and captain of the *Tallahassee,* had a reputation for recklessness. Although he had considerable naval experience, he was actually a colonel in the Confederate cavalry, and like Semmes, he longed to create havoc in New York. He knew which ships were in port from newspapers that he had taken from captured ships, and he hoped to set fire to the ships in the harbor, blast the navy yard in Brooklyn, and then escape into Long Island Sound. Later, he claimed that he gave up the plan only because he did not have a pilot to take the *Tallahassee* through treacherous Hell Gate.[10]

During these unpleasant days, the president called for five hundred thousand more men for the army. The call for troops prompted John Mullaly to publish an article called "The Coming Draft" in his paper, now named the *Metropolitan Record and New York Vindicator,* which resulted in his arrest for counseling Governor Seymour and others to resist the draft. The political aspects of the arrest were minimized, however, when the court ruled in a preliminary hearing that even though Mullaly had urged the governor "to resist the draft," these were 'mere preliminaries" because the draft would not go into effect until September. Although Mullaly toned down his comments about the draft after this incident, he continued to express his belief that the South had the right to select its own government and that the North "in the endeavor to force her into a compulsory Union is violating the principle of universal suffrage, which we claim to be the foundation of our democratic system. By this right we shall continue to stand, for it is a right older and more valuable than even the Union itself."[11]

Recruiting was always difficult. Despite inducements, there were never enough men to win the war. The New York Stock Exchange even appropriated a thousand dollars to help spur enlistments after its board heard General Hancock tell about the army's manpower needs.[12] To make matters worse, recruiters from other towns and counties in the state descended on the city, erected booths in parks and squares, and with offers of higher bounties took men the city needed to fill its own quota. The National Affairs Committee of the Common Council complained that "men are constantly taken from under our noses and we are powerless." The committee estimated that half of the quotas of adjoining counties and towns under the last call were filled by men signed up in New York City. A campaign to clear out the interlopers' booths was fruitless. Closed one day, they returned the next.[13]

The city of Brooklyn was a special annoyance. Orison Blunt indignantly advised the Common Council that nine-tenths of the residents of

Brooklyn made their incomes in Manhattan and paid no taxes there. Nonetheless, they obtained credit for one-fourth of the men recruited in New York simply because the cities were adjoining and some residents might have been claimed by Manhattan. Blunt believed with some reason that this principle could have been applied just as well to Jersey City or Hoboken.

Although the recruiting of immigrants was not as productive as generally supposed, brokers and agents from out of town were also busy at Castle Garden offering inducements to new arrivals. The Board of Supervisors reacted to this robbery of men with exasperation, erected a recruiting office nearby, and printed placards in German as well as English offering bounties. But the small number of men gained hardly compensated for the expense.

When Orison Blunt, a member of the Special Committee on Volunteering, complained to Admiral Paulding that the mustering officer of the Marine Corps was signing up substitutes for persons residing outside the county, the admiral showed no sympathy. He needed men and did not care where they came from. Finally, Blunt, concerned that the city had become a general rendezvous for outside recruiting agents, appealed to Mayor Gunther for help and enclosed a proposed ordinance to stop the practice and facilitate raising the city's quota. The mayor endorsed the proposal and forwarded it to the Board of Councilmen, which also gave its approval. But the Board of Aldermen, despite entreaties, failed to act on the measure.[14] Another irritant for recruiters was an ad that appeared requesting Yale alumni in the city to meet "to devise and adopt methods of mutual insurance against the draft."[15] This ad underscored the fact that young men of privilege easily evaded the call to serve their country.

The worst month of the election year for the Republicans eventually ended. Yet at the beginning of September, General Dix, vacationing on Long Island, received an urgent message from the War Department ordering him to proceed to New York immediately "to aid in preserving the peace of the city." Happily, it was a false alarm. Apparently someone in the War Department had misjudged public opinion in New York or feared the results of excessive jubilation in the city streets. The news was that Atlanta had fallen.[16]

Even the Common Council celebrated the good news, passing a resolution recommending illuminations for the recent success of the Union army. Mayor Gunther, however, refused to approve the resolution for which he received the hearty approval of the *Daily News*. The resolution required citizens to light a tallow candle in their windows. The mayor feared that those who did not comply might be denounced as disloyal. His veto message commented, "I do not see how those who have always held that the Federal Government has nothing to do with the domestic institutions of the States, can be expected to rejoice over victories, which whatever they may be, surely are not Union victories. If those victories were to unite the States, and were a sure harbinger of peace, I would be pleased if I could issue such a proclamation as would induce the poorest citizen to part with his last mite for the purchase of a single tallow candle to celebrate the event." This sour statement so riled the *Herald* that it suggested that Gunther should be mayor of Richmond. But Samuel Morse was among two hundred citizens who publicly expressed their esteem for the mayor and gave him their unqualified approval. Illumination, they said, was a manifestation of joy. Rejoicing over domestic strife was nothing less than political degeneration.[17]

Gunther saw the illumination episode as simply campaign politics. The administration claimed that the recent military success was the result of the Emancipation Proclamation and that this new policy would produce a succession of victories. In that event, Gunther was sure he would be called upon to light up the city every fortnight. The mayor doggedly proclaimed his attachment to the "Union as it was and the Constitution as it is" and denounced the president for demanding that the southern people abandon their constitutional rights. He argued that the difference between the two political parties in the North was that one called for unconditional surrender of states' rights while the other claimed that "peace may be restored on the basis of the Federal Union."[18]

Although the mayor was criticized for his decision, the *Tribune* sardonically absolved him, saying that "no human creature should be held responsible for want of brains." The paper regarded his lack in this respect a great misfortune rather than a fault. Yet Gunther did not lack brains. The timing of his statement may have been bad and his idealistic views may have been impossible to achieve, but they did not reflect lack of intelligence. This unique Tammany politician yearned for the practical application of Christian love and forgiveness in a nation filled with hatred, which was too much to expect in the real world.

Despite Mayor Gunther's sentiments, the mood of the nation changed and the Republicans capitalized on the military victory. Greeley, now effervescent, was suddenly a Lincoln supporter, and thousands

of other citizens had an abrupt change of heart. Inconsistent or not, reluctant or not, Radical Republicans flocked to Lincoln's banner. The conservative Thurlow Weed, recently so pessimistic, astutely recognized the
shift. He took a suite of rooms at the Astor House adjoining the Republican State Committee to be near the center of activity. The hotel was also
headquarters for Raymond's direction of the national campaign. And
John Jacob Astor, Jr., politely wrote a jarring note to McClellan telling
him that he would not vote for him even though he retained affectionate
personal feelings.[19]

During September Frémont met with a delegation of Republicans
in New York who urged him to give up his race as a third-party presidential candidate. He swallowed the bitter pill and gracelessly withdrew
from the campaign with a swipe at Lincoln's administration as a political, military, and financial failure. The genial Cochrane, the vice-presi-
dential candidate, on friendlier terms with Lincoln, gave up the race
graciously.

"True" Democrats rallied to the side of Lincoln, too. Some people
may have called them "War" Democrats, the definitions were never exact, but it was a faction loyal to the administration. In a meeting at
Cooper Institute, James Worrall, a Pennsylvanian, spoke to an audience
of such Democrats and took aim at August Belmont, chairman of the
Democratic party, as an agent of the Rothschilds: "There is not a people
or government in Christendom in which the paws, or fangs, or claws of
the Rothschilds are not plunged to the very heart of the treasury."[20]

Francis Lieber wrote campaign literature with a passion. He aimed
much of his work at New York City in an attempt to minimize the heavy
Democratic influence. As a German immigrant, he appealed to the German-Americans in the city to vote for the Union party. A campaign pam-
phlet, *Lincoln or McClellan,* also printed as *Lincoln oder McClellan? Au-
freuf an die Deutschen in Amerika,* referred to the distress caused by lack
of union in the fatherland and drew an obvious comparison. The address proved to be very popular, and the *Tribune* could not seem to produce enough copies. Finally, a copy was posted on the *Tribune* bulletin
board and large numbers of "Dutchmen" read the address there. Lieber
was surprised that this piece was so popular and was a trifle annoyed because his most acclaimed writing was his least profound.[21]

The trend toward Lincoln, however, did not represent sentiment in
New York City. Veterans formed McClellan Legions, and Colonel Lionel

d'Epineuil, who had led the Epineuil Zouaves at the start of the war, campaigned among army men on active service. Manton Marble urged McClellan to keep up a "diligent friendly correspondence with all your old friends in the army," a tactic he said had worked for Franklin Pierce, who had kept up a lively correspondence with army officers he had known in Mexico. The Young Men's Democratic Union Club at 534 Broadway vibrated with energy. Its slogan was "Peace upon the basis of the Union," and a banner hanging in front of Tammany Hall read, "Union as it was and Constitution as it is." In McClellan parades around town workingmen ironically carried signs which ridiculed Lincoln as a "railsplitter." Charles Rogers, a dry goods clerk, watched the "War Eagles" parade for Lincoln one night, but a McClellan torchlight procession the next night impressed him as both larger and better.[22]

McClellan received as much advice from newspaper editors as did Lincoln. J. H. Van Evrie, editor of the *Day-Book*, told the general that if he showed more hostility to abolition the peace men would support him. The *Herald* was supposedly neutral in the campaign, but Albert Ramsey wrote McClellan that an excellent feeling existed toward him in the *Herald* office: "All personal pique seems to have been overcome, and the former kind feelings reestablished." Ramsey said that Bennett doubted that McClellan could win the election and did not want to commit his paper. "Now," Ramsey wrote, "he can serve us better if his paper be not committed either way."[23]

If Bennett was neutral in the campaign, he showed it in a strange way. He thought that both Lincoln and McClellan had been tried in their jobs and found wanting. Nevertheless, not long after Ramsey wrote to McClellan, a *Herald* editorial ripped into Lincoln: "The imbecility of Old Abe, his mismanagement of the war and total incompetency exhibited at almost every state of the present struggle, have alienated many whose sympathies are with the Republican party."[24]

Although the Republicans appeared to be incompetent, the Democrats campaigned under a cloud of suspicion. William Aspinwall considered sympathy with the rebels the curse of the Democratic party, and he told Samuel Barlow that it was a weight the party must shake off. "I would see," he wrote, "that some McClellan Club in New York & other prominent points, burnt as much powder as the Republicans in celebrating the victories announced from time to time — As matters now stand they make the noise & get the credit; and will get the votes too unless this is controlled."[25] The advice was sound, but Barlow's outspoken views since the start of the war had done their share in arousing suspicions against the Democrats. His antiwar comments may have been acceptable in New York City, but they were not acceptable many other places in the North. It was a little late for him to initiate a show of enthusiasm for the war.

John A. Stevens, Jr., urged Chase to speak in New York during the campaign, but the former secretary of the treasury, proud and sensitive, clearly indicated that he did not have the best relations with New York commercial circles. He told Stevens that if he could flatter himself into believing that the businessmen of the city had an interest in his views, he would "try to overcome my extreme repugnance to address a New York audience." But he had no evidence that such interest existed, and he was not sorry. He did not want to speak in the city without "preparation that every word may be taken down as spoken." Chase felt that he could not speak freely in the city, as he did in the West, without his words being distorted.[26]

In the midst of the campaign, gold speculators hoped to force the price of gold to 300. They came close with a high of 285 in July. By September, however, General Philip Sheridan was raising havoc in the Shenandoah Valley and the price of gold began to fall. Then Assistant Treasurer Cisco received authority to sell gold late in the season. On October 31, he started selling and continued until election day. The fall of the price of gold and the success of the Union army led a gentlemen's furnishing store to advertise its entire stock at reduced prices, but it may have been a merchandising stunt. When gold moved up again, Macy's prices remained low.[27]

The dapper August Belmont spoke at Cooper Institute in November and stressed that the Republicans would try to prolong the war. He pictured the South fighting to the last extremity "if the fatal policy of confiscation and forcible emancipation is to be persisted in, and that is the policy to which Mr. Lincoln and his party are pledged, should they be able to keep themselves in power."[28]

A few days before the election, a large outdoor meeting with three speakers' stands was held by antiadministration bankers and merchants at Wall and Broad streets. Among those who lent their names to the occasion were rich William Aspinwall and William B. Astor as well as Assistant Treasurer John J. Cisco. Samuel Tilden, one of the speakers, said that Lincoln believed that abolition of slavery was preferable to the happiness of the white race and denied that the South could ever be restored on that basis.[29]

Fernando Wood did not let a cold deter him from campaigning until the last minute. At a meeting of the Workingmen's Independent Democratic Club of the Twenty-second Ward, he blithely instilled fear in the hearts and minds of his listeners by saying that Lincoln wanted to free slaves so they could take the place of white laborers in the North. The black man would be raised at the expense of the white. In contrast, he said, Democrats proposed a government of white men, not blacks.[30]

As election day approached, memories of the draft riots revived, and wild rumors of anticipated violence swept the city. Some reports were more than rumors. The previous July, the *Richmond Whig* had issued a call for men to infiltrate the North. "Philadelphia, and even New York," the paper said, "is not beyond the reach of a long and brave arm. The moral people of these cities cannot be better taught the virtues of invasion than by the blazing light of their own dwellings."[31] Secretary of State Seward forwarded to City Hall a reliable report that Confederates planned to set fire to principal cities in the North on election day. The *Daily News* immediately denounced Seward's letter as "humiliating," a "palpable electioneering trick." An editorial said the people were weary of fables of conspiracy. The continued cry of "wolf" might be intended to throw the citizenry off guard when the real wolf came in the guise of administration fraud and violence at the polls. "No man would dare apply the torch in the midst of that excited populace." If the administration would only cease issuing inflammatory proclamations and mysterious dispatches, the election would be peaceful.[32]

General Butler, the "Beast" of New Orleans, was sent to the city by Stanton with troops from Virginia. The need for troops to maintain order was questionable, and Butler's jurisdiction in relation to that of his superior, the capable General Dix, was unclear. Copperheads regarded Butler as an "unscrupulous minister of arbitrary measures" who would produce a reign of terror. New Orleans, said the *Daily News*, gave "no diploma to tyranny that will entitle its holder to practice in New York."[33]

Butler, a clever and controversial politician, was an odd choice to bring tranquillity to the city at this tense time. Certainly his appearance could be interpreted as an effort to tip the scales in favor of the Union party presidential nominee. Butler's personal and political qualities

were questionable. Formerly a Democrat, currently a staunch administration man, he could be expected to come down heavily on the side of
the Radical Republicans if a difficult situation arose. It was almost beyond belief that he had been a Breckinridge Democrat from Massachusetts who had repeatedly supported Jefferson Davis for president at the
Democratic National Convention at Charleston in 1860.[34]

Butler's infamous occupation of New Orleans had bolstered his
family's fortunes and shocked northerners as well as southerners. He
had even forbidden silent prayer in New Orleans churches because he
was sure the people prayed for the Confederacy. But Butler was bright
and ambitious and enjoyed the limelight and the clashes that always surrounded him. Many could doubt his honesty, but few could doubt that
he possessed ability and strength. He had admirers in New York City,
who believed that he was a presidential possibility, but the city's Copperheads, including Mayor Gunther, could be forgiven for anticipating the
worst. When Butler received his orders to go to New York, Grant's military secretary said, "His name alone would be a terror to those who plotted against the republic." Butler reported officially to General Dix, the
commanding officer of the Department of the East. Nevertheless, their
authority seemed to overlap, and their relationship remained confused.
Butler was supposed to be in the city to meet any emergency that arose.
This was, of course, an insult to Dix. Butler told Secretary of War Stanton that he would "coddle" General Dix until it became necessary to be
something else, "and of that you must leave me to judge."[35]

Still, Dix was a politician and a strong man, and although modest
and of a completely different temperament than Butler, he was not to be
taken lightly. Any thought by Stanton or anyone else in Washington that
Dix was weak because he did not want to alarm the populace with a display of military force was mistaken. Dix knew the city and was a good
judge of its moods. He had grave reservations about the need for Butler
and his troops. And he was not naive about the mischief Butler could
create. When Butler arrived, Dix suggested that he take his troops to
northern New York and Vermont, which were considered vulnerable to
attack by Confederates in Canada. Butler knew it was an attempt to side-
line him. He appealed to Stanton and remained in the city. Dix won the
next round, however, when he received Stanton's approval to send about
three thousand of Butler's five thousand troops upstate to Albany, Buf-
falo, and Troy.

Butler set up his headquarters in the city on November 4, first at the Fifth Avenue Hotel, then at the larger Hoffman House. Judge Henry Dean, a bitter foe of the administration, publicly announced that Butler would be hanged if he marched up Broadway. When Butler arrived safely, he took the trouble to send for Dean, who, according to Butler, promised to correct his "pronouncement." It was the kind of outrageous situation that Butler enjoyed.

Morgan Dix stopped at his father's house on Twenty-first Street the next day and found everyone in a turmoil. General Dix had asked for additional troops, but he had not asked for such an intrusion and was disturbed by Butler's nervy assumption of authority. Dix was not sure whether he or Butler was to have command of New York, but he had already stopped Butler from issuing an inflammatory proclamation. According to Morgan Dix, Butler "telegraphed to Washington apparently with the idea of getting authority thence to issue what orders he liked best, and father at once telegraphed also . . . and Thurlow Weed has been telegraphing and everybody seems to be completely stirred up."[36]

Butler intended to take over the state militia in the city commanded by Major General Charles Sandford. Members of the militia were generally opposed to the administration, and Sandford refused to report to Butler. The situation calmed the day before the election, when Stanton, at the request of Lincoln, warned Butler against any "collision" between United States forces and the New York militia, adding, "as General Dix the commanding officer of the Dept. does not approve of the order proposed by you to be issued in reference to the Militia of the State . . . it had better not be issued." Dix had won the day.[37]

Frustrated in his martial ambitions, Butler turned his attention to Wall Street, searching for a Confederate conspiracy to devalue the currency. Butler thought there might be a move to run up the price of gold, which would affect the price of food and other necessities and cause discontent among the working classes. He telegraphed Stanton, "One thing is certain, that the gold business is in the hands of a half dozen firms who are all foreigners or secessionist." Butler's mistrust of speculators was not entirely unfounded. Within recent weeks, H. J. Lyons's brokerage firm had bought more than $10 million worth of gold and gave the appearance of disloyal behavior. Lyons was born in the South, was an officer in a Kentucky bank, had numerous business connections in the South, and had opened his office less than a year before. Referring to

Lyons's history, Butler told Stanton, "This shows that there is something behind him."

Butler sent for Lyons, and with his customary ability to put the fear of God into people, frightened the financier about the consequences of his gold buying. By the time Butler finished, Lyons meekly said he did not think he would buy any more gold and he would sell what he owned that day.[38]

Butler also levied his wrath on a few other New York branches of brokerage houses, including Vickers and Company of Liverpool, two Washington houses, and a Baltimore house. Butler's efforts were minimal, however, and though he may have temporarily cast a spell over the gold speculators, the price of gold did not immediately drop. While Butler searched for conspirators, two Confederates were actually plotting the destruction of the city in rooms one floor above his in his hotel. Butler would have gloried in their capture if he had only known about them.

The day before the election, an overly optimistic Albert Ramsey wrote to McClellan that confidence in the Democrats was perceptible in Wall Street and the radicals were frightened. "The army vote," he erroneously reported, "is clearly with us." He said soldiers discarded their Lincoln badges when they arrived home. And he did not think Lincoln would get thirty thousand votes in the city.[39]

Although it was a foregone conclusion that Lincoln would not carry New York City, Ramsey ignored the genuine enthusiasm for the president in some quarters. He apparently did not attend the huge outdoor meeting on Wall Street at the end of the campaign at which bankers and merchants mingled with mechanics and day laborers to express their support for Lincoln. Members of the Corn Exchange and New York Produce Exchange appeared in a body, and the rich, old Democrat Peter Cooper joined hands with Republicans Moses Grinnell and George Opdyke. Even fainthearted David Dudley Field, so recently opposed to the president, was there. It was a perfect example of the danger of generalizing about the attitudes of New Yorkers.[40] The final hours of the campaign were filled with rallies, torchlight parades, charges, and countercharges. The Loyal Ladies of the Union held a grand meeting at the Church of the Messiah, where the guest speaker, Charles Sumner, spoke with his usual grandiloquence. He was warmly applauded when he said that although he had often heard that clergymen and women had nothing to do with politics, the remarks came from those whose views were not acceptable to either clergymen or women. Sumner touched a raw nerve when he said that if Lincoln was slow, McClellan was slower. But McClellan had his moments of exhilaration while he reviewed a huge demonstration of the Democratic clubs of the city from his balcony at the Fifth Avenue Hotel.[41]

Contrary to expectations, the rainy, foggy election day was quiet. Ballots were cast from sunrise to sunset, but the long lines at the polls moved slowly. Edmund Stedman stood in the rain for two hours to vote for Lincoln. Dix had troops ready for any emergency. They were kept out of sight, mostly stationed on ships in both rivers so they would not incite the trouble they were supposed to prevent. Offshore, Butler's men stood by in critical areas. Potential trouble spots were Wall Street, the telegraph cable across the North River, the High Bridge for the Harlem Railroad, "Mackrelville," the Irish slum on the lower East Side, and the Battery. The men did not enjoy their duty. They were confined, cold, and often hungry because provisions ran low on board ships. Butler ordered his troops if it became necessary to take action, to "fire no blank cartridges while the enemies of law and order are within range." Despite Butler's love for dramatics, he acted with uncharacteristic discretion, probably because Dix helped keep him in line. Fortunately, no major incidents occurred.[42]

The Democratic chairman, August Belmont, had an embarrassing day. Once during the campaign, that social gadabout had attended the opera at the Academy of Music, and between the acts he was overheard saying that he would bet a thousand dollars on McClellan to win the election and another thousand that gold would reach 300 by election day. Somehow, Belmont's offers to bet found their way into newspapers before the election. A letter to the editor of the *Times*, signed "Union," asserted that Belmont had been offered a bet of $2,000 to $1,000 and the Democratic chairman declined because he wanted odds of three to one, which was not exactly a display of confidence in his candidate. Belmont replied publicly without confirming or denying the charge by offering a different bet. He was willing to put up $10,000 to be deposited in the New York Trust Company under the terms that if Lincoln won the election, the country would be at war during his term or he would be forced into a disgraceful peace with separation. Belmont offered to deposit the same amount for a bet that if McClellan was elected, the Union would be restored within his term. He seemed to be trying to work himself out of an awkward situation.

No one appeared to take Belmont's bets, but they gave the election inspector at the polls an excuse to challenge Belmont's right to vote. The state law prohibited gambling on an election for public office. The inspector's effrontery enraged Belmont, who had been standing in line for two hours. George Templeton Strong waited in the same line a little behind Belmont and enjoyed the scene as Belmont left in a storm. But even Strong had to admit that the challenge on such a ground was unusual.[43]

General Butler telegraphed Lincoln, "The quietest city ever seen."[44] The grog shops and Gold Room closed, and the New York Stock Exchange did little business. Nevertheless, the voters of the city did not support Lincoln. The Democrats piled up a big vote, aided by the recent naturalization of citizens in the city and possibly some fraud in the lower wards.

Henry Raymond waited anxiously for the outcome at the National Committee Headquarters at the Astor House while crowds peacefully gathered at Printing House Square to watch for the latest returns. The next day, when the results were definite, the president had lost the metropolis by about thirty-seven thousand votes, which was a strong, antiadministration showing. The consolation for the Republicans came when they carried the state by a slim margin of not much more than six thousand votes for Lincoln and defeated Governor Seymour for reelection by about nine thousand votes. The Republican Reuben Fenton would be the next governor. Jubilant Lincoln men at the Astor House went wild with the thought that Democrats and "pseudo-peace men" had been defeated.[45] Still, the "pseudo-peace men" had dominated the city.

Samuel Barlow, dismayed by the results, was sure that Lincoln's reelection endorsed every "fallacy & monstrosity which the folly of fanaticism of the Radicals may invent, including miscegenation, negro equality, territorial organization and subjugation." He had been convinced that the Democratic party could have supported Lincoln if he had only ignored slavery.[46]

The disappointed editors of the *Daily News* hoped that Lincoln's reelection would provide the president with an opportunity to atone for the wrongs he had committed against liberty and justice. The list of his wrongs was long, including his suppression of habeas corpus, trial by jury, a free press, free speech, and full enjoyment of conscience. "Let Mr. Lincoln be *President* for the next term; hitherto he has been a dictator," said the paper. The election had a different effect on another anti-administration newspaper. The *Journal of Commerce* announced its withdrawal from the world of politics. But the *Metropolitan Record* had no intention of giving up expressing political views. The paper forecast "repeated conscriptions, increased taxation, and many more years of war" as a consequence of the election. And the editor predicted that the South "will be independent when the North lies prostrate under intolerable oppression. . . . We shall continue to write as we have heretofore done until the pen be stricken from our hand."[47]

The price of gold rose about 12 percent to 259½ with the first news of Lincoln's reelection. The rationale for the rise was that Lincoln would prolong the war and issue more greenbacks. Soon, however, second thoughts prevailed and the price dropped to 252.[48]

Butler's performance during the election may not have accomplished anything, but that did not stop him from taking the opportunity for self-aggrandizement. He remained in the city a few days after his troops left to receive accolades, and they came forth. Former mayor Opdyke as chairman of "loyal citizens of New York" applauded Butler for "the influence which they believe your presence here has exerted in preserving the peace of the city during the recent election." And others were quick to extol the general's virtues. David Dudley Field entertained Butler at dinner as did James W. White, whose guest list included Archbishop John McCloskey, John Hughes's successor. The final tribute before Butler departed was a banquet in his honor at the Fifth Avenue Hotel at which Henry Ward Beecher gave a toast and proposed Butler's nomination for president in 1868.[49]

Political analysts in the city who studied the returns in the national election did not worry about publicly insulting voters because of their ethnic origin or occupation. A review of ward voting trends by one emerging political scientist indicated that the native-born, intelligent, orderly, and more prosperous professional people voted for Lincoln. The "vicious and ignorant" voted for McClellan. The First Ward in the vicinity of the Battery, with "nearly as many rum holes as houses," went ten to one against Lincoln. The Eleventh Ward, near Rivington Street, a tenement house area of "ignorant Germans" and the domicile of "rag pickers and bone gatherers," went heavily for McClellan. The Fourteenth Ward, the site of brothels and rum shops between Canal and Houston streets, was five to one for McClellan. The Eighteenth Ward, which ran from Fourteenth Street to Twenty-sixth Street near the East River, where much of the rioting took place the previous year, filled with liquor shops and a "degraded population," was another McClellan stronghold. The heaviest vote for McClellan came from the area close to the Bowery in the Seventeenth Ward, inhabited by Germans and the Irish of "Mackrelville." In contrast, the Ninth Ward, bounded on the north by Fourteenth Street, where a large number of "intelligent native born mechanics and business people" lived, gave Lincoln a strong vote. The Fifteenth Ward, east of Sixth Avenue, whose residents were intelligent and orderly, according to the analyst, was the only ward in the city to give Lincoln a majority. The Republicans envied the Democratic organization in the city, which consistently beat them at the polls. The Republicans believed their mistake was to place too much emphasis on ideas and too little on organization. Winning the Irish vote was practically impossible for Republicans, but postelection results indicated to them that they should try to gain a larger share of the German vote. The Germans were believed to be more intelligent than the Irish and with an instinctive hatred for slavery. Some suggested setting up Union party headquarters in the heavily German Eleventh and Seventeenth wards with reading rooms for laboring men.[50]

The election may have stimulated recruiting in the city. Whatever the reason, the chairman of the Volunteer Committee, Orison Blunt, reported that there were now plenty of volunteers and substitutes. Anyone who wanted a substitute simply wrote his name in the committee book and paid $220, $430, or $650 for a two-, three-, or four-year substitute. Bounty brokers were not pleased with this arrangement, which cut them out of a commission. Nevertheless, the bounty brokers did a good business with those unaware of Blunt's system. Brokers continued to advertise for large bounties and usually received $50 dollars from the recruit for their services. The citizens were pleased that Blunt had minimized the threat of a draft call and reduced the profits of the bounty brokers. They were not so pleased when they heard that the Board of Supervisors had voted him a gold medal, a service of silver plate, and $50,000 to be paid by the city treasury for his work.[51]

With the election out of the way, the city looked forward to Thanksgiving. As the holiday approached, the most renowned master bakers of the city gathered at the Astor House under the auspices of the Loyal League Club. Lorenzo Delmonico, Alexander Stetson, and James Kelly were among those who passed a resolution to roast all poultry free of charge that was sent to them by interested families for soldiers in the field. The Union League Club also wanted soldiers and sailors to have a good Thanksgiving dinner and inaugurated a fund-raising campaign, which collected more than $56,000 and sent almost fifty thousand turkeys to the Army of the Shenandoah, more than thirty thousand to the Atlantic Squadron, and 225,000 pounds of turkey and other poultry to the Armies of the Potomac and James, along with doughnuts, cakes, fruit, and cheese.[52]

There was a feeling of relief in the city that the anticipated violence on election day had not taken place. Yet the relief was premature. The havoc makers were merely off schedule and postponed their appearance until later in the month. They had an elaborate plan to destroy the city. The scheme of destruction was not perpetrated by angry, ignorant mobsters but by Confederate officers working under the general authorization of Jefferson Davis. Jacob Thompson, one of the "peace negotiators" with whom Greeley had met at Niagara Falls, had served as secretary of the interior under President Buchanan. Now, operating with the blessing of Davis, he envisioned Confederate saboteurs burning New York City.

Colonel Robert Martin of Kentucky, formerly one of Morgan's Raiders, led a team of daring young men made up of Lieutenant John Headley, another Morgan Raider, Captain Robert Kennedy, who had recently escaped from a military prison and had suffered a leg wound at Shiloh, and Lieutenants John Ashbrook, James Harrington, James Chenault, John Price, and another man whose name is unknown. Captain E. Longmire, an accomplice, was already in New York City arranging for a supply of "Greek fire." The explosive was a mixture of phosphorus in a bisulfide of carbon.

Later in October, the saboteurs left Toronto with false papers and arrived in New York City with the intention of carrying out their infamous deed on election day. They took rooms in various hotels throughout the city under assumed names. It was not unusual for a southerner to register at a hotel in New York. Thousands of people had arrived from the South since the start of the war, and they attracted no special attention. The gossip at the New York Club was that many new female arrivals from the South "of good social standing" had increased the harlotry of the city as the only alternative to starving.[53]

The army's Department of the East had issued a general order that all arrivals from insurgent states must register at its headquarters, but it was generally ignored. Many of the newcomers did not even hesitate to criticize the administration.

Martin, Headley, and Kennedy supposedly met with James McMaster of the rabid *Freeman's Journal,* who was said to have assured them that there was a supporting army of "about twenty thousand" ready to help at the critical moment. Although it is difficult to believe, a private secretary of Governor Seymour was allegedly present and told the southerners that the governor would cooperate. Certainly Seymour, despite his strong antiadministration views, would never have entertained such notions.

The heavy troop concentrations surrounding the city on election day convinced the conspirators to delay their actions until Thanksgiving. The progress of the Union army in Georgia discouraged some of the group and incensed others. Price and the unknown man backed off from the enterprise and Longmire vanished. The others continued to plot in a small house near Central Park that belonged to a southern female refugee or at Headley's room at the Astor House, where he was registered as W. S. Haines. Originally, they intended to attack government buildings, but that was difficult because they were guarded. Instead, they decided that hotels were an easier setting for the start of their conflagration.

Headley picked up the supply of Greek fire from a chemist in Greenwich Village. The group decided to start the fires on the evening of November 25, the day after Thanksgiving. Each man was assigned four hotels and instructed to heap the bedding together and then pour on the Greek fire. To avoid notice, they were to keep the windows and doors tightly closed. The St. James Hotel at Broadway and Twenty-sixth Street was the first to report a fire at 8:43 P.M. Soon the magnificent St. Nicholas Hotel at Broadway and Spring Street was in trouble. Then an unscheduled fire started at Barnum's Museum. Kennedy, well under the influence of liquor, went upstairs in the museum to look around the city for evidence of his group's handiwork. On the way down, he threw a vial of phosphorus on the stairs to add to the confusion. A lecture was under way on the fifth floor, and a near panic ensued when an usher shouted, "Fire!" In a short time, however, it was under control.

The astute Barnum realized what a fire could do to his business. He immediately wrote a letter to the editor of the *Times,* which appeared on the front page the next morning. He said that stories of "slight damage" to the museum were incorrect. There was not even a scorch visible, and he explained precautions against fire. He had a twenty-four-hour watch, water buckets always ready, and a large fire hose. He never allowed an uncovered light, the building was heated by a steam furnace in the cellar, and his sense of security was so great that he insured the museum for one-third less than the true value.

During the night, however, fire alarms went out from nine other hotels. A young woman discovered a fire in a room at the LaFarge Hotel, which disturbed the benefit performance for the Shakespeare Monument Fund at the Winter Garden next door. While the three Booths, Edwin, Junius Brutus, and John Wilkes, were mesmerizing the audience in *Julius Caesar,* someone spread the word of fire. The play stopped, and Edwin Booth avoided a panic by pleading for order. The audience, which had paid double price for the seats, soon calmed down and the play continued with the audience unaware of the excitement throughout the city. At Niblo's, *Corsican Brothers* was interrupted when the Metropolitan Hotel started to smoke.[54]

Volunteer firemen worked diligently, and as the hours passed it became obvious that the fires were not coincidental. Hotel managers commenced room-by-room checks. At nine o'clock the next morning the last fire was found at the Astor House during an inspection.

Through the night rumors spread of a Confederate attack, and for once they were correct. But it was an attack that fizzled. The Confederates had done their work poorly. In each instance, the saboteurs had made the mistake of suffocating their fires by making sure that the windows and doors were closed. The Greek fire needed oxygen to encourage the blaze. Instead, they created more smoke than fire. Little damage was done, and no lives were lost. The six-story, million-dollar St. Nicholas Hotel suffered the most, requiring repairs amounting to a reported $10,000.

General Dix immediately issued General Order 92 announcing that the perpetrators would be tried by a military court or commission and if found guilty they would be executed within twenty-four hours. A second order, General Order 93, revived the previous order that required persons arriving from rebel states to register. Anyone who failed to do so would be regarded as a spy. In addition, keepers of hotels and boardinghouses were requested to submit names of people registering from insurgent states to the Department of the East. Almost at once, numerous people rushed to the army office at 37 Bleecker Street to register their names.

Mayor Gunther, always sensitive to the rights of southerners, did not care for Dix's order to apply military law against the culprits. Even if his city were reduced to ashes, he did not want any hasty trials. He recommended to the Common Council that $25,000 be appropriated for the conviction of rebel incendiaries according to due process of law in a civilian court. The Board of Supervisors accepted Gunther's principle, but appropriated only $5,000. Gunther's desire for a fair trial at a time when passions were high was courageous.[55]

Some arrests were made shortly after the incident, but the suspects were released when they provided information that supported their innocence. The guilty Confederates, apparently satisfied with their sloppy work, took a sleeper to Toronto by way of Albany. Detectives pursued the southerners to Toronto, but only one man was eventually caught. The unfortunate Kennedy was later arrested in Detroit and returned to New York for trial by a military commission. He was sent to Fort Lafayette at the Narrows, where he wrote Benjamin Wood and James McMaster for help, but both men spurned him.

The *Daily News,* thankful that the city had been spared, did not remind its readers that the paper had regarded Seward's warning as an electioneering trick. Instead, it said that if attempts to set fire to the city had been successful, the result would have been intense hostility to the Confederacy. "New York in ashes," the newspaper said, "would have been more deadly to the Southern cause than New York in the fullness of strength and grandeur."[56]

Sometime during the winter of 1864–65 another attempt at conspiracy allegedly took place in the city. John Wilkes Booth had a wild plan to capture the president and other high-ranking officials and turn them over to Jefferson Davis for a price. He was said to have met Samuel Knapp Chester, a character actor, had a few drinks with him at the House of Lords, a tavern on Houston Street, then made another stop at an oyster bar. After a walk up Broadway, Wilkes discussed his plot with

Chester under a street lamp. Booth saw his scheme as a way to make a fortune, but Chester was sensible enough to refuse the opportunity.[57]

The year had been fraught with confusion and contradiction, dramatic action and distressing frustration. And another disturbing innovation had been brought on by the war. A number of female students attended sessions at the Bellevue Hospital Medical College, which some saw as "repugnant to the sentiments of polite society, and by so doing have necessarily lost that command for gallant attentions which all gentlemen are so ready to accord to the fairer sex." Not everyone agreed, and the young women continued their studies. A "Mother of the New School," wrote, "I understand from the Bible that God made man and woman equal in all things."[58]

Serious women demonstrated their courage at another institution. The Medical College for Women and Hospital for Women and Children at 724 Broadway near Eighth Street completed its first year with a sense of purpose and achievement. Eighteen females had enrolled in the college that many had regarded as merely an experiment. The war had been the impetus for its founding. The trustees believed that women who answered the country's call for service would be more efficient if they had a proper medical education. They also believed that half-educated midwives could not compete with well-trained modern physicians.[59]

The year had also brought military and political triumphs that could not be reversed. As December came to an end, the city did not present a picture of exhaustion from war, government oppression, or suffering from heavy taxes. In the Christmas season, attractively decorated shops did a brisk business. Expensive laces, embroideries, and shawls found eager customers. Macy's did an active trade in bracelets, earrings, fancy pins, and other costume jewelry. Confectioners and fancy fruit stores were busy, and Tiffany thrived. Someone counted thirty-five florists on Broadway from Canal Street to the Fifth Avenue Hotel on Twenty-third Street. Despite horrible poverty in the city, toy shops profited from the sale of such luxuries for lucky children as dolls that babbled and roosters that crowed. The war was not over, but as the chimes rang out from Trinity Church on Christmas Eve the worst seemed over. General Sherman gave the north a Christmas present when he occupied Savannah on December 22, and hope existed that the end of the war was really in sight.

16
Victory

Conservative Republican Thurlow Weed and Radical Republican George Opdyke had sniped at each other for years. Their rivalry often centered on jobs, contracts, and power rather than their presumed differences of principle. The intraparty feuding, distracting and often petty, finally erupted into a libel suit when the irritable Opdyke decided he could no longer endure Weed's slanderous remarks.

Near the close of 1864, the case of *Opdyke* v. *Weed* came to trial in the New York Supreme Court. Opdyke, the plaintiff, claimed $50,000 for injury to his character by alleged libelous charges by Weed published in the *Albany Evening Journal* and reprinted in the *New York World*. Perhaps it was a sign that the war was winding down. Victory was within grasp of the North, and two Republican politicians could enjoy the luxury of pursuing their private battle.

Weed had unquestionably said some unpleasant things about Opdyke. He had called him a swindler and said he had engaged in a secret partnership involving army clothing and gun contracts. Opdyke, he said, had sold shoddy blankets and made more "than any fifty sharpers, Jew or Gentile, in the city of New York." Allegedly, Opdyke had made money from the draft riot by swearing falsely that he had no interest in a gun factory destroyed by mobsters and then was a member of an auditing committee that investigated the loss and allowed a profitable indemnity of $190,000. The claim had been made in the name of the managing partner, but the mayor, according to Weed, had improperly used his influence. Even worse, Opdyke had supposedly received a substantial sum from the federal government for guns he reported had been destroyed. In another age, this case might have been considered a frivolous legal battle between two jealous men. The suit was significant, however, because Opdyke and Weed typified a large class of men who had taken advantage of the war, low ethical standards, and political influence to make excessive profits.

The trial opened before a crowded courtroom, and the antagonists presented a sharp contrast. Weed, the defendant, appeared calm and confident. Instead of backing away from the charges, he suggested that the court also look into the sale of the office of surveyor of the port of New York by Opdyke for $10,000. Opdyke, stiff and petulant, strived to save his honor. The trial continued into the new year, and before it was over, Opdyke seemed more on the defensive than Weed. It was a classic case of the pot calling the kettle black.

Both sides were represented by eminent counsel, and the spectators looked forward to a good show. Edwards Pierrepont, Weed's attorney, said in his opening remarks that he had struggled to avoid a court case between the two men, but he found that "it was as impossible to prevent this trial as to prevent the rebellion or the fall of Fort Sumter. We had reached a state of corruption in the public administration of affairs in this city to that degree that it could be borne no longer." The lawyer stressed that Weed denied nothing in Opdyke's complaint and that the defendant, who held no ill will, had made his remarks only after careful consideration. He also declared that Weed had been attacked first as "the father of the lobby," a "corrupter of public morals," and "contriver of various corrupt schemes." If these charges were true, Pierrepont wondered for the benefit of the court why Opdyke had not begun criminal prosecution instead of instituting a civil case. The motive for the suit, he argued, had to be Opdyke's inordinate love of money.[1]

To escape the claim of personal libel, Pierrepont was anxious to show at the outset that the dispute was a public question that concerned public morality and political responsibility. He even broadened the case to include freedom of the press. "Give a verdict," he told the jury, "which will muzzle the press and you will find next year it is dead." This additional argument gave Pierrepont the opportunity to appear sanctimonious in his defense of one of the great political fixers of his time. Former Judge Emott's opening statement for Opdyke took the opposite position, emphasizing the private aspect of the case, which, he said, was not a political libel suit. It was a question affecting the private character of the plaintiff. His client had suffered pain and anguish from Weed's false and malicious charges, and he intended to collect damages.[2]

After almost three weeks of confusing, contradictory, and inconclusive testimony, neither Opdyke nor his lawyers was completely convincing in making their case. And Opdyke's involvement in war contracts provided room for suspicion of his activities. Pierrepont's summation in defense of Weed claimed that the great question to decide was whether a man serving in a public office as a trustee and guardian should gain financially by fraudulent use of his position. Emott concluded his case for Opdyke on much narrower grounds. His main argument involved malice. Weed had struck at Opdyke, Emott said, because Weed hated Opdyke.

After hours of deliberation through the night, the foreman of the jury reported to the court that it was hopeless to expect any agreement among the jurors. The judge discharged the jury, but Weed came out of the trial looking better than Opdyke. A horde of people gathered around Weed in the courtroom to shake his hand and congratulate him. Newspapers also gave Weed a boost by reporting that jurors could not agree whether Weed should pay six cents for nominal charges or be acquitted.[3]

Yet both Weed and Opdyke were greedy politicians with an eye for personal gain at public expense, and there were undoubtedly elements of truth in the charges that each flung against the other. Although Weed was not a public official, he was intimately involved in government affairs, and today both men would certainly be found guilty of conflict of interest. In 1865, however, this messy trial was merely a symptom of the times. Profiteers were everywhere, and fine distinctions in ethical relations between business and government were roughly drawn. Bilking the government was routine practice.

The government was vulnerable to these skillful moneymaking sharks. One of the best ways to turn a fast dollar early in 1865 was to sell whiskey. In mid-1864, the federal government levied a tax of a $1.50 a gallon on whiskey and announced that the tax would be increased to $2.00 in February 1865. Since no provision was made for retroactive collections, hoarders immediately built up their stocks to make a financial killing. Profits were enormous, and the government lost millions in revenue. Among the whiskey hoarders was none other than Thurlow Weed.[4]

As the war entered its fourth year, these eager profiteers displayed their success in garish ways, ranging from expensive hairdos, extravagant clothes and jewelry to handsome carriages, elaborate parties, and imposing new mansions. The established rich, fearing the invasion of their sacred privileges, called the new rich "the sybarites of shoddy." George Templeton Strong snobbishly said, "Not a few ladies in most sumptuous turn-outs, with liveried servants, looked as if they might have been cooks or chambermaids a few years ago."[5]

Henry Bellows detected a disturbing change in the people. Everyone seemed to have settled down after the election and assumed an attitude of perfect confidence. They were as little concerned with the war "as if it were in Mexico." A desire for ease and pleasure "burst out with a vehemence." The new rich, Bellows said, "more indulgent of folly," spent their mornings gambling in petroleum, gold, and mining stocks, their afternoons in their sporting equipages, and their evenings at card tables. The levity and recklessness alarmed him. Morals, decorum, refinement, and moderation were ridden down just as "Sheridan rode down Gen. Early in the Shenandoah." Ben Butler, he feared, was not the model man, who would represent the spirit of reconstruction in the coming years. And inflated paper currency produced wild schemes as careless hands squandered money as if it were water. "People's consciences," Bellows wrote, "have suffered the same depreciation as the paper dollar and their decisions are not worth half their face." The police were inactive, dress was "melodramatic," the streets were even dirtier, and vice was shameless. All of this made religious life more difficult. "What kind of sentiments," he asked, "are to have power with the new time and the new civilization?"[6] He wondered whether the people's moral intelligence matched their general intelligence. He was perplexed and disconcerted.

Despite political fixers and profiteers and superficial trends, the war had fundamentally changed the attitudes of some people in the city giving hope for human progress. Often men and women did not realize that a mental revolution was taking place in their lives until something occurred to make them conscious that their outlook had undergone a drastic conversion. Such a realization shook Morgan Dix when he read the news on the morning of February 1 that Congress had approved the proposed Thirteenth Amendment to the Constitution, which would abolish slavery forever. He accepted the news with "humble gratitude to Almighty God." Then the thought dawned on him that he was not the same man he was four years ago. "How strange the changes of time!" he wrote in his diary. "4 years ago I was an out and out ultra-Southern and pro-slavery."[7] Others in the city had undoubtedly undergone the same experience. Yet some still believed that there was no provision in the Constitution to permit Congress or the president to dictate to any state on the issue of slavery. They were not happy with the congressional proposal.[8]

Neither modern thought nor war riches improved the city's deplorable sanitary conditions. Garbage piled high in the gutters, and dead animals and human excrement were a common sight in the streets along with the latest fashions. Cattle driven to almost two hundred slaughterhouses in the city added to the filth. Outhouses and cesspools in courtyards behind tenement houses were rarely drained and contributed to the spread of disease. On Fortieth Street between Broadway and Seventh Avenue, three latrines were within thirty feet of each other, and the stench made the house unfit for living. In other houses, waste matter ran into cellars. The conditions at Rivington and Ninth streets were especially revolting. The war had made it easier to neglect the lives of those who were later called the "other half."

In the spring of 1865, smallpox spread in the poor areas of the city although vaccination could have easily prevented the epidemic. The Citizens Association supported a study of sanitation, and in a two-week period twelve hundred cases of smallpox were discovered. In 1862, the Board of Commissioners of Health in the city had concluded that smallpox could be eliminated by compulsory vaccination and submitted a bill for that purpose to the state legislature, where it was stalled. Little was done in the intervening years to control the disease. Inspectors found a woman tending bar while serving as a nurse for her husband who suffered from the sickness. One woman with smallpox sold candy, and a girl making cigars and a woman selling vegetables had scabs falling from their skin.[9]

In tenement house areas such as Mulberry Street typhus ran a strong second to smallpox, and diarrhea, cholera infantum, and typhoid fever also took their toll. The Citizens Association report charged that the poor population of the city was like an army camp without regulations. The inspectors claimed that at least half a million people were "literally submerged in filth and half stifled in an atmosphere charged with all the elements of death."[10]

The few rules and regulations that existed for public health were generally ignored. "Its Board of Health, the Mayor and Common Council," the report continued, "is an unwieldy body, without a shadow of qualifications for its duties. Its Commissioners of Health have limited powers, and are equally incompetent." Most of the politically appointed health wardens were liquor dealers, who had no medical knowledge and avoided infected areas as much as possible. One health warden advised a family stricken with smallpox to "burn camphor on the stove and hang bags of camphor about the necks of children." Some families failed to report smallpox cases for fear the patient would be sent to a public hospital, which was often considered a fate worse than death. Others did not even report deaths because doing so created fear and odium among neighbors in congested houses. The Citizens Association made sensible recommendations. It called for formation of a health board independent of political influence and partisan control made up of businessmen with executive ability and medical men with knowledge of disease and prevention. Medical inspectors should be medical doctors who could intelligently investigate causes of disease. The association also recommended that the health board and police department establish a close alliance so that orders would be obeyed. Dr. Stephen Smith reported the findings to a joint committee of the senate and assembly in Albany, and they created a brief sense of horror but little permanent improvement. Nevertheless, the adverse publicity stirred the Bureau of Sanitary Inspection to life, and it arranged for the removal of eight hundred cartloads of night soil, one hundred dead horses, about two hundred dead dogs, and more than six thousand barrels of offal in less than a week.[11]

The horrifying conditions in the streets attracted less intense interest in some quarters than the drop in the price of gold. As the Union army advanced in February, gold, contrary to expectations, remained firmly above 200. By mid-March, however, the price dropped to 175, and then a panic resulted in further drops in the next two months until it reached 145. The days of Dixie-loving speculators were over.[12]

Another era had come to an end in the city, too. The war had dealt a severe blow to shipbuilding and the merchant marine. They would never be the same again. Confederate attacks on Union ships had caused owners to make broad-scale transfers to foreign registries. There were five thousand fewer merchant ships flying the American flag since the start of the war, and the volume of shipping had plummeted 60 percent. The great shipbuilding era in the city would have probably ended anyway because property on Manhattan had become too valuable for shipyards.[13]

The end of the war was clearly in sight as Lincoln entered his second term of office. Even the dyed-in-the-wool southern sympathizer Samuel Barlow admitted that the Confederates had reached the end of their rope.[14] After much agony, the chaos of the early war years had been replaced by a powerful and well-organized war machine in the North. The overwhelming advantage of greater manpower as well as industrial might and ingenuity, as Samuel Morse had predicted at the start of the war, finally produced results. Much had been learned about the management of large forces. The Sanitary Commission was only one example. It now operated steamships, hospital cars, wagons, trains, and homes for recuperation. Under the careful eye of its treasurer, George Templeton Strong, the commission expended more than $1 million a month to perform these services.

Lincoln's solemn and beautiful inaugural speech ended with words that became among his best known: "With malice toward none, with charity for all, with firmness in the right as God gives us to see the right, let us strive on to finish the work we are in, to bind up the nation's wounds, to care for him who shall have borne the battle and for his widow and orphan, to do all which may achieve and cherish a just and lasting peace among ourselves and with all nations." Yet these charitable words did not please everyone. Both the *World* and the *Daily News* were quick to denounce the speech, accusing Lincoln of substituting piety for politics in a disjointed address that was barren of ideas and presented no plan for the future. The *World* said it published the speech with "a blush of shame and wounded pride."[15]

Although victory was in sight, the draft was still in effect and there were complaints that New York City's quota was too high. David Turnure claimed that one-fifth of the city's voting population was subject to the draft yet the quota in "abolition districts" was only one-fifteenth. Although his figures may not have been accurate and he was not an objective observer, he convinced himself that the injustice was a matter of revenge against city Democrats by Governor Fenton.[16]

Mayor Gunther heard numerous complaints from poor mechanics and laboring men who had been drafted and forced to leave their destitute families. He felt that a rigorous and unfair enforcement of the draft had produced innumerable evils, and he proposed to the Common Council that it apply to the state legislature for authority to issue $20 million worth of bonds to attract volunteers and "thus alleviate the burden of military service, now so unequally imposed, and prevent the distress and horrors" connected with the draft.[17] But the proposal was not acted on.

Bounty brokers still searched diligently for recruits. Newspapers reported that youths had been drugged and kidnapped into the army. Innocent young men were allegedly enticed into dens on West Cherry, Greenwich, and Houston streets, given bad liquor, and then passed a physical examination by corrupt doctors while they were still in a stupor. Reports also claimed that boys were drugged on their way to school and later awakened on Rikers Island in uniform. Criminals convicted of minor offenses were given the option of joining the army instead of going to jail, and some of them became bounty jumpers. Occasionally a bounty broker was arrested, but most of them were left untouched by the war. Stories of organized bounty rings were common. The *Herald* alleged that an extensive ring included supervisors, recruiting officers, doctors, bounty brokers, and policemen, who shared in the profits, but there was no proof.

In March, there were drawings for the draft in some city districts, but by the middle of the month the draft was officially postponed. Recruits were at "dead-low water," and authorities threatened a renewal of the draft if quotas for volunteers were not met. There was a deficiency of 755 men in the Twenty-second Ward, and citizens met at National Hall to encourage recruitment. Fernando Wood was present and found himself in the strange position of trying to encourage recruits for the war he despised. But he had a rationale. He placed his appeal on the strictly practical consideration that by volunteering one could escape the draft. He believed the ward had been unfairly treated in comparison with richer wards that paid higher bounties. There was some truth in his words because it was true that extra "hand money" was distributed by rich individuals in some districts to increase the number of volunteers.[18]

Wood could always find reasons for the positions he adopted. After years of upholding slavery, he was now able to rationalize abolition. "Even men like me," he wrote George Shea, "would consent to abolish slavery if peace could thereby be restored to our disturbed country."[19] But it was a little late for his views to have any effect.

In a few days, the war would only be an unhappy memory for Fernando Wood. In high spirits, he sailed for Europe with his wife and daughter on the *City of London*. The family planned to tour Ireland, Switzerland, and the Holy Land and return home in the fall. Wood's exit as the Union army triumphed was well timed to avoid aspersions about his wartime doubts and Copperhead politics. Still, he was always a captivating personality, and he left the country with a fond farewell from a host of friends. A private dinner was given for him at the Astor House by some of his political intimates as a "token of personal respect."[20] Another politician had already made a less graceful exit from the country. In January, the former presidential candidate George McClellan had departed. August Belmont advised him not to leave for Europe so soon after the election, but the little general did not heed the advice.

Even more astonishing and of deeper significance than these departures was the vote of two city congressmen in the House of Representatives. James Brooks and Winthrop Chanler voted against the proposed Thirteenth Amendment to prohibit slavery. The war had not changed their opinions.

In February, the twenty-year-old Confederate officer Robert Kennedy had been found guilty of attempting to burn down the city by a court-martial. The trial was held at General Dix's headquarters and ended with the expected verdict of "death by hanging." In the weeks before he faced the gallows, Kennedy spent his time handcuffed in a large room at Fort Lafayette. His emotions ran the gamut from bravado to bitterness. An attempt to set fire to his room only made his life more uncomfortable as he was restricted further by an extra pair of handcuffs and leg irons. Before going to the gallows on March 25, young Kennedy wrote kind and generous letters to his mother and to the officers at the fort. Prisoners and special guests witnessed his final walk to the gallows. The agony of the proceedings was prolonged when a review of his case was read. Kennedy interrupted frequently, saying, "It's a damned lie." At the end of the review, Kennedy denied that he was ever intentionally a spy and said, "Gentlemen, this is judicial murder." Then, trying to be lighthearted, he added, "Colonel, can't you give me a drink before I go up?" The drink was not forthcoming. A soldier placed a black cap over his head, and soon it was all over. The city quickly forgot the adventurous young man, not much more than a boy, who had looked upon his acts as valorous deeds of a Confederate officer in time of war.[21]

Soon the city was caught up in a wild and spontaneous celebration. Grant had taken Richmond. Telegraphic dispatches with the good news arrived about ten o'clock on the morning of April 3. At first, it seemed impossible. Skeptics wanted confirmation, and confirmation came with each successive telegram. The city had not been so excited since the mass meeting at Union Square at the start of the war. The Board of Aldermen immediately adjourned with three cheers and went out into the street to celebrate. George Strong rushed to Trinity Church to make sure the chimes rang. The regular bell ringer was away, but recruits clanged the bells. Newsboys shouted in the streets, "Richmond Ours!" Boats in the harbor broke out bunting, and lights glowed. Guns fired at the foot of Wall Street. Everywhere, in restaurants, bars, stages, and railroad cars, crowds exulted over the news. The usual staid reserve of Morgan Dix, rector of Trinity Church, was shattered. He was so excited he did not know what to do. He said, "Couldn't sit down, couldn't stand up, couldn't stay in, couldn't stay out; felt like 'running, leaping, and praising God.' " He offered a Thanksgiving prayer by himself and then rushed uptown and downtown and waited in the street for the arrival of more news bulletins.[23]

Wall Street was overjoyed, the price of gold dropped 9 percent, and the general security market strengthened. Impromptu meetings took place in the financial district and at Union Square. Soldiers, especially wounded soldiers, were given free drinks at every turn. At the Astor House a wounded soldier from Minnesota suddenly became the object of affection, and revelers collected about a hundred dollars for him. Then the crowd danced wildly around him singing, "Rally round the flag." At City Hall both boards of the Common Council met and immediately adjourned amid three cheers. Strangers joined together to sing the doxology, "John Brown," and "The Star Spangled Banner." Men hugged each other, cried, and laughed. Sixteen men were seen four abreast, arm in arm, and each one sang a different song.[23] In the evening some houses lighted Chinese lanterns and gas jets. The Atheneum Club sparkled, and the Union League Club put up decorations. Lights from the *Times* building shined toward Park Row. No celebration had been planned. It was a genuine outburst of emotion.

Enthusiastic members of the Union League Club listened to more speeches and congratulated each other on the victory. George Templeton Strong noticed that Hamilton Fish was there, "beaming and gushing, and shaking everybody's hands with fervor." Strong remembered that two years before Fish's talk had been discouraged and disloyal. "If you want to know which way the wind blows," Strong noted in his diary, "throw up Hamilton Fish."[24]

The next day, the Board of Aldermen set up a special committee to celebrate the occasion formally and communicated that desire to the mayor. Gunther, true to his Copperhead instincts, said once again that he was opposed to celebrating victories gained over fellow citizens. He suggested that Jefferson's birthday would be a more fitting reason for festivities. It would demonstrate amity to the South, he said, rather than subjugation. He thought a celebration would increase bitterness in the South whereas he wanted to show affection and goodwill. He was ready to restore "personal freedom now thrown down by military power, to disavow the cruel policy of confiscation and vengeance, and to re-establish the integrity and powers of the State governments." That, he believed, would be the only way to enjoy the blessings of liberty. But his unusual magnanimity and Christian forbearance were too much for most citizens that day. The board ignored the mayor, and plans for a celebration went on.[25]

Gunther is one of the least-known mayors of the city of New York. Yet he was an intriguing character who deserves credit for consistently upholding his independent views. His detestation of the war showed most clearly in this moment of final victory. Turning his back on the opportunity to "wave the flag" was hardly standard behavior for a working politician.

An odd celebrant of imminent peace swam from Governor's Island to the Battery. He was Captain William Robert Webb of the Second North Carolina Cavalry, who had been held as a prisoner. He came ashore in his wet, gray uniform with yellow collar and cuffs and yellow striped trousers. He openly admitted that he had escaped from the prison stockade and wandered around the city without anyone restricting him.[26]

On Wall Street, joy was tempered with trepidation about the effect peace would have on business. No one could deny that war had produced many material benefits. Peace could bring depression. As the end of the ordeal approached, however, a buoyant spirit rose on the stock exchange. The mercurial forecasts of financiers now hailed the arrival of peace as the beginning of a new, substantial, and enduring prosperity. This was contrary to gloomy opinions expressed on and off the floor of the exchange just a short time before. In the next few days, government securities were strong and railways advanced as gold dropped another 2 or 3 percent.

Shortly after midnight on April 10, newsboys shouted, "Surrender of Lee's army, ten cents and no mistake." Headlines declared "Victory," "Peace," "Surrender of Lee and His Whole Army." It seemed incredible that the war was over. Yet it was true. Another day of rejoicing began, but it was a trifle less volcanic than on the day of Richmond's fall. Georgeanna Woolsey and her mother were surprised to see the lack of enthusiasm uptown. Women moved in and out of dry goods shops as if it were an ordinary day. The Woolseys said to each other, "Come, let us see what Wall Street is doing," and took the Fulton Street omnibus to the neighborhood of the customhouse. The scene was different there. Thousands of men and scarcely any women blocked the streets. The men were singing, "Praise God from whom all blessings flow."²⁷

The board of the stock exchange enthusiastically appointed a committee of one to buy an American flag, "the best and most beautiful manufacture to adorn the room of the Board of Brokers."²⁸ A joint committee of the Common Council met and Councilman Lent said it was of no consequence whether Mayor Gunther signed their celebratory resolution. The citizens, he said, were determined to celebrate regardless of what the mayor did. The councilman moved that all citizens illuminate their houses on April 20. The committee also appointed a committee to go to Washington to try to postpone the draft.

Although no flags were seen in front of the *Daily News* building or the *Day-Book* office, they were rare exceptions. Flags flew all over the city. Even Mayor Gunther succumbed to the spirit of jubilation and signed a proclamation designating April 20 as the official day of celebration. His words sounded as though he was giving permission to Copperheads to join the festivities. "The time for rejoicing has come," he said. "Let any patriot rejoice. Let any man opposed to the war, because the war was in conflict with his principles or his feelings rejoice."²⁹

But there was no celebration on the twentieth. The day of thanksgiving turned into a day of sorrow. On the fifteenth, black-bordered columns told that Lincoln had been shot. The *Times* wrote, "At this moment of writing, we have only a partial announcement of the facts, and have neither the data nor the spirit to comment." The first accounts of the shooting did not say that the president was dead and left a slight hope. But the hope was short-lived.

Woodward Hudson, the seven-year-old son of the managing editor of the *Herald,* had awakened early on the morning of the fifteenth. He

The city that bitterly criticized Abraham Lincoln mourns his death. (Courtesy of the New-York Historical Society)

saw the black borders on the front pages of the *Times* and *Tribune* and asked what they meant. His father had come home early the night before, worn out from work, and was not aware of the news. He was shaving at the time. When he realized the significance of the boy's question, he put down his razor and tears came to his eyes.[30]

Helen Grinnell would never forget her feeling when her husband told her the president had been assassinated. She sank into a chair unable to speak and felt as though she was in a horrible dream. "The nation is paralyzed," she wrote that day, "we do not know which way to turn or what is to become of us."[31]

Morgan Dix, deeply affected by the sad news, went to Trinity Church, but he had no intention of preaching. He asked the people at the church to pray. That same day, Mayor Gunther declared, "The death of the President of the United States may well excite your profound grief and amazement." He recommended that businesses suspend operation and that public mourning be observed. Edmund Stedman said that the city was converted into a "vast mausoleum."[32]

The Board of Aldermen passed a resolution expressing grief over the "dreadful calamity," which "dashed the cup of gladness from our lips." But the board members, who had never shown any enthusiasm for Lincoln, added, "He was fast becoming the idol of our people, including those who, at the commencement of his career, doubted the wisdom and integrity of his motives."[33] At times of bereavement, politicians can be very generous.

A deeper personal tragedy struck Edwin Booth. The brother of Lincoln's assassin was a loyal Union man, who was stunned when he heard about the deed committed by a loved member of his family. Booth was appearing as Sir Edward Mortimer in an old melodrama, *The Iron Chest,* in Boston. The theater closed, and after deputy marshals searched his trunks and questioned him, Edwin Booth returned to his home on Nineteenth Street in New York City, where he joined a grief-stricken mother and sister. His family had never been stable, and throughout his life he had feared that something terrible might happen, but this act was beyond his wildest fears. The event had an ironic side for Edwin Booth. Earlier in the year, he had seen a young man at a railroad in Jersey City being pushed by a crowd between the platform and train. Booth quickly grabbed him by the coat collar and saved him from being crushed to death or suffering horrible injury. The young man recognized his rescuer and introduced himself. He was Robert Lincoln, the president's son.

The distraught Booth remained at home. His brother Junius was arrested in Philadelphia under an erroneous suspicion of complicity in the murder and taken to Washington. Edwin did not know what had happened to John Wilkes until news arrived on the twenty-sixth that he had died of a bullet wound in a Virginia barn. And Edwin could not help but lament over his own dreams and ambitions that were suddenly washed away. He received hundreds of vilifying letters, and a friend said that for days his sanity hung in the balance. In desperation, Booth sent for Henry Bellows to give him spiritual comfort.

Occasionally, Booth took a walk at night along dark streets where he could not be recognized. Later, he wrote to a friend, "Oh, how little did I dream, my boy, when on Friday night I was as Sir Edward Mortimer exclaiming, 'Where is my honor now? Mountains of shame are piled upon me!' that I was not acting but uttering the fearful truth." Crushed and despondent, Booth was certain that his career on the stage was over. But during the worst weeks, friends rallied around him and strangers gave him unexpected sympathy. Maria Daly did not agree with those who said that Booth should never act again. "I said," she wrote, "that he suffered doubly ... I thought nothing should be added. The melancholy Dane: he will look and act more naturally than ever." Eventually, Edwin Booth returned to the stage, the only way he knew to make a living, and triumphed once again.[34]

After the first news of the assassination had arrived, crowds gathered in the streets to wait for the latest word. Assuming that Seward had also been killed, George Templeton Strong wrote, "I have heard it said fifty times today: These madmen murdered the two best friends they had in the world."[35] The board of the New York Stock Exchange expressed the sentiment that the president had been murdered at a time when the "amiable impulses of his heart were prompting his efforts." In the confusion that followed the assassination and the uncertainty about the consequences for the Union, the board reaffirmed its "unceasing" support of the government.[36]

Flags were now at half staff. Black crepe replaced colorful bunting, and black rosettes were pinned on curtains. Little business was done during the time of mourning, and even the arrests for drunkenness and disorder declined. On Easter Sunday, the nineteenth, clergymen eulogized the late president. Maria Daly, who still held Lincoln responsible for Chancellorsville and Fredericksburg, was inclined to believe the Lord took second place in His own house that day. The city had become too maudlin for her. She did not repent for her harsh feelings about the president, and the competitive display of mourning by her neighbors struck her as ridiculous. More seriously, she convinced herself that the assassination would not have taken place if there had been higher standards for selecting government officials. "We would have wiser men and more able rulers and not political tricksters to run the business of government with the intent to make for themselves so much per cent out of the business."³⁷

Spring rains cleaned the streets, and the city looked its best. On the twenty-fourth, the president's body arrived in the city by ferry from Jersey City. A solemn procession, accompanied by the Seventh Regiment, made its way to City Hall. The hearse was drawn by six gray horses covered with black cloth, and a groom in mourning walked alongside each horse. The president's body was laid near the Governor's Room, where thousands quietly paid their respects. Only four years before, the gaunt Lincoln had courteously thanked Mayor Wood for his kind reception in the city by people "who do not by a large majority agree with me on political sentiment." It was all over now. Victory and tragedy mingled in the city just as strong support for the president had mingled with doubts and outright opposition. At Union Square an ecumenical outdoor service was held. Reverend Stephen Tyng was joined by Archbishop McCloskey and Rabbi Samuel Isaacs, who read from the Scriptures.

The next day, another funeral procession for Lincoln attracted thousands of onlookers. In the afternoon, Morgan Dix performed a marriage ceremony for a couple at St. Paul's while the bell in the tower tolled and outside bands played dirges.³⁸ He found the entire scene incongruous. That evening, after a long day of ceremonies, Henry Bellows wrote to William Cullen Bryant asking him to write a memoir of the late president: "You can do a justice nobody else will, to the tender beauty of Mr. Lincoln's character. You can make people feel the lesson which his simplicity and integrity, his disinterestedness and purity, commend to them in all their political duties." Bellows had always given Lincoln the benefit of the doubt from their earliest association, and his respect for the president increased throughout the war. Bellows was undoubtedly impressed by Bryant's literary ability, but oddly he had turned to a man who had written bitterly about the ineffective president in the *Evening Post*. And less than a year before Bryant had privately written to John Murray Forbes that he was so disgusted with Lincoln's behavior that he could not muster "respectful terms to write him."[39] Perhaps, as George Templeton Strong said, "Death has suddenly opened the eyes of the people. A hero has been holding a high place among them. But this hero has been despised and rejected by a third of this community, and only tolerated by the other two-thirds."[40]

The voters of the city had expressed their opposition to the president and the war in election after election. The poor and middle classes were important elements in the life of the city when they cast their votes, but numbers did not always tell the complete story. Class counted. Yet the few rich frequently agreed with the many poor who wanted to call a halt to the war.

Definitions are difficult to draw, and common labels are unsatisfactory. War or Peace Democrats, radical or conservative Republicans, loyalists or disloyalists were all classifications that had severe limitations. There were too many practical considerations, too many overlapping thoughts, and too many shifts in opinion from day to day. Loyalists one day often teetered on the brink of disloyalty the next, and their principles were frequently motivated by profit. The emotions of the city were volatile, and the fine line between loyalty and disloyalty was sometimes hard to distinguish. Spirits roared up and down. New York City was a fast-moving town then as now, and the mood of the city was always susceptible to the latest success or defeat. Heroes were worshiped, villains were scorned, and both were quickly forgotten. The passing opinions of city leaders as well as ordinary men and women were ill founded more often than not, and their actions did not always follow their words. Casual conversation without knowledge, a universal practice, created many illusory hopes and fears.

One often-expressed fear was that blacks would flood from the South to take the jobs of white workers. An exodus did take place, but it was by whites, not blacks. The black population in the city had dropped to 9,945 in 1865, a decline of about 2,500 since 1860. In the latter part of the war and the immediate postwar period, droves of white southerners headed for New York City to escape the devastation that surrounded their old homes. Even the widow of Jefferson Davis eventually found refuge there. A Marylander wrote, "New York is filled with Confederates. They appear to have one idea which is that the South is ruined and no longer habitable. They rush to New York as the center of wealth and they expect to obtain profitable employment at the hands of the very people who have persistently oppressed them." A medical doctor in Alabama decided New York City was the best place to get away from freedmen. The city attracted him "as a population without political principle, without morals, without religion, & without negroes, & would therefore suit my present state of mind reasonably well." Benjamin Wood, still sensing sinister motives, believed Radical Republicans promoted this movement of whites north so their party could control the South. Whatever the reason, many former Confederates would do well in New York City in the years to come.[41]

The city merchants were ready to reestablish their friendly commercial connections with the South. When business profits were involved, they were willing to forgive and forget. Soon after the end of hostilities, the city sent relief supplies to Savannah, and the Produce Exchange justified this humane effort as a way to rebuild "cordial business, commercial and political relations with the City of New York." But New York businessmen wanted to work with the South on their own terms. The war had not removed their inherent fear of excessive power in the hands of the federal government, and they were aware that over-centralization in Washington, D.C., was a new threat that had come out of the war. Radical Republican steps in Congress to intervene in the affairs of the South with government loans and other direct aid did not please them. As a result, they generally preferred to support President Johnson, who seemed to have a sense of limits. The South, they believed, should look once again to New York City for the supply of capital. In adopting this attitude, the city found itself in a rivalry with such cities as Philadelphia and Boston, which were anxious to reassert their own commercial power. These cities took the opposite political approach. They joined forces with Radical Republicans in Congress to maintain the increased power of the national government. Their businessmen, as a rule, believed that close association with the Radicals and the force of the federal government would help them overcome New York's commercial dominance in the country. But they would find in time that, despite their philosophy, the business leadership of New York City was too mighty to surpass.[42]

Opinions clashed during the terrible war years while the city prospered. The value of real estate increased and notwithstanding the awful poverty, there were more jobs, labor began to be heard, and although admittedly meager, there were more opportunities for women to broaden their opportunities in life. Business was not hurt by the withdrawal of southern trade and, in meeting the demands of war, faced large challenges and consolidated its organizations. Banking systems improved.

For two years, by a quirk of circumstances, a Republican was mayor in the heavily Democratic city. Although he did not represent the political views of the majority of citizens, he was an energetic executive who strongly supported the war for the Union at a critical time. Still, he never forgot to serve his own interests and was quick to feud with the national administration. He did his best to replace the president and even though Opdyke was a Republican, Lincoln could hardly consider him a supporter.

More representative of the common people were the two mayors who bitterly opposed the war. Fernando Wood, frequently referred to as a scoundrel, was a clever and imaginative politician with a following that never lost faith in him. Although he favored secession for the city at the start of the war and opposed passage of the Thirteenth Amendment to abolish slavery late in the war, his positions on these issues did not have any lasting effect on his political future. He returned to the House of Representatives in 1867 and served until his death in 1881. His character was ever suspect, and his ambitions appeared to rule his decisions. Nonetheless, who can tell how much principle and sincerity lurked in his inner soul. Certainly he remained consistent in his admiration of the South and desire for peace.

C. Godfrey Gunther was an even more unusual mayor for a city at war. He did not appear to possess either the suaveness or audacity of Wood, and his election may have been a fluke. But he did not hesitate to speak his mind against the war even as the tide turned in favor of the North. His hatred for the war was as deep-seated and genuine as his love for states' rights. Gunther lived in comfortable obscurity after the war, but no one could say that he had not lived by his principles.

New York City, of course, stood for more than its political leaders. Its influence extended far beyond the borders of Manhattan Island. Its financiers, merchants, lawyers, intellectuals, clergymen, journalists, scientists, and working people attracted national attention. Their views carried weight across the country, and they sounded many discordant notes. They were often at odds with the president and placed unnecessary pressure on him. Even when they worked diligently for the Union, their concepts of the Union differed.

In the light of history, the words of Samuel Morse, August Belmont, Archbishop Hughes, Horace Greeley, Maria Daly, or Samuel Barlow do not always ring with a resonance that we approve today. Yet we know the end of the story. We know that the Union was preserved, slavery was abolished, and Lincoln is revered. They did not. There were many paths to take during those trying years. Intelligent men and women had good reason to differ. And they did. It is possible that compromise, conciliation, or peaceful secession might have been a better way. We can admire Abraham Lincoln's strength of character and be thankful for him, but his path was not the only one. New Yorkers were often a thorn in the president's side, but they were not as inspired by him as we are today. He was often misunderstood, as he well knew. Some saw him as a radical while others saw him as a conservative. He could never please them all.

Nevertheless, the southern-minded dissidents in the city presented nagging questions. Despite the confusion of the times, despite widespread ignorance, did they see the fundamental issue more clearly than those quick to take up arms? Were they more sensitive and prescient? Those who sought to prevent the war may have had a more vivid imagination and a truer sense of the barbarism of war. They did not envision an easy or glorious victory, only bloodshed and destruction. They did not have to see bloated and battered bodies on a battlefield or piles of discarded arms and legs behind surgeons' tents to know that war was hell. They saw war itself as the issue, not secession or slavery. War was the crime. Would it have been wiser to compromise? Would time have eventually solved the critical problems for the politicians? Despite arbitrary arrests, freedom of expression was rampant in the city, and these questions were volubly aired but never answered.

The compromisers may have been more sensitive than those who lived under the false illusions of military solutions. Perhaps they were not so outrageous to offer alternatives to the North and South that could have avoided the slaughter of hundreds of thousands of young men. Historians often denounce compromises as signs of weakness before wars, as in the Civil War, and then find that politicians actively engage in compromises after wars. The sequence seems wrong. If the immorality of war is to enter the consciousness of modern men and women, they must learn the intricacies of compromise.

The world is full of irony; it is one of the few consistent elements in life. Rascals can do good, and saints can do harm. The rascal Fernando Wood might have been more noble in his deepest thoughts than the self-righteous William Cullen Bryant. Self-righteousness, North and South, was the enemy of tolerance and peace. Although generalities about New York City are almost impossible to make, a blanket description of self-righteousness could never be attached to its inhabitants. They were self-strivers who were too apt to regard principles less important than practicalities. And their practical, self-interested minds sought peace. Hard-headed realists, rather than idealists, longed for tranquillity. Still, their sensitivity to the horror of war was matched by their insensitivity to the evils of slavery. They expected that someday, somehow, a political settlement of the slavery issue would come without bloodshed. Other nations had abolished slavery without resorting to mass slaughter. Tragically, this did not happen in the United States. Unwilling to solve one immoral problem, slavery, the nation resorted to another immorality, war.

Would the nation have been worse off to follow the sentiments of the majority in New York City? The seeds for better understanding were certainly present in a city that lived with so many differences within itself. New Yorkers' unheroic pleas for compromise, if accepted, might have minimized the immediate strains and led to a long-term settlement. Their self-interest might have proven a firmer foundation than the ideals of those who were eager for war. Unfortunately, no one listened to Gerard Hallock of the *Journal of Commerce* when he called for courage to prevent the carnage that was sure to come. Those who are ready to meet others halfway rarely attract attention. Their reason is too often seen as a sign of weakness. Perhaps the real evil is that myths of the glory of war continue, and we refuse to learn from history. The belief persists that war, inherently immoral, is a moral necessity.

But the other side of the story cannot be neglected. The city also contained devoted Unionists such as the Bellowses, Woolseys, Dixes, Strongs, and a host of others who fought and sacrificed for the war they hated. Frequently they were truly heroic. Disgruntled or otherwise, more than a hundred thousand men from the city joined the Union forces. Often the volunteers who fought and suffered came from the same elements of society that loudly denounced the war. Men and women do not always act on their sentiments, and the Irish-Americans were a vivid example of this paradox.

Elitists had expressed their dissatisfaction with the course of events, yet they organized the Union Defense Committee, the United States Sanitary Commission, and the hyperactive National War Committee. Enthusiastically or reluctantly, they gave financial, moral, and military support to preserve the Union. And some gave their lives.

The clashes of opinion throughout the war did not detract from the strength of the city. The reverse seemed to be true. New York was a diverse place, and the diversity could be called democracy in action in a time of crisis. In the end, the city that continually badgered the president and enraged the administration became a disappointment to the South and rallied around the Union. The city answered the reveille, but it was a strange reveille.

ABBREVIATIONS
NOTES
BIBLIOGRAPHY
INDEX

Abbreviations

CU	Cooper Union
HEH	Henry E. Huntington Library
LC	Library of Congress
MA	Municipal Archives, New York City
MHS	Massachusetts Historical Society
NYAM	New-York Academy of Medicine
NYHS	New-York Historical Society
NYPL	New York Public Library
NYSE	New York Stock Exchange Archives
TA	Trinity Church Archives
WI	Webb Institute

Notes

Chapter 1. The Long Wait

1. Samuel A. Pleasants, *Fernando Wood of New York* (New York: Columbia Univ. Press, 1948), 11–27; George Fort Milton, *Abraham Lincoln and the Fifth Column* (New York: Vanguard, 1942), 242.

2. Alexander B. Callow, Jr., *The Tweed Ring* (New York: Oxford Univ. Press, 1966), 17.

3. John Bigelow, ed., *Letters and Literary Memorials of Samuel J. Tilden,* 5 vols. (Port Washington, N.Y.: Kennikat Press, 1971), 1:127.

4. Edward S. Martin, *The Life of Joseph Hodges Choate as Gathered Chiefly from His Letters,* 2 vols. (New York: Scribner's, 1920), 1:181.

5. "Editor's Easy Chair," *Harper's New Monthly Magazine* 25, no. 146 (1862): 274.

6. Paul Migliore, "The Business of Union: The New York Business Community and the Civil War" (Ph.D. diss., Columbia University, 1973), 15–20.

7. "The Trade and Prospects of New York City," *Harper's Weekly* 5, no. 212 (1861): 34.

8. Henry Hall, *Report on the Ship-Building Industry of the United States* (Washington, D.C.: U.S. Government Printing Office, 1884), 116; Henry Whittemore, ed., *Advance Sheets of Origin and Progress of Steam Navigation in America* (New York: Original and Progressive Publishing Co., n.d.).

9. Migliore, "Business of Union," 15–20.

10. Carl Bode, ed., *Struggles and Triumphs or Forty Years' Recollections of P. T. Barnum* (New York: Penguin, 1981), 103.

11. J. Miller, *The 1866 Guide to New York City* (1866; rpt. New York: Schocken Books, 1975), 35.

12. Ralph M. Hower, *History of Macy's of New York, 1858–1919: Chapters in the Evolution of the Department Store* (Cambridge, Mass.: Harvard Univ. Press, 1943), 38, 121–93; Junius H. Browne, *The Great Metropolis: A Mirror of New York* (1869; rpt. New York: Arno, 1975), 289–93.

13. Miller, *1866 Guide,* 67–68; Nat Brandt, "New York Is Worth Twenty Richmonds," *American Heritage* 22, no. 6 (1971): 289–93; Edward K. Spann, *The New Metropolis: New York City, 1840–1857* (New York: Columbia Univ. Press, 1981), 94–116.

14. George C. D. Odell, *Annals of the New York Stage*, 15 vols. (New York: Columbia Univ. Press, 1927–49), 7:305; Alan Downer, ed. *The Autobiography of Joseph Jefferson* (Cambridge, Mass.: Belknap Press of Harvard Univ. Press, 1964), 142–56.

15. Gerald Astor, *The New York Cops: An Informal History* (New York: Scribner's, 1971), 31.

16. Robert Ernst, *Immigrant Life in New York City, 1825–1863* (New York: Columbia Univ. Press, 1949), 40.

17. Hower, *History of Macy's*, 40–63; Edward Hungerford, *The Romance of a Great Store* (New York: McBride, 1922), 4–25.

18. Robert Neil Mathis, "Gazaway Bugg Lamar: A Southern Businessman and Confidant in New York City," *New York History* 56, no. 3 (1975): 298–313.

19. M. R. Werner, *It Happened in New York* (New York: Coward-McCann, 1957), 179.

20. Ernst, *Immigrant Life*, 170–84.

21. Pleasants, *Wood*, 99.

22. Howard C. Perkins, ed., *Northern Editorials on Secession*, 2 vols. (Gloucester, Mass.: Peter Smith, 1964), 1:454–55, 494; quotes from *New York Evening Day-Book*, Jan. 24, 1861, and *New York Herald*, March 7, 1861.

23. H. G. Ludlow to S. F. B. Morse, May 5, 27, 1861, Samuel F. B. Morse Papers, LC.

24. Samuel Barlow to Samuel Tilden, June 1860, Samuel Tilden Papers, NYPL.

25. Roy P. Basler, ed., *The Collected Works of Abraham Lincoln*, 8 vols. (New Brunswick: Rutgers Univ. Press, 1953), 3:522–50.

26. Margaret Clapp, *Forgotten First Citizen: John Bigelow* (Boston: Little, Brown, 1947), 136.

27. John A. Hardy, secretary to August Belmont, to Samuel Tilden, Aug. 2, 1860, Tilden Papers.

28. Frank L. Klement, *The Limits of Dissent* (Lexington: Univ. of Kentucky, 1970), 45.

29. *New York Times*, Oct. 12, 1860.

30. Albon P. Man, Jr., "Labor Competition and the New York Draft Riots of 1863," *Journal of Negro History* 36, no. 4 (1951): 367–405.

31. *New York Herald*, Sept. 19, 1860.

32. Alfred H. Satterlee Diary, Oct. 3, 23, 1860, NYPL.

33. James M. McPherson, *The Negro's Civil War* (New York: Pantheon, 1965), 272.

34. Satterlee Diary, Nov. 6, 1860; Allan Nevins, ed., *Diary of the Civil War, 1860–1865: George Templeton Strong* (New York: Macmillan, 1962), 58–60; McPherson, *Negro's Civil War*, 272.

35. Satterlee Diary, Nov. 9, 1860; William Cullen Bryant II and Thomas G. Voss, eds., *The Letters of William Cullen Bryant, 1858–1864*, 4 vols. (New York: Fordham Univ. Press, 1984), 4:186.

36. John G. Nicolay and John Hay, *Abraham Lincoln: A History*, 10 vols. (New York: Century, 1914), 2:95.

37. Satterlee Diary, Nov. 20, Dec. 7, 1860; Bryant and Voss, eds., *Letters*, 4:186; Nevins, ed., *Diary of the Civil War*, 63.

38. *New York Tribune*, Nov. 28, Dec. 17, 1860; Ralph Ray Fahrney, *Horace Greeley and the Tribune in the Civil War* (New York: DaCapo, 1970), 1, 49.

39. *New York Times*, Dec. 26, 1860; *New York World*, Dec. 15, 1860; *New York Herald*, Feb. 1, 1861; Perkins, ed., *Northern Editorials*, 1:475–76; William Harlan Hale, *Horace Greeley: Voice of the People* (New York: Harper, 1950), 232.

40. De Alva S. Alexander, *A Political History of the State of New York*, 4 vols. (1909; rpt. Port Washington, N.Y.: Ira J. Freedman, 1969), 2:337–38.

41. David M. Potter, *Lincoln and His Party in the Secession Crisis* (New Haven: Yale Univ. Press, 1942), 69–71; Irving Katz, *August Belmont: A Political Biography* (New York: Columbia Univ. Press, 1968), 86–88; Alexander, *Political History*, 2:341.

42. Bryant and Voss, eds., *Letters*, 4:187.

43. John Dix to Horatio Seymour, Dec. 26, 1860, Fairchild Collection, NYHS; *Proceedings of an Union Meeting Held in New York, An Appeal to the South* (New York: John H. Duyckinck, 1860), NYHS; Florence E. Gibson, *The Attitudes of New York Irish toward State and National Affairs* (New York: Columbia Univ. Press, 1951), 113; James J. Heslin, " 'Peaceful Compromise' in New York City, 1860–1861," *New-York Historical Society Quarterly* 44, no. 4 (1960): 349–62.

44. Bigelow, ed., *Letters of Tilden*, 1:147–48.

45. *Proceedings of the Board of Aldermen of the City of New York*, Oct. 1, 1860–JAN. 4, 1861, 80:873–85.

46. Allan Nevins, *The Emergence of Lincoln*, 2 vols. (New York: Scribner's, 1950), 2:412.

47. Hower, *History of Macy's*, 63, quoting advertisement in *New York Herald*, Dec. 22, 1860.

Chapter 2. The New Year

1. *New York Times*, Jan. 3, 1861.

2. Georgeanna M. W. Bacon, ed., *Letters of a Family during the War for the Union, 1861–1865*, 2 vols. (New York: Privately printed, 1899), 1:33; Anne L. Austin, *The Woolsey Sisters of New York: A Family's Involvement in the Civil War and a New Profession (1860–1900)* (Philadelphia: American Philosophical Society, 1971), 14–22.

3. James W. Hudnut, *Semi-Centennial History of New York Life Insurance Company* (New York: Published by the company, 1895), 64–73.

4. *New York Times*, Jan. 5, 1861.

5. Ibid.

6. *Proceedings of the Board of Aldermen*, 81:10–26.

7. Ibid.

8. August Belmont, *A Few Letters and Speeches of the Late Civil War* (New York: Privately printed, 1870), 19.

9. Mathis, "Gazaway Bugg Lamar," 308.

10. Nicolay and Hay, *Lincoln*, 2:418.

11. *Proceedings of the Board of Aldermen*, 81:34–35.

12. Perkins, ed., *Northern Editorials*, 1:396; *New York Herald*, Jan. 8, 1861; *New York Times*, Jan. 8, 1861; Pleasants, *Wood*, 113–17; Wood Gray, *The Hidden Civil War: The Story of the Copperheads* (New York: Viking, 1964), 213–14.

13. Nevins, ed., *Diary of the Civil War*, 66, 105.

14. Pleasants, *Wood*, 117; Mathis, "Gazaway Bugg Lamar," 307.

15. *New York Herald*, Jan. 9, 1861; *New York Times*, Jan. 9, 1861.

16. *New York Times*, Jan. 9, 1861.

17. Ibid., Jan. 10, 1861.

18. Ibid, Jan. 14, 1861.

19. Werner, *It Happened in New York*, 182.

20. *New York Times*, Jan. 4, 11, 1861.

21. Draft of letter from Peter Cooper to Abraham Lincoln, March, 20, 1861, Peter Cooper Papers, Cooper Union, New York City.

22. Potter, *Lincoln and His Party*, 123–24; Heslin, "Peaceful Compromise," 349–61.

23. Harold E. Hammond, ed., *Diary of a Union Lady, 1861–1865* (New York: Funk and Wagnalls, 1962), 5; Harold E. Hammond, *A Commoner's Judge: The Life and Times of Charles Patrick Daly* (Boston: Christopher, 1954), 159.

24. William Howard Russell, *My Diary North and South* (1863; rpt. New York: Harper, 1954), 7; Stewart Mitchell, *Horatio Seymour of New York* (Cambridge, Mass.: Harvard Univ. Press, 1938), 226.

25. Belmont, *A Few Letters*, 5–7.

26. Samuel Tilden to Editors, *New York World*, Jan. 29, 1861, Tilden Papers; Alexander Flick, *Samuel Jones Tilden: A Study in Political Sagacity* (Port Washington, N.Y.: Kennikat Press, 1963), 118–33.

27. Edward Lind Morse, ed., *Samuel F. B. Morse: His Letters and Journals*, 2 vols. (New York: Kennedy Galleries/DaCapo, 1973), 2:414.

28. *New York Times*, Jan. 16, 1861.

29. Ibid.

30. *New York Herald*, Jan. 11, 1861.

31. Martin, *Life of Choate*, 1:217–18; Alfred G. Jones Diary, Feb. 1861, Alfred Goldsborough Jones Papers, NYPL.

32. Justin Kaplin, *Walt Whitman: A Life* (New York: Simon & Schuster, 1980), 260–61.

33. Basler, ed., *Works of Lincoln*, 4:229–31.

34. *New York Times*, Feb. 21, 1861.

35. Basler, ed., *Works of Lincoln*, 4:232–33.

36. *New York Times*, Feb. 21, 1861.

37. Brother Basil Leo Lee, *Discontent in New York City, 1861–1865* (Washington, D. C.: Catholic University of America Press, 1943), 32; Werner, *It Happened in New York*, 182.

38. Joel H. Silbey, *A Respectable Minority: The Democratic Party in the Civil War Era, 1860–1868* (New York: Norton, 1977), 25–32.

39. Clapp, *Forgotten First Citizen*, 142.

40. Horace Greeley to unidentified, March 14, 1861, Horace Greeley Papers, NYPL; Chester L. Barrows, *William M. Evarts, Lawyer, Diplomat, Statesman* (Chapel Hill:

Univ. of North Carolina Press, 1941), 97; Brainerd Dyer, *The Public Career of William M. Evarts* (Berkeley: Univ. of California Press, 1933), 45; Glyndon G. Van Deusen, *Horace Greeley: Nineteenth Century Crusader* (Philadelphia: Univ. of Pennsylvania Press, 1953), 256 –60.

41. W. M. Gooding to Henry Bellows, March 25, 1861, Henry Bellows Papers, MHS.

42. Nevins, ed., *Diary of the Civil War*, 105.

43. *New York Times*, March 6, 1861; *Journal of Commerce*, March 5, 1861.

44. Martin, *Choate*, 1:217.

Chapter 3.   Fort Sumter

1. Henry Clews, *Twenty-Eight Years in Wall Street* (New York: J. S. Ogilvie, 1887), 39, 73–79.

2. Peter Cooper to Senator John Sherman, Feb. 4, 1861, Cooper Papers.

3. Henry W. Domett, *A History of the Bank of New York, 1784–1884* (New York: Published by the Directors, 1884), 95–96.

4. Salmon P. Chase, *Diary and Correspondence of Salmon P. Chase* (Washington, D. C.: American Historical Association, 1902), 493.

5. Mathis, "Gazaway Bugg Lamar," 310.

6. *New York Herald*, April 11, 1861; *New York Evening Post*, April 10, 1861; *New York Times*, April 5, 1861; *New York World*, April 30, 1861.

7. *New York Times*, April 26, 27, 30, 1861.

8. Edward Robb Ellis, *The Epic of New York City* (New York: Coward-McCann, 1966), 317.

9. *New York Herald*, April 4, 1861.

10. Ibid.

11. Ibid., April 1, 6, July 6, 8, 13, 1861; Richard O'Connor, *The Scandalous Mr. Bennett* (New York: Doubleday, 1962), 29–30, 39; Don C. Seitz, *The James Gordon Bennetts, Father and Son* (Indianapolis: Bobbs-Merrill, 1928), 185–97; Browne, *Great Metropolis*, 495; Hale, *Greeley*, 63, 226–51; Matthew Hale Smith, *Sunshine and Shadow in New York* (Hartford: Burr, 1868), 656.

12. *New York Times*, March 4, 15, 1861.

13. Ibid., April 9, 1861; Martin, *Choate*, 1:219.

14. *New York Times*, April 11, 1861.

15. *Journal of Commerce*, April 12, 1861; *New York Daily News*, Feb. 20, March 13, 14, 20, April 12, 1861.

16. *New York Times*, April 12, 1861.

17. *New York Herald*, April 12, 1861.

18. Ellis, *Epic*, 292.

19. Nevins, ed., *Diary of the Civil War*, 118; Edmund C. Stedman, ed., *The New York Stock Exchange*, 2 vols. (New York: New York Stock Exchange Historical Society, 1905), 1:131; Martin, *Choate*, 1:219; Bacon, ed., *Letters of a Family*, 1:37.

20. Morgan Dix, *Memoirs of John Adams Dix*, 2 vols. (New York: Harper, 1883), 1:9.

21. Louis M. Starr, *Bohemian Brigade: Civil War Newsmen in Action* (New York: Knopf, 1954), 30.

22. Barrows, *Evarts*, 101.

23. *New York Times,* April 16, 1861; *Journal of Commerce,* April 15, 1861; Pleasants, *Wood,* 119.

24. *New York Times,* April 16, 1861; Nevins, ed., *Diary of the Civil War,* 121.

25. *New York Times,* April 16, 1861.

26. "Threats to Burn New York," *Frank Leslie's Illustrated Newspaper* 11, no. 286 (1861): 403; Chase, *Diary and Correspondence,* 2:493-96.

27. New York Stock and Exchange Board Minutes, April 17, May 11, 1861, NYSE Archives, New York City; *New York Times,* April 16, 1861; Joseph B. Bishop, *A Chronicle of One Hundred and Fifty Years: The Chamber of Commerce of the State of New York, 1768-1918* (New York: Scribner's, 1918), 71.

28. Francis Brown, *Raymond of the Times* (New York: Norton, 1951), 276; Starr, *Bohemian Brigade,* 31.

29. Morgan Dix Diary, April 18, 1861, Archives of the Parish of Trinity Church of the City of New York, New York City.

30. Barrows, *Evarts,* 102; Dix, *Memoirs,* 9.

31. *New York Times,* April 22, 1861.

32. Lawrence Kehoe, ed., *Complete Works of the Most Reverend John Hughes, Archbishop of New York, Comprising His Sermons, Letters, Lectures, Speeches, etc.* 2 vols. (New York: Catholic Publication House, 1864), 1:12, 2:i-xiii, 513; Henry A. Brann, *Most Reverend John Hughes, First Archbishop of New York* (New York: Dodd, Mead, 1892), 154, 435. See also John R. G. Hassard, *Life of the Most Reverend John Hughes, D.D.: First Archbishop of New York, with Extracts from His Private Correspondence* (New York: Appleton, 1866), and Richard Shaw, *Dagger John* (New York: Paulist Press, 1977).

33. Alfred Janson Bloor Diary, April 21, 1861, NYHS; Nevins, ed., *Diary of the Civil War,* 125-28; James McCullough Farr, *A Short History of the Brick Presbyterian Church in the City of New York, 1768-1943* (New York: Brick Church, 1943), 4-5. See also Shepherd Knapp, *A History of the Brick Presbyterian Church in the City of New York* (New York: Brick Church, 1909).

34. *Proceedings of the Board of Aldermen,* 82:56-58; Edgcumb Pinchon, *Dan Sickles, Hero of Gettysburg and "Yankee King of Spain"* (Garden City, N.Y.: Doubleday, 1945), 152; Bayrd Still, *Mirror for Gotham* (New York: New York University Press, 1956), 179; James G. Wilson, ed., *The Memorial History of the City of New York,* 4 vols. (New York: New York History Company, 1892-93), 3:484; O'Connor, *Scandalous Mr. Bennett,* 39-40.

35. Perkins, ed., *Northern Editorials,* 2:717.

36. Samuel Morse to Cornelia Goodrich, April 21, 1861, Thomas F. Madigan Collection, NYPL.

37. John L. O'Sullivan to Samuel Tilden, May 6, June 5, 25, July 16, 1861, Sept. 19, 1864, Tilden Papers.

38. Nevins, ed., *Diary of the Civil War,* 127, 132.

39. *Reports, Resolutions and Documents of the Union Defense Committee of the Citizens of New York* (New York: N.p., 1862); John Perry Pritchett, Francis Katzman, and Howard Dellon, "The Union Defense Committee of the City of New York during the Civil War,"

New-York Historical Society Quarterly 30, no. 3 (1946): 142–60; *New York Times*, April 21, 1861; Bacon, ed., *Letters of a Family*, 1:39–44; Titus Coan to Mother, April 21, 1861, Titus Coan Papers, NYHS; New York Stock and Exchange Board Minutes, April 18, 1861.

40. Dix, *Memoirs*, 13.

41. Sylvia Dannett, ed. *Noble Women of the North* (New York: Yoseloff, 1959), 48.

42. Wilson, *Memorial History*, 3:488n; Wheaton J. Lane, *Commodore Vanderbilt: An Epic of the Steam Age* (New York: Knopf, 1942).

43. John Crosley Brown, *A Hundred Years of Merchant Banking: A History of Brown Brothers and Company* (New York: Privately printed, 1909), 224–25.

44. Dix Diary, April 23, 1861.

45. *New York Times*, April 22, 1861.

46. Brown, *Raymond of the Times*, 202; Wilson, *Memorial History*, 3:494.

47. Dr. Howard Rusk, "Bellevue Hospital, Pioneer in Medical Practice Training," *New York Times*, May 23, 1948, Bellevue Hospital Miscellaneous Papers, NYAM; Dannett, ed., *Noble Women*, 30–61; Agatha Young, *The Women and the Crisis: Women of the North in the Civil War* (New York: McDowell, Obolensky, 1959), 72–76; Dorothy Clarke Wilson, *Lone Woman Doctor: The Story of Elizabeth Blackwell, the First Woman Doctor* (Boston: Little, Brown, 1970), 387–89.

48. Ellis, *Epic*, 296.

Chapter 4. Recruits

1. Judith Lee Hallock, "The Role of the Community in Civil War Desertion," *Civil War History* 29, no. 2 (1983): 123–34; John Hope Franklin, *From Slavery to Freedom: A History of American Negroes* (New York: Knopf, 1967), 268.

2. New York Stock and Exchange Board Minutes, April 18, 1861; William J. Roehrenbeck, *The Regiment That Saved the Capital* (New York: Thomas Yoseloff, 1961), 54–64.

3. Bacon, ed., *Letters of a Family*, 1:39.

4. Dix Diary, April 21, 22 1861; *New York Daily News*, April 23, 1861; *Frank Leslie's Illustrated Newspaper*, April 27, 1861.

5. Mrs. Henry Bellows to Russell Bellows, May 5, 1861, Bellows Papers; Dix, *Memoirs*, 18.

6. Dix Diary, May 5, 1861.

7. Ibid., June 8, 1861.

8. Charles A. Ingraham, *Elmer E. Ellsworth and the Zouaves of '61* (Chicago: University of Chicago Press, 1925), 2–7; Lowell Limpus, *History of the New York Fire Department* (New York: Dutton, 1940), 226–28.

9. George Bliss, "Autobiography of George Bliss," 146, typescript NYHS.

10. Pritchett, Katzman, and Dellon, "Union Defense Committee," 144–54.

11. Nevins, ed., *Diary of the Civil War*, 152.

12. Domett, *Bank of New York*, 97; Basler, ed., *Works of Lincoln*, 5:240–43.

13. [Brooks Brothers], *Established 1818, Brooks Brothers Centenary, 1818–1918* (New York: Cheltenham Press, 1918), 18–32; James A. Rawley, *Edwin D. Morgan, 1811–1883: Merchant in Politics* (New York: Columbia Univ. Press, 1955), 154.

14. *New York Times,* April 29, 1861; Lee, *Discontent,* 55.

15. *New York Times,* May 23, 1861.

16. Hammond, ed., *Diary of a Union Lady,* 22.

17. *New York Times,* June 15, 1861.

18. Margaret Leech, *Reveille in Washington* (New York: Harper, 1941), 85.

19. *New York Times,* May 21, 24, 1861; *New York Herald,* July 1, 1861.

20. Dix Diary, May 25, 27, 1861; Archbishop John Hughes to Thurlow Weed, April 21, 1861, Thurlow Weed Papers, NYHS; Hassard, *Hughes,* 443; Howard R. Marraro, "Lincoln's Italian Volunteers from New York," *New York History* 24, no. 1 (1943): 56–67; Leech, *Reveille in Washington,* 70–85.

21. Mrs. Daniel Sickles to "My own dear Dan," April 20, 1861, Daniel Sickles Papers, NYHS; Pinchon, *Sickles,* 152–62.

22. Dix Diary, June 24, 1861.

23. *New York Times,* April 25, 1861.

24. Basler, ed., *Works of Lincoln,* 4:375.

25. Rawley, *Morgan,* 139–49.

26. Dix Diary, May 26, 1861; Martin, *Choate,* 1:221; Ingrahm, *Ellsworth,* 158–61.

27. Van Deusen, *Greeley,* 276.

28. Belmont, *A Few Letters,* 32.

29. Alfred H. Satterlee Diary, June 1, 1861 NYPL; Emmons Clark, *History of the Seventh Regiment of New York, 1806–1889,* 2 vols. (New York: Seventh Regiment, 1890), 2:38.

30. Perkins, ed., *Northern Editorials,* 2:798.

31. Henry Bellows to Russell Bellows, May 2, 1861, Bellows Papers.

32. Louisa Lee Schuyler Papers, NYHS; Henry Bellows to son, April 25, 1861, Bellows Papers.

33. George W. Adams, *Doctors in Blue: The Medical History of the Union Army in the Civil War* (New York: Henry Schuman, 1952), 4; William Quentin Maxwell, *Lincoln's Fifth Wheel: The Political History of the United States Sanitary Commission* (New York: Longmans, Green, 1956), 2–8.

34. Henry Bellows to Mrs. Bellows, May 16, 20, 1861, Bellows Papers.

35. Ibid., May 20, 1861.

36. Henry Bellows to Mrs. Bellows, second letter (by hand of Cyrus Field), May 20, 1861, Bellows Papers.

37. Maxwell, *Lincoln's Fifth Wheel,* 8.

38. Plan of organization, Sanitary Commission, June 13, 1861, Bellows Papers.

39. Mrs. Bellows to Henry Bellows, 1861, ibid.

40. Henry Bellows to Russell Bellows, June 20, 1861, ibid.

41. *New York Times,* June 7, 1861; Adams, *Doctors in Blue,* 16.

42. Bacon, ed., *Letters of a Family,* 1:64.

43. Hassard, *Hughes,* 442; Jane E. Mottus, *New York Nightingales: The Emergence of Nursing Profession at Bellevue and New York Hospital, 1850–1920* (Ann Arbor: Research Press–Studies in American History and Culture, Univ. of Michigan, 1981), 23–34.

44. Bacon, ed., *Letters of a Family*, 1:78–85.

45. Miller, *1866 Guide*, 4.

46. Kathleen L. Endres, "The Women's Press in the Civil War: A Portrait of Patriotism, Propaganda, and Prodding," *Civil War History* 30, no. 1 (1984): 31–53.

47. Justin G. Turner and Linda Levitt Turner, eds., *Mary Todd Lincoln: Her Life and Letters* (New York: Knopf, 1972), 86.

48. Bloor Diary, July 4, 1861; George Winston Smith and Charles Judah, *Life in the North during the Civil War: A Source History* (Albuquerque: Univ. of New Mexico Press, 1966), 45; Bryant and Voss, eds., *Letters*, 4:222n.

49. *New York Times*, June 16, 1861.

50. Barrows, *Evarts*, 104.

51. Carleton Mabee, *The American Leonardo: The Life of Samuel F. B. Morse* (New York: Knopf, 1957), 417.

52. *New York Times*, July 17, 18, 19, 1861.

53. Ibid., July 20, 21, 1861.

54. Lee, *Discontent*, 70; Kenneth P. Williams, *Lincoln Finds a General*, 2 vols. (New York: Macmillan, 1949), 1:96.

55. Bacon, ed., *Letters of a Family*, 1:123.

56. Satterlee Diary, July 22, 1861; Dix Diary, July 22, 1861; *New York Times*, July 22, 23, 1861; *New York Herald*, July 22, 23, 1861; *New York Tribune*, July 22, 23, 1861.

57. John Bigelow, *Retrospections of an Active Life*, 5 vols. (New York: Baker and Taylor, 1909), 1:361; F. L. Olmsted to William Cullen Bryant, July 31, 1861, Bryant-Godwin Papers, NYPL; *New York Times*, July 24, 1861.

58. *New York Evening Post*, July 23, 1861; *New York Times*, July 24, 1861.

59. *New York Times*, July 26, 27, 28, 1861.

60. J. A. Stevens, Jr., to J. A. Stevens, July 27, 1861, John A. Stevens Papers, NYHS; Clapp, *Forgotten First Citizen*, 147.

61. Van Deusen, *Greeley*, 276; Starr, *Bohemian Brigade*, 49–54.

62. Hassard, *Hughes*, 446.

63. *New York Daily News*, Aug. 16, 30, 1861; Gibson, *Attitudes of New York Irish*, 134; Pleasants, *Wood*, 124.

64. Francis Lieber to A. D. Bache, July 11, 1862, Francis Lieber Papers, HEH.

65. A. H. Livermore to Henry Bellows, Aug. 29, 1861, Bellows Papers.

Chapter 5. Money

1. Letter from New York bank presidents to Governor Edwin Morgan, May 13, 1861; Governor Edwin Morgan to J. A. Stevens and other bank presidents, May 18, 1861, Stevens Papers.

2. Maunsell B. Field, *Memories of Many Men and Some Women: Being Personal Recollections of Emperors, Kings, Queens, Princes, Presidents, Statesmen, Authors and Artists, at Home and Abroad during the Last Thirty Years* (New York: Harper, 1874), 253–55; Nicolay and Hay, *Lincoln*, 6:228; "The National Loan," *Harper's Weekly* 5, no. 247 (1861): 594.

3. Ellis Paxson Oberholtzer, *Jay Cooke, Financier of the Civil War*, 2 vols. (Philadelphia: George W. Jacobs, 1907), 1:151–53.

4. *New York Times*, Aug. 3, 16, 23, 1861; Lee, *Discontent*, 52, 64, 83, 85.

5. *Reports, Resolutions and Documents of the Union Defense Committee*.

6. *New York Times*, Aug. 11, 26, Sept. 11, Oct. 23, Dec. 11, 1861; Lee, *Discontent*, 168.

7. *Harper's Weekly* 5, no. 256 (1861): 738–39.

8. New York Stock and Exchange Board Minutes, Oct. 23, 1861.

9. Lane, *Commodore Vanderbilt*, 175.

10. Glyndon G. Van Deusen, *Thurlow Weed, Wizard of the Lobby* (Boston: Little, Brown, 1947), 273, 285–87.

11. Thurlow Weed to Fernando Wood, Oct. 29, 1861, Fernando Wood Papers, NYPL.

12. Robert I. Warshow, *Jay Gould: The Story of a Fortune* (New York: Greenberg, 1947), 56.

13. John K. Winkler, *Morgan the Magnificent: The Life of J. Pierpont Morgan (1837–1913)* (New York: Vanguard, 1930), 56–57.

14. John Nevin, *Gideon Welles* (New York: Oxford Univ. Press, 1973), 362–63.

15. *The Wealth and Biography of the Wealthy Citizens of the City of New York* (New York: New York Sun Office, 1855), NYHS.

16. P. H. Watson to Abram Hewitt, Jan. 12, 1862; Hewitt to Watson, Jan. 27, 1862, Abram Hewitt Papers, CU; "The Old Ship-Builders of New York," *Harper's New Monthly Magazine* 65, no. 386 (1882): 223–41.

17. Abram Hewitt to Capt. W. B. Franklin, May 11, 1861, Hewitt Papers.

18. *New York Times*, Oct. 2, 1861; Hower, *History of Macy's*, 90.

19. Odell, *Annals of the New York Stage*, 7:377–429; Bode, *Struggles and Triumphs*, 276.

20. Odell, *Annals of the New York Stage*, 7:358–63.

21. Ibid., 352–438, *New York Times*, Dec. 21, 1861.

22. Kaplan, *Walt Whitman*, 264.

23. *New York Times*, Dec. 21, 1861, quoting notice in *New York Herald*.

Chapter 6. Maritime Affairs

1. *New York Times*, Oct. 24, 28, Nov. 1, 1861; *New York World*, Nov. 1, 1861; Barrows, *Evarts*, 103–7; Nicolay and Hay, *Lincoln*, 5:9–10; Dyer, *Evarts*, 53–57; Matthew Page Andrews, *Women of the South in War Time* (Baltimore: Remington, 1927), 428–30.

2. *New York World*, Nov. 9, 1861.

3. Andrews, *Women of the South*, 430.

4. Martin, *Choate*, 1:235–36, *Proceedings of the Board of Aldermen*, 84:177.

5. *New York Herald*, July 1, 1861.

6. Bigelow, *Retrospections*, 1:422–24.

7. *New York Times*, Oct. 18, 19, 1861; Glyndon G. Van Deusen, *William Henry Seward* (New York: Oxford Univ. Press, 1967), 309–13; Rawley, *Morgan*, 169.

8. *New York Times*, Dec. 5, 6, 9, 1861.

9. *Proceedings of the Board of Aldermen*, 84:341–47.

10. *New York Times*, Dec. 13, 16, 17, 18, 21, 31, 1861; D. P. Crook, *The North, the South and the Powers, 1861–1865* (New York: Wiley, 1974), 114, 150–54; Van Deusen, *Seward*, 313.

11. "A Looker On" to Moses Taylor, Chairman, Loan Committee, Dec. 24, 1861, NYHS; Allan Nevins, *History of the Bank of New York (1784–1934)* (New York: Privately printed, 1934), 59–72.

12. Brown, *A Hundred Years of Merchant Banking*, 227.

13. *New York World*, Dec. 30, 1861; Bigelow, *Retrospections*, 2:473–74.

14. *New York Times*, Dec. 15, 25, 1861.

Chapter 7. Mayoral Election

1. *New York Times*, Nov. 4, 1861.

2. *New York Daily News*, Sept. 1, 1861.

3. Nevins, ed., *Diary of the Civil War*, 168; Factbook, Municipal Reference Library, New York City.

4. *New York Times*, Dec. 1, 2, 1861.

5. Pleasants, *Wood*, 126–31.

6. Frederick Seward to Fernando Wood, Nov. 29, 1861, Wood Papers.

7. *New York World*, Nov. 27, 1861.

8. Dix Diary, Oct. 30, Nov. 1, 1861.

9. Pleasants, *Wood*, 130.

10. *New York Times*, Dec. 4, 1861.

11. David Mitchell Turnure Journal, Nov. 30, Dec. 4, 1861, NYHS.

12. *New York World*, Dec. 4, 1861.

Chapter 8. Despair

1. *New York Times*, Jan. 3, 4, 7, 13, 1862; Smith and Judah, *Life in the North*, 199; Allan Nevins, *The War for the Union*, 4 vols. (New York: Scribner's, 1959–71), 2:506.

2. George Opdyke, *Official Documents, Addresses, Etc. of George Opdyke, Mayor of the City of New York, during the Years 1862 and 1863* (New York: Hurd and Houghton, 1866), 1; Thurlow Weed Barnes, *Memoir of Thurlow Weed*, 2 vols. (Boston: Houghton Mifflin, 1884), 2:412; Rawley, *Morgan*, 169; Nevins, ed., *Diary of the Civil War*, 196.

3. Opdyke, *Official Documents*, 1–10.

4. D. T. Valentine, ed., *Manual of the Corporation of the City of New York* (New York: Edmund Jones, 1862), 146.

5. Jones Diary, March 3, 1862, Jones Papers.

6. *New York Times*, March 13, 16, 1862; Domett, *History of the Bank of New York*, 97.

7. Allan Nevins, *Abram S. Hewitt, with Some Accounts of Peter Cooper* (New York: Harper, 1935), 216–18.

8. Francis B. Wheeler, *John Flack Winslow and the Monitor* (Poughkeepsie: Privately printed, 1893), 34–40.

9. Opdyke, *Official Documents*, 30.

10. Lane, *Commodore Vanderbilt*, 174–79.

11. Ibid.

12. Ibid, 180–82.

13. J. Howley, "William H. Webb—Shipbuilder" (Senior thesis, Princeton University, 1946), 63, WI.

14. Fahrney, *Greeley and the Tribune*, 99.

15. George Dow to "My dear Thomas," March 20, 1862, George Dow Papers, NYHS.

16. Albert Uhlmann, *Maiden Lane: The Story of a Single Street* (New York: Maiden Lane Society, 1931), 88.

17. Nevins, *War for the Union*, 2:508; Stedman, ed., *New York Stock Exchange*, 1:147 –48; *New York Times*, March 24, 1862.

18. *New York Times*, April 12, 1862.

19. *New York Times*, May 23, 1862; Nevins, ed., *Diary of the Civil War*, 207.

20. Jane Benedict, comp., *The Story of the First Fifty Years of the Mount Sinai Hospital, 1852–1952* (New York: Mount Sinai Hospital, 1944), 34; Joseph Hirsh and Beka Doherty, *The First Hundred Years of the Mount Sinai Hospital, 1852–1952* (New York: Random House, 1952), 40–41.

21. *Proceedings of the Board of Aldermen*, 86:363; *New York Times*, Nov. 16, 1862; Page Cooper, *The Bellevue Story* (New York: Thomas Crowell, 1948), 78.

22. Claude Edwin Heaton, *The First One Hundred Twenty-five Years of the New York University School of Medicine* (New York: New York University School of Medicine, 1966, 13 –19; Robert J. Carlisle, ed., *An Account of Bellevue Hospital with a Catalogue of the Medical and Surgical Staff* (New York: Society of the Alumni of Bellevue Hospital, 1893), 77.

23. John Shrady, ed., *The College of Physicians and Surgeons of New York and Its Founders, Officers, Instructors, Benefactors and Alumni*, 2 vols. (New York: Lewis, 1911).

24. Henry Bellows to Russell Bellows, June 9, 1862; Dr. William Van Buren to Henry Bellows, Sept. 12, 1863, Bellows Papers.

25. Henry Bellows to Russell Bellows, June 9, 1862, Bellows Papers.

26. Ibid.

27. Heaton, *First One Hundred Twenty-five Years*, 18–19.

28. Bernard B. Nadell, "History of Bellevue Hospital," typescript, Bellevue Miscellaneous Papers, NYAM.

29. Titus Coan to Mother, Oct. 19, 1862, Coan Papers.

30. Heaton, *First One Hundred Twenty-five Years*, 16–19; Annual Announcement and Circular, Bellevue Hospital Medical College, 1861–62 and 1863–64, NYAM; College of Physicians and Surgeons Catalogue, 1863, NYAM.

31. Hammond *Diary of a Union Lady*, 127, Henry Bellows to "My dear Joe," Feb. 1, 1862, Bellows Papers.

32. Henry Bellows to Russell Bellows, May 10, 1862; Mrs. Bellows to son, May 17, 1862; Mrs. Bellows to Henry Bellows, March 11, 1862, Bellows Papers.

33. Laura Wood Roper, *FLO: A Biography of Frederick Law Olmsted* (Baltimore: Johns Hopkins Univ. Press, 1973), 191–206.

34. Henry Bellows to Russell Bellows, May 21, 1862, Bellows Papers.

35. Bacon, ed., *Letters of a Family*, 1:342–43, 362–67.

36. Hammond, ed., *Diary of a Union Lady*, 132.

37. Bacon, ed., *Letters of a Family*, 1:367.

38. *New York Times*, May 13, 1862.

39. Starr, *Bohemian Brigade*, 104–6.

40. Francis Lieber to Alexander Bache, May 9, June 18, July 6, 1862, Lieber Papers; "Editor's Easy Chair," *Harper's New Monthly Magazine* 25, no. 147 (1862): 418–24.

41. Gustavus Myers, *The History of Tammany Hall* (New York: Boni and Liveright, 1917), 196.

42. *Proceedings at the Mass Meeting of Loyal Citizens on Union Square . . .* (New York: Committee on Arrangements, 1862); Opdyke, *Official Documents*, 60.

43. Hammond, ed., *Diary of a Union Lady*, 160–70.

44. Morse, ed., *Morse*, 2:419.

45. Ibid., 420.

46. Barnes, *Memoir of Thurlow Weed*, 2:420.

47. Katz, *Belmont*, 114.

48. Bigelow, *Retrospections*, 1:504.

49. Nevins, *War for the Union*, 2:169.

50. Barrows, *Evarts*, 107.

51. Malcolm Ives to James Gordon Bennett, July 3, 1862, James Gordon Bennett Papers, LC; *New York Times*, Sept. 26, 1862; *Proceedings of the Board of Aldermen*, 87:244.

52. C. H. Marshall to "His Excellency Abr. Lincoln," 1862, Miscellaneous MSS, WI.

53. Howley, "William H. Webb," 64–65.

54. Richard Delafield to Horatio Seymour, Jan. 26, 1863, Richard Delafield Letter Press Book, NYHS.

55. Ibid.

56. Ibid.

57. A. S. Hewitt to Secretary of War, May 31, 1862, Hewitt Papers.

58. *Harper's Weekly* 7, no. 329 (1863): 242.

59. George Walton Dalzell, *The Flight from the Flag* (Chapel Hill: Univ. of North Carolina Press, 1940), 140–41.

60. Ibid., 238–47.

61. Opdyke, *Official Documents*, 122–57; *Proceedings of the Board of Aldermen*, 89:25.

62. Charles Sumner to John A. Stevens, Jr., April 17, 1862 (possibly 1863), Stevens Papers.

63. *New York Times*, Jan. 3, 1862.

64. Mrs. Kirkland to Henry Bellows, Aug. 7, 1862, Bellows Papers.

65. Nicolay and Hay, *Lincoln*, 6:115.

66. Bacon, ed., *Letters of a Family*, 1:456.

67. *Proceedings of the Board of Aldermen*, 88:46–55, *New York Times*, Oct. 6, 11, Dec. 7, 1862.

68. *New York Times*, July 16, Oct. 17, 1862.

69. George Opdyke to William Cranston, Dec. 29, 1862, Letterbook, Mayoralty Correspondence, MA.

70. *New York Daily News*, Nov. 1, 1864; Smith, *Sunshine and Shadow*, 37.

71. Odell, *Annals of the New York Stage*, 7:433–38.

72. Still, *Mirror for Gogham*, 178.

Chapter 9. Emancipation

1. Hiram Barney to Norman Judd, July 4, 1862, Hiram Barney Papers, HEH.

2. Basler, ed., *Works of Lincoln*, 5:153.

3. *New York Times*, Feb. 21, 1862.

4. Henry Bellows to "My dearest Bartol," Aug. 18, 1862, Bellows Papers.

5. Peter Cooper to Nahum Capen, Nov. 19, 1861, Cooper Papers.

6. Edward Dicey, *Spectator in America* (Chicago: Quadrangle, 1971), 283.

7. August Belmont to S. L. M. Barlow, Aug. 26, 1862, Samuel Barlow Papers, HEH.

8. Albert V. House, "The Samuel Latham Mitchell Barlow Papers in the Huntington Library," *Huntington Quarterly* 28, no. 4 (1965): 341–52.

9. *New York Tribune*, Aug. 20, 1862; Peter A. Isely, *Horace Greeley and the Republican Party, 1853–1861* (Princeton: Princton Univ. Press, 1947), 332.

10. Basler, ed., *Works of Lincoln*, 5:388–89n; *New York Tribune*, Aug. 25, 1862.

11. Crook, *The North, the South, and the Powers*, 263.

12. Henry Bellows to "My dear King," July 4, 1862, Bellows Papers.

13. Bryant and Voss, eds., *Letters*, 4:212, 262, 268, 438–44; Robert Harper, *Lincoln and the Press* (New York: McGraw-Hill, 1951), 75, 100.

14. Bryant and Voss, eds., *Letters*, 4:445; Allan Nevins, *The Evening Post* (1922; rpt. New York: Russell, 1968), 287–88.

15. Nevins, ed., *Diary of the Civil War*, 256.

16. Benedict, comp., *First Fifty Years of the Mount Sinai Hospital*, 34.

17. Nevins, ed., *Diary of the Civil War*, 251.

18. *New York Times*, Sept. 17, 1862.

19. Martin, *Choate*, 1:240–41.

20. Ibid., 242.

21. *New York Times*, Aug. 9, 1862.

22. Ibid., Sept. 12, 17, 1862.

23. George Opdyke to John Kennedy, July, 29, Sept. 28, 1862, Mayoralty Correspondence.

24. *New York Times*, Aug. 2, 1862.

25. Joseph George, Jr., " 'A Catholic Family Newspaper' Views the Lincoln Administration: John Mullaly's Copperhead Weekly," *Civil War History* 24, no. 2 (1978): 112–32; Shaw, *Dagger John*, 344; Roi Ottley and William J. Weatherby, eds., *The Negro in New York: An Informal Social History* (New York: New York Public Library, 1967), 110–22.

26. George Opdyke to General Harvey Brown, Sept. 9, 1862, to Secretary of War Stanton, Sept. 12, 1862, to Lincoln, Sept. 18, 1862, to George Hope, Oct. 28, 1862, to Rear Admiral Paulding, Dec. 27, 1862, all in Mayoralty Correspondence.

27. Hassard, *Hughes*, 443 quoting letter from Hughes to Seward, Aug. 13, 1862.

28. Opdyke, *Official Documents*, Aug. 27, 1862; Choate to wife, Aug. 27, 1862, Joseph Choate Papers, LC; *New York Times*, Sept. 20, 1862.

29. National War Committee Papers, Aug. 30, 1862, NYHS.

30. Moses H. Grinnell to Opdyke, Sept. 6, 1862, National War Committee Papers, Turnure Journal, Sept. 28, 1862.

31. National War Committee Papers, Aug. 30, 1862.

32. Report No. 3, Proceedings of the National War Committee, 1862; Opdyke to Belmont, Sept. 11, 1862, ibid.

33. John A. Stevens, Jr., to John A. Stevens, Dec. 1, 1861, Stevens Papers.

34. John C. Frémont to Opdyke, Sept. 5, 1862; telegram from Edwin Stanton to Opdyke, Sept. 5, 1862, National War Committee Papers.

35. Minutes, National War Committee, Aug. 29, 1862–Feb. 3, 1863, ibid.

36. National War Committee File, Oct. 10, 1862; William Alexander to National War Committee, Nov. 28, 1862; Gen. George Stoneman Plan of Operation; Report No. 5, all in ibid.

37. *New York Times*, Sept. 11, 1862.

38. Ibid., Sept. 15, 1862.

39. Hiram Barney, "Memories," Barney Papers.

40. *New York Times*, Sept. 25, 1862.

41. *Proceedings of the Board of Aldermen*, 88:12; Opdyke, *Official Documents*, 99.

42. Hassard, *Hughes*, 440; Mabee, *American Leonardo*, 424.

43. George Dow to "My dear Henry," Aug. 15, 1862, Dow Papers.

44. Bigelow, *Retrospections*, 1:474.

45. Turnure Journal, Sept. 24, 1862.

46. Ibid., April 4, 5, 1862.

47. Hammond, ed., *Diary of a Union Lady*, 182.

48. Gibson, *Attitudes of New York Irish*, 141.

49. Endres, "Women's Press in the Civil War," 31–53.

50. Manton Marble to E. D. Beach, May 21, 1863, Manton Marble Papers, LC; George T. McJimsey, *Genteel Partisan: Manton Marble* (Ames: Iowa State Univ. Press, 1971), 39–45.

51. Nevins, *War for the Union*, 2:238

52. Basler, ed., *Works of Lincoln*, 5:444.

53. Bigelow, *Retrospections*, 1:545–46.

54. *New York Times*, Sept. 26, 1862; Kehoe, ed., *Works of Hughes*, 1:13–14, 2:540; Shaw, *Dagger John*, 345–47.

55. *New York Times*, Sept. 29, 1862.

56. Ibid., Nov. 8, 12, 14, 15, 17, 1862.

57. Ibid., Sept. 24, 26, 1862.

58. Endres, "Women's Press in the Civil War," 190.

59. *New York Times*, Oct. 8, 1862.

60. Mitchell, *Horatio Seymour*, 226.

61. Sidney D. Brummer, *Political History of New York State during the Period of the Civil War* (New York: Longmans Green, 1911), 238.

62. *New York Times*, Oct. 2, 1862.

63. Greeley to Schuyler Colfax, Nov. 16, 1862, Greeley Papers.
64. Turner and Turner, eds., *Mary Todd Lincoln*, 137–39.
65. *New York Times*, Oct. 14, Nov. 4, 1862.
66. August Belmont to Samuel Barlow, Oct. 12, 1862, Barlow Papers.
67. Bigelow, ed., *Letters of Tilden*, 1:166–67; *New York Times*, Nov. 4, 1862.
68. *New York Times*, Oct. 7, 1862.
69. Hammond, *Commoner's Judge*, 166.
70. *New York Times*, Oct. 28, Nov. 1, 1862.
71. Ibid., Nov. 5, 1862.
72. Ibid., *New York Herald*, Dec. 13, 1862.
73. *New York Times*, Nov. 5, 1862.
74. Ibid., Nov. 6, 7, 1862; Brown, *Raymond of the Times*, 232–38.
75. Henry Bellows to Russell Bellows, Nov. 9, 1862, Bellows Papers.
76. *New York Times*, Nov. 5, 6, 1862.
77. Nicolay and Hay, *Lincoln*, 6:194n.
78. Thomas Seymour to Horatio Seymour, Nov. 8, 1862, Fairchild Collection.
79. Belmont, *A Few Letters*, 75.
80. Samuel Barlow to Horatio Seymour, Nov. 8, 1862 Fairchild Collection.
81. Basler, ed., *Works of Lincoln*, 5:553–54.
82. Samuel Barlow to Horatio Seymour, Dec. 2, 1862, Fairchild Collection; House, "Barlow Papers," 341–52.
83. Titus Coan to "Hattie," Dec. 1, 1862, Coan Papers.
84. Crook, *The North, the South, and the Powers*, 265–66.
85. Fahrney, *Greeley and the Tribune*, 140–41.
86. Van Deusen, *Seward*, 362.
87. *New York Times*, Dec. 26, 1862.

Chapter 10. Loyalty

1. Morse, ed., *Morse*, 2:424.
2. Smith and Judah, *Life in the North*, 92.
3. Tilden to Editors, *Evening Post*, Feb. 7, 1863, Tilden Papers; Bigelow, *Letters of Tilden*, 1:169; Katz, *Belmont*, 120; Denis T. Lynch, *"Boss" Tweed: The Story of a Grim Generation* (New York: Blue Ribbon, 1931), 242–43.
4. Plan of Operation of the Loyal Publication Society, Feb. 14, 1863; John A. Stevens, Jr., to J. M. Forbes, Feb. 17, 1863, both in Stevens Papers; Frank Friedel, *Francis Lieber: Nineteenth Century Liberal* (Baton Rouge: Louisiana State Univ. Press, 1947), 345–48; Peyton McCrary, "The Party of Revolution: Republican Ideas about Politics and Social Change," *Civil War History* 30, no. 4 (1984): 330–50.
5. Vallandigham to Greeley, Jan. 10, 1863, Greeley Papers.
6. James White to Horace Greeley, Feb. 9, 1863, ibid.
7. Henry Bellows to Jonathan Sturges, Dec. 11, 1863, Bellows Papers; George M. Frederickson, *The Inner Civil War, Northern Intellectuals and the Crisis of the Union* (New York: Harper, 1965), 134–36.

8. David Turnure Journal, Jan.–Dec. 1863.

9. Opdyke, *Official Documents*, 147–61; Martha Lamb, *History of the City of New York*, 3 vols. (New York: Valentine's Manual, 1921), 3:774.

10. Bishop, *Chronicle of One Hundred and Fifty Years*, 77.

11. Reginald Townsend, *Mother of Clubs, Being the History of the First Hundred Years of the Union Club of the City of New York* (New York: Privately printed, 1936), 70–71; Dixon Wecter, *The Saga of American Society: A Record of Social Aspiration, 1607–1937* (New York: Scribner's, 1970), 153.

12. Henry Bellows, *Historical Sketch of the Union League Club of New York* (New York: Club House, 1879), 53–54; Nevins, ed., *Diary of the Civil War*, 285; Roper, *FLO*, 214; McPherson, *Negro's Civil War*, 163–99.

13. *Proceedings of the Board of Aldermen*, 89:96.

14. Dix Diary, Jan. 23, 24, 26, 1863; "Some Impressions," *Trinity Church Newsletter*, Sept.–Oct. 1981; Odell, *Annals of the New York Stage*, 7:605; Bode, ed., *Struggles and Triumphs*, 311–12; M. R. Werner, *Barnum* (New York: Harcourt, Brace, 1923), 253–69; J. G. Randall and David Donald, *The Civil War and Reconstruction* (Boston: Heath, 1961), 486.

15. Hiram Barney to Salmon Chase, March 28, 1863, Barney Papers.

16. Brummer, *Political History of New York*, 304–7.

17. J. H. E. Whitney, *The Hawkins Zouaves (Ninth NYV)* (New York: Published by the author, 1866), 180–85; *New York Times*, May 6, 1863.

18. *New York Times*, June 11, 12, 1863; Edward A. Pollard, *Southern History of the War: The First Year of the War*, 2 vols. (1862–63); rpt. Freeport: Books for Libraries, 1969), 1:213.

19. *New York Times*, May 10, 1863.

20. Ibid., Feb. 5, 25, March 23, 1863.

21. *Proceedings of the Board of Aldermen*, 93:84–87.

22. Nevins, ed., *Diary of the Civil War*, 300.

23. *New York Times*, March 8, 1863; Klement, *Limits of Dissent*, 134–35.

24. Clement Vallandigham to Manton Marble, May 12, 15, 1863, Marble Papers.

25. Horatio Seymour to unknown, May 16, 1863, Fairchild Collection.

26. *New York Times*, June 4, 1863.

27. Ibid.

28. Ibid., June 4, 7, 1861.

29. T. J. Barnett to S. L. M. Barlow, May, 16, 23, June 10, 1863, Barlow Papers.

30. George Opdyke to John Putney, March 30, 1863, Opdyke Letterbook, Mayoralty Correspondence.

31. Delafield to Seymour, July 3, 1863, Delafield Letter Press Book.

32. Delafield to unknown, Feb. 18, 1863, ibid.

33. General Wool to Gov. Seymour, July 6, 1863, Fairchild Collection; General Wool to Gov. Seymour, June 30, July 6, 1863, Madigan Collection.

34. Opdyke to Major General John E. Wool, July 3, 1863, Opdyke Letter Press Book, Mayoralty Correspondence.

35. Delafield to Wool, June 19, 1863, Delafield Letter Press Book.

36. John A. Stevens to General Ward Barnett, March 10, 1863, Stevens Papers; Opdyke Letter Press Book, 389, May 1863, Mayoralty Correspondence.

37. *New York Times,* June 20, 1863.

38. Ibid., June 16, 1863.

39. Odell, *Annals of the New York Stage,* 7:577; Harnett T. Kane, *Spies for the Blue and Gray* (New York: Ace, 1954), 127–38.

40. Titus Coan to "Hattie," July 13, 16, 1863, Coan Papers.

41. Hammond, ed., *Diary of a Union Lady,* 244.

Chapter 11. Riot

1. George Opdyke to Frank Howe, July 8, 1863, Opdyke Letterbook, Mayoralty Correspondence.

2. Gibson, *Attitudes of New York Irish,* 147.

3. George, " 'A Catholic Family Newspaper,' " 124.

4. *New York Daily News,* July 13, 1863; Ellis, *Epic,* 297; Nicolay and Hay, *Lincoln,* 7:17.

5. Man, "Labor Competition," 375–405; Pleasants, *Wood,* 143; Nicolay and Hay, *Lincoln,* 7:17; Adrian Cook, *The Armies of the Streets: The New York City Draft Riots of 1863* (Lexington: University Press of Kentucky, 1974), 50–51; McJimsey, *Genteel Partisan,* 49.

6. Nevins, ed., *Diary of the Civil War,* 333.

7. Fitz John Porter to Manton Marble, July 13, 1863, Marble Papers.

8. Nicolay and Hay, *Lincoln,* 7:16–19n.

9. Opdyke to Acton, July 13, 1863; to Seymour, July 13, 1863; two telegrams to Seymour, July 13, 1863; to Wool, July 13, 1863; to Sandford, July 13, 1863; Opdyke Proclamation, July 13, 1863; Opdyke to Stanton, July 13, 1863; to Paulding, July 13, 1863, Opdyke Letterbook, Mayoralty Correspondence.

10. Dix Diary, July 14, 1863; *New York Times,* July 15, 16, 1863.

11. *New York Times,* July 14, 19, 1863; Cook, *Armies of the Streets,* 77; Ottley and Weatherby, eds., *Negro in New York,* 118.

12. Dix, *Memoirs,* 1:74.

13. Martin, *Choate,* 1:255–56; *New York Times,* July 28, 1863.

14. Hirsh and Doherty, *First Hundred Years of the Mount Sinai Hospital,* 42; Cooper, *Bellevue Story,* 79.

15. Bacon, ed., *Letters of a Family,* 1:537–39.

16. Frederick Van Wyck, *Recollections of an Old New Yorker* (New York: Liveright, 1932), 30.

17. Kaplan, *Walt Whitman,* 292; Bacon, ed., *Letters of a Family,* 1:541.

18. *New York Times,* July 14, 1863.

19. Jones Diary, July 14, 1863, Jones Papers.

20. *New York Daily News,* July 14, 1863.

21. Field, *Memories of Many Men,* 260, Nevins, ed., *Diary of the Civil War,* 339.

22. Hiram Barney to unknown, July 14, 1863, Barney papers.

23. Uhlmann, *Maiden Lane,* 90.

24. Henry Bellows to Henry Stebbins, July 15, 1863, Bellows Papers.

25. Stuyvesant Square Home Guard Minutes, July 15–21, 1863, Stuyvesant Square Home Guard Papers, NYHS.

26. Sworn statement of Ellen Parker, Aug. 10, 1863, Letterbook, Mayoralty Correspondence.

27. Resolution adopted by Board of Councilmen and Board of Aldermen, July 15, 1863; *Proceedings of the Board of Aldermen*, 91:80–81.

28. *New York Tribune*, Sept. 3, 1863.

29. Kehoe, ed., *Works of Hughes*, 2:541; *New York Times*, July 18, 1863; Nicolay and Hay, *Lincoln*, 7:25.

30. Martin, *Choate*, 1:259; Hammond, ed., *Diary of a Union Lady*, 251.

31. *New York Times*, July 29, 1863.

32. Letter with clipping from L. Kehoe, associate editor, *New York Tablet*, to J. A. Stevens, Jr., July 25, 1863; L. Kehoe to J. A. Stevens, Esq., Dec. 8, 1863, Stevens Papers.

33. Cook, *Armies of the Streets*, 176, 194–203; William Lofton, "Northern Labor and the Negro during the Civil War," *Journal of Negro History* 34, no. 3 (1949): 251–73.

34. Opdyke to A. T. Stewart, July 30, 1863; to Stock Exchange members, Aug. 12, 1863, Mayoralty Correspondence.

35. *Report of the Committee of Merchants for the Relief of the Colored People Suffering from the Late Riots in the City of New York* (New York: G. A. Whitehorne, 1863), NYHS.

36. Lofton, "Northern Labor," 267.

37. Croswell Bowen, *The Elegant Oakey* (New York: Oxford Univ. Press, 1956), 18–71; Migliore, "Business of Union," 293.

38. Opdyke to Sidney Roberts, July 28, 1863, Opdyke Letterbook, Mayoralty Correspondence.

39. Horatio Seymour to President Lincoln, Aug. 3, 1863, in Basler, ed., *Works of Lincoln*, 6:370n; Draft letter, Manton Marble to President Lincoln, 1863, Marble Papers; *Proceedings of the Board of Aldermen*, 91:80.

40. John A. Stevens, Jr., to S. P. Chase, July 21, 1863, Stevens Papers.

41. Basler, ed., *Works of Lincoln*, 6:369–70n.

42. "Resumption of the Draft in New York," *Harper's Weekly* 7, no. 349 (1863): 562–63.

43. Dix Diary, July 20, 1863; *The War of the Rebellion: Official Records of the Union and Confederate Armies*, 128 vols. (Washington, D.C.: U.S. Government Printing Office, 1880–1901), Ser. 3, Vol. 3, p. 672.

44. Harriet Seaver to Titus Coan, Sunday, 1863, Coan Papers.

45. *New York Herald*, Oct. 5, 1863; *New York Times*, Aug. 26, 28, 29, Sept. 1, 6, 7, 8, 11, 17, 1863; Lee, *Discontent*, 109; *Report of the Committee on Substitutes and Relief of the Board of Supervisors* (New York: William L. S. Harrison, Printer to the County, 1863), NYHS.

46. New York City Draft Board, Miscellaneous Papers, LC; Migliore, "Business of Union," 302.

47. Milton, *Abraham Lincoln and the Fifth Column*, 138.

48. Rodman Gilder, *The Battery* (Boston: Houghton Mifflin, 1936), 208.

Chapter 12. Living

1. Edward Pessen, "The Egalitarian Myth and the American Social Reality: Wealth, Mobility, and Equality in the 'Era of the Common Man,' " *American Historical Review* 76, no. 4 (1971): 989–1034; Still, *Mirror for Gotham,* 175; Smith and Judah, *Life in the North,* 200–29; Emerson D. Fite, *Social and Industrial Conditions in the North during the Civil War* (New York: Ungar, 1963), 184.

2. Memorial to President Lincoln about health of the city, June 29, 1864, 468, Mayoralty Correspondence; *New York Times,* May 2, 14, 15, Nov. 15, 20, 1864; Carlisle, ed., *Bellevue Hospital,* 63.

3. Choate to wife, n.d., Choate Papers; Martin, *Choate,* 1:252.

4. Laura Stedman and George Gould, *Life and Letters of Edmund Clarence Stedman,* 2 vols. (New York: Moffat, Yard, 1910), 1:325.

5. Theodore Francis Jones, ed., *New York University* (New York: New York Univ. Press, 1933), 29n.

6. Smith and Judah, *Life in the North,* 219; Fite, *Social and Industrial Conditions,* 187; Philip S. Foner, *History of the Labor Movement in the United States,* 2 vols. (New York: International Publishers, 1947), 1:341.

7. *New York Herald,* Oct. 3, 1863.

8. Foner, *History of Labor,* 1:341–57; Hammond, *Commoner's Judge,* 180.

9. Hower, *History of Macy's,* 65; Hungerford, *Romance of a Great Store,* 15–22.

10. Charles E. Rogers Diary, Feb. 23, May 24, 1864, NYPL.

11. Foner, *History of Labor,* 1:341–57.

12. Fite, *Social and Economic Conditions,* 124.

13. Howley, "William H. Webb," 65–66.

14. Opdyke, *Official Documents,* 52, 147.

15. Fite, *Social and Industrial Conditions,* 166–67n; Allan Nevins, *Hamilton Fish: The Inner History of the Great Administration* (New York: Dodd, Mead, 1937), 86–87.

16. Winkler, *Morgan the Magnificent,* 62.

17. Randall and Donald, *Civil War,* 481; Nevins, *War for the Union,* 3:259, 508; Smith and Judah, *Life in the North,* 203.

18. Pollard, *Southern History,* 2:84.

19. Henrietta M. Larson, *Jay Cooke, Private Banker* (Cambridge, Mass.: Harvard Univ. Press, 1936), 154; James K. Medberry, *Men and Mysteries of Wall Street* (1870; rpt. Wells, Vt.: Fraser Publishing, 1968), 244–46.

20. New York Stock and Exchange Board Minutes, Dec. 14, 1863, New York Stock Exchange Papers.

21. Henry Bellows to H. G. Stebbins, July 15, 1863, ibid.

22. Frederick L. Collins, *Money Town: The Story of Manhattan Toe, That Golden Mile Which Lies between the Battery and the Fields* (New York: G. P. Putnam, 1946), 219–22; Warshow, *Jay Gould,* 56.

23. Oberholtzer, *Jay Cooke,* 1:234, 259–62, 282, 309–10.

24. Fite, *Social and Economic Conditions,* 47, 128–30.

25. Nevins, *War for the Union,* 3:369.

26. Ibid., 342–43; Kenneth J. Blume, "The Flight from the Flag: The American Government, the British Caribbean, and the American Merchant Marine, 1861–1865," *Civil War History* 32, no. 1 (1986): 44–55.

27. Earl S. Pomeroy, "The Visit of the Russian Fleet in 1863," *New York History* 24, no. 4 (1943): 512–24; Marshall B. Davidson, "A Royal Welcome for the Russian Navy," *American Heritage* 11, no. 4 (1960): 38–43, 107; H. J. Kushner, "The Russian Fleet and the American Civil War: Another View," *Historian* 34, no. 4 (1972): 633–49; "The Russian Ball," *Harper's Weekly*, Nov. 21, 1863.

28. Henry Bellows to Russell Bellows, Oct. 4, 1863, Bellows Papers.

29. *New York Herald*, Oct. 2, 24, 1863.

30. George Opdyke to James Brown, Dec. 1, 1863; to Admiral Lisovski, Dec. 1, 1863, Opdyke Letterbook, Mayoralty Correspondence.

31. Merle Curti, *The Growth of American Thought* (New York: Harper, 1943), 443–67.

32. Jerome Mushkat, "Ben Wood's 'Fort Lafayette,' " *Civil War History* 21, no. 2 (1975): 160–71.

Chapter 13. A New Mayor

1. *New York Times*, Nov. 1, 1863.

2. "The City," *Harper's Weekly* 7, no. 363 (1863): 786.

3. Basler, ed., *Works of Lincoln*, 7:4–5n.

4. Lee, *Discontent*, 274; Nevins, ed., *Diary of the Civil War*, 375.

5. Matthew Breen, *Thirty Years of New York Politics Up-to-Date* (New York: published by the author, 1899), 50.

6. Factbook, Municipal Reference Library, New York City.

7. *New York Herald*, Nov. 8, 1864; Wilson, ed., *Memorial History*, 3:511n.

8. *New York Tribune*, Nov. 30, 1863.

9. Mary Gunther Day, "Your Grandmother's People," typescript, New Haven, 1966, NYHS.

10. *Proceedings of the Board of Aldermen*, 93:12.

Chapter 14. Political Embarrassments

1. Brummer, *Political History of New York*, 420; Van Deusen, *Greeley*, 310; Fahrney, *Greeley and the Tribune*, 180–202.

2. John A. Stevens, Jr., to S. P. Chase, Sept. 15, 1863, Stevens Papers.

3. John A. Stevens, Jr., to L. E. Crittenden, Dec. 31, 1863, ibid.

4. Hiram Barney to Edward Pierce, Feb. 14, 1861, Barney Papers; David Donald, ed., *Inside Lincoln's Cabinet: The Civil War Diaries of Salmon P. Chase* (New York: Longmans, Green, 1954), 279n.

5. Blume, "Flight from the Flag."

6. Barney to Lincoln, Jan. 9, 1864, Barney Papers; Field, *Memories of Many Men*, 304.

7. Basler, ed., *Works of Lincoln*, 7:268n; Rawley, *Morgan*, 195.

8. Opdyke to James Hamilton, Nov. 3, 1863, Miscellaneous Papers, NYPL.

9. *Harper's Weekly* 8, no. 373 (1864): 114.

10. John A. Stevens, Jr., to S. P. Chase, April 18, 1863, Stevens Papers.

11. Peter Cooper, Francis Lieber, and others to National Executive Committee of Union and Republican parties, March 21, [1864], Stevens Papers.

12. Basler, ed., *Works of Lincoln*, 7:259–60n.

13. Hammond, ed., *Diary of a Union Lady*, 178.

14. Bliss, "Autobiography," 166–77.

15. Ottley and Weatherby, *Negro in New York*, 122; George, " 'A Catholic Family Newspaper,' " 128–29.

16. Phyllis F. Field, *The Politics of Race in New York: The Struggle for Black Suffrage in the Civil War Era* (Ithaca: Cornell Univ. Press, 1982), 158.

17. Henry Bellows to Mrs. Lane, Nov. 27, 1863, Bellows Papers; Bacon, ed., *Letters of a Family*, 2:568–70; Werner, *It Happened in New York*, 193.

18. Gunther Proclamation, April 2, 1864, Letterbook, Mayoralty Correspondence.

19. "The Metropolitan Fair," *Harper's Weekly*, 8 no. 381 (1864): 246; Dix Diary, April 3, 1864.

20. Hammond, ed., *Diary of a Union Lady*, 279.

21. Dix Diary, April 3, 12, 1864; Nevins, ed., *Diary of the Civil War*, 417n, 430–32; Dannett, *Noble Women of the North*, 273–75; Wilson, *Memorial History*, 3:508–9.

22. William S. Myers, *General George Brinton McClellan: A Study in Personality* (New York: Appleton, 1934), 410; see also Stephen W. Sears, *George B. McClellan, the Young Napoleon* (New York: Ticknor & Fields, 1988).

23. Oberholtzer, *Jay Cooke*, 401–10.

24. Domett, *History of the Bank of New York*, 98–99.

25. Stedman and Gould, *Life and Letters*, 1:341–42.

26. Board Minutes, New York Stock Exchange, May 14, 1864, New York Stock Exchange Papers.

27. S. L. M. Barlow memorandum about letter to Weed, May 1864, Barlow Papers.

28. Mayor Gunther to General Dix, May 9, 1864, Letterbook, Mayoralty Correspondence; Charles Halpine to Horatio Seymour, May 5, 1864, Fairchild Collection; *New York Times*, May 10, 11, 1864.

29. *New York Times*, May 18, 19, 1864.

30. *New York Times*, May 19, 20, 1864.

31. Ibid., May 21, 24, 1864; McJimsey, *Genteel Partisan*, 52.

32. John T. Morse, ed., *Diary of Gideon Welles*, 3 vols. (Boston: Houghton Mifflin, 1911), 2:36–37; Dix, *Memoirs*, 1:99–100; *War of the Rebellion*, Ser. 3, Vol. 4, p. 388; Mitchell, *Seymour*, 358; *New York Times*, May 19, 24, June 28, 1864.

33. Marble to Cassidy, draft, July 1864, Marble Papers.

34. *New York Times*, May 19, 1864.

35. Barnett to Barlow, Nov. 23, 1863, March 20, May 24, June 4, 1864, Barlow Papers.

36. *New York Times*, May 22, 1864.

37. Barnes, *Memoir of Weed*, 446.

38. Nevins, ed., *Diary of the Civil War*, 455−57.

39. Bishop, *Chronicle of One Hundred and Fifty Years of the Chamber of Commerce*, 81−84.

40. Basler, ed., *Works of Lincoln*, 7:412−15; Field, *Memories of Many Men*, 300; Nicolay and Hay, *Lincoln*, 9:91−94.

41. Randall and Donald, *Civil War*, 350.

42. William M. Barney, *Flawed Victory* (Lanham, Md.: University Press, 1980), 167−68; Randall and Donald, *Civil War*, 350−52; Oberholtzer, *Jay Cooke*, 326−44; Harold van B. Cleveland, Thomas F. Huertes, et al, *Citibank, 1812−1970* (Cambridge, Mass.: Harvard Univ. Press, 1985), 27.

43. Charles H. Brown, *William Cullen Bryant, A Biography* (New York: Scribner's, 1971), 460.

44. Basler, ed., *Works of Lincoln*, 7:404 − 10n: Bryant and Voss, eds., *Letters*, 4:364−70.

45. Brown, *Bryant*, 459−63.

46. Godwin to Bryant, July 31, 1865, Bryant-Godwin Papers; Brown, *Bryant*, 459−63.

47. Amasa Parker to Samuel Tilden, July 7, 1864, Tilden Papers.

48. Turnure Journal, Jan. 16, 1865.

49. John A. Stevens, Jr., to William Alexander, Aug. 13, 1864; Edgar Conkling to Stevens, Sept. 7, 1864, Stevens Papers.

50. *New York Sun*, June 30, 1889.

51. Alford Erbe to John A. Stevens, Jr., 1864, Stevens Papers.

52. Gunther to Sandford, July 11, 12, 1864, Letterbook, Mayoralty Correspondence.

53. Dix Diary, July 10−15, 1864.

54. Thomas W. Egan to M. F. Odell, July 30, 1864, Madigan Collection.

55. Edward C. Kirkland, *The Peacemakers of 1864* (New York: Macmillan, 1927), 67−76.

56. Basler, ed., *Works of Lincoln*, 7:435 and n.; Fahrney, *Greeley and the Tribune*, 161n.

57. Basler, ed., *Works of Lincoln*, 7:441n.

58. C. A. Dana to H. J. Raymond, July 26, 1864, George E. Jones Papers, NYPL.

59. John Hay to Henry Raymond, April 20, 1865, Henry J. Raymond Papers, NYPL.

60. VanDeusen, *Greeley*, 308; Barrows, *Evarts*, 123.

61. Barrows, *Evarts*, 123; Van Deusen, *Greeley*, 308.

62. Robert Bormer to Greeley, May 1862, Greeley Papers; Basler, ed., *Works of Lincoln*, 7:482−83n.

63. Basler, ed., *Works of Lincoln*, 7:489−90.

64. Kirkland, *Peacemakers,* 105.

65. Brown, *Raymond of the Times,* 259-60; Smith and Judah, *Life in the North,* 119.

66. Brown, *Raymond of the Times,* 261.

67. Gunther Pronouncement, Mayor's Office, Aug. 1, 1864, Letterbook, Mayoralty Correspondence.

68. Basler, ed., *Works of Lincoln,* 7:461n, 514-15n.

69. Greeley to Opdyke, Aug. 18, 1864, Stevens Papers.

70. Bryant and Voss, eds., *Letters,* 4:387-88.

71. Morse, ed., *Diary of Welles,* 2:97, 142; Brown, *Raymond of the Times,* 263.

Chapter 15. Presidential Election

1. Ethan Allen to S. L. M. Barlow, July 20, 1864, Barlow Papers; Elbert B. Smith, *Francis Preston Blair* (New York: Macmillan, 1980), 344; Nicolay and Hay, *Lincoln,* 9:246-49.; Myers, *McClellan,* 433-35.

2. Kirkland, *Peacemakers,* 115-16; *New York Times,* Aug. 8, 1864.

3. Nicolay and Hay, *Lincoln,* 9:254.

4. Herbert Mitgang, ed., *Washington in Lincoln's Time by Noah Brooks* (New York: Rinehart, 1958), 110.

5. Mitchell, *Seymour,* 372.

6. Myers, *History of Tammany Hall,* 206.

7. Kirkland, *Peacemakers,* 137; Brummer, *Political History of New York,* 420-21.

8. Hiram Barney to William Fessenden, Aug. 31, 1864; draft of Barney resignation, June 14, 1864, Barney Papers.

9. Brown, *Bryant,* 466.

10. Mary E. Thomas, "The CSS Tallahassee: A Factor in Anglo-American Relations, 1864-1866," *Civil War History* 21, no. 2 (1975): 148-59; Dalzell, *Flight from the Flag,* 182-87.

11. George, " 'A Catholic Family Newspaper,' " 127.

12. Board Minutes, New York Stock Exchange, July 13, 1864, New York Stock Exchange Papers.

13. *Proceedings of the Board of Aldermen,* 93:236.

14. *Proceedings of the Board of Aldermen,* 97:55-57; *Report of Special Committee on Volunteering . . .* 1864 (New York: William L. S. Harrison, 1864), NYHS.

15. *New York Times,* Aug. 23, 1864.

16. Dix Diary, Sept. 3, 1864.

17. *Proceedings of the Board of Aldermen,* 95:351-54; *New York Herald,* Oct. 1, 1864; *New York Times,* Nov. 29, 1864; *New York Daily News,* Nov. 10, 1864.

18. Mayor's Communications, Filed Papers, City Clerk, Sept. 29, 1864, Mayoral Correspondence.

19. John Jacob Astor to McClellan, Sept. 29, 1864, George B. McClellan Papers, LC; Nevins, ed., *Diary of the Civil War,* 513; Van Deusen, *Weed,* 310.

20. Katz, *Belmont,* 145.

21. Friedel, *Lieber,* 351-53.

22. Corresponding Secretary, Young Men's Democratic Union Club, to McClellan, Sept. 19, Oct. 8, 1864, McClellan Papers; Rogers Diary, Nov. 4, 5, 1864, Col. Lionel d'Epineuil to Manton Marble, Aug. 26, 1864, Marble Papers.

23. J. H. Van Evrie to McClellan, Sept. 14, 1864; Albert Ramsey to McClellan, Oct. 18, 1864, McClellan Papers.

24. Nevins, *War for the Union*, 4:137.

25. William Aspinwall to S. L. M. Barlow, Sept. 26, 1864, Barlow Papers.

26. *New York Sun*, June 30, 1889.

27. *New York Times*, Oct. 21, 1864; Brummer, *Political History of New York*, 438; Hower, *History of Macy's*, 110.

28. Katz, *Belmont*, 146.

29. *New York Daily News*, Nov. 1, 1864.

30. Ibid., Nov. 7, 1864.

31. Edward G. Longacre, "The Union Army Occupation of New York City," *New York History* 65, no. 2 (1984): 133–57.

32. *New York Daily News*, Nov. 4, 1864.

33. Ibid., Nov. 7, 1864.

34. Robert S. Holzman, *Stormy Ben Butler* (New York: Collier, 1961), 37–39.

35. Ibid, 142–43.

36. Dix Diary, Nov. 5, 1864.

37. Longacre, "Union Army Occupation," 141–49.

38. Ibid., 143–44.

39. Albert Ramsey to McClellan, Nov. 7, 1864, McClellan Papers.

40. *New York Times*, Nov. 5, 1864; Barrows, *Evarts*, 123–24.

41. *New York Times*, Nov. 5, 6, 1864.

42. Stedman and Gould, *Life and Letters*, 347; Dix, *Memoirs*, 1:94–95; Nicolay and Hay, *Lincoln*, 9:373.

43. *New York Times*, Nov. 3, 1864; Katz, *Belmont*, 147; Nevins, ed., *Diary of the Civil War*, 510.

44. Nicolay and Hay, *Lincoln*, 9:375.

45. Brummer, *Political History of New York*, 439; Van Deusen, *Seward*, 398; Brown, *Raymond of the Times*, 267.

46. LaWanda Cox and John H. Cox, *Politics, Principle, and Prejudice* (New York: Free Press, 1963), 44.

47. *New York Daily News*, Nov. 10, 11, 1864; George, " 'A Catholic Family Newspaper,' " 127.

48. *New York Times*, Nov. 10, 1864.

49. Longacre, "Union Army Occupation," 156–57.

50. *New York Times*, Nov. 20, 1864.

51. Ibid., Nov. 16, Dec. 26, 27, 1864.

52. Ibid., Nov. 13, 1864; Bellows, *Historical Sketch of the Union League Club*, 69.

53. *New York Times*, Nov. 13, 1864; Nevins, ed., *Diary of the Civil War*, 521–22n; see Nat Brandt, *The Man Who Tried to Burn New York* (Syracuse: Syracuse Univ. Press, 1986).

54. *New York Times*, Nov. 27, 1864; Odell, *Annals of the New York Stage*, 7:638–39.

55. Gunther Proclamation, Nov. 30, 1864, Letterbook, Mayoralty Correspondence; *New York Times*, Nov. 27–29, 1864.

56. *New York Daily News,* Nov. 28, 1864.

57. Jim Bishop, *The Day Lincoln Was Shot* (New York: Perennial/Harper, 1955), 67–68.

58. *New York Times,* Dec. 11, 18, 25, 1864.

59. Second Annual Announcement and Constitution of the New York Medical College for Women and Hospital for Women and Children, 1864, MA.

Chapter 16. Victory

1. *The Great Libel Suit* (New York: Wynkoop and Hollenbeck, n.d. [1865]), 6–11; *New York Times,* Dec. 9, 14, 1864, Jan. 6, 7, 1865.

2. *Great Libel Suit,* 6, 127, 131.

3. *New York Times,* Jan. 12, 1865; *Great Libel Suit,* 156.

4. Van Deusen, *Weed,* 289; Randall and Donald, *Civil War,* 487.

5. Nevins, ed., *Diary of the Civil War,* 567.

6. Henry Bellows to Russell Bellows, Feb. 12, 1865, Bellows Papers.

7. Dix Diary, Feb. 1, 1865.

8. Turnure Journal, Jan. 1865.

9. *Memorial of Board of Commissioners of Health of the City of New York on Subject of Compulsory Vaccination with a View to Exterminate the Small-Pox* (New York: Tafton, 1862).

10. *New York Times,* March 16, 1865.

11. *New York Times,* March 16, 24, 1865.

12. *New York Times,* March 10, 19, April 13, 1865.

13. Hall, *Report on the Ship-Building Industry,* 116; Barney, *Flawed Victory,* 164.

14. Dix Diary, March 14, 1865.

15. *New York World,* March 6, 1865; *New York Daily News,* March 6, 1865.

16. Turnure Journal, Feb. 1865.

17. *Proceedings of the Board of Aldermen,* 97:590–91.

18. *New York Times,* Oct. 23, 1864, Feb. 21, March 1, 1865.

19. Fernando Wood to George Shea, Jan. 15, 1865, Wood Papers.

20. Invitation to George Shea from Wood dinner committee, March 16, 1865, ibid.

21. *New York Times,* Feb. 28, March 26, 27, 1865.

22. Leicester C. Lewis, *A History of the Parish of Trinity Church in the City of New York* (New York: Columbia University Press, 1950), 56.

23. Ibid.

24. Nevins, ed., *Diary of the Civil War,* 573–75.

25. *Proccedings of the Board of Aldermen,* 98:23–24; *New York Times,* April 5, 1865.

26. Gilder, *The Battery,* 208–9.

27. Bacon, ed., *Letters of a Family,* 1:655.

28. Board Minutes, New York Stock Exchange, April 10, 1865, New York Stock Exchange Papers.

29. Gunther Proclamation, April 12, 1865, Letterbook, Mayoralty Correspondence.

30. Starr, *Bohemian Brigade,* 347.

31. Helen (Lansing) Grinnell Diary, April 15, 1865, NYPL.

32. Dix Diary, April 15, 1865; Gunther Proclamation, April 15, 1865, Letterbook, Mayoralty Correspondence; Stedman, *Life and Letters*, 1:352–53.

33. *Proceedings of the Board of Aldermen*, 98:11.

34. Richard Lockridge, *Darling of Misfortunes* (New York: Blom, 1971), 153–58; Eleanor Ruggles, *Prince of Players: Edwin Booth* (New York: Norton, 1953), 173–201; Hammond, ed., *Diary of a Union Lady*, 361.

35. Nevins, ed., *Diary of the Civil War*, 584.

36. Board Minutes, New York Stock Exchange, April 17, 1865, New York Stock Exchange Papers.

37. Hammond, *Commoner's Judge*, 192.

38. Dix Diary, April 25, 1865. TA.

39. Henry Bellows to W. C. Bryant, April 25, 1865, Bryant-Godwin Papers.

40. Nevins, ed., *Diary of the Civil War*, 587.

41. Daniel E. Sutherland, "Exiles, Emigrants, and Sojourners: The Post Civil War Confederate Exodus in Perspective," *Civil War History* 31, no. 3 (1985): 237–56.

42. Migliore, "Business of Union," 388–407.

Bibliography

Manuscript Collections

Barlow, Samuel. Papers. Huntington Library, San Marino, California.

Barney, Hiram. Papers. Huntington Library, San Marino, California.

Bellevue Hospital, Miscellaneous Papers. New-York Academy of Medicine.

Bellows, Henry. Papers. Massachusetts Historical Society, Boston.

Bennett, James Gordon. Papers. Manuscript Division, Library of Congress.

Bloor, Alfred Janson. Diary. New-York Historical Society.

Bryant, William Cullen. Papers. Bryant-Godwin Papers. Rare Books and Manuscripts Division, Astor, Lenox and Tilden Foundations, New York Public Library.

Choate, Joseph. Papers. Manuscript Division, Library of Congress.

Coan, Titus. Papers. New-York Historical Society.

Common Council National Affairs Committee, Municipal Archives, New York City.

Cooper, Peter. Papers. Cooper Union Library, New York City.

Delafield, Richard. Letter Press Book. New-York Historical Society.

Dix, Morgan. Diary. Archives of the Parish of Trinity Church of the City of New York, New York City.

Dow, George. Papers. New-York Historical Society.

Fairchild Collection. New-York Historical Society.

Greeley, Horace. Papers. Horace Greeley Papers. Rare Books and Manuscripts Division. Astor, Lenox and Tilden Foundations, New York Public Library.

Grinnell, Helen (Lansing). Diary. Rare Books and Manuscripts Division, Astor, Lenox and Tilden Foundations, New York Public Library.

Hewitt, Abram. Papers. Cooper Union Library, New York City.

Jones, Alfred G. Papers. Alfred Goldsborough Jones Papers. Rare Books and Manuscripts Division, Astor, Lenox and Tilden Foundations, New York Public Library.

Jones, George E. Papers. Rare Books and Manuscripts Division, Astor, Lenox and Tilden Foundations, New York Public Library.

Lieber, Francis. Papers. Huntington Library, San Marino, California.

Madigan, Thomas F. Collection. Rare Books and Manuscripts Division, Astor, Lenox and Tilden Foundations, New York Public Library.

Marble, Manton. Papers. Manuscript Division, Library of Congress.

Marshall, C. H. Miscellaneous Papers. Webb Institute, Glen Cove, New York.

Mayoralty Correspondence, Papers. Municipal Archives, City of New York.

McClellan, George B. Papers. Manuscript Division, Library of Congress.

Morgan, Edwin. Papers. New-York Historical Society.

Morse, Samuel F. B. Papers. Manuscript Division, Library of Congress.

National War Committee. Papers. New-York Historical Society.

New York City Draft Board. Miscellaneous Papers. Manuscript Division, Library of Congress.

New York Stock Exchange. Papers. New York Stock Exchange Archives, New York City.

Porter, Fitz John. Papers. Manuscript Division, Library of Congress.

Raymond, Henry J. Papers. Rare Books and Manuscripts Division, Astor, Lenox and Tilden Foundations, New York Public Library.

Rogers, Charles E. Diary. Rare Books and Manuscripts Division, Astor, Lenox and Tilden Foundations, New York Public Library.

Satterlee, Alfred H. Diary. Rare Books and Manuscripts Division, Astor, Lenox and Tilden Foundations, New York Public Library.

Schuyler, Louisa Lee. Papers. New-York Historical Society.

Sickles, Daniel. Papers. New-York Historical Society.

Stevens, John A. (Sr. and Jr.) Papers. New-York Historical Society.

Stuyvesant Square Home Guard. Papers. New-York Historical Society.

Tilden, Samuel. Papers. Rare Books and Manuscripts Division, Astor, Lenox and Tilden Foundations, New York Public Library.

Turnure, David Mitchell. Journal. New-York Historical Society.

Webb, William. Miscellaneous Papers. Webb Institute, Glen Cove, New York.

Weed, Thurlow. Papers. New-York Historical Society.

Wood, Fernando. Papers. Rare Books and Manuscripts Division, Astor, Lenox and Tilden Foundations, New York Public Library.

Books

Adams, George. *Doctors in Blue: The Medical History of the Union Army in the Civil War.* New York: Henry Schuman, 1952.

Alexander, De Alva S. *A Political History of the State of New York.* 4 vols. 1909. Reprint. Port Washington: Ira J. Friedman, 1969.

Knapp, Shepherd. *A History of the Brick Presbyterian Church in the City of New York.* New York: Brick Church, 1909.

Lamb, Martha. *History of the City of New York.* 3 vols. New York: Valentine's Manual, 1921.

Lane, Wheaton J. *Commodore Vanderbilt: An Epic of the Steam Age.* New York: Knopf, 1942.

Larson, Henrietta M. *Jay Cooke, Private Banker.* Cambridge, Mass.: Harvard Univ. Press, 1936.

Lee, Brother Basil Leo. *Discontent in New York City, 1861 – 1865.* Washington, D.C.: Catholic Univ. of America Press, 1943.

Leech, Margaret. *Reveille in Washington.* New York: Harper, 1941.

Lewis, Leicester C. *A History of the Parish of Trinity Church in the City of New York.* New York: Columbia Univ. Press, 1950.

Limpus, Lowell. *History of the New York Fire Department.* New York: Dutton, 1940.

Lockridge, Richard. *Darling of Misfortunes.* New York: Blom, 1971.

Lynch, Denis T. *"Boss" Tweed: The Story of a Grim Generation.* New York: Blue Ribbon, 1931.

Mabee, Carleton. *The American Leonardo: The Life of Samuel F. B. Morse.* New York: Knopf, 1957.

Martin, Edward S. *The Life of Joseph Hodges Choate as Gathered Chiefly from His Letters.* 2 vols. New York: Scribner's, 1920.

Maxwell, William Quentin. *Lincoln's Fifth Wheel: The Political History of the United States Sanitary Commission.* New York: Longmans, Green, 1956.

McJimsey, George T. *Genteel Partisan: Manton Marble.* Ames: Iowa State Univ. Press, 1971.

McPherson, James M. *The Negro's Civil War.* New York: Pantheon, 1965.

Medberry, James K. *Men and Mysteries of Wall Street.* 1870. Reprint. Wells, Vt.: Fraser Publishing, 1968.

Miller, J. *The 1866 Guide to New York City.* 1866. Reprint. New York: Schocken Books, 1975.

Milton, George Fort. *Abraham Lincoln and the Fifth Column.* New York: Vanguard, 1942.

Mitchell, Stewart. *Horatio Seymour of New York.* Cambridge, Mass.: Harvard Univ. Press, 1938.

Mitgang, Herbert, ed. *Washington in Lincoln's Time by Noah Brooks.* New York: Rinehart, 1958.

Morse, Edward Lind, ed. *Samuel F. B. Morse: His Letters and Journals.* 2 vols. New York: Kennedy Galleries/DaCapo, 1973.

Morse, John T., ed. *Diary of Gideon Welles.* 3 vols. Boston: Houghton Mifflin, 1911.

Mottus, Jane E. *New York Nightingales: The Emergence of Nursing Profession at Bellevue and New York Hospital, 1850–1920*. Ann Arbor: Research Press–Studies in American History and Culture, University of Michigan, 1981.

Mushkat, Jerome. *The Reconstruction of the New York Democracy, 1861–1874*. Madison, N.J.: Fairleigh Dickinson Univ. Press, 1981.

———. *Tammany: The Evolution of a Political Machine, 1789–1865*. Syracuse: Syracuse Univ. Press, 1971.

Myers, Gustavus. *The History of Tammany Hall*. New York: Boni and Liveright, 1917.

Myers, William S. *General George Brinton McClellan: A Study in Personality*. New York: Appleton, 1934.

Nevin, John. *Gideon Welles*. New York: Oxford Univ. Press, 1973.

Nevins, Allan. *Abram S. Hewitt, with Some Accounts of Peter Cooper*. New York: Harper, 1935.

———. *The Emergence of Lincoln*. 2 vols. New York: Scribner's, 1950.

———. *The Evening Post*. 1922. Reprint. New York: Russell, 1968.

———. *Hamilton Fish: The Inner History of the Grant Administration*. New York: Dodd, Mead, 1937.

———. *History of the Bank of New York (1784 – 1934)*. New York: Privately printed, 1934.

———. *The War for the Union*. 4 vols. New York: Scribner's, 1959–71.

———, ed. *Diary of the Civil War, 1860–1865: George Templeton Strong*. New York: Macmillan, 1962.

———, et al. *The Century, 1847–1946*. New York: Century Association, 1947.

Nicolay, John G., and John Hay. *Abraham Lincoln: A History*. 10 vols. New York: Century, 1914.

Oberholtzer, Ellis Paxson. *Jay Cooke, Financier of the Civil War*. 2 vols. Philadelphia: George W. Jacobs, 1907.

O'Connor, Richard. *The Scandalous Mr. Bennett*. New York: Doubleday, 1962.

Odell, George C. D. *Annals of the New York Stage*. 15 vols. New York: Columbia Univ. Press, 1927–49.

Opdyke, George. *Official Documents, Addresses Etc. of George Opdyke, Mayor of the City of New York, during the Years 1862 and 1863*. New York: Hurd and Houghton, 1866.

Ottley, Roi, and William J. Weatherby, eds. *The Negro in New York: An Informal Social History*. New York: New York Public Library, 1967.

Perkins, Howard C., ed. *Northern Editorials on Secession*. 2 vols. Gloucester, Mass.: Peter Smith, 1964.

Pinchon, Edgcumb. *Dan Sickles, Hero of Gettysburg and "Yankee King of Spain."* Garden City, N.Y.: Doubleday, 1945.

Whittemore, Henry, ed. *Advance Sheets of Origin and Progress of Steam Navigation in America*. New York: The Original and Progressive Publishing Company, n.d.

———. *To Moses Taylor, Esq., Chmn. Loan Committee from "A Looker On."* New York, December 24, 1861, NYHS.

Reports

Bellevue Hospital Medical College. *Annual Announcement and Circular.* 1861–62, 1863–64.

College of Physicians and Surgeons, New York—Medical Department of Columbia College. *Annual Announcement of Lectures*, 1860–61.

Hall, Henry. *Report on the Ship-Building Industry of the United States*. Washington, D.C.: U.S. Government Printing Office, 1884.

Memorial of Board of Commissioners of Health of the City of New York on Subject of Compulsory Vaccination with a View to Exterminate the Small-Pox. New York: Tafton, 1862.

Proceedings at the Mass Meeting of Loyal Citizens on Union Square, N.Y., 15th Day of July, 1862. Under the auspices of the Chamber of Commerce of the State of New York, the Union Defense Committee of the Citizens of New York, the Common Council of the City of New York and Other Committees of Loyal Citizens. New York: Committee on Arrangements, 1862.

Proceedings of a Union Meeting Held in New York, An Appeal to the South. New York: John H. Duyckinck, 1860. NYHS.

Report of the Committee of Merchants for the Relief of Colored People Suffering from the Late Riots in the City of New York. New York: G. A. Whitehorne, 1863. NYHS.

Report of the Committee on Substitutes and Relief of the Board of Supervisors. New York: William L. S. Harrison, Printer to the County, 1863. NYHS.

Report of Special Committee on Volunteering, Embracing a Complete Statement of Operations in Filling the Quota of the County of New York under the Call of the President, Dated July 18, 1864 for 500,000 Men. New York: William L. S. Harrison, 1864. NYHS.

Reports, Resolutions and Documents of the Union Defense Committee of the Citizens of New York. New York: N.p., 1862. NYHS.

Report on the National Bank Currency Act, Its Defects and Its Effects. New York: New York Clearing House, 1863.

Second Annual Announcement and Constitution of the New York Medical College for Women and Hospital for Women and Children, 1864. MA.

Public Documents

Proceedings of the Board of Aldermen of the City of New York, Vols. 80–97, 1860–65.

Newspapers, 1860–65

Frank Leslie's Illustrated Newspaper
Journal of Commerce
New York Daily News
New York Evening Day-Book
New York Evening Post
New York Herald
New York Sun
New York Times
New York Tribune
New York World

Periodicals, 1860–65

Harper's Weekly
Harper's New Monthly Magazine

Index

359

THE CIVIL WAR AND NEW YORK CITY

was composed in 10 on 13 Baskerville on a Merganthaler Linotron 202
by Partners Composition;
and Craw Modern display type provided by Dix Type, Inc.;
printed by sheet-fed offset on 50-pound, acid-free Glatfelter B-16;
Smyth-sewn and bound over binder's boards in Holliston Roxite B,
with dust jackets printed in two colors
by Edwards Brothers, Inc.;
designed by Victoria Lane;
and published by

SYRACUSE UNIVERSITY PRESS
SYRACUSE, NEW YORK 13244-5160